Measuring National Well-being 2012

In replacement of 'Social Trends'

Contents:

Measuring National Well-being - Our Relationships, 2012

Author Name(s): Chris Randall Office for National Statistics

Abstract

This article is published as part of the ONS Measuring National Well-being Programme. The programme aims to produce accepted and trusted measures of the well-being of the nation - how the UK as a whole is doing. This article on 'Our relationships' is the first in a series which aims to explore in more detail the different domains that have been considered as important for the measurement of National Well-being. It firstly focuses on close family relationships, both the form that those relationships take as well as the quality of those relationships. However, these relationships do not operate in isolation, and for this reason friendships and other relationships in the wider community and the workplace are also analysed.

Introduction

The amount and quality of social connections with people around us are an essential part of our well-being. The importance of relationships for an individual's well-being as well as for society more generally cannot be overlooked when making an assessment of the nation's well-being.

This was highlighted in the ONS National Debate on Measuring National Well-being. When people were asked what mattered most for the measurement of National Well-being, 'personal relationships' was one aspect that people considered as most important.

Previous research has also shown that personal relationships are vitally important to an individual's well-being and should be considered when making any assessment of National Well-being.

'The frequency of contact with others and the quality of personal relationships are crucial determinants of people's well-being. People get pleasure from spending time with others – be it family, friends or colleagues – and activities are typically more satisfying when shared with others. Furthermore, social networks provide material and emotional support in times of need' (Kahneman and Krueger, 2006).

'Social connections, including marriage, of course, but not limited to that, are among the most robust correlates of subjective well-being. People who have close friends and confidants, friendly neighbours and supportive co-workers are less likely to experience sadness, loneliness, low self-esteem and problems with eating and sleeping…Subjective well-being is best predicted by

the breadth and depth of one's social connections. In fact, people themselves report that good relationships with family members, friends or romantic partners — far more than money or fame — are prerequisites for their own happiness' – (Helliwell and Putnam, 2004).

Key points

Personal relationships and loneliness

- In a survey in April and June 2011, adults aged 16 and over in Great Britain were more likely to be satisfied with their personal relationships than with their life overall (8.3 and 7.4 out of 10 respectively): and those with higher levels of satisfaction with their personal relationships tend to have higher levels of overall life satisfaction.
- In July 2011 around 1 in 20 adults aged 16 and over in Great Britain reported being completely lonely in their daily lives.

Family relationships

- In 2011, two-thirds (66 per cent) of adults aged 16 and over in England reported spending time most days or every day together with their family.
- When asked in April and August 2011, adults aged 16 and over in Great Britain with a partner or spouse reported higher levels of life satisfaction than those who were single or were separated or divorced.
- In 2011, more than 9 in 10 (91.1 per cent) adults aged 16 and over in Great Britain reported levels of satisfaction with the well-being of their child or children of 7 or more out of 10.

Friendships

- In 2011, over 4 in 10 (42 per cent) adults aged 16 and over in England reported spending time most days or every day together with their friends.
- In October 2011, just under half (47.3 per cent) of adults aged 16 and over in Great Britain reported being highly satisfied (9 to 10 out of 10) with their relationships with their friends.
- About two thirds of adults aged 16 and over in the UK reported being satisfied with their social life in 2008/09, although younger and older people reported higher levels of satisfaction than those between the ages of 25 and 54.

Community

- In 2009–10, over 80 per cent of adults aged 16 and over in England reported that many or some of the people in their neighbourhood could be trusted.
- In 2010–11 nearly 8 in 10 adults aged 16 and over in England reported that they felt they belonged strongly or very strongly to their neighbourhood.
- In 2010/11, 45.7 per cent of adults aged 16 and over in England were involved with a group, club or organisation which had people who got together to do an activity or to talk about things in the 12 months prior to interview.

Workplace relationships

- Just under 9 in 10 (87 per cent) of the working population of the EU-25 in 2004 reported that they were satisfied with the people that they worked with compared with just over 9 in 10 (91 per cent) in the UK.

Personal relationships and loneliness

Personal relationships are very important to an individual's well-being. They provide emotional and material support and help people's ability to deal with difficult times in their lives.

Experimental statistics from the Office for National Statistics (ONS) Opinions Survey looked at the levels of subjective well-being in the British population in 2011. In April and June 2011, adults aged 16 and over in Great Britain were asked to rate their satisfaction with their personal relationships from 0 to 10 where 0 represented not at all satisfied and 10 completely satisfied. The average reported satisfaction with personal relationships was higher than for overall life satisfaction. Overall, the average (mean) rating for satisfaction with personal relationships was 8.3, this compares with an average (mean) rating of 7.4 for overall life satisfaction. Over half (58.7 per cent) rated their satisfaction with their personal relationships as high (9 to 10 out of 10), while more than a quarter (27.1 per cent) rated their satisfaction as medium (7 to 8 out of 10) with the remaining 14.2 per cent rating their satisfaction as low (0 to 6 out of 10).

Figure 1

Satisfaction with personal relationships compared with life satisfaction,(1) 2011(2)

Great Britain

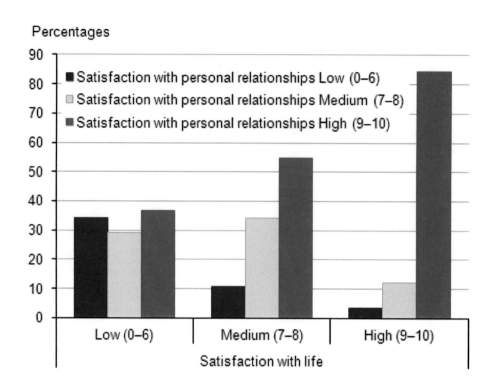

Source: Opinions (Omnibus) Survey - Office for National Statistics

Notes:
1.   Adults aged 16 and over were asked 'Overall, how satisfied are you with your life nowadays?' and 'Overall, how satisfied are you with your personal relationships?'
2.   Data for April and June 2011.

Overall satisfaction with life and personal relationships are related. Of those who reported a high satisfaction with life (9 to 10 out of 10), 84.2 per cent also reported a high satisfaction with their personal relationships (Figure 1). Conversely, 34.3 per cent of those who reported a low satisfaction with life (0 to 6 out of 10) also had low satisfaction with their personal relationships. However it must be noted that a similar proportion (36.6 per cent) who reported a low satisfaction with life also had a high satisfaction with their personal relationships, which indicates that there are other factors that impact on overall individual well-being.

Inadequate levels of social relationships may lead to people experiencing loneliness in life. However the feeling of loneliness is subjective and a person may experience this even when in the company of family and friends. In July 2011, the ONS Opinions Survey asked adults aged 16 and over in Great Britain on a scale of 0 to 10 how lonely they felt in daily life. Just over a third (33.5 per cent) of respondents who answered this question recorded not being lonely at all in their daily life (0 out of 10), while 4.5 per cent recorded being completely lonely in their daily life (10 out of 10).

Apart from looking at a person's relationship overall, it is also important to look at specific relationships, namely those with family, friends and the wider community.

Family relationships

Just under half (49.2 per cent) of all adults aged 16 and over in Great Britain were married or in a civil partnership in 2010, with a further 11.3 per cent cohabiting. A quarter (25.0 per cent) were single (never married), while 2.5 per cent were married or in a civil partnership but not living as a couple. 5.7 per cent were divorced or their civil partnership was dissolved and 6.4 per cent were widowed or their civil partner had died.

The proportions of the adult population who are either married or widowed continue to decline and the proportions who are either single or divorced continue to rise. One of the main reasons for the decrease in the married population and the increase in the single population is the growth of cohabitation by unmarried couples. In the early 1960s in Britain fewer than 1 in 100 adults under 50 are estimated to have been cohabiting at any one time, compared with 1 in 6 in 2010. Cohabitation may be seen as a precursor or an alternative to marriage. The average age at first marriage is increasing and there has been a general decrease in the annual number of marriages since the early 1970s. A large increase in divorces was observed during the 1970s. The Divorce Reform Act 1969 came into effect in England & Wales on 1 January 1971 which made it easier for couples to divorce upon separation. The percentage of marriages ending in divorce has generally increased for those marrying between the late 1960s and the early 1990s[1] (ONS, 2011a).

Figure 2

Spending time most days or everyday with family:(1) by age, 2011

England

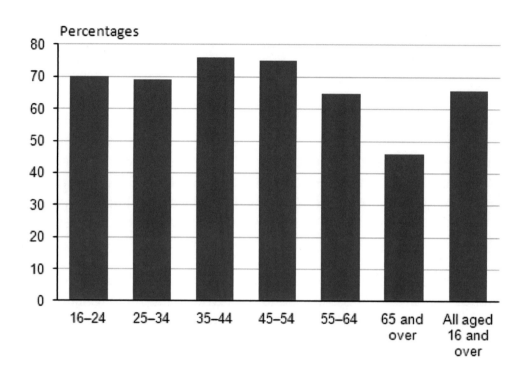

Source: Environment, Food and Rural Affairs

Notes:
1. Sample composed of 1,769 adults aged 16 and over, who were asked how often in the two weeks prior to interview they had spent time together with their family.

The 2011 survey of public attitudes and behaviours towards the environment run by the Department for Environment, Food and Rural Affairs (Defra) asked people how often in the previous two weeks they had spent time together with family. Two-thirds (66 per cent) of respondents reported having spent time with family every day or most days during the two weeks prior to interview (Figure 2). This is an increase from 61 per cent in 2007. There was variation by age group with those aged 65 and over much less likely to report spending time with family every day or most days (46 per cent) than other age groups (Defra, 2011).

It is also important to look at the quality of family relationships. Having a positive relationship with family is an important factor in influencing people's satisfaction with life and emotional well-being. The ONS Opinions Survey (April and August 2011) showed that adults aged 16 and over in Great Britain who were either married or in civil partnerships, cohabiting with their partners, or were widowed, reported very similar average (mean) ratings for satisfaction with their lives. These average (mean) ratings were higher than those for separated or divorced people and for those who were single (ONS, 2011b).

According to the British Household Panel Survey (BHPS)[2], a very high proportion of adults aged 16 and over in the UK reported that they are somewhat, mostly, or completely satisfied with their spouse or partner (92.3 per cent in 2008–09). In each year since 2002–03 approximately 9 in 10 reported this level of satisfaction with their spouse or partner and over half reported that they were completely satisfied. In 2008–09 men were more likely than women to report being somewhat, mostly or completely satisfied with their relationship with a partner or spouse in 2008–09 at 93.8 per cent compared with 91.0 per cent of women.

Figure 3

Partnerships that reported being extremely happy or perfect: by duration of partnership, (1) 2009(2) United Kingdom

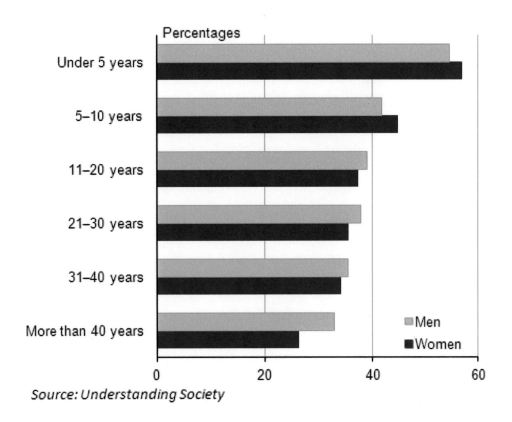

Source: Understanding Society

Notes:
1. Sample composed of 5,384 men and 6,441 women (unweighted).
2. Wave 1 data which was carried out across 2009–2010. This research makes use of data from participants interviewed in 2009.

According to data from *Understanding Society* (Wave 1, Year 1), the successor to the BHPS, happiness with a partnership declines with the duration of the relationship. This applies to both men and women aged 16 and over in the UK but the decline is steeper for women than for men (Figure 3). For those who had been together for less than 5 years, a similar proportion of both men and women reported their partnership as being extremely happy or perfect (54.4 per cent of men and 56.9 per cent of women). However, for those who had been together for more than 40 years, just 32.9 per cent of men and 26.4 per cent of women reported their partnership as being extremely happy or perfect (Understanding Society, 2011).

People's relationships with their children and in turn their children's experience of family life and their general well-being is also extremely important. In April and June 2011, the ONS Opinions Survey asked adults aged 16 and over in Great Britain how satisfied they were with the well-being of their child or children on a scale of 0 to 10. Over 9 in 10 (91.1per cent) reported a rate of 7 out of 10 and over with the most common response being 10 out of 10.

Figure 4

Predicted probability that a child (1) is completely happy with family life: by relationship with parents (2,3)

United Kingdom

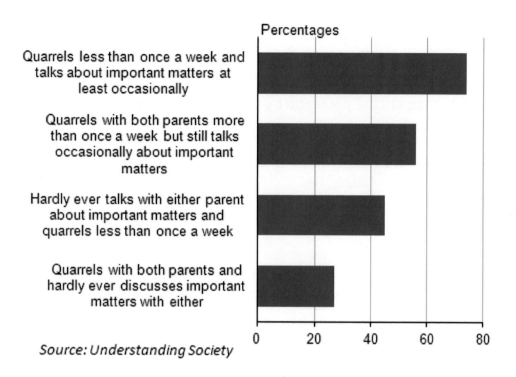

Source: Understanding Society

Notes:
1. These are predictions assuming the child is a 'typical' child age 12 years old.
2. Sample of 2,082 children aged 10 to 15 (unweighted).
3. Wave 1 data which was carried out across 2009–2010. This research makes use of data from participants interviewed in 2009.

From a child's perspective, data for 10 to 15 year olds from *Understanding Society* (Wave 1, Year 1) shows a strong relationship between how happy a child is with their family life and the frequency with which they quarrel with their parents and discuss important matters with them. For example, children who quarrel with their parents less than once a week and discuss important matters with them at least occasionally have a 73.6 per cent chance of reporting being completely happy with their family life (Figure 4). Children who quarrel with their parents more than once a week, and hardly ever discuss important matters with them have only a 26.9 per cent chance of rating themselves completely happy with their families (Understanding Society, 2011).

Financial problems are often cited as a common cause of disagreement between people in both new and established relationships. A YouGov survey in 2011 asked 2,425 adults aged 18 and over in Great Britain 'Do you think times of recession or economic trouble makes people's personal relationship stronger, makes them more likely to break down, or makes no difference?' Around 6 in 10 men and women (58 per cent and 63 per cent respectively) felt that it made relationships more likely to break down and 11 per cent of men and 7 per cent of women reporting that it made relationships stronger (Yougov, 2011).

Notes

1. For more information on changes in the poulation by marital status over time see Population Estimates by Marital Status

2. The survey period for the BHPS was September to March with around 90 per cent of the interviews collected in September to December.

Friendships

Friends are part of a person's support system and, unlike family, are chosen by the individual. They may often give advice on decisions and are companions in life who share interests and secrets.

Figure 5

Spending time most days or everyday with friends:(1) by age, 2011

England

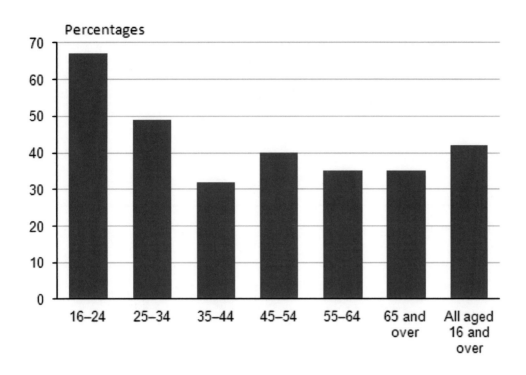

Source: Environment, Food and Rural Affairs

Notes:

1. Sample composed of 1,769 adults aged 16 and over, who were asked how often in the two weeks prior to interview they had spent time together with their friends.

Adults aged 16 and over in England were asked in the 2011 survey of public attitudes and behaviours towards the environment how often in the previous two weeks they had spent time together with friends. Over 4 in 10 adults (42 per cent) spent time with friends every day or most days (Figure 5). This was an increase from 37 per cent in 2007. Proportionately, younger people were more likely to report spending time with friends than older people; 67 per cent of 16 to 24 year-olds spent time with friends on most or every day in the two weeks prior to interview, compared with 35 per cent of those aged 55 to 64 and 65 and over. The lowest proportion of people spending time with friends on most or every day was those in the 35 to 44 age group (32 per cent). This may be due to having young children to look after and work commitments (Defra, 2011).

Table 1

Satisfaction with relationships with friends:(1) by gender, 2011

Great Britain

	Low	Medium	High
	(0–6)	(7–8)	(9–10)
All aged 16 and over	12.1	40.4	47.3
Men	13.2	43.1	43.8
Women	11.4	37.9	50.8

Percentages

Table source: Office for National Statistics

Table notes:
1.   1 Data is at October 2011.

In October 2011, the ONS Opinion Survey asked adults aged 16 and over in Great Britain to rate their satisfaction of their relationships with friends from 0 to 10. Almost half (47.3 per cent) reported a high satisfaction rating (9 to 10 out of 10) with 40.4 per cent reporting a medium satisfaction rating (7 to 8 out of 10) (Table 1). The average (mean) rating was 8.2.

Satisfaction with friends varied by gender and age with 43.8 per cent of men reporting a high satisfaction compared with 50.8 per cent of women, while 37.9 per cent of women reported a medium satisfaction compared with 43.1 per cent of men. Older people were more likely to report high satisfaction with their relationships with friends (56.4 per cent for those aged 65 to 74 and 54.3 per cent for those aged 75 and over) compared with lower age groups that ranged from 42.3 per cent for those aged 16 to 24 to 49.1 per cent for those aged 55 to 64.

According to the Princes' Trust Youth Index 2012, young people aged 16 to 25 were more satisfied with their relationships with family and friends in 2012 than they were in 2011 with the level of contentment rising from 78 to 80 points for family and 75 to 77 points for friends (Prince's Trust, 2012).

A person's social life consists of a combination of various components such as activities, people and places. While all of these are required to define a social life, the nature of each component is different for every person. Having a satisfactory social life may add to an individual's sense of well-being.

According to the BHPS,[1] nearly 7 in 10 (67.0 per cent) adults aged 16 and over in the UK were somewhat, mostly or completely satisfied with their social life in 2008–09. This was the same proportion as in 2002–03.

Social life satisfaction varied by age. In 2008–09 those aged 16 to 24 and 55 and over were more likely to report that they were somewhat, mostly or completely satisfied with their social life (75.7 per cent and 71.7 respectively). This compares with 58.2 per cent of those aged 35 to 44, 62.1 per cent aged 45 to 54 and 63.2 per cent of those aged 25 to 34. Lower satisfaction with social life for these age groups may be due to people having less time for socialising because of work or family commitments.

The presence of children in the family obviously has an effect. Three-quarters (75.2 per cent) of couples with no children and 71.8 per cent of couples with non-dependent children were somewhat, mostly or completely satisfied with their social life. This is higher than the equivalent figures for couples with dependent children (62.2 per cent) and lone parents with dependent children (50.8 per cent).

Two decades ago, most people would probably have used a landline phone or letter to contact friends to arrange a meeting. With the advent of new technology such as the Internet and mobile phones there are now other preferred ways of getting in touch; this is reflected in the proportions from Ofcom's Adults Media Literacy publication for 2005 and 2010 in Figure 6.

Figure 6

Selected preferred communication method for making contact with friends to arrange a meeting (1)

United Kingdom

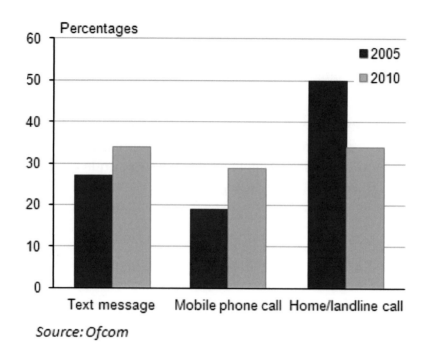

Source: Ofcom

Notes:
1.   Adults aged 16 and over (3,244 in 2005 and 2,117 in 2010).

Between 2005 and 2010, the proportion of adults aged 16 and over in the UK using a home/landline phone to contact friends to arrange a meeting decreased from 50 per cent to 34 per cent. Over the same period, those using text messages to contact friends to arrange a meeting increased from 27 per cent to 34 per cent, while those making a call from a mobile phone increased from 19 per cent to 29 per cent (Figure 6) (Ofcom, 2010)

Preferences for ways of getting in touch with a friend to arrange to meet vary considerably across different demographic groups. In 2010, adults aged less than 45 were more likely to send a text (62 per cent of those aged 16 to 24, 51 per cent of those aged 25 to 34 and 44 per cent of those aged 35 to 44). Adults aged 45 and over were more likely to make a call using the home/landline phone (37 per cent of those aged 45 to 54; 58 per cent of those aged 55 to 64 and 71 per cent of those aged 65 and over). Men were more likely to make a mobile phone call (34 per cent of men compared with 24 per cent of women) while women are more likely to send a text (39 per cent of women compared with 28 per cent of men) (Ofcom, 2010)

Social networking is also a way of increasing contact with friends and family. According to Ofcom, around half of all internet users in 2010 reported that using the internet had increased the contact they had with friends (53 per cent) or family (50 per cent) who live further away. Around a quarter (26 per cent) had increased contact with friends who live nearby and just under a fifth (18 per cent) family who live nearby. Just over a quarter (27 per cent) of internet users say they have increased contact with people with whom they share personal interests and hobbies, while 17 per cent of internet users say they have increased contact with people with different interests and hobbies (Ofcom, 2010).

Notes

1. The survey period for the BHPS was September to March with around 90 per cent of the interviews collected in September to December.

Community

Trusting other people is the foundation of most personal relationships and is a key determinant of well-being. Trust is important because people cannot get close to and maintain friendships or relationships without it.

According to the Citizenship Survey[1], half (50 per cent) of all adults aged 16 and over in England in 2009–10 reported that many of the people in their neighbourhood could be trusted and just over a third (34 per cent) reported that some could be trusted. Older age groups were more likely than younger age groups to report trust in people their neighbourhood. For example, just over 9 in 10 (91 per cent) aged 65 to 74 reported that many or some people could be trusted in their neighbourhood compared to 72 per cent of those aged 16 to 24 (DCLG, 2011).

The ONS Opinions Survey asked adults aged 16 and over in Great Britain in September 2011 to rate on a scale of 0 to 10 to what extent they felt most people could be trusted, the average (mean) rating was 5.8. Just under 6 in 10 (58.4 per cent) felt their extent of trust was low (0 to 6 out of 10), while 36.6 per cent rated their extent of trust as medium (7 to 8 out of 10) with the remaining 4.9 per cent rating their extent of trust as high (9 to 10 out of 10) (DCLG, 2011).

A feeling of belonging to a local community can influence people's sense of identity and may also contribute to an individual's sense of well-being.

Figure 7

Whether people feel that they belong strongly to their neighbourhood (1)

England

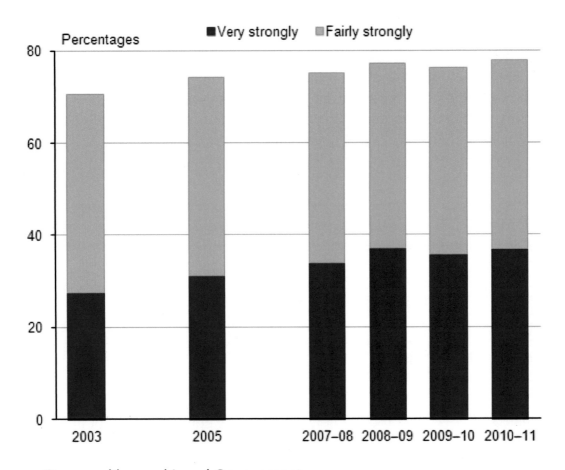

Source: Communities and Local Government

Notes:
1. Excludes respondents who answered 'don't know' and those with missing answers.

In 2010–11, 78 per cent of adults aged 16 and over in England felt they belonged strongly to their neighbourhood (Figure 7): the proportion of people who said they belonged strongly to their neighbourhood in 2010-11 was higher than in the period 2003 to 2007–08 (between 70 per cent and 75 per cent), but very similar to later years (77 per cent for 2008–09 and 76 per cent for 2009–10)[1] (DCLG, 2011).

The proportion of people who felt strongly they belonged to a neighbourhood varied by age, with a higher proportion of older people reporting that they belonged strongly to a neighbourhood. For example, around 87 per cent of people aged 65 and over felt strongly that they belonged to their neighbourhood, compared to 66 per cent of those aged 25 to 34.

Being involved in groups or activities outside of the home is a good way of meeting and communicating with other people. According to the Taking Part Survey in England in 2010/11, in the 12 months prior to interview, 45.7 per cent of adults aged 16 and over were involved with a group, club or organisation which had people who got together to do an activity or to talk about things. There was very little difference in the proportion of men and women who were involved in these groups (44.5 per cent and 46.9 per cent respectively). The most frequently reported activity groups were sports and exercise groups and hobbies or social clubs (DCMS, 2011).

Figure 8

Participation in selected activity groups:(1,2) by gender, 2010/11

England

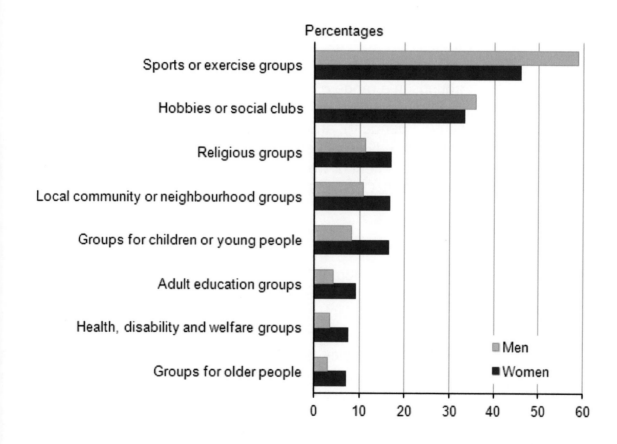

Source: Culture, Media and Sport

Notes:
1. Adults aged 16 and over that reported that they had been involved with a group of people who get together to do an activity or to talk about things in the 12 months prior to interview.
2. Groups not included in the chart are Environmental, Political, Trade Union, Other groups and excludes those who answered don't know.

A higher proportion of men reported that they were involved with a sports or exercise group than women (58.9 per cent and 46.0 per cent respectively) (Figure 8). Around the same proportion of men and women participated in hobbies or social clubs (35.9 per cent of men and 33.2 per cent of women). However a higher proportion of women participated in some groups compared with men: for example, religious groups (16.8 per cent compared with 11.2 per cent), local community or neighbourhood groups (16.7 per cent and 10.7 per cent) and groups for children and young people (16.4 per cent and 8.2 per cent) (DCMS, 2011).

When people from different ethnic or religious backgrounds mix socially it can make communities more cohesive so that the communities may suffer less from problems associated with anti-social behaviour, crime and lack of trust. Any reduction in problems is likely to improve the well-being of residents.

Tab 2 (30.5 Kb Excel sheet)   * This table can be found on page 22

In 2010–11, around 8 in 10 (82 per cent) people mixed socially at least once a month with people from different ethnic or religious backgrounds in a range of settings (excluding at home) (Table 2). People were most likely to mix socially with people from different backgrounds at the shops (64 per cent), followed by work, school or college (54 per cent), and then a pub, club, café or restaurant (45 per cent). Men were more likely than women to have met people from other backgrounds at work, school or college (58 per cent of men and 50 per cent of women) or in a pub, club, café or restaurant (50 per cent of men and 41 per cent of women) (DCLG, 2011).

Notes

1. The Citizenship Survey (formerly known as the Home Office Citizenship Survey, or HOCS) has been commissioned every two years since 2001. Approximately 10,000 adults in England and Wales (plus an additional boost sample of 5,000 adults from minority ethnic groups) are asked questions covering a wide range of issues, including race equality, faith, feelings about their community, volunteering and participation. Since 2007, the survey moved to a continuous design, allowing the provision of headline findings on a quarterly basis.

Working relationships

Another important form of relationship is that between work colleagues. Good workplace relationships can help make the working environment enjoyable and add to a person's well-being and may also improve productivity. A special Eurobarometer asked adults aged 15 and over who were working in December 2004 about their satisfaction with the people they work with. Just under 9 in 10 (87 per cent) of the working population of the EU-25 reported that they were satisfied with the people that they worked with compared with just over 9 in 10 (91 per cent) in the UK. Conversely, 8 per cent of the working population of the EU-25 reported that they were not satisfied with the people that they worked with compared with 4 per cent in the UK (Eurobarometer, 2005).

Figure 9

Employees perception of relations with management,(1) 2004

United Kingdom

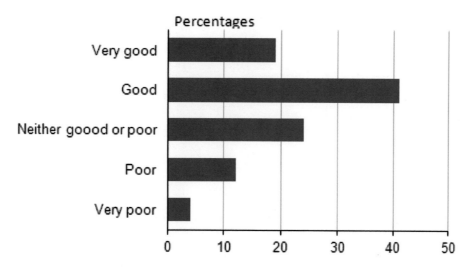

Source: Workplace Employment Relations Survey, ESRC, Acas,
Policy Studies Institute

Notes:
1. All employees in workplaces with 10 or more people were asked 'In general, how would you describe relations
    between managers and employers here'?

Another important relationship within the workplace is that of employers and managers. The quality
of the relationship between a manager and employee can significantly impact the performance of the
workforce. According to the 2004 Workplace Employment Relations Survey[1], just under 1 in 20 (19
per cent) of employees in workplaces with 10 or more people in the UK reported that relationships
between managers and employers were very good, while just over 4 in 10 (41 per cent) reported
relations as good. Just over 1 in 10 (12 per cent) described relations as poor and 4 per cent as very
poor (WERS, 2004).

Notes

1. This is the latest data available and employment and economic conditions will have changed over time.

About the ONS Measuring National Well-being Programme

NWB logo 2

This article is published as part of the ONS Measuring National Well-being Programme.

The programme aims to produce accepted and trusted measures of the well-being of the nation - how the UK as a whole is doing. It is about looking at 'GDP and beyond' and includes:

- greater analysis of the national economic accounts, especially to understand household income, expenditure and wealth
- further accounts linked to the national accounts, including the UK Environmental Accounts and valuing household production and 'human capital'
- quality of life measures, looking at different areas of national well-being such as health, relationships, job satisfaction, economic security, education environmental conditions
- working with others to include the measurement of the well-being of children and young people as part of national well-being
- measures of 'subjective well-being' - individuals' assessment of their own well-being
- headline indicators to summarise national well-being and the progress we are making as a society

The programme is underpinned by a communication and engagement workstream, providing links with Cabinet Office and policy departments, international developments, the public and other stakeholders. The programme is working closely with Defra on the measurement of 'sustainable development' to provide a complete picture of national well-being, progress and sustainable development.

Background notes

1. Details of the policy governing the release of new data are available by visiting www.statisticsauthority.gov.uk/assessment/code-of-practice/index.html or from the Media Relations Office email: media.relations@ons.gsi.gov.uk

Copyright

This document is also available on our website at www.ons.gov.uk.

References

1. DCLG, 2011- DCLG - Citizenship Survey.

2. DCMS, 2011 - Taking Part Survey - DCMS - Taking Part Survey.

3. Defra, 2011 - Survey of public attitudes and behaviours towards the environment DEFRA: Statistics.

4. Eurobarometer, 2005 - Special Eurobarometer 223 - Eurobarometer.

5. Ofcom, 2010 - Media Literacy Publications and Research - Ofcom: Media Literacy.

6. ONS, 2011a - Population Estimates by Marital Status.

7. ONS, 2011b - Initial investigation into Subjective Well-being from the Opinions Survey.

8. Prince's Trust, 2012 - Prince's Trust Youth Index 2012 - Prince's Trust Youth Index 2012.

9. Understanding Society, 2011 - Understanding Society: Early findings from the first wave of the UK's household longitudinal study.

10. WERS, 2004 - 2004 Workplace Employment Relations Survey - BIS: Workplace Employment Relations Survey.

11. YouGov, 2011 - YouGov/Sunday Times Magazine Survey Results - Yougov archives.

Table 2

Proportion of people mixing with others from different ethnic or religious backgrounds:(1) by location, ethnicity, sex and age, 2010-11

England   Percentages

	Home or their home	Work, school or college	Child's crèche, nursery or school	Pub, club, café or restaurant	Group, club or organisation	Shops	Formal volunteering	Informal volunteering	Place of worship	Any mixing (excluding at home)
All	36	54	17	45	33	64	19	15	15	82
Men	37	58	15	50	37	64	20	15	14	83
Women	34	50	19	41	29	64	19	16	16	80
16 to 24	54	79	9	67	47	74	25	19	14	92
25 to 34	49	73	28	61	38	73	18	16	19	92
35 to 49	37	68	33	50	35	69	22	18	15	88
50 to 64	29	49	8	37	28	60	19	14	13	80
65 to 74	20	11	3	26	24	52	17	12	14	65
75 and over	13	2	1	13	16	40	11	7	16	52
Ethnic Minority Groups[2]	63	73	33	59	44	85	23	25	46	95
White	32	51	15	44	31	61	19	13	11	80

1 Percentage mixing at least once a month.

2 Ethnicity figures based on all samples, other figures based on core sample.

Source: Citizenship Survey, Department for Communities and Local Government

Measuring National Well-being - What we do, 2012

Author Name(s): Carla Seddon Office for National Statistics

Abstract

This article describes what we do in work and leisure activities and looks at the balance between them. These were common themes in the national debate on measuring national well-being. The extent and the importance of each type of activity vary between individuals. Getting the right balance across all aspects of work and leisure is important in determining an individual's well-being.

Introduction

Do we live to work or work to live? Across the UK people live many different lifestyles based on individual choices, characteristics, personal preferences and circumstances. Individuals divide their time between various tasks and activities, including paid or unpaid employment, volunteering and various leisure activities. What we do in life shapes our lifestyles, our relationships with others and our overall well-being.

In Haworth's paper Life, Work Leisure and Enjoyment he says that *'Research into lived experience, work, leisure, and enjoyment is central to our understanding of happiness and well-being'*. (Haworth, 2010)

This article is published as part of the ONS Measuring National Well-being Programme. The programme aims to produce accepted and trusted measures of the well-being of the nation - how the UK as a whole is doing.

Key points

Labour Market: Employment, Unemployment and Economic Inactivity

Many studies have found evidence that those in employment have higher rates of well-being than those who are unemployed.

- The proportion of working age people in employment in the UK in October to December 2011 was 70.3 per cent, the unemployment rate was 8.4 per cent and economic inactivity stood at 23.1 per cent.

- In April to September 2011, adults in the UK aged 16 and over who were unemployed reported lower well-being (average ratings of 6.5, 6.8 and 6.8 out of 10 respectively for 'life satisfaction', 'worthwhile' and 'happy yesterday' questions) than those in employment (7.5, 7.8 and 7.4 out of 10 respectively).

Labour Market: Hours worked by those in Employment

Some studies have found that life satisfaction rises as the number of hours worked increases, but this effect can be reversed if these hours are excessive.

- The proportion of all those in employment in the UK working more than 45 hours a week decreased by 6.8 per cent between October to December 2011 and October to December 1996.
- Women are more likely to than men to work shorter hours. In October to December 2011 in the UK, 9.7 per cent of women work over 45 hours a week compared with 27.8 per cent of men. This is because more women work part time than men.

Job Satisfaction

- In 2009/10, 77.8 per cent of employed people in the UK reported being somewhat, mostly or completely satisfied with their job.

Work-life Balance

Obtaining the correct balance between work and home can help increase and maintain levels of well-being.

- In April and June 2011, 48.4 per cent of adults aged 16 and over in Great Britain reported relatively low satisfaction with their work-life balance (between 0 and 6 on a scale of 0 to 10).

Informal care-giving

Some research shows that those who care for others have lower scores for well-being indicators than non-carers.

- In 2009/10, the majority of adult carers aged 16 and over in the UK spent less than 35 hours per week undertaking caring responsibilities; for those caring for 35 hours or more, 5 per cent provide less than 50 hours; for 10 per cent time spent varies and 12 per cent provide 50 or more hours.

Volunteering

Studies have questioned whether volunteering improves the happiness and wellbeing of those who volunteer.

- In 2010/11, 39 per cent of adults aged 16 and over in England reported that they had formally volunteered at least once in the previous 12 months compared with 55 per cent who had informally volunteered.

- In England in 2008/09, 62 per cent of regular formal volunteers were motivated to volunteer because they 'wanting to improve things/help people'.

Leisure: Free Time

Spending time participating in leisure activities can have a positive effect on an individual's well-being.

- In 2009–10, 62.6 per cent of respondents in the UK reported being somewhat, mostly or completely satisfied with the amount of leisure time they had.
- In 2010/11, the most commonly reported free time activities by adults aged 16 and over in England were watching TV (87.6 per cent), spending time with friends and family (83.5 per cent) and listening to music (73.7 per cent).
- During 2010, adults aged 16 and over in the UK spent on average 4 hours 2 minutes daily watching television and 2 hours 53 minutes listening to the radio.

Leisure: Arts and Culture

- In England in 2010/11, 46.3 per cent of adults aged 16 and over had visited a museum or gallery in the last year, a continuation of the upward trend since 2006/07 (41.5 per cent). Meanwhile, 39.7 per cent had visited a public library, a decrease from 2005/06 (48.2 per cent).
- In 2010/11, 56.8 per cent of adults aged 16 and over in England had visited a heritage site as a child compared with 70.7 per cent who visited as an adult.

Leisure: Sports and physical activities

Engaging in sports and physical activities is thought to have a positive effect on the well-being of those who participate.

- In 2010/11, 54.1 per cent of adults aged 16 and over in England had participated in some type of sport or physical activity in the 4 weeks before interview. A higher proportion of men (61.8 per cent) participated than women (46.7 per cent).
- In England in 2010/11, 11.6 per cent of adults aged 16 and over had only exercised using a digital exercise device. A higher proportion of women (14.7 per cent) only exercised using a digital exercise device then men (8.3 per cent).

Holidays and Travel

Taking holidays can help to increase an individual's level of well-being.

- In 2010 there were 56 million visits abroad by UK residents. One in three visits (66 per cent) were for holidays, one in five (20 per cent) to visit friends and relatives and one in ten (12 per cent) for business purposes.
- In 2010, 119 million trips were made within the UK, nearly half (57 million) were holiday trips, 43 million were to visit friends and relatives and nearly 17 million were business trips.
- In Great Britain in 2010, 20 per cent of all trips were for shopping purposes while commuting journeys made up 16 per cent of all trips.

Labour Market: Employment, Unemployment and Economic Inactivity

A large part of many adult's lives, at least between the ages of 16 and 64, is spent either working or looking for employment. This section looks at information related to the labour market, including the trend in the numbers in employment, those unemployed, those who are not active in the labour market, usual hours worked and how satisfied those in employment are with their jobs. In addition there is some analysis of time spent in caring for others.

Various studies have been conducted regarding the relationship between well-being and employment status. In general many of these agree that those in employment have higher rates of well-being than those who are unemployed. *'Studies consistently show a large negative effect of individual unemployment on Subjective Well-Being. Models which treat life satisfaction scales as a continuous variable, tend to find that the unemployed have around 5–15% lower scores than the employed (e.g. Di Tella et al., 2001; Frey & Stutzer, 2000, 2002; Helliwell, 2003; Stutzer, 2004).'* (Dolan, Peasgood, White, 2008).

It has also been suggested that one of the reason for this is that the structure and purpose of employment plays a factor in improving well-being. *'The social psychologist Maria Jahoda (1982, 1984, 1986, Haworth 1997 Chapter 2) in her ground breaking analysis of employment and unemployment, argued for the centrality of the social institution of employment in providing five categories of psychological experience which are conducive to well-being and that, to the extent that the unemployed are deprived of these experiences, this contributes to the decline in their well-being. These experiences are: time structure, social contact, collective effort or purpose, social identity or status and regular activity'* (Haworth, 2010).

Figure 1: Levels of economic activity and inactivity (1)

United Kingdom

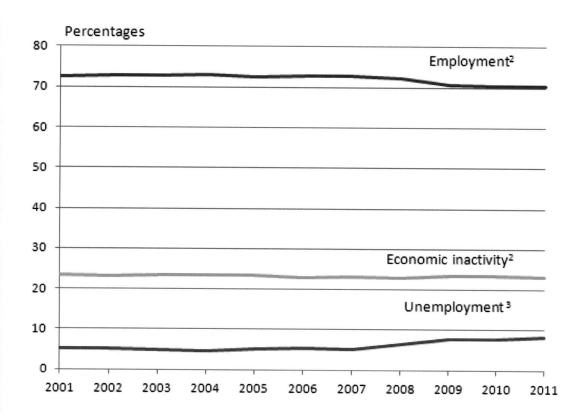

Source: Labour Force Survey - Office for National Statistics

Notes:
1. Data are at October to December each year and are seasonally adjusted.
2. Men and women aged 16 to 64.
3. Total unemployed as a percentage of economically active for all those aged 16 and over.

Over the last 10 years, the proportion of people of working age who are economically active has been quite stable. Since 2008 there has been a shift from employment to unemployment. Data from the Labour Force Survey (LFS) shows that in the UK in October to December 2011 the proportion of working age (16 to 64) people in employment was 70.3 per cent, slightly down from 70.5 per cent for the same quarter of the previous year and also lower than it was in October to December 2001

(72.6 per cent) (Figure 1). In the same period the unemployment rate[1] was 8.4 per cent, up from 7.9 per cent for the same quarter of the previous year and 5.2 per cent in October to December 2001. Economic inactivity[2] stood at 23.1 per cent in October to December 2011, down from the 23.4 per cent the same period in both the previous year and October to December 2001. (ONS, 2012a)

In October to December 2011, male employment stood at 75.3 per cent down from 75.7 per cent in the same period the previous year and a decrease from 79.1 per cent in October to December 2001. Male unemployment was 9.0 per cent, up from 8.5 per cent in October to December 2010 and 5.7 per cent in the same period of 2001. Male inactivity was 17.1 per cent in October to December 2011, slightly up from 17.0 per cent in the same period of 2010 and an increase from 16.0 per cent in 2001. Over the same time periods female employment stood at 65.4 per cent in 2011, a slight increase from 65.3 per cent in 2010 and down from 66.2 per cent in 2001. Female unemployment was 7.7 per cent in October to December 2011, up from 7.2 per cent in 2010 and 4.5 per cent 2001. Female economic inactivity was 29.1 per cent in 2011, down from 29.6 per cent in October to December 2010 and 30.6 per cent in 2001. The estimated percentage of those aged 16 and over who were unemployed in October to December 2011, at 8.4 per cent, was at its highest level since July to September 1995. Unemployment rates for men (9.0 per cent) is the highest proportion since January to March 2010 and for women (7.7 per cent) is the highest since January to March 1994.

The LFS report 'Older workers in the labour market - 2011' also showed that over the past decade an increasing number of older people (those aged 65 and over) are in work. This increase was in both full-time and part-time employment. Of those aged 65 and over in October to December 2010, 2.7 per cent (270,000) worked full-time, up from 1.2 per cent in January to March 2001 and 6.1 per cent (600,000) worked part-time, an increase from 3.4 per cent in January to March 2001. The 870,000 workers aged 65 and over made up 3.0 per cent of all workers in October to December 2010. This percentage has doubled over the last decade when it was 1.5 per cent in January to March 2001, with 412,000 people aged 65 and over in work. For further information see 'Older workers in the labour market – 2011'. (ONS, 2011a)

A release on young people covering employment rates since 1992 for those in and out of education compared to older people, the types of jobs that young people in or out of education are doing and the pay differences between young and older workers was released on 29 February 2012. For further information see 'Young people in work – 2012'. (ONS, 2012b)

In October to December 2011 the LFS showed there were almost 9.3 million people aged 16 to 64 who were economically inactive (that is not in employment and not available or looking for work). Of the economically inactive population, almost a quarter (24.5 per cent) are students, another quarter are looking after the family or home (24.9 per cent) and a third quarter are long term sick (22.7 per cent). Almost 16.5 per cent of the economically inactive population are retired, 1.8 per cent are temporarily sick, 0.7 per cent are discouraged workers and 8.8 per cent are inactive for other reasons. Just over 7 million (75.6 per cent) of economically inactive people do not want a job compared to over 2 million (24.4 per cent) who want a job but are unavailable for work.

Interactive maps are available showing the percentage of economically active and inactive residents at local authority level.

Results from analysis of the subjective well-being questions asked on the Annual Population Survey (APS) between April and September 2011 support the theory that in the UK adults aged 16 and over who are unemployed report lower well-being than those who are in employment. The average ratings for the 'life satisfaction', 'worthwhile' and 'happy yesterday' questions were significantly lower for unemployed people (6.5, 6.8 and 6.8 out of 10 respectively) than for employed people (7.5, 7.8 and 7.4 out of 10 respectively). The results also demonstrated that the length of time in unemployment led to lower average ratings, with subjective well-being decreasing as the duration of unemployment increased. For example, the average rating for 'life satisfaction' was 6.9 out of 10 for people who had been unemployed for up to 6 months, decreasing to 6.2 out of 10 for those unemployed for 6 to 12 months, and to 6.0 out of 10 for people whose length of unemployment exceeded 12 months. For further information and data see: Measuring Subjective Wellbeing in the UK, Analysis of experimental subjective well-being data from the Annual Population Survey, April - September 2011 (ONS, 2011b)

While employment and unemployment can have an effect on well-being, work can also have an effect on our health as will be discussed in the Measuring National Well-being: Health to be published later this year.

Notes

1. The unemployment rate is calculated, in accordance with international guidelines, as the percentage of all economically active people aged 16-64.

2. Economically inactive include people who are neither in employment or unemployment. This includes those looking after a home, retired or permanently unable to work.

Labour Market: Hours worked by those in Employment

Some studies find that life satisfaction rises as hours worked increases and that there are links with lower satisfaction amongst men who work part time hours. While other studies have found no such links. However Meier and Stutzer (2006) found *'an inverse U-shaped curve between life satisfaction and hours worked (including when fixed effects are controlled for) suggesting that well-being rises as hours worked rise but only up to a certain point before it then starts to drop as hours become excessive'*. (Dolan, Peasgood, White, 2008)

Figure 2: Usual weekly hours of work (1),(2) (all in employment)

United Kingdom

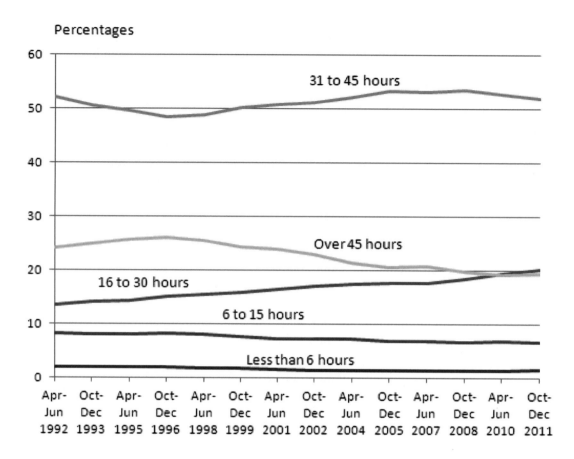

Source: Labour Force Survey - Office for National Statistics

Notes:
1.   Main job only
2.   Data are seasonally adjusted

According to the LFS, of all those in employment in the UK in October to December 2011, 1.6 per cent worked less than 6 hours per week, 6.8 per cent worked 6 to 15 hours per week, 20.2 per cent worked 16 to 30 hours a week, 52.1 per cent worked 31 to 45 hours per week and 19.4 per cent worked over 45 hours per week (Figure 2). Since comparable records began in April to June 1992 there has been a downwards trend in those usually working 6 to 15 hours with an overall fall of 1.4 per cent. Over the same period those working 16 to 30 hours have shown an overall increase of 6.7 per cent. Those working 31 to 45 hours is at the same level now as 20 years ago (52.1 per cent) although the level dropped to 48.5 per cent in 1996 and steadily increased to 53.7 per cent in 2009 before beginning to fall again. Those working over 45 hours has shown a sharp downwards trend since 1996 with an overall decrease of 6.8 per cent since October to December 1996. Lastly those working less than 6 hours have remained stable over the last 20 years with levels remaining between 1.6 and 2.1 per cent.

Figure 3: Usual weekly hours of work (1) (all in employment) by sex (2), October to December 2011

United Kingdom

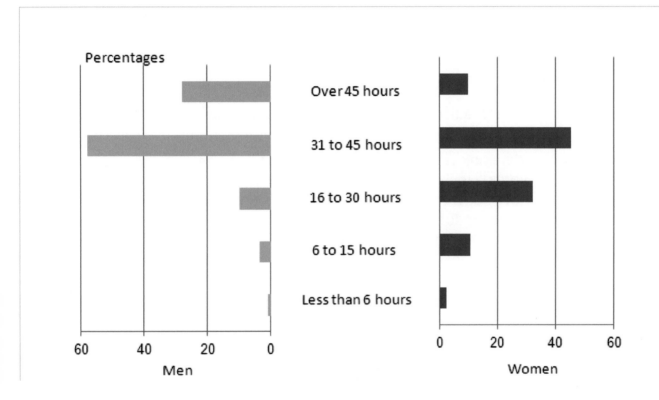

Source: Labour Force Survey - Office for National Statistics

Notes:
1.   Main job only.
2.   Data is seasonally adjusted.

Females are more likely than males to work shorter hours. In October to December 2011, 2.4 per cent of females worked less than 6 hours per week compared with 0.8 per cent of males (Figure 3). The percentage of females working 6 to 15 hours a week was 10.4 per cent compared with 3.6 per cent of males. A further 32.1 per cent of females work 16 to 30 hours a week in comparison with 9.9 per cent of males; 45.4 per cent of females compared with 57.9 per cent of males worked 31 to 45 hours a week and 9.7 per cent of females work over 45 hours compared with 27.8 per cent of males.

An analysis of hours worked in the Labour Market released in December 2011 showed that, in the second quarter of 2011, the average number of usual hours worked for people in employment in the UK stood at around 36.3 per week, down 4.7 per cent from 38.1 hours per week in 1992. This change was driven by a mixture of structural changes in the economy, and more flexibility in the hours chosen by employees or offered by employers (including more part-time working). For further information and data about hours worked in the Labour Market see 'Hours worked in the Labour Market- 2011'. (ONS, 2011c)

It could be suggested that the satisfaction with hours worked is dependent on whether the number of hours worked are voluntarily chosen by the individuals working them. From an individual's perspective, a lowering of underemployment and overemployment[1] may benefit physical and psychological well-being. According to the analysis of the LFS 'Characteristics of the underemployed and the overemployed in the UK' between Q1 2001 and Q1 2010 (not seasonally adjusted) underemployment levels declined gradually from the beginning of the decade until 2005, when they began to increase. However, overemployment increased gradually from 2000 until 2003 and then began to drop slightly until 2005. There was a small peak in overemployment in Q4 2007, but this was followed by a sharper decline up to Q2 2009. This could be because labour demand (hours of work required by employers) decreased as the economy contracted resulting in more people being underemployed as they were working fewer hours than preferred. For further information see 'The Economic and Labour Market Review, Vol 4 No7'. (ELMR, 2010)

Links to further Labour Market publications which you might find useful can be found in the notes section below.

Notes

1. Based on the ILO definition and data from the LFS,employed people (aged 16 or over) are classified as underemployed if: they are willing to work more hours because they want a job additional to their current job, want another job with longer hours, or want more hours in their current job; they are available to start working longer hours within 2 weeks and their 'constructed hours' during the reference week did not exceed 40 hours (if they are under 18 years of age) or 48 hours (if they are over 18 years of age). There is no international definition for overemployment, but in this article, employed people (aged 16 or over) are classified as overemployed if: they want to work fewer hours, either in a different job or in their current job and they would accept less pay for shorter hours, either in a different job or in their current job.

2. For Further Labour Market information you may find the below publications and links useful:

   Graduates in the Labour Market, 2011

Labour Market Flows

Labour Market Statistics, tables including age, disputes etc

Mothers in the Labour Market, 2011

People with disabilities in the Labour Market, 2011

Sickness Absence in the Labour Market, February 2011

The relationship between hours worked in the UK and the economy (359.9 Kb Pdf)

Young people's education and labour market choices aged 16/17 to 18/19

Job Satisfaction

Job satisfaction describes how content an individual is with his/her job. It is necessary for the large majority of those in the workforce to work, but each individual's satisfaction with their job varies. There are several sources of information which can be used to examine satisfaction with jobs.

Table 1: Satisfaction with Job (1)

United Kingdom

Percentages (2)

Responses[3]	2002/03	2005/06	2008/09	2009/10[4]
Somewhat, mostly or completely satisfied	68.8	70.0	71.9	77.8
Completely satisfied	11.9	11.9	11.5	18.5
Mostly satisfied	25.6	27.7	30.1	42.9
Somewhat satisfied	31.3	30.3	30.3	16.4
Neither satisfied nor dissatisfied	15.7	15.6	15.6	7.0
Somewhat dissatisfied	8.2	7.3	7.4	8.0
Mostly dissatisfied	4.2	4.4	3.4	4.1
Completely dissatisfied	3.0	2.8	1.8	3.1

Table source: British Panel Household Survey/
Understanding Society

Table notes:

1. Responses to " How dissatisfied or satisfied are you with.........Your job (if in employment)"
2. The percentages are of those who responded.
3. Responses to earlier waves of the BHPS differ. However, they have always been on a 7 point scale varying from completely (or very) satisfied to completely (or very) dissatisfied.
4. Understanding Society -- the UK Household Longitudinal Study--surveys approximately 40,000 households in the United Kingdom. The sample is randomly allocated to monthly samples across this period. While each wave of the survey takes two years to complete, the waves overlap so that sample members are interviewed annually. Wave 1 data collection took place between January 2009 and January 2011. Around 8,400 households which were former participants of the British Household Panel Survey (BHPS) are part of Understanding Society from Wave 2 2010-2011.

According to Understanding Society (US) in the UK in 2009/10 77.8 per cent of employed people are somewhat, mostly or completely satisfied with their job (Table 1). In 2009/10, 7.0 per cent stated that they were neither satisfied nor dissatisfied with their job. A further 15.2 per cent stated that they were somewhat, mostly or completely dissatisfied with their jobs. The proportions who were somewhat, mostly or completely satisfied with their job in response to the earlier British Household Panel Study (BHPS) were 71.9 per cent in 2008/09: this had increased gradually from 68.8 per cent in 2002/03. Note that comparisons between the 2009/10 US results and the earlier BHPS results should be treated with care as there is some variation in the samples, surveys and questions. (US, 2011)

Respondents in the April and June 2011 ONS Opinions Survey were asked the question 'Overall, how satisfied are you with your work situation?' Of those surveyed, 37.7 per cent stated that they had low satisfaction (between 0 and 6 on a scale of 0 to 10) with their work situation. A further 29.0 per cent stated that they had medium satisfaction (between 7 and 8 on the scale) with their work situation and 33.3 per cent had high satisfaction (9 to 10 on the scale). The same survey showed that 40.1 per cent of respondents had low satisfaction with the amount of time they had to do the things they like doing, 33.3 per cent had medium satisfaction and 26.6 per cent had high satisfaction. (ONS, 2011d)

Aspects of work appear to be rated differently in Britain and in the United States, according to findings from the Gallup-Healthways Well-Being Index for the United Kingdom. When the United States and the UK are compared across six key areas of wellbeing, the UK score lower than the USA with the largest difference being in workers' perceptions of their workplaces. Gallup classifies those who answer yes to all four items in the Work Environment Index as having a good work environment. In total, 35 per cent of UK workers report having a good work environment compared with 47 per cent of American workers and UK employees give their workplaces lower ratings than USA workers across all four work environment measures. In the UK less than half who work for an employer say their supervisor is more like a partner than a boss (42.1 per cent), compared with the majority of USA workers (55.8 per cent). UK workers are also less likely than those in the USA to say that they are satisfied with their job and that they get to use their strengths at work, 87.7 per cent of USA respondents stated they were satisfied with the job they did, compared with 83.8 per cent of UK respondents, while 84.4 per cent of USA respondents stated they got to use their strengths to do what they did best everyday compared with 80.3 per cent of UK respondents. Finally, 78.7 per cent of US respondents agreed that their supervisor always creates an open/ trusting environment compared with 77.1 per cent in the UK[1]. (Gallup, 2011)

Notes

1. Results are based on telephone interviews conducted as part of the Gallup-Healthways Well-Being Index survey Jan.2-March 31,2011, with random sample of 3,933 adults, aged 18 and older, living in the United Kingdom, selected using random-digital-dial sampling.

Work-life Balance

There are 1,440 minutes in every day. The 2005 Time Use Survey showed that in 2005 adults aged 16 and over in Great Britain spent on average 491 minutes (8 hours, 11 minutes) per day sleeping,

170 minutes (2 hours 50 minutes) on paid work, 82 minutes (1 hour 22 minutes) eating and drinking and 44 minutes per day on personal care such as washing and dressing. This means that over a third of our day (36 per cent) is spent sleeping /resting, a fifth (23 per cent) is spent on free time, 13 per cent is spent on paid work /study, 13 per cent on domestic work, 9 per cent is spent on meals and personal care and the remaining 6 per cent is spent travelling. It should be noted that these averages include all those aged 16 and over whether they work or not. (ONS, 2005)

Obtaining and maintaining the correct balance between working life and home life can be beneficial to an individuals overall well-being. *'It is plausible to expect individual differences to condition the impact of work–family balance on individual well-being and work outcomes. For example, work imbalance may have more severe effects on quality of life for some individuals than for others.'* (Greenhaus, Collins, Shaw, 2002)

Figure 4: How satisfied are you with the balance between the time you spend on your paid work and the time you spend on other aspects of your life? (1),(2)
Great Britain

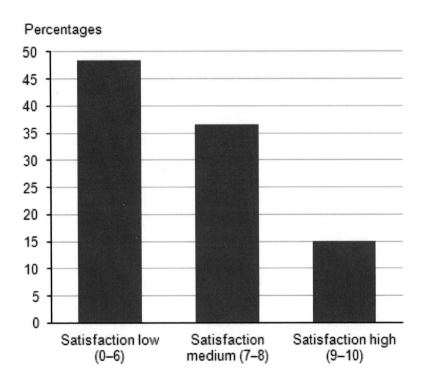

Source: Opinions (Omnibus) Survey - Office for National Statistics

Notes:

1.   Data at June 2011.

2.   Respondents were asked 'How satisfied are you with the balance between the time you spend on your paid work and the time you spend on other aspects of your life?'.

Figure 4 illustrates the results from the June 2011 Opinions survey when respondents were asked the question 'How satisfied are you with the balance between the time you spend on your paid work and the time you spend on other aspects of your life'. Nearly half of those surveyed (48.4 per cent) reported relatively low satisfaction with their work-life balance (between 0 and 6 on a scale of 0 to 10 where 0 equals not at all and 10 equals completely). A further 36.6 per cent stated that they had medium satisfaction (between 7 and 8 on the scale) with their work-life balance while 15.1 per cent had high satisfaction (9 to 10 on the scale). (ONS, 2011d)

According to a quarterly survey among UK employees, conducted in June 2011, commissioned by the Chartered Institute of Personnel and Development (CIPD), the proportion of employees agreeing or strongly agreeing they achieve the right work-life balance has increased to 58 per cent from 56 per cent for the previous quarter. Voluntary sector employees are most likely to agree this is the case (60 per cent), followed by those in the private sector (59 per cent) and those in the public sector (53 per cent). Men are significantly less likely to agree they achieve the right work-life balance (53 per cent) than women (64 per cent). People working in small organisations are more likely to agree they achieve the right balance between their work and home lives than those employed by medium-sized or large organisations. Sole traders are most likely to agree this is the case. In all, 35 per cent of employees agree or strongly agree that their organisation provides them with support to help them manage their work-life balance, with public sector employees most likely to agree this is the case (39 per cent), followed by those in the voluntary sector (36 per cent) and those in the private sector (34 per cent). Just over a third (35 per cent) of employees agreed that their manager provides support to help them manage their work-life balance. Public sector employees are most likely to agree this is the case (46 per cent) with private sector staff least likely to (33 per cent). (CIPD, 2011)

Apart from paid employment individuals spend time on things which might be considered as 'unpaid work' as well as being other aspects of what people do and value. These include informal care for those who need help and both formal and informal volunteering.

Informal care-giving

There has been little research conducted into the effect that providing care has on the carers well-being however, *'The evidence from the few studies that examined the effects of the amount of time engaged in informal care-giving suggests that more care is associated with worse GHQ[1] scores (Hirst, 2003, 2005), lower happiness (Marks, Lambert, & Choi, 2002; van den Berg & Ferrer-i-Carbonell, forthcoming) and more depressive symptoms (Marks et al., 2002)'.* (Dolan, Peasgood, White, 2008)

It is difficult to identify carers as a sub-group of the population. Although there are 2.3 million inactive people who look after family or the home, not all those provide care for other people. Also some of those who currently care for someone are active in the labour force.

According to the 2009/10 Family Resource survey most adult carers aged 16 and over are employed (31 per cent full time, 14 per cent part time) or self-employed (5 per cent full time, 3 per cent part time), rather than unemployed (4 per cent) or retired (23 per cent), permanently sick or disabled (6 per cent), or classed under another form of economic inactivity (14 per cent). The majority of all carers spend less than 35 hours per week undertaking their caring responsibilities: 27 per cent less than 5 hours; 34 per cent 5, but less than 20 hours; 7 per cent 20, but less than 35 hours; and 5 per cent for whom it varies, but less than 35 hours. Of those undertaking caring responsibilities of 35 hours or more per week, 5 per cent provide at least 35 but less than 50 hours; for 10 per cent time spent varies but is more than 35 hours; and more than 1 in 10 provide 50 or more hours per week (12 per cent). For further information and data about statistics see: 'Family Resource Survey 2009-10'. (DWP, 2010)

Notes

1. General Health Questionnaire (GHQ, Goldberg & Williams, 1988), which also contains several items measuring SWB. In general in the GHQ the higher the score, the more severe the condition.

Volunteering

Volunteering takes many forms and is performed by a wide range of people. It could be said that volunteering and helping others improves the happiness and wellbeing of the volunteers, but is this the case or are happier people more likely to volunteer in the first place? Furthermore, although Thoits and Hewitt (2001) did find a positive relationship between well-being and volunteering *'it also seemed to be the case that happier people tended to do more voluntary work, questioning the argument that volunteering is the cause of greater well-being'* (Dolan, Peasgood, White, 2008).

It has also been stated that volunteers tend to have more favourable human, cultural and social capital resources than non-volunteers and that all these are indicators of higher well-being (Choi, Kim, 2010)

Table 2: Participation in voluntary activities, 2001 to 2010-11

England

Percentages

	2001	2003	2005	2007/08	2008/09	2009/10	2010/11
At least once a month							
Informal volunteering[1]	34	37	37	35	35	29	29
Formal volunteering[2]	27	28	29	27	26	25	25
Any volunteering[3]	47	50	50	48	47	42	41
At least once in last year							
Informal volunteering	67	63	68	64	62	54	55
Formal volunteering	39	42	44	43	41	40	39
Any volunteering	75	73	76	73	71	66	65

Table source: Citizenship Survey - Department for Communities and Local Government

Table notes:
1. Informal volunteering: Giving unpaid help as an individual to people who are not relatives.
2. Formal volunteering: Giving unpaid help through groups, clubs or organisations to benefit other people or the environment.
3. Participated in either formal or informal volunteering.

According to the Citizenship Survey in England in 2010/11, 39 per cent of adults aged 16 and over reported that they had volunteered formally[1] at least once in the 12 months prior to interview, a smaller proportion than in all years between 2003 and 2007/08 but unchanged compared with 2008/09 and 2009/10 (Table 2). Twenty-five per cent of people reported that they volunteered formally at least once a month in 2010/11, a lower level than all years between 2001 and 2007/08 but unchanged compared with 2008/09 and 2009/10. In 2010/11, levels of informal volunteering[2], both in the previous year and on a regular basis, were higher than levels of formal volunteering. Fifty five per cent of people volunteered informally at least once in the 12 months prior to interview, and 29 per cent volunteered informally at least once a month. As with informal volunteering during the previous year, the level of monthly informal volunteering (29 per cent) was also lower than in all years prior to 2009/10 (when levels ranged from 34 per cent to 37 per cent). This followed a notable decline between 2008/09 and 2009/10 (from 35 per cent to 29 per cent). (DCLG, 2011)

In England in 2010/11, 39 per cent of men and 38 per cent of women engaged in formal volunteering. Those aged 35 to 49 years volunteered the most with 43 per cent, followed by 42 per cent for 50- to 64-year-olds, 41 per cent for 65- to 74-year-olds, 38 per cent for 16- to 25-year-olds, 33 per cent for 26- to 34-year-olds, and 28 per cent among those aged 75 years and over.

In Northern Ireland in 2007, 21 per cent of adults aged 16 and over were formal volunteers, this equates to an estimated 282,067 individuals. Informal volunteers accounted for 35 per cent of the individuals surveyed of which almost a third were also formal volunteers (31 per cent). This equates to an estimated 470,111 individuals who had been engaged as informal volunteers over the last 12 months when questioned in 2007. An estimated 145,734 individuals were both formal and informal volunteers. Females were more likely than males to be formal volunteers. As a proportion of all formal volunteers 6 out of every 10 were females (61 per cent). (VDA, 2007)

A Third Sector Research Centre (TSRC) working paper discusses the selection of methods of measuring and definitions of volunteering. It suggests that for the purposes of academic research and policy analysis and decision making there is considerable variation in the estimates derived from different surveys. Estimates range between 20 per cent and 50 per cent as the lower and upper bounds of annual involvement in volunteering (inclusive definition[3]), and between 10 per cent and 30 per cent for involvement on a monthly basis (on restrictive definitions[4]). For an overview of data and sources of information about volunteering in the UK see 'Individual voluntary participation in the United Kingdom: an overview of survey information', TSRC working paper 6. (TSRC, 2011)

According to the 2008/09 Citizenship survey the most popular motivation for regular formal volunteers in England to start volunteering was 'wanting to improve things/help people' (62 per cent), feeling 'the cause was really important' to them (40 per cent), wanting to 'meet new people/ make friends' (33 per cent). People started volunteering because they had spare time (33 per cent) and 32 per cent wanted to make use of existing skills. The most common benefit cited by regular formal volunteers was 'getting satisfaction from seeing the results' (65 per cent); 'enjoying it' (64 per cent), meeting people and making friends (55 per cent), it gave them a 'sense of personal achievement'(32 per cent), and it gave them a chance to do things they were good at (30 per cent). (DCLG, 2009)

Notes

1. Formal volunteering: Giving unpaid help through groups, clubs or organisations to benefit other people or the environment.

2. Informal volunteering: Giving unpaid help as an individual to people who are not relatives.

3. Definitions of volunteering vary through different surveys, however an inclusive definition usually relies on a basic survey question clarifying whether the respondent did unpaid voluntary work

during 12 months preceding the survey thereby approximating annual rate of involvement in volunteering.

4. Definitions of volunteering vary through different surveys, however a restrictive definition focuses on those who did unpaid voluntary work with frequency of at least once a month.

Leisure: Free Time

Roberts (1999) provides one definition of leisure as '*Existing in what is left over; in time that remains when paid work and other obligatory activities have been done,*'. (Roberts, 1999)

Therefore, leisure, or free time, is a period spent on non-compulsory activities when individuals can choose to do the things they enjoy according to their preferences and lifestyles. Spending time participating in leisure activities and doing the things they enjoy can have a positive effect on an individual's well-being. '*Participation in both physical and non- physical leisure activities has been shown to reduce depression and anxiety, produce positive moods and enhance self-esteem and self-concept, facilitate social interaction, increase general psychological wellbeing and life satisfaction, and improve cognitive functioning*'. (Haworth, 2010)

Table 3: Satisfaction with amount of leisure time (1)

United Kingdom

Percentages (2)

Responses[3]	2002/03	2005/06	2008/09	2009–10[4]
Somewhat, mostly or completely satisfied	60.6	58.1	62.9	62.6
Completely satisfied	20.9	17.5	18.0	15.6
Mostly satisfied	17.6	17.6	20.8	26.7
Somewhat satisfied	22.1	22.9	24.2	20.2
Neither satisfied nor dissatisfied	18.8	19.0	18.7	12.8
Somewhat dissatisfied	12.0	13.3	10.9	14.3
Mostly dissatisfied	6.0	6.5	5.2	6.5
Completely dissatisfied	2.6	3.2	2.3	3.9

Table source: British Panel Household Survey/
Understanding Society

Table notes:

1. Responses to " How dissatisfied or satisfied are you with.........The amount of leisure time you have"
2. The percentages are of those who responded.
3. Responses to earlier waves of the BHPS differ. However, they have always been on a 7 point scale varying from completely (or very) satisfied to completely (or very) dissatisfied.
4. Understanding Society -- the UK Household Longitudinal Study--surveys approximately 40,000 households in the United Kingdom. The sample is randomly allocated to monthly samples across this period. While each wave of the survey takes two years to complete, the waves overlap so that sample members are interviewed annually. Wave 1 data collection took place between January 2009 and January 2011. Around 8,400 households which were former participants of the British Household Panel Survey (BHPS) are part of Understanding Society from Wave 2 2010-2011.

The Understanding Society Survey (US) asked respondents 'How dissatisfied or satisfied are you with the amount of leisure time you have'. In the UK, in 2009–10, 62.6 per cent of respondents reported that they were somewhat, mostly or completely satisfied (Table 3), 12.8 per cent were neither satisfied nor dissatisfied and 24.7 per cent were somewhat, mostly or completely dissatisfied.

  In the earlier British Household Panel Survey (BHPS) there was an increase in those who were somewhat, mostly or completely dissatisfied with the amount of leisure time they had from 60.6 per cent in 2002/03 to 62.9 per cent in 2008/09. It should be noted that there are some issues of comparability between the earlier BHPS and those from US. (US, 2011)

Figure 5: Selected activities performed in free time: (1), (2) by age, 2010/11

England

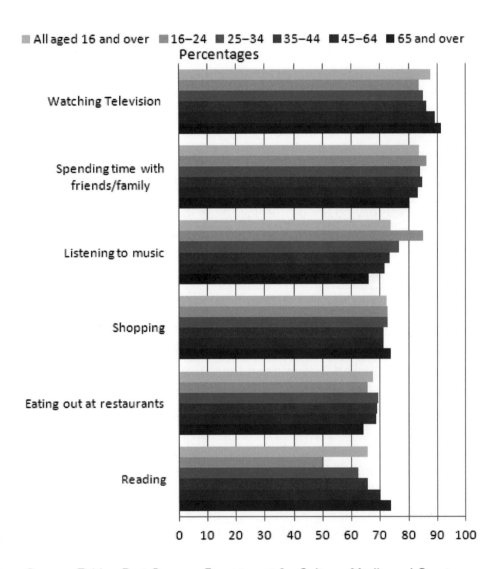

Source: Taking Part Survey - Department for Culture, Media and Sport

Notes:
1. Respondents were shown a list of activities and asked to pick the things they did in their free time. The most popular activities performed by all adults aged 16 and over are shown in the table.
2. Figures exclude refusals and 'Don't know'.

Data from the Taking Part Survey show that in England in 2010/11 the most commonly reported free time activity is watching TV (87.6 per cent of adults aged 16 and over), followed by spending time with friends or family (83.5 per cent) and listening to music (73.7 per cent) (Figure 5). There was however some variation with age. The same three most common activities were reported for all age groups from 25 to 64. The proportion reporting reading as one of their activities increased with age, so that is was the third most popular for those aged 65 and over, while listening to music decreased with age so that it was the second most common activity for those aged 16 to 24. (DCMS, 2011)

The percentages who reported spending time with family and friends, using the internet/ emailing, going to the cinema, going to pubs/clubs/bars, or playing sport or exercising all also decreased with age.

The three most commonly reported activities were the same for men as for all individuals (87.4 per cent watching TV, 80.2 per cent spending time with family and friends and 73.0 per cent listening to music). However for women listening to music is the fourth most reported activity (74.4 per cent) while shopping is the third (a top three of 87.8 per cent watching TV, 86.7 per cent spending time with family and friends and 81.4 per cent shopping).

As seen in Figure 5 spending time with family and friends is a popular way for individuals to use their free time; this use of leisure time could be particularly beneficial to their well-being as *'It would appear that, overall, socialising with family and friends is positively associated with Subjective Well-being (e.g. Lelkes, 2006; Pichler, 2006) and that this positive effect applies into older age (Ritchey, Ritchey, & Dietz, 2001), and remains even when controlling for levels of life satisfaction in previous periods (Baker et al., 2005)'*. (Dolan, Peasgood, White, 2008). The relationship between spending time with friends and family and individuals' well-being is further investigated in the Reporting on National Well-being article 'Our Relationships'

In 2009, according to the Northern Ireland Life and Times Survey, 73 per cent of adults aged 18 and over in Northern Ireland watched TV, DVD's or video's daily. More men (74 per cent) watched these than women (72 per cent). Those aged between 35 and 44 watched least (59 per cent) compared with 82 per cent of those aged 65 years and over. For other age groups 68 per cent of 18- to 24-year-olds watched daily compared with 74 per cent of 25- to 34-year-olds, 77 per cent of 45- to 54-year-olds, and 78 per cent of those aged 55 to 64. (NILT, 2009)

Also in Northern Ireland in 2009, 57 per cent of adults listened to music, 34 per cent spent time on the internet or computer and 27 per cent read books on a daily basis. Additionally when looking at activities adults engaged in at least several times a month, 36 per cent spent time shopping, 36 per cent got together with relatives, 40 per cent got together with friends and 11 per cent when to the movies.

Table 4: Average time per day (1) spent using communications services

United Kingdom

		Minutes per day
	2005	2010
Television	219	242
Radio	185	173
Internet - fixed	15	28
Phone - fixed	15	12
Phone - mobile	7	13

Table source: Ofcom / BARB / RAJAR / Nielsen Netratings (home use only)

Table notes:

1. Daily figures were calculated from monthly data on the assumption that there are 30.4 days in the average month; the exception was for internet consumption where the quoted figures relate to May 2005 and May 2010, and 31 days were used; the internet consumption figures include the use of online applications such as streaming media and only include use at home; mobile telephony figures are estimated assuming that the average time taken to send and receive a text message is 35 seconds.

According to Ofcom's Communications Market Report, television and radio continued to play a large role in the total time consumers spend on communications services each day during 2010 (Table 4). Adults aged 16 and over in the UK spent 242 minutes (4 hours 2 minutes) daily watching television on a TV set, up by 23 minutes from 2005, while radio accounted for 173 minutes (2 hours 53 minutes) per day, down by 12 minutes over the same period. Fixed-line calls accounted for 12 minutes per person per day, while a similar amount of time (13 minutes) was spent on mobile phone calls and texting on a mobile. Internet activities undertaken on a fixed internet connection (using web and applications) experienced the largest increase in average daily use, nearly doubling from 15 minutes in 2005 to 28 minutes in 2010. (Ofcom, 2011)

Leisure: Arts and Culture

Arts and culture encompasses a wide selection of activities in which people both participate, such as playing a musical instrument, and engage, for example attending a musical performance. The distinction between participating and being in the audience is blurring with the connectivity provided by the latest generation of mobile phones and other web-enabled devices. The arts and culture are popular with many choosing to spend their free time watching television, listening to music, visiting historic sites, museums and galleries, going to the cinema, attending concerts, participating in arts and crafts or playing musical instruments.

Some research studies have found links between arts and culture and wellbeing, for instance that culture helps to strengthen social ties in the community and therefore contributes towards individual and organisational self-esteem which ultimately nurtures well-being (European Commission 2009) and that '*Claims that the arts are good for individuals take many forms. The arts have been said to improve health, mental well-being, cognitive functioning, creative ability and academic performance*'. (Guetzkow, 2002)

Figure 6: Proportion who have visited a museum, gallery or archive, a public library, a heritage site or engaged with the arts in the last year, 2005/06 to 2010/11

England

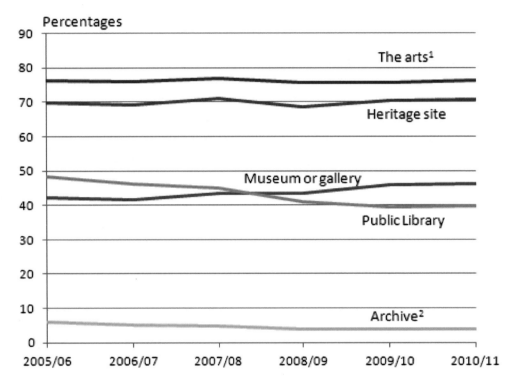

Source: Taking Part Survey, Department for Culture, Media and Sport

Notes:
1. The respondent is asked if they have participated in a given list of arts activities or attended a given list of arts events eg: Theatre, singing, street arts etc
2. An Archive is a place containing records, documents, or other materials of historical interest

In 2010/11 according to the Taking Part Survey in England, 46.3 per cent of adults aged 16 and over had visited a museum or gallery in the last year: a significant increase from 2008/09 (43.4 per cent) and a continuation of the upward trend since 2006/07 (41.5 per cent) (Figure 6). Meanwhile, 39.7 per cent of adults had visited a public library in the last year, a decrease from 2005/06 (48.2 per cent). However the steady decline in library visits observed between 2005/06 and 2008/09 has now stabilised, with no significant change observed between 2008/09 (41.1 per cent) and 2010/11 (39.7 per cent). In 2010/11, 70.7 per cent of adults had visited a heritage site in the last year, relatively unchanged from 2005/06 (69.9 per cent) while 76.2 per cent of adults had engaged with the arts[1] at least once in the last year, unchanged from 2005/06 (76.3 per cent). In 2010/11, 4.0 per cent of adults visited an archive, not a significant change from 3.8 per cent in 2009/10 but a significant decrease from 5.9 per cent in 2005/06.

The Continuous Household Survey in Northern Ireland in 2010/11 shows that 41 per cent of adults aged 16 and over visited a museum in the previous 12 months, an increase from 32 per cent in 2009/10 and 2007/08 and up from 26 per cent in 2008/09. In 2010/11, 32 per cent visited a public library at least once a year, a steady increase from 29 per cent in 2009/10, 26 per cent in 2008/09 and 27 per cent in 2007/08. Also in Northern Ireland, 80 per cent of adults engaged with the arts in 2010/11, an increase from 76 per cent in 2009/10 and 71 per cent in 2008/09 and 2007/08. In 2010/11, 52 per cent of adults, aged 16 and over read for pleasure, 50 per cent participated in sport and physical activity in the previous 12 months, 6 per cent participated in painting, drawing, printmaking and sculpture, 5 per cent participated in dance (other than ballet), 8 per cent played a musical instrument for their own pleasure and 3 per cent played a music instrument to an audience[2]. (DCALNI, 2010)

Data from the Scottish Household Survey show that in 2010, 85 per cent of adults aged 16 or over were engaged in culture in the last 12 months. Cultural engagement is defined as those who have participated in a cultural activity or who have attended or visited a cultural event or place. Eighteen per cent visited a historic site in 2010 which was, down from 20 per cent in 2007 . Thirty per cent of adults visited museums, galleries and archives in 2010 (unchanged since 2007) and 28 per cent visited a library - a decrease from 31 per cent in 2007. In 2010, 61 per cent of adults read for pleasure, while 51 per cent went to the cinema and 43 per cent went to the theatre or music concerts. Seventeen per cent of adults engaged in arts and crafts and 10 per cent played a musical instrument, while 29 per cent engaged in theatre, dance or classical music, 26 per cent played a musical instrument, acted, sung or danced, 13 per cent wrote stories, poems, plays or music, and 9 per cent participated in painting or drawing[3]. (SG, 2010)

The Arts in Wales survey shows that between 2005 and 2010 the proportion of the Welsh adults aged 16 and over engaging in the arts increased with 86 per cent normally attending arts events at least once per year, an increase from 76 per cent in 2005, and 39 per cent normally participating in an art form at least once a year, an increase from the 20 per cent recorded in 2005. Over this period the largest increases were recorded for attendance at cinema, live music events, art galleries and exhibitions, plays and musicals and participation in visual arts and crafts, music and dance. Women were more likely to attend and participate in the arts (90 per cent) than men (87 per cent). (ACW, 2010)

Figure 7: Adult and childhood participation in culture and sport (1), (2), 2010/11

England

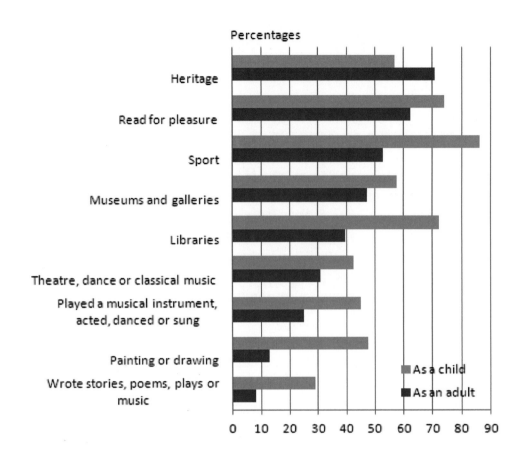

Source: Taking Part Survey - Department for Culture, Media and Sport.

Notes:

1. Figures exclude people who have participated for the purposes of paid work or academic study.

2. Respondents were asked if they participated in these activities when they were growing up and now as an adult.

Figure 7 shows that in 2010/11 a higher proportion of adults aged 16 and over in England had participated in culture and sport when they were children than as an adult with the exception of visiting a heritage site where 56.8 per cent of adults had visited a heritage site as a child while 70.7 per cent had visited as an adult in the last 12 months. In England in 2010/11, 46.3 per cent of adults aged 16 and over, had visited a museum or gallery in the last 12 months while 57.7 per cent had visited as a child aged 11 to 15. There was a relationship between visiting museums or galleries as a child and as an adult. Of those who had visited a museum or gallery as a child 57.3 per cent had also visited as an adult, but among those adults who had not visited as a child, only 32.5 per cent had visited as an adult. For visiting heritage sites, the influence of childhood participation is less marked than it is for other sectors. Among those adults who had visited a heritage site as a child,

82.3 per cent also visited as an adult. However, 59.0 per cent of adults who did not visit a heritage site as a child had visited as an adult. In 2010/11, 53.0 per cent of adults had participated in sport in the last 4 weeks (prior to interview); 86.0 per cent had done so as a child. Among those adults who had participated in sport as a child, 56.4 per cent had also participated in the last 4 weeks. Meanwhile, among those adults who did not play sport as child, only 36.3 per cent had participated in the last 4 weeks. (DCMS, 2011)

Notes

1. Participated in art activities or attended art events.

2. Please note that figures for England, Scotland, Northern Ireland and Wales are not directly comparable with each other due to different surveys, methods, selections and questions.

3. Note that there are considerable differences between the percentage of adults who attended heritage sites from DCMS "Taking Part Survey" and the Scottish Household Survey figures on the "percentage who have visited a place of historic or archaeological interest in the last 12 months". This is likely to be due to differences in the ways in which questions were asked and how variables were defined between the 2 surveys.

Leisure: Sports and physical activities

As we can see in Figure 7 many adults and children participate in sport or physical activities in their free time where they aim to use, maintain or improve physical fitness and provide themselves with entertainment either through casual or organised participation

There have been a number of studies regarding the effect of exercise and physical activities on the well-being of those who engage and participate in them. '*The psychological effects associated with physical activity have been the topic of numerous scientific studies, conducted mainly since the early 1970s. The general conclusion from this research is that physical activity can enhance the participants' sense of well-being*'. (Biddle, Ekkekakis, 2005). The outcome of many of these studies seem to agree that there is a correlation between the two: '*Establishing one or more plausible mechanisms could help to show that the relationship between physical activity and well-being goes beyond statistical association, providing evidence that physical activity can, in fact, cause positive changes in well-being*'. (Biddle, Ekkekakis, 2005)

Figure 8: Percentage of adults who have participated in sport or recreational physical activities during the last 4 weeks and 12 months: by sex, 2010/11

England

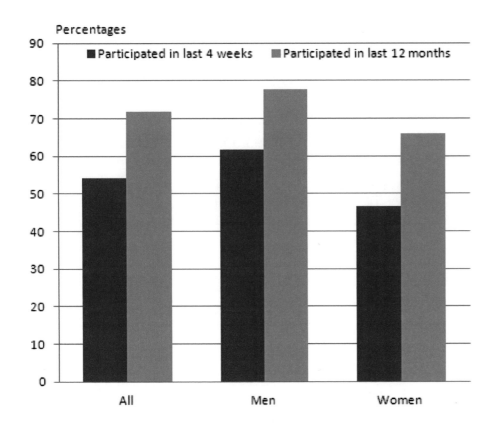

Source: Taking Part Survey - Department for Culture, Media and Sport

The Taking Part survey shows that in England in 2010/11, 54.1 per cent of adults, aged 16 and over had participated in some type of sport or recreational physical activity in the last four weeks while 71.7 per cent had done so in the last 12 months (Figure 8). A higher proportion of men participated in sport or recreational physical activity than women, both in the last four weeks (61.8 per cent compared with 46.7 per cent) and in the last 12 months (77.7 per cent compared with 65.9 per cent).

In England in 2010/11, the top sport or recreational physical activities[1] undertaken in the last four weeks were attending the gym (14.6 per cent); indoor swimming (14.4 per cent); cycling (10.6 per cent); running (7.6 per cent); keep fit, (7.1 per cent); and outdoor football (7.1 per cent).

The most popular activities for adults in the last 12 months were indoor swimming (31.6 per cent); the gym (21.8 per cent); cycling (18 per cent); outdoor swimming (13.6 per cent) snooker, pool, billiards[2] (13.5 per cent); and tenpin bowling (13.0 per cent).

In England in 2010/11, 89.7 per cent of all children had participated in sport in the last four weeks prior; 85.4 per cent of 5- to 10-year-olds and 94.5 per cent of 11- to 15-year-olds. These figures are not significantly different to 2008/09. Swimming, diving or lifesaving was the most common sport amongst 5- to10-year-old children, with almost half (48.3 per cent) of all children in this age group doing this in the last four weeks. More than a third had played football (35.9 per cent), and more than a quarter (28.0 per cent) had been cycling. Football was the most common sport amongst 11- to 15-year-olds, with half (50.0 per cent) of all children this age group having played in the last four weeks. Basketball (27.3 per cent) was the second most common, followed by swimming, diving or lifesaving (26.6 per cent).

Data from the Continuous Household Survey shows that in Northern Ireland in 2010/11, 50 per cent of adults aged 16 and over participated in sports or recreational physical activities in the last 12 months. Males were more likely to have participated (57 per cent) than females (44 per cent). One in five respondents (20 per cent) participated in swimming[3] in the 12 months prior to the survey. This was the most popular sport/physical activity followed by keep fit (15 per cent), golf (10 per cent) and jogging (10 per cent). (DCALNI, 2010)

The Scottish Household Survey shows that in Scotland in 2010, 51 per cent of adults, aged 16 and over participated in sport in the four weeks prior to interview. The most popular activities included swimming (17 per cent), keep fit/aerobics (13 per cent), multigym/weight training (11 per cent) and running and dancing, both at 10 per cent. Males (57 per cent) were more likely to participate than females (46 per cent). (SG, 2010)

In Wales in 2008/09, according the Active Adult Survey run by Sports Council Wales, 56 per cent of adults aged 15 and over participated in sport or physical recreation activity in the four weeks prior to interview. The data suggests a decrease from 2004-05 (59 per cent). Participation decreases with age: 73 per cent of 15- to 24-year-olds participated in an activity at least once, compared with 37 per cent of those aged 65 and over. Males (62 per cent) are more likely to participate than females (51 per cent). (SCW, 2009)

Figure 9: Percentage of adults who have done active sport in the last 4 weeks or used a digital exercise device (1): by sex, 2010/11

England

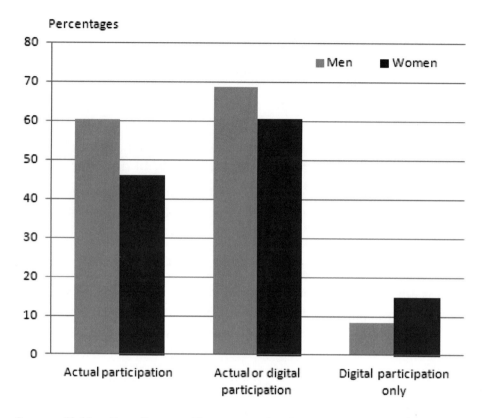

Source: Taking Part Survey - Department for Culture, Media and Sport

Notes:

1.   Digital exercise device eg Wii fit.

In England in 2010/11, 53.0 per cent of adults aged 16 and over, had taken part in active sport in the last four weeks, 64.6 per cent of adults had participated in active sport or used a Wii Fit or similar digital exercise device and 11.6 per cent of adults had only exercised using a Wii Fit or similar digital exercise device (Figure 9). Men (60.4 per cent) reported a higher percentage of active sport participation than women (45.9 per cent). A higher proportion of women (14.7 per cent) only exercised using a digital exercise device than men (8.3 per cent).

For further information on sporting activities in England at Local Authority level see small area estimates of participation.

Notes

1. Gym includes health, fitness, gym or conditioning activities; indoor swimming includes diving; cycling includes cycling for health, recreation, training and competition purposes; running includes jogging, cross-country and road running and keep fit includes aerobics and dance exercise (including exercise bikes).

2. Does not include bar billiards.

3. Swimming includes diving; keep fit includes aerobics, yoga and dance exercises; golf includes pitch and putt/putting.

Holidays and Travel

To make use of their free time many people choose to take holidays and travel to take time away from normal employment or education. A holiday can be described as a non-working trip or stay away from one's normal home.

Holidays could be seen as prolonged periods of leisure time and therefore as leisure activities have been said to increase well-being it could be assumed that taking a holiday would also lead to increased levels of well-being; '*Links have been made between access to and participation in tourism and happiness, quality of life and wellbeing. There is an underlying assumption that holidays are times and spaces in which participants should be happy*'. (McCabe, Joldersma, Chunxiao, 2009). Some studies which have been conducted have found some evidence to support this theory, '*Numerous studies have concentrated on health, wellbeing and quality of life to ascertain if there is a relationship between holidays and measures of subjective or self-reported wellbeing states. Gilbert and Abdullah (2004) found small increases in reported subjective wellbeing (SWB) amongst general population of holidaymakers*'. (McCabe, Joldersma, Chunxiao, 2009).

The number and destination of holidays taken and travel for other purposes, such as commuting and business trips, is discussed in this section.

Figure 10: UK residents visits abroad: by purpose of visit

United Kingdom

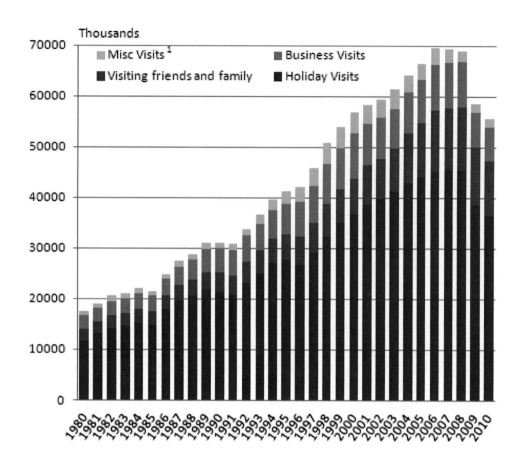

Source: International Passenger Survey (IPS) - Office for National Statistics

Notes:

1. Visits for miscellaneous purposes include those for study, to attend sporting events, for shopping, health, religious or other purposes, together with visits for more than one purpose when no one purpose predominates.

According to data from the International Passenger Survey for UK residents the most common reason for travel to other countries was to take a holiday (Figure 10). Between 1980 and 2005 there was a steady increase in the number of UK residents travelling abroad for all purposes and this growth was generally resilient to challenging economic and social pressures. However a combination of factors, such as difficult economic conditions and unfavourable exchange rates, have led to a levelling off of this growth between 2006 and 2008 and a decline over the past two years.

In 2010 there were 56 million visits abroad by UK residents. One in three visits (66 per cent) were for holidays, one in five (20 per cent) to visit friends and relatives and one in ten (12 per cent) for business purposes. Between 2009 and 2010, total visits fell by 5 per cent: with holidays falling by 5 per cent, business trips by 4 per cent and visiting friends and relatives by 6 per cent. However there is a much larger fall in visits when compared with 2008, total visits fell by 19 per cent in 2010 when compared with 2008; holiday visits by 20 per cent, visiting friends and relatives by 12 per cent and business trips by 26 per cent. (ONS, 2011e)

There are differences between residents of the UK and the EU when it comes to holidays and how many holidays are taken. Information in a Eurobarometer report shows that 46 per cent of EU citizens aged 15 and over who had been on holiday during 2010 had made one holiday trip and 26 per cent had taken two such trips. In comparison for UK citizens, 42 per cent had one holiday trip and 27 per cent had taken two. A further 11 per cent of EU holidaymakers had made three holiday trips in 2010 compared with 13 per cent for those in the UK and 9 per cent of EU residents had made four such trips compared to 10 per cent in the UK. Finally for the EU, 6 per cent had taken more than five holidays, while from the UK 8 per cent had five or more holidays. (EB, 2011)

Table 5: Domestic trips: by purpose

United Kingdom

Trips (millions)

	2006	2007	2008	2009	2010
All Trips	126.3	123.5	117.7	126.0	119.4
Holiday, pleasure/ leisure	53.3	53.7	52.0	60.7	56.6
Holiday, visiting friends or relatives	25.9	23.1	23.5	23.7	22.1
All Holidays	79.2	76.8	75.4	84.3	78.7
Other visits to friends or relatives	23.7	24.7	20.6	20.8	20.6
All Visits To Friends Or Relatives	49.6	47.8	44.1	44.4	42.8
Attend conferences	1.9	1.9	1.9	1.7	1.3
Attend exhibition/ trade show/ agricultural	0.7	0.8	0.7	0.7	0.5
Conduct paid work/on business	16.6	16.1	15.7	15.5	15.1
All Business Travel	19.2	18.8	18.2	18.0	16.9
Travel/ Transport is my business	0.8	0.4	0.7	0.5	0.6
Other/School trip/Missing	3.4	2.8	2.7	2.5	2.6

Table source: Visit England/ Visit Wales/ Visit Scotland/ Northern Ireland Tourist Board

In 2010, 119 million trips were made within the UK (Table 5) a decrease of over 6 million trips compared with 2009, the year of the 'staycation', when there had been an increase of almost 9 million holiday trips within the UK compared with 2008. In the UK in 2010 nearly half of all trips (57 million) were holiday trips for pleasure and leisure and many of the other trips (43 million) were made to visit friends and relatives, either as a holiday (22 million) or for other reasons (21 million). There were nearly 17 million business trips made in the UK in 2010, a decrease of just over one million since 2009 and a continuation of the downward trend since 2006. (VE, VW, VS, NITB, 2010)

Table 6: Average number of trips (trip rates) per person per year: by trip purpose, 1995/97 to 2010 (1)

Great Britain

Trips

	1995/97	2005	2006	2007	2008	2009	2010
Commuting	174	161	160	162	156	147	150
Business	39	37	35	33	30	30	29
Education	68	66	62	63	62	61	59
Escort education	48	48	44	44	43	44	47
Shopping	237	206	219	186	198	193	193
Other escort	84	97	97	86	96	91	91
Personal business	110	109	105	98	103	103	98
Visiting friends at private home	144	123	119	110	109	109	103
Visiting friends elsewhere	46	47	49	48	47	48	46
Entertainment/ public activity	40	52	49	48	43	44	47
Sport: participate	23	17	16	18	20	20	18
Holiday: base	10	12	11	11	11	12	11
Day trip	20	27	28	28	30	28	28
Other including just walk	44	42	45	38	44	43	41
All purposes	1,086	1,044	1,037	972	992	973	960

Table source: National Travel Survey -
Department for Transport

Table notes:
1.   There is an apparent under-recording of short trips in 2007 and 2008 compared to other years.

According to the National Travel Survey shopping is the type of trip that people in Great Britain make most often, with an average 193 shopping trips each in 2010, 20 per cent of all trips (Table 6). These trips tend to be shorter than average (4.3 miles in 2010) and therefore shopping only accounted for 12 per cent of distance travelled. Commuting journeys made up 16 per cent of trips and business reasons accounted for a further 3 per cent in 2010. These trips tend to be longer than average, so make up a higher proportion of the average distance travelled, at 20 per cent and 10 per cent respectively. Most of the decline in overall trips between 1995/97[1] and 2010 is because of a fall in shopping and visiting friends. People in Great Britain made 18 per cent fewer shopping trips per year in 2010 than they did in 1995/97 and visits to friends declined by 22 per cent over the same period: the fall entirely due to a decrease in visits to private homes rather than elsewhere. The trend of falling numbers of shopping trips over time is associated with a switch from more frequent, short shopping trips on foot, to longer, less frequent car trips. (DFT, 2011)

On average, females make more trips than males, but males travel much further each year. In 2010, females made 5 per cent more trips than males (984 per year compared with 935). However, males travelled 23 per cent further than females, averaging 7,426 miles a year compared with 6,051 miles.

In 2008-10 on average, Northern Ireland residents travelled 5,976 miles per year over the three-year reporting period. Each person made an average of 905 journeys each year, some 6 per cent less than the average for Great Britain. Twenty two per cent of all journeys in Northern Ireland in 2008–2010 were for leisure purposes (for example to visit friends, to take part in entertainment or sport activities, to go on holiday or day trips), 20 per cent for shopping and 16 per cent for commuting. Journeys to services, such as the bank, doctor or library made up 13 per cent of all journeys. In terms of miles travelled, almost a third (31 per cent) of the total distance travelled was for leisure purposes, just over a fifth (21 per cent) for commuting, 14 per cent for shopping and 11 per cent for personal business. Nearly a tenth (8 per cent) of the total distance travelled was for business travel. (DRDNI, 2010)

The downsides of commuting were mentioned in responses to the National Well-being Debate. However, there is very little research evidence regarding the effect of commuting on well-being. The following comment suggests that commuting time needs to be offset by potential benefits, such as commuters' level of earnings, the area and the houses in which they live and should take into account whether commuting by car or by public transport. '*Despite the adversities of commuting, some of its elements can serve as enhancements to well-being, such as privacy, protected time, and the symbolic value of personal vehicles and freedom.*' (Novaco, Gonzalez, 2009)

According to the Labour Force Survey, in 2009 in the UK around three in four, or 75 per cent of workers take less than half an hour to travel from home to work. However, commuting patterns are vastly different between workers in London and those working in the rest of the UK. People working in London, in particular central London, tend to travel longer to get to work, with more than half (56 per cent) needing to commute for more than 30 minutes to get to work every day. By contrast, only 20 per cent of those working in the rest of the UK need to travel for more than 30 minutes to reach their workplace. For further information and data about commuting to work see 'Commuting to work - 2011'. (ONS, 2011f)

Notes

1.   1995/97 represents 3 years of combined data.

About the ONS Measuring National Well-being Programme

NWB logo 2

This article is published as part of the ONS Measuring National Well-being Programme.

The programme aims to produce accepted and trusted measures of the well-being of the nation - how the UK as a whole is doing. It is about looking at 'GDP and beyond' and includes:

- greater analysis of the national economic accounts, especially to understand household income, expenditure and wealth
- further accounts linked to the national accounts, including the UK Environmental Accounts and valuing household production and 'human capital'
- quality of life measures, looking at different areas of national well-being such as health, relationships, job satisfaction, economic security, education environmental conditions
- working with others to include the measurement of the well-being of children and young people as part of national well-being
- measures of 'subjective well-being' - individuals' assessment of their own well-being
- headline indicators to summarise national well-being and the progress we are making as a society

The programme is underpinned by a communication and engagement workstream, providing links with Cabinet Office and policy departments, international developments, the public and other stakeholders. The programme is working closely with Defra on the measurement of 'sustainable development' to provide a complete picture of national well-being, progress and sustainable development.

Find out more on the Measuring National Well-being website pages.

Background notes

1. Details of the policy governing the release of new data are available by visiting www.statisticsauthority.gov.uk/assessment/code-of-practice/index.html or from the Media Relations Office email: media.relations@ons.gsi.gov.uk

Copyright

References

1. ACW, 2010 – Arts in Wales Survey

2. CIPD, 2011 – Employee Outlook: Summer

3. DCLG, 2009 - Citizenship Survey: Volunteering and Charitable Giving Topic Report

4. DCLG, 2011 - Citizenship Survey

5. DCSM, 2011 - Taking Part Survey

6. DCALNI, 2010 – Findings from the Continuous Household Survey

7. DHSSPSNI, 2011 - Health Survey Northern Ireland: First Results from the 2010/11 Survey

8. DFT, 2011 – The National Travel Survey

9. DRDNI, 2010 – Travel Survey for Northern Ireland

10. DWP, 2010 - Family Resource Survey

11. EB, 2011 – Flash Eurobarometer, Survey on the attitudes of Europeans towards tourism

12. ELMR, 2010, 'The Economic and Labour Market Review, Vol 4 No7' - Characteristics of the underemployed and the overemployed in the UK

13. Gallup, 2011- The Gallup- Healthways Well-being Index

14. NILT, 2009 – Northern Ireland Life and Times

15. Ofcom, 2011 – The Communications Market Report

16. ONS, 2005 – Time Use Survey 2005: How we spend our time.

17. ONS, 2011a - Older Workers in the Labour Market

18. ONS, 2011b - Measuring Subjective Wellbeing in the UK, Analysis of experimental subjective well-being data from the Annual Population Survey, April - September 2011

19. ONS, 2011c - Hours worked in the Labour Market

20. ONS, 2011d - Measuring Subjective Wellbeing in the UK, Investigation of subjective well-being data from the ONS Opinions Survey

21. ONS, 2011e - International Passenger Survey

22. ONS, 2011f - Commuting to work

23. ONS, 2012a - Labour Force Survey

24. ONS, 2012b - Young people in work

Measuring national well-being: Households and families, 2012

Author Name(s): Ian Macrory: Office for National Statistics

Abstract

This article is published as part of the ONS Measuring National Well-being Programme. The programme aims to produce accepted and trusted measures of the well-being of the nation - how the UK as a whole is doing. 'Households and families' is the third in a series which aims to explore in more detail the different domains that have been considered as important for the measurement of National Well-being. It firstly focuses on family and household formation and then on individual aspects of these such as marriage and divorce.

Introduction

A household is defined as a person living alone or a group of people who live and eat together. Families are defined by marriage, civil partnership or cohabitation, or the presence of children in the household.

Individuals live in different types of households and families during their lifetime. Most people begin life living with their parents and later they may set up home alone typically with other non-related adults or by starting a family. Families are started when people form partnerships or marry or when they have children. Analysing the population by household and family type is important for many different organisations in the public and private sectors, including policy makers dealing with issues like health, housing and benefits. Problems such as unemployment and poverty can often be better understood by looking at the characteristics of households and families. Information about households and families also shows how society is changing. This chapter provides the latest data on the number and composition of households and families in the United Kingdom and Great Britain and looks at trends over time.

Key points

Household composition

- There were 25.5 million households in Great Britain in 2011, an increase of 9.2 million since 1961 and 1.6 million since 2001
- Average household size in Great Britain has decreased from 3.1 persons in 1961 to 2.4 persons in 2011

- A smaller proportion of households in Great Britain have children living in them in 2011 than in 1961, and those households with children have fewer children living in them

Families

- In 2011 there were an estimated 17.9 million families in the UK, an increase from 17.0 million in 2001: with the increase of 0.7 million cohabiting couple families and 0.4 million lone parent families offset by a decrease of 0.3 million in the number of married couple families
- There were an estimated 50.7 million people living in families in the UK in 2011, an increase from 48.8 million in 2001
- The most common type of family in the UK in 2010 was a married couple with or without children, although the proportion had decreased from an estimated 72.4 per cent of all families in 2001 to 67.2 per cent in 2011
- In the UK families consisting of a cohabiting couple with or without children increased from 12.5 per cent of all families in 2001 to 16.0 per cent 2011 and lone parent families increased from 14.8 per cent in 2001 to 16.1 per cent in 2011
- The most common type of family with children in the UK contained one child at the time of the survey in 2011 (46.3 per cent of all families with children)

Marriages

- Around two-thirds of marriages (68.2 per cent) in 2010 in England and Wales were by civil ceremony, a similar proportion to 2008 but an increase compared with 1981 when only 49.0 per cent of marriages were by civil ceremony

Divorces and dissolution

- In England and Wales between 1990 and 2010 the total number of children of divorcing couples of all ages decreased from nearly 153,000 to just over 104,000: partly because of the overall decrease in the number of divorces and partly because the average number of children involved in each divorce had reduced

Births

- In 2010 there were 723,200 live births registered in England and Wales compared with 783,200 in 1971 and 706,200 in 2009
- The age distribution of women giving birth in England and Wales has changed considerably. In 1971 women in the 20 to 24 age category were the largest group giving birth, accounting for 36.5 per cent of all live births. By 2010 this proportion had fallen to 19.0 per cent, and the 30 to 34 age

category, whose proportion had doubled to 28 per cent between 1971 and 2010, accounted for more live births than any other group
- In 1971 91.6 per cent of births in England and Wales were within marriage, by 2010 this had decreased to 53.2 per cent

Conceptions and abortions

- Provisional estimates for 2010 suggest that the number of conceptions in England and Wales had increased by 1.4 per cent compared with 2009
- In England and Wales between 1991 and 2010 the number of conceptions by women younger than 30 decreased markedly while the number by women aged 30 and over increased
- The proportion of conceptions resulting in legal abortions has shown a small decline in 2010 (1.0 per cent), which is not reflected in all age groups. The biggest increase was in under 16's where there was a 4.5 per cent rise

Children and young people

- In England as at December 2011 there were 1.3 million registered child–care places available at any one time
- In England in 2011 there were 90,000 children classified as being 'looked after' at any time during the year, an increase of more than 7,000 since 2007

Carers and caring

- Sixty one per cent of adult informal carers in the UK in 2009/10 were providing care to someone living outside their own household. Parents outside of the household were the main recipients of informal care

Household composition

Most households consist of a single family or someone living alone (as shown in Tables 1 and 2). This first section looks at people living in private households and excludes those living in institutions such as care homes, prisons, hospitals and other communal establishments.

There were an estimated 25.5 million households in Great Britain in 2011, an increase of 1.6 million from 2001 and of 9.2 million since 1961. The proportion of households with three or more people living in them has fallen from 57 per cent in 1961 to 35 per cent in 2011. Consequently the average household size, which was 3.1 people in 1961, had fallen to 2.4 people by 2001 and has remained at that level since, as seen in Table 1. (ONS, 2011a)

Table 1: Households (1) by size

Great Britain

Percentages

	1961	1971	1981	1991	2001	2011
One person	*12*	*18*	22	27	29	29
Two people	*30*	*32*	32	34	35	35
Three people	*23*	*19*	17	16	16	16
Four people	*19*	*17*	18	16	14	13
Five people	9	8	7	5	5	4
Six or more people	7	6	4	2	2	2
All households (=100%) (millions)	16.3	18.6	20.2	22.4	23.9	25.5
Average household size (number of people)	3.1	2.9	2.7	2.5	2.4	2.4

Table source: Office for National Statistics

Table notes:

1. Data are at Q2 (April - June) each year and are not seasonally adjusted. A household is defined as a person living alone, or a group of people living at the same address who have the address as their only or main residence and either share one main meal a day or share living accommodation (or both).

Part of the decrease in average household size in Great Britain can be attributed to a reduction in the proportion of families with children, and the decrease in the number of children within those families with children as shown in Table 2. (ONS, 2011a)

Table 2: Households: (1,2) by type of household and family

Great Britain

Percentages

	1961	1971	1981	1991	2001	2011
One person households	12	18	22	27	29	29
One family[3] households						
Couple[4]						
No children	26	27	26	28	29	28
1–2 dependent children[5]	30	26	25	20	19	18
3 or more dependent children[5]	8	9	6	5	4	3
Non-dependent children only[6]	10	8	8	8	6	6
Lone parent[4]						
Dependent children[5]	2	3	5	6	7	7
Non-dependent children only[6]	4	4	4	4	3	3
Two or more unrelated adults	5	4	5	3	3	4

Percentages

	1961	1971	1981	1991	2001	2011
Multi-family households	*3*	*1*	*1*	*1*	*1*	*1*
All households						
(=100%) (millions)	16.3	18.6	20.2	22.4	23.9	25.5

Table source: Office for National Statistics

Table notes:
1. Data are at Q2 (April–June) each year and are not seasonally adjusted.
2. For 2001 to 2010, a household is defined as a person living alone, or a group of people living at the same address who have the address as their only or main residence and either share one main meal a day or share living accommodation (or both). For 2011 it is defined as one person living alone, or a group of people (not necessarily related) living at the same address who share cooking facilities and share a living room or sitting room or dining area.
3. A family is a married, civil partnered or cohabiting couple with or without children, or a lone parent with at least one child. Children may be dependent or non-dependent.
4. These households may contain individuals who are not family members. Couples include a small number of same-sex couples and civil partners.
5. Dependent children are children (aged under 16, or aged 16 to 18 in full-time education) living with their parent(s), excluding all children who have a spouse, partner or child living in the household. These families may also contain non-dependent children.
6. Non-dependent children are those living with their parent(s), and either (a) aged 19 or over, or (b) aged 16 to 18 who are not in full-time education or who have a spouse, partner or child living in the household. Non-dependent children are sometimes called adult children.

The proportion of households consisting of one family with children decreased from 54 per cent to 38 per cent between 1961 and 2011. Over the same time period the proportion of households containing couples with one or two dependent children went down from 30 per cent to 18 per cent (from about 4.9 million to 4.5 million households) and those with 3 or more dependent children from 8 per cent to 3 per cent of all households (from about 1.3 million to 0.8 million households). However, most of this change happened before 2001 and there was little change in the proportions of different types of one family household between 2001 and 2011.

Another contributor to the reduction in average household size, as shown in Tables 1 and 2, is the increase in the proportion of people living alone. In 2011, 29 per cent of all households in Great Britain contained just one person, the same proportion as in 2001, but a considerable increase since 1961 when only 12 per cent of households were one person living alone. However, most of this increase occurred in the 30 years between 1961 and 1991. Increases since 1991 have been slower, with a rise in the proportion of single person households of only 2 percentage points.

In 2010 there were around 25 million households in Great Britain. Of these, less than 1 per cent were people buying a house for the first time. According to the Council of Mortgage Lenders (CML) there were just over 200,000 loans made to first-time buyers in 2010, accounting for 37 per cent of all mortgages (Figure 1). This was an increase of fewer than 8,000 on 2008 when loans to first-time buyers reached their lowest level since the 1974 figure of 198,000. However, in 1974 they accounted for 44 per cent of all mortgages whereas by 2008 only 37 per cent of loans were made to first-time buyers.

Figure 1: Mortgages by type (1,3,4)

Great Britain: Number of mortgages

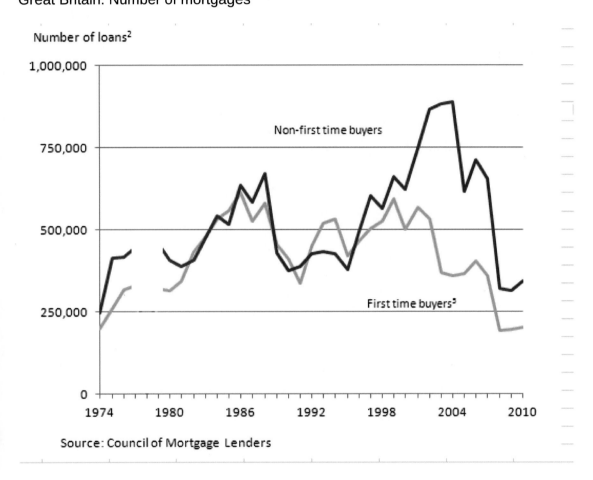

Notes:

1. Data are not available for 1978.
2. Totals shown are estimates grossed up from the sample of lenders reporting to reflect total market size.
3. Figures pre-April 2005 are taken from the Survey of Mortgage Lenders or, prior to 1992 Q2 (annually prior to 1993), the Building Societies 5% sample of mortgage completions. RMS figures are not strictly comparable with earlier ones because of material differences in reporting methodologies and the samples of lenders contributing data.
4. Prior to April 2005, estimates of the proportion of first time buyers and movers exclude cases where the previous tenure of buyers is not known.
5. First time buyer numbers will include some buyers who have previously owned a property before, but are not in owner-occupation at the time of this purchase. Estimates from the Survey of English Housing suggest that that around 20% of stated first-time buyers may in fact fall into this category.

At the start of the credit crisis in 2008, the number of first-time buyers fell sharply to 192,000, a drop of 46.6 per cent on the previous year. By 2010, the figure had recovered slightly and stood at 200,000. This figure is still down by more than two thirds from the historic peak of 613,000 seen in 1986. Non-first time buyer figures showed a similar fall followed by a slight recovery. In 2008, there were 334,000 such buyers, a fall of more than half (51.0 per cent) from the previous year, and decline of 61.3 per cent from the historic peak of 887,000 seen in 2004. By 2010, the figure stood at 343,000.

It has become more difficult for first-time buyers to obtain a mortgage. As recently as 2007, first-time buyers paid deposits averaging 10 per cent of a property's purchase price, but by 2009 this had risen to 25 per cent and now stands at around 20 per cent. CML figures indicate that, by 2010, the average deposit was £26,000, representing 79 per cent of the average annual income from which the mortgage was paid. In 2007 the average deposit was £13,000, or 37 per cent of annual income. This represents a significant increase in difficulty for those wishing to become owner occupiers.

The number of unassisted first-time buyers has also declined sharply, from around 69 per cent of all first-time buyers in 2005 Q3 to 36 per cent in 2011 Q3. For first-time buyers under 30 the decline is even greater, from 64 per cent to 22 per cent over the same period. Since 2005, when the CML began collecting the data, the median age of all first-time buyers has been around 29. By contrast, the median age for unassisted first-time buyers rose from 30 to 33 between 2008 and 2009 and remains at this level. (Council of Mortgage lenders, 2011)

People living alone by age

In 2011 in the UK, there were just over 7.7 million people living alone, compared with just over 7.0 million in 2001.

The percentage of all households in the UK that are single occupant has not varied greatly between 2001 and 2011. It was at its lowest for this period in 2001 (29.4 per cent) and its highest in 2011 (30.2 per cent). However, within the group of people living alone, there have been changes in the age profile (Figure 2).

Figure 2: Number of people living alone: by age group

United Kingdom

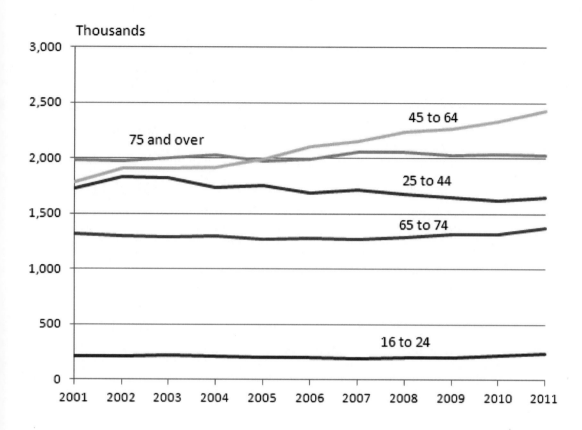

Source: Labour Force Survey - Office for National Statistics

Those in the 16 to 24 age group had the biggest year on year percentage increase in 2011, up by 6.7 per cent to 240,000. However, the number of 45 to 64 year olds have shown the strongest growth since 2001 with a 36.2 per cent increase to 2.4 million.

As a proportion of those living alone during the period from 2001 to 2011, the groups made up of 16 to 24 year olds and those aged 65 or over have shown relatively small variation (less than 2 percentage points from peak to trough in each case). By contrast, the proportion of single person households occupied by 45 to 64 year olds had a relatively large span of 6.1 percentage points (25.4 per cent of the total in 2001 and 31.5 per cent in 2011). This is more pronounced than the variation in the 25 to 44 year old group that was at its highest as a proportion in 2002 (25.3 per cent) and its lowest in 2011 (21.3 per cent), a difference of 2 percentage points. (ONS, 2011a)

Families

The previous sections examined the composition of households in Great Britain and the UK. This section describes the different types of family[1] in the UK and the people who live in them.

Previous research has found that having children does not have a significant effect on people's happiness, but that it does have a positive effect on overall life satisfaction (Haller and Hadler, 2006). This could suggest that people regard having children as an important part of their overall well-being, even if the presence of children does not improve people's day-to-day emotions. See also Measuring subjective well-being in the UK: Analysis of subjective well-being data from the Annual population survey, April - September 2011.

The Office for National Statistics (ONS) 'Initial investigation into Subjective Well-being data from the Opinions Survey' report showed that there was no significant difference between the average ratings for the 'life satisfaction' and 'happy yesterday' questions for people who live in households without children and those who live in households with children. Neither did these two groups have a significant difference between the average ratings to the 'anxious yesterday.' However, the average ratings for the 'worthwhile' question improved significantly for people living in households with children. The lowest rating for the 'worthwhile' question was given by people living in households where no children are present (7.6 out of 10). This increases to between 7.8 and 7.9 out of 10 for people living with two or more children in their household. This finding suggests that although the presence of children does not alter overall life satisfaction or improve day-to-day emotions, it may bring an increased sense of meaning and purpose to people's lives, therefore increasing average scores for the 'worthwhile' question. (ONS 2011b)

In 2011 there were about 17.9 million families in the UK, an estimated increase of 0.9 million (5.4 per cent) since 2001. The growth in the number of families between 2001 and 2011 is driven by increases in the numbers of cohabiting couples by 0.7 million and of lone parent families by 0.4 million. The second of these is despite a small decrease in the number of lone father families. These increases were offset by a reduction of 0.3 million in the number of married couple families with dependent children. However married couples with no children and those with non-dependent children both showed a very small increase. Between 2001 and 2011 the number of people living in families increased by 3.9 per cent, from 48.8 million to 50.7 million (Table 3).

Table 3: Families (1) and number of people living in families (2,3): by family type

United Kingdom

Percentage and numbers

	Families		Dependent children	
	2001	2011	2001	2011
Married couple family	72.4	67.2	74.7	69.4
Civil partnership family[4,5,6]	-	0.3	-	0.2
Cohabiting couple family[6]	12.5	16.0	11.7	15.4
Same sex cohabiting couple family[6]	0.3	0.4	0.2	0.3
Lone mother family	12.7	14.2	11.7	13.2
Lone father family	2.1	1.9	1.7	1.6
All families (millions = 100%)	17.0	17.9	48.8	50.7

Table source: Office for National Statistics

Table notes:
1. A family is a married, civil partnered or cohabiting couple with or without children, or a lone parent with at least one child. Children may be dependent or non-dependent.
2. Dependent children are those living with their parent(s) and either (a) aged under 16, or (b) aged 16 to 18 in full-time education, excluding children aged 16 to 18 who have a spouse, partner or child living in the household.
3. Non-dependent children are those living with their parent(s), and either (a) aged 19 or over, or (b) aged 16 to 18 who are not in full-time education or who have a spouse, partner or child living in the household. Non-dependent children are sometimes called adult children.
4. Civil partnerships were introduced in the UK in December 2005.
5. The people in families figure for civil partner families is not considered reliable for practical purposes.
6. Families with no children and non-dependent children only have been added together for civil partner couple families and same sex cohabiting couple families to improve the robustness of the estimates.

Married couple families remained the most common in the UK, although there had been a decrease between 2001 and 2011 in the proportion of families of this type from 72.4 to 67.2 per cent of all families. There had been an increase between 2001 and 2011 in the proportion of families which included cohabiting couples from 12.5 per cent to 16.0 per cent of all families, and in families headed by a lone parent from 14.8 per cent to 16.1 per cent of all families. The growth in lone parent families was in those headed by a lone mother, as both the proportion and number of families headed by a lone father fell.

Of all those individuals (both adults and children) living in families just over 69.4 per cent (35.2 million) lived in a married couple family in 2011, while the proportions living in cohabiting families and lone parent families were both around 15 per cent (7.8 million and 7.5 million individuals respectively). In addition, in 2011 there were approximately 63,000 same sex cohabiting families and 59,000 civil partner families.

In 2011 there were an estimated 7.6 million families with dependent children, an increase of 0.2 million (2.6 per cent) since 2001. The number of dependent children living in families in 2011 was 13.2 million, a decrease of 0.9 per cent on the 2001 figure. (ONS, 2011c)

Table 4: Families (1) and dependent children (2)

United Kingdom

Percentages

	Families			Dependent children	
	2001	2011		2001	2011
Married couple family					
One child	24.2	24.2		13.4	13.9
Two children	29.5	26.0		32.8	30.0
Three or more children	11.8	9.4		21.7	18.1
Total married couple family	65.4	59.6		68.0	62.0
Cohabiting couple family					
One child	5.8	7.6		3.2	4.4
Two children	3.6	4.9		4.0	5.6
Three or more children	1.6	2.0		2.9	4.0
Total cohabiting couple family	10.9	14.5		10.1	14.0
Lone parent family					
One child	12.6	14.5		7.0	8.4
Two children	7.6	8.2		8.5	9.5
Three or more children	3.3	3.1		6.3	6.2
Total lone parent family	23.6	25.8		21.9	24.0
All families					
One child	42.5	46.3		23.7	26.7
Two children	40.8	39.1		45.4	45.1

Percentages

	Families		Dependent children	
	2001	2011	2001	2011
Three or more children	16.7	14.6	30.9	28.2
Total all families	100.0	100.0	100.0	100.0

Table source: Office for National Statistics

Table notes:

1. Excludes a small number of Civil Partnership and same-sex cohabiting couple families. A family is a married, civil partnered or cohabiting couple with or without children, or a lone parent with at least one child. Children may be dependent or non-dependent.

2. Excludes dependent children who do not live in families.

The majority of dependent children in the UK live in families of which there are three main types: a married couple, a cohabiting couple or a lone parent family. The proportions of these types of family with dependent children have changed between 2001 and 2011. Married couple families decreased from 65.4 per cent of all families with dependent children in 2001 to 59.6 per cent in 2011 (Table 4). The numbers of these families had also gone down from 4.8 million in 2001 to 4.5 million 2011. The proportion of cohabiting couple families with dependent children increased between 2001 and 2011, from 10.9 per cent to 14.5 per cent, and lone parent families from 23.6 per cent to 25.8 per cent of all families with dependent children.

Of all dependent children living in families, 62.0 per cent (8.2 million) lived in a married couple family in 2011 a decrease from 68.0 per cent (9.0 million) in 2001. The proportion living in cohabiting couple families increased from 10.1 per cent (1.3 million) in 2001 to 14.0 per cent (1.8 million) in 2011. Over the same time period the proportion of dependent children living in lone parent families increased from 21.9 per cent to 24.0 per cent (2.9 million to 3.2 million).

At the time of the survey in 2011 families with one dependent child remained the most common at 46.3 per cent of all families with dependent children. This was an increase from 42.5 per cent in 2001, driven by growth in cohabiting and one parent families, and part of a trend towards smaller families. The proportion of families that currently consists of a married couple with one child was almost unchanged at 24.2 per cent of all families, while those with two or more children both decreased. Similarly, while both cohabiting couple and lone parent families increased overall, the greatest growth in both groups came from among those with one child. In both groups those with three or more children either showed the lowest growth (cohabiting couples) or fell (lone parent families). Over half of all cohabiting couple and lone parent families had a single dependent child at the time of the survey. However, for married couple families the most frequent number of dependent children was two. The proportion of all families with three or more dependent children decreased from 16.7 per cent in 2001 to 14.6 per cent in 2011. Note that all these types of family could also have non-dependent children, and the survey only shows the number of children in the family at the time of the survey. (ONS, 2011a)

Marriages and civil partnerships

The previous sections showed estimates of households and families at specific points in time. The next sections discuss the events which can cause changes to household and family types, such as marriage, civil partnership[2], divorce, dissolution of civil partnerships and births.

ONS's 'Analysis of experimental subjective well-being data from the Annual Population Survey, April - September 2011' report showed that people who are not in a partnership report lower average ratings for the 'life satisfaction', 'worthwhile' and 'happy yesterday' questions and higher average ratings for the 'anxious yesterday' question.

People who are married or in civil partnerships reported the highest average levels of life satisfaction (7.7 out of 10), significantly higher than cohabiting couples (7.5 out of 10). Cohabiting couples reported significantly higher average ratings for the 'life satisfaction' question than single people (7.3 out of 10). People who are widowed had an average rating of 6.8 out of 10. The lowest average rating for the 'life satisfaction' question were reported by people who are divorced or separated, including those who have dissolved civil partnerships (6.6 out of 10); see also Measuring National Well-being Our relationships article.

The Marriage Act 1836 and the Registration Act 1836 came into force in 1837 in England and Wales providing the statutory basis for regulating and recording marriages. There were 118,100 marriages registered in 1838, the first full year of civil registration in England and Wales. Annual numbers of marriages generally rose steadily from the 1840s to the 1940s, apart from peaks and troughs around the two world wars.

The provisional number of marriages registered in England and Wales in 2010 was 241,100, an increase of around 8,700 since 2009 and the highest figure since 2005 (Figure 3).

Figure 3: Marriages: by previous marital status

England and Wales

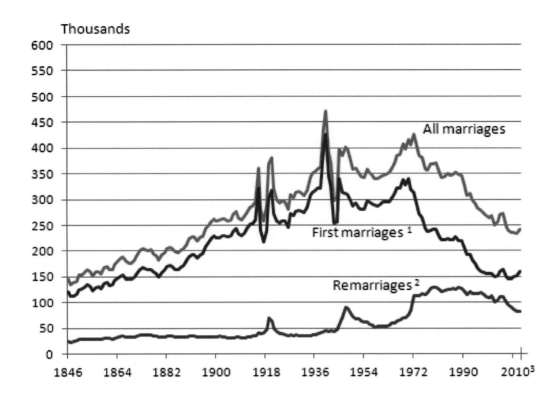

Source: Office for National Statistics

Notes:

1. For both parties.
2. For one or both parties.
3. Figures for 2010 are provisional.

The number of marriages in England and Wales that were the first for both partners peaked in 1940 at 426,100, when 91 per cent of all marriages were the first for both partners. First marriages fell below three-quarters (73 per cent) of all marriages in 1972 and continued to decrease, reaching a low of 58 per cent of all marriages in 1996. Provisional figures for 2010 show that there were around

158,980 marriages which were the first for both partners, two-thirds (66 per cent) of all marriages. The last time the proportion of marriages that were first marriages for both parties was this high was in 1977. The 2010 figure is, in part, driven by an increase of 8.7 per cent in the number of first marriages since 2007 coupled with a 7.9 per cent decrease in remarriages during the same period.

Remarriages rose by about a third between 1971 and 1972, following the introduction of the Divorce Reform Act 1969 in England and Wales, and continued an upward trend until 1989, after which they began falling. Provisional estimates for 2010 show that 34 per cent of all marriages (82,100) were remarriages for one or both parties. Although this was a slight increase on 2009 it was nonetheless in line with the prevailing downward trend that has been apparent since the mid 1990's, although during this time there have been some year-on-year increases.

In England and Wales marriage rates have been in steady decline since 2003 reaching their lowest level in 2009 since they were first calculated in 1862. In 2010, the provisional marriage rate for both men and women increased slightly. The rate for men was 21.8 men marrying per 1,000 unmarried men aged 16 and over, up from 21.4 in 2009. The provisional marriage rate for women in 2010 was 19.8 women marrying per 1,000 unmarried women aged 16 and over, up from 19.3 in 2009. (ONS 2009)

In both Scotland and Northern Ireland the number of marriages increased between 2009 and 2010: in Scotland from 27,524 to 28,480, a rise of 3.5 per cent, while in Northern Ireland the number of marriages increased to 8,156 from 7,931 an increase of 2.8 per cent.

During the 1990's civil ceremonies overtook religious ceremonies as the most common form of marriage in England and Wales, from 49 per cent in 1991 to 62 per cent in 1999. Of the 241,100 marriages that were registered in England and Wales in 2010, more than two-thirds (68 per cent) were solemnised in civil, as opposed to religious, ceremonies and for the first time more than half (52 per cent) of all marriages were in Approved Premises. As well as the changes in the type and place of ceremony there has also been a change in the seasonal distribution of marriages: in 1981 62 per cent of marriages took place between April and September but this had risen to 70 per cent in 2010.

The Civil Partnership Act 2004 came into force on 5 December 2005 in the UK, when couples could give notice of their intention to form a civil partnership. The Act enables same-sex couples aged 16 and over to obtain legal recognition of their relationship. The first day that couples could formally form a partnership was 19 December 2005 in Northern Ireland, 20 December 2005 in Scotland and 21 December 2005 in England and Wales.

The total number of partnerships formed since the Civil Partnership Act came into force in December 2005 until the end of 2010 is 46,622. The highest number of civil partnerships registered in one year in the UK was 16,106: this was in 2006 the first full year of registration. The following year registrations dropped by almost half to 8,728, in 2009 there were 6,281 registrations and in 2010 there were 6,385 civil partnerships. This represents a very small increase of 1.7 per cent between 2009 and 2010.

The number of civil partnerships increased in all countries of the UK between 2009 and 2010, apart from Scotland where the number of civil partnerships fell by 6.6 per cent to 465. There was an increase of 1.7 per cent in England (5,536 partnerships in 2010), 9.8 per cent in Wales (268 partnerships in 2010) and 20.8 per cent in Northern Ireland (116 partnerships in 2010). (ONS, 2010a)

Divorce and dissolution

Another way in which family structures change is following divorce, or for civil partnerships dissolution. Between 1918 and 1938 the number of divorces each year in England and Wales gradually increased from 1,100 to 6,300. Following the 1937 Divorce Act, which extended the grounds on which divorce was allowed, numbers increased considerably throughout the 1940s to a peak of around 60,300 in 1947. Although the number of divorces then fell to 22,700 in 1958, there was a further increase during the 1960s.

The Divorce Reform Act (1969) which came into effect in January 1971 and was subsequently consolidated into the Matrimonial Causes Act 1973, had a considerable impact on divorce numbers in England and Wales. In 1972 there were 119,000 divorces, an increase of almost 60 per cent on the previous year. From 1972 onwards there was a generally upward trend in divorces in England and Wales, reaching the highest recorded number of 165,000 in 1993.

The numbers of divorces were variable between 1993 and 2002, and there was a consistent downward trend from 2003 to 2008, including a sharp drop between 2004 and 2005. After a sharp fall between 2008 and 2009 divorces were higher in 2010 than in 2009. In 2009 there were about 113,900 divorces in England and Wales compared with 121,700 in 2008, a decrease of 6.4 per cent. In 2010 this rose to 119,600, a 4.9 per cent increase, the first increase since 2003. It should be noted that over this period the number of marriages also declined and this may have contributed to a fall in divorces.

In Scotland, there were fewer than 10,200 divorces registered in 2009/10, a fall of 9.8 per cent on the previous year. In Northern Ireland in 2010, 2,600 divorces were recorded, an increase of 19.5 per cent compared with the previous year (Scottish Government, 2010a; NISRA, 2010a).

In order to obtain the dissolution of a civil partnership, a couple must have been in a registered partnership or a recognised foreign relationship for at least 12 months. In 2010 there were, according to provisional estimates, 509 civil partnership dissolutions granted in the UK, an increase from 353 in 2009, 180 in 2008 and 41 in 2007 (ONS, 2010b). There were more dissolutions granted to female couples than male throughout the UK in 2010: 60 per cent of dissolutions in England and Wales, 56 per cent in Scotland and 67 per cent in Northern Ireland being granted to female couples. 2010 was the first year any civil partner dissolutions were recorded in Northern Ireland. In Scotland the gender of individuals receiving a dissolution was not collected until September 2010. For this reason the General Register Office for Scotland (GROS) inferred the gender of individuals from the names on the divorce decree. In many circumstances this would be straightforward but in some cases a name or both names may be gender neutral. (ONS, 2010b)

As already discussed family type is changed when divorce occurs, and when a divorcing couple already have children together this affects the family type in which those children live. There has been a considerable change not only in the number of children living in families affected by divorce but also in the distribution of their ages. The total number of children of divorcing couples was

104,000 in 2010. This was a decrease of 40.7 per cent from the historic peak of 1993 when the figure was 176,000. However, 2010 is the first year to show a year on year increase since 2003. The decrease since the peak is partly because of the overall decrease in the number of divorces and partly because the average number of children involved in each divorce had reduced (ONS 2011d).

Figure 4: Number of children (1) of divorced couples: by age (2) group

England and Wales

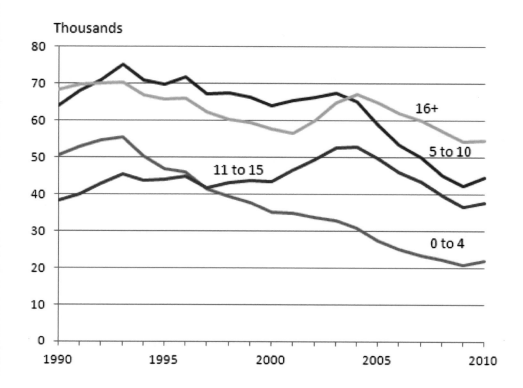

Source: Office for National Statistics

Notes:
1. Children are those treated as children of the family, and can include children born outside marriage, children of previous marriages, adopted and step children.
2. Ages are those at petition to divorce.

There was also a change in the ages at which children were affected by divorce. This is particularly noticeable for children aged 0 to 4, where after an increase to about 55,500 in 1993, numbers fell in each year to reach 21,900 in 2010. By 2004, the highest number of children who were affected by divorce were those aged 16 and over. From 2004 onwards numbers in each of the age groups decreased (Figure 4).

Notes

1. A family is a married or cohabiting couple living together with or without children or a lone parent living with his or her children. A family could also consist of grandparent(s) with their grandchild or grandchildren if the parent(s) are absent.

2. Civil partners have equal treatment to married couples in a number of legal matters such as tax, employment benefits, pension benefits, maintenance and recognition for immigration and nationality purposes.

Conceptions, births and abortions

Births

One of the largest changes over time, as noted above, is in the types of family which have dependent children: there has been a decrease in the proportion living in married couple families and an increase in the proportion that are living in cohabiting couple and lone parent families. This section examines changes in the numbers of children born within and outside marriage, together with the changes in the ages of their mothers. There is also a discussion of the differences over time in the registration of their births and how this relates to the change in the types of family with dependent children.

The number of births in England and Wales increased year-on-year in most years between 2001 and 2010, rising from 594,600 in 2001 to 723,200 in 2010. However, in spite of the considerable increase, the total number of births has still not reached the level seen in 1971 when there were 783,200 births, although birth numbers have been higher such as in 1961 and 1947; see also Measuring National Well-being Population article.

Table 5: Live births: by age of mother and registration type (1)

England and Wales

| | Age of mother at birth | | | | | | |
	Under 20	20-24	25-29	30-34	35-39	40 and over	All ages
All live births							
1971	82.6	285.7	247.2	109.6	45.2	12.7	783.2
1981 [3]	56.6	194.5	215.8	126.6	34.2	6.9	634.5
1991	52.4	173.4	248.7	161.3	53.6	9.8	699.2
2001	44.2	108.8	159.9	178.9	86.5	16.3	594.6
2008	44.7	136.0	193.0	192.5	116.2	26.4	708.7
2009	43.2	136.0	194.1	191.6	114.3	27.0	706.2
2010	40.6	137.3	199.2	202.5	115.8	27.7	723.2
Outside Marriage							
1971	21.6	22.0	11.5	6.3	3.2	1.1	65.7
1981 [3]	26.4	28.8	14.3	7.9	27.3	0.9	81.0
1991	43.4	77.8	52.4	25.7	9.8	2.1	211.3
2001	39.5	68.1	56.8	45.2	23.3	5.1	238.1
2008	42.0	97.7	82.6	54.4	34.6	9.5	320.8
2009	40.9	100.1	85.6	55.8	34.1	9.6	326.2
2010	38.9	103.4	90.8	60.6	35.0	10.2	338.8
Within Marriage							
1971	61.1	263.7	235.7	103.4	42.1	11.6	717.5

	Age of mother at birth						
	Under 20	20-24	25-29	30-34	35-39	40 and over	All ages
1981 [3]	30.1	165.7	201.5	118.7	31.5	6.0	553.5
1991	8.9	95.6	196.3	135.5	43.8	7.7	487.9
2001	4.6	40.7	103.1	133.7	63.2	11.1	356.5
2008	2.7	38.2	110.4	138.1	81.6	16.9	387.9
2009	2.3	35.9	108.5	135.8	80.2	17.4	380.1
2010	1.7	34.0	108.5	141.9	80.8	17.6	384.4

Table source: Office for National Statistics

Table notes:

1. The Human Fertilisation and Embryology Act 2008 contained provisions enabling two females in a same-sex couple to register a birth from 1st September 2009 onwards. Due to the small numbers in 2009 and 2010, births registered to a same-sex couple in a civil partnership (22 in 2009, 335 in 2010) are included with marital births while births registered to a same-sex couple outside a civil partnership (2 in 2009, 140 in 2010) are included with births outside marriage.
2. Figures have been rounded to the nearest one hundred.
3. For 1981 data the processing was delayed due to the late submission of registrations. As a result the data for 1981 is estimated and figures for age of mother are based on a ten per cent sample.

The average age for women giving birth in England and Wales has increased from just over 26.6 years in 1971 to 29.5 years in 2010 (ONS, 2010c) and this is reflected in the age distribution in Table 5. In 1971, nearly four out of five of all live births (79 per cent) were to women aged under 30: by 2010 about half of all live births (52 per cent) were to women in this age group. Comparing live births in 1971 and 2010, the number of live births decreased for women in each of the three age groups under 20, 20 to 24 and 25 to 29 and increased for women in each of the three age groups 30 to 34, 35 to 39 and 40 and over.

The balance between numbers of registrations of births outside and within marriage has also altered, reflecting the change in family structure discussed earlier in this article. More than five times as many babies were born outside marriage in 2010 compared with 1971. In 1971 there were 65,700 live births outside marriage in England and Wales, 8.4 per cent of all live births in that year. Live births outside marriage increased both numerically and as a proportion of all births reaching 338,800 (46.8 per cent) in 2010. Over the same time period the number of live births within marriage had decreased by 46.0 per cent from 717,500 to 384,400.

However, the increases and decreases in overall births, and those within and outside marriage were not the same for all age groups. The number of births within marriage in the under 20 age group decreased from 61,100 in 1971 to 1,700 in 2010 (a decrease of 97 per cent), and the 20 to 24 age group decreased from 263,700 in 1971 to 34,000 in 2010 (a decrease of 230,000 or 87 per cent). In the older age groups there have been increases in the number of live births within marriage: for example in the 35 to 39 age group the increase between 1971 and 2009 was 38,600 live births (from 42,100 to 80,700 or 92 per cent).

By contrast, live births outside marriage have generally increased in all age groups although there is some variation in individual age groups in particular decades. The increase was most noticeable between 1981 and 1991: during this period it varied by age group with mothers aged under 20, and 40 and over showing the smallest increases. However it should be noted that births in the 40 and over age group represent only around 1.4 per cent of those giving birth outside of marriage at that time.

For births outside marriage, the increase in age of mothers is less marked (the proportion of under 30s has fallen from 84 per cent of births to 69 per cent, a much smaller decrease than that of births within marriage).

Conceptions and Abortions

Information about conceptions[1] also shows a change in age structure (Table 6). Provisional estimates in 2010 indicate that there were 909,200 conceptions in England and Wales, an increase of nearly 13,000 (1.4 per cent) from 896,300 in 2009. The number of conceptions in 2010 was also higher than in 1991 and 2001. There was an increase in the overall rate of conception between 2009 and 2010 of one additional conception per 1,000 women (from 81 to 82 conceptions per 1,000 women aged 15 to 44, see footnote 4 to table 6).

Table 6: Conceptions: (1) by age of woman at conception

England and Wales (2)

Age of woman at conception

	Under 16	Under 18	Under 20	20-24	25-29	30-34	35-39	40 and over	All ages
Numbers (thousands)									
1991	7.5	40.1	101.6	233.3	281.5	167.5	57.6	12.1	853.7
2001	7.9	41.0	96.0	161.6	199.3	196.7	92.2	17.8	763.7
2008	7.6	41.4	103.3	198.5	237.8	207.1	115.6	26.5	888.6
2009	7.2	38.3	97.9	199.5	242.2	213.3	116.5	26.8	896.3
2010	6.7	34.6	91.7	201.6	247.3	222.4	118.3	27.9	909.2
Rates (conceptions[3] per thousand women in age-group)									
1991	8.9	44.6	64.1	120.2	135.1	90.1	34.4	6.6	77.7
2001	8.0	42.7	60.8	102.5	114.2	96.7	44.3	9.6	70.3

Age of woman at conception

	Under 16	Under 18	Under 20	20-24	25-29	30-34	35-39	40 and over	All ages

Rates (conceptions[3] per thousand women in age-group)

	Under 16	Under 18	Under 20	20-24	25-29	30-34	35-39	40 and over	All ages
2008	7.8	40.7	60.1	108.7	133.2	121.7	58.1	12.6	79.9
2009	7.5	38.3	57.3	108.5	133.8	125.9	60.1	12.8	80.9
2010	7.0	35.5	54.6	108.6	134.1	129.4	62.9	13.5	82.3

Percentage terminated by abortion

	Under 16	Under 18	Under 20	20-24	25-29	30-34	35-39	40 and over	All ages
1991	51.1	39.9	34.5	22.2	13.4	13.7	22.0	41.6	19.4
2001	55.8	45.7	40.4	29.7	18.4	14.6	20.4	34.6	23.2
2008	61.5	49.4	42.4	28.0	17.4	12.8	16.3	30.0	21.8
2009	59.8	48.8	41.9	27.1	16.5	12.4	15.8	29.1	21.0
2010	62.5	49.9	42.8	27.3	16.4	12.6	15.9	28.2	20.8

Table source: Office for National Statistics

Table notes:
1. Conception figures are estimates derived from birth registrations and abortion notifications.
2. Data are for residents of England and Wales.
3. Revised mid–2002 to mid–2008 population estimates published on 13 May 2010 have been used in the calculation of conception rates. Figures may therefore differ from those published previously. Rates for women of all ages, under 16, under 18, under 20 and 40 and over are based on the population of women aged 15-44, 13-15, 15-17, 15-19 and 40-44 respectively.

However, these increases were not uniform across age groups. Between 2009 and 2010 conception rates (per 1,000 women) showed a noticeable increase only among those age groups where women were aged 30 and over. Women in their 20's showed almost no increase in the rate per 1,000 and the rate among those in the teenage age groups fell. This pattern was also shown in the longer-term trend. All the age groups 30 and over showed increases between 1991 and 2010 and all age groups below 20 showed decreases. The 25 to 29 age group showed the smallest fall in conception rate from 135.1 per thousand to 134.1 per thousand.

Women in the 25 to 29 age group continue to have the highest number and rate per 1,000 of conceptions. However, while those in the 20 to 24 age group had the second highest number and rate of conceptions in 1991, by 2010 they had been replaced by those in the 30 to 34 age group: this group having previously had the third highest number of conceptions and rates per 1,000 in 1991.

The proportion of conceptions resulting in legal abortions has shown a small decline in 2010 (1.0 per cent) to 20.8 per cent of all conceptions. This proportion varies between age groups. The proportions of conceptions resulting in legal abortion were highest in the lower age groups and generally decreased with age, reaching a minimum of 12.6 per cent in the 30 to 34 age group. The proportion then shows significant increases for the 35 to 39 (15.9 per cent) and the 40 and over age groups (28.2 per cent). In girls aged under 16, 62.5 per cent of pregnancies were terminated legally. Slightly less than a half of conceptions (49.9 per cent) in women aged under 18 led to a legal abortion according to provisional estimates for 2010. The overall percentage of conceptions leading to a legal abortion was almost unchanged between 2009 and 2010, falling from 21.0 per cent to 20.8 per cent.

Between 1991 and 2010 the percentage of conceptions resulting in legal abortion increased by 1.4 percentage points, from 19.4 per cent to 20.8 per cent in England and Wales. However, the largest increases over this time period were in the younger age groups which include girls and women up to the age of 30. For those aged 30 and over, there were decreases in all age groups, with a particularly marked fall in the 40 and over age group from 41.6 per cent in 1991 to 28.2 per cent in 2010.

In Scotland there has been a fall in the number and rate of abortions for the past two years, 12,826 in 2010 compared with 13,108 in 2009 and 13,902 in 2008 (representing rates of 12.3 per 1000 women aged 15–44 in 2010, 12.6 in 2009 and 13.3 in 2008). This fall is a change to the overall pattern of increase since the implementation of the 1967 Abortion Act, although small dips for short periods have been observed before.

As in previous years, the rate of terminations in 2010 was highest in younger women, 16–19 (21.4 per 1000) and those aged 20–24 (22.4 per 1000). Lower rates are seen in the older age groups; women aged 25–29 (15.3 per 1000); aged 30–34 (10.8 per 1000); aged 35–39 (6.3 per 1000) and in women aged over 40 (2.1 per 1000). (Scottish Government, 2010b).

In Northern Ireland, abortion is illegal and is only considered lawful in exceptional circumstances. As there are such a small number of abortions, and in order to protect patient confidentiality, there are no comparable conception figures for Northern Ireland. (NISRA 2010b)

Notes

1. Conception estimates include pregnancies that result in one or more live births or stillbirths or which are terminated by a legal abortion. They do not include miscarriages or illegal abortions.

Children and young people

Childcare is very important to many families, particularly where one or both parents are working. It can be provided informally by family, friends or neighbours, or formally by a registered childminder or childcare company: many parents and guardians use a combination of both formal and informal childcare.

Table 7: Registered child-care places and providers, 31 December 2011

England

Thousands

Providers	Childminders		Childcare on: non-domestic premises		All	
Provision on:[1]	Places[2]	[3]	Providers[2]	Places[3]	Providers[2]	Places[3]
All registers	53.6	267.9	16.5	686	70.2	955.7
EYR and CCR	3.1	14.6	1.6	70.1	4.8	85
EYR and VCR	0	0	0.1	6.7	0.2	6.8
EYR only	0.2	0.7	7.5	260.9	7.8	262
EYR total	56.9	283.2	25.9	1,023.80	83	1,309.40

Table source: Office for Standards in Education

Table notes:
1. Register(s): Ofsted register care provided for children on two registers, the Early Years Register (EYR) and the Childcare Register, which has a compulsory (CCR) and voluntary (VCR) component. People can apply to join one register or both registers at the same time. Most childcare providers caring for children aged under eight must register with Ofsted unless the law says they are not required to do so. If a childcare provider is not required to register with Ofsted, then in some circumstances they may choose to do so by joining the voluntary part of the Childcare Register (VCR).
2. Providers are the number of providers registered on the database at the at the end of the relevant period. As not all providers inform Ofsted that they have ceased provision, this number is likely to be higher than the actual number of providers.
3. Registered places are the number of children that may attend the provision at any one time. Registered places are not the number of places occupied, nor the number of children who may benefit from receiving places through providers offering sessions at different times of the day. Place numbers are only collected for providers on the Early Years Register. For these providers, the numbers show the total places available for children under eight. Averages are used for a very small number of providers whose place numbers are not available at the time of the analysis. There are very small discrepancies in totals due to rounding.

In England in December 2011 there were more than 96,000 registered childcare providers: including around 10,000 childminders and nearly 2,000 childcare providers on non-domestic property who are signed to the voluntary childcare register and not listed above (Table 7). Between them they were responsible for providing more than 1.3 million childcare places. Registered childminders and home childcare providers account for more than two-thirds of providers, 58,000 and 10,000 respectively, but less than a quarter of all places, around 283,000. Instead the majority of childcare is provided by those using non-domestic property, for example by nurseries and crèches or pre and after school clubs. These provide more than a million childcare places. As a childcare place may be shared by more than one child during a week the actual number of children receiving childcare may be higher. However it should also be noted that these are spaces and not all available spaces may be taken up. (Ofsted 2011)

Children can come under the responsibility of their local authority if their parents or guardians are having difficulty looking after them. 'Looked after' children can be placed with foster carers, placed for adoption or remain with their parents. In 2011 there were nearly 91,000 children who were looked after in England, an increase of more than 7,000 since 2007, most of which came from increases of instances of 'Abuse or neglect', followed by 'Family dysfunction'.

Table 8: Children looked after (1) at 31 March, by need for care (2,3)

England

Thousands

	2007	2008	2009	2010	2011
Abuse or neglect	48.7	48.4	49.1	51.5	53.8
Child's disability	3.1	3.0	3.0	2.9	2.9
Parents illness or disability	4.4	4.1	3.9	3.9	3.9
Family in acute stress	7.1	7.3	7.6	8.3	8.5
Family dysfunction	9.3	9.3	9.9	11.3	12.7
Socially unacceptable behaviour	2.5	2.3	2.2	2.2	2.2
Low income	0.2	0.2	0.2	0.2	0.3
Absent parenting	8.2	8.1	8.5	7.8	6.7
Total	83.5	82.5	84.3	88.2	90.9

Table source: Children, Schools and Families

Table notes:
1. Excludes children looked after exclusively under one or more agreed series of short term placements at any time during the years ending 31 March.
2. The most applicable category of the eight 'Need Codes' at the time the child started to be looked after rather than necessarily the entire reason they are looked after.
3. Placement and category of need relate to child's latest episode of care during the year.

Although the number of children being looked after has increased year-on-year since 2008, this may be due to increased intervention by social services rather than an increase in any of the categories stated. The most common reason for a child being looked after was 'Abuse or neglect' which accounted for nearly 60 per cent of all cases (Table 8). The next most common reason was 'Family dysfunction' (14 per cent) although family reasons, excluding parental illness or disability, between them accounted for nearly 31 per cent of cases. Disability, either the child's or the parent's disability or illness, accounted for just over 7 per cent of all looked after children.

During the same period (2007 to 2011) the number of looked after children in Scotland increased from 14,000 to 16,000, although a category of need breakdown is not available.

Wales had 5,415 children who began to be looked after in 2011. This is a decrease on the previous year's figure of 5,160 but higher than the 2007 figure of 4,640.

Carers and caring

Informal carers are adults or children who provide any regular service or help to someone who is sick, disabled or elderly, but not in a paid capacity. Many carers balance their caring responsibilities with paid work. Those in full-time employment made up the largest group (36 per cent) of carers in the UK in 2009/10, regardless of whether they were providing care within or outside their household (Figure 5). The next largest group was those in retirement (23 per cent), followed by those who were economically inactive (20 per cent) and then those in part-time employment (17 per cent). The proportion of male carers in full-time employment was much higher than the proportion of female carers (47 per cent compared with 28 per cent) but the reverse was true for those in part-time employment (8 per cent of men and 23 per cent of women), this may reflect that traditionally women are more likely than men to be in part-time employment. However, there was little difference between men and women who reported caring in retirement (25 per cent and 22 per cent respectively).

Sixty one per cent of adult informal carers in the UK in 2009/10 were providing care for someone living outside their own household. Family members were the main recipients of informal care from both household and non-household members. There were some similarities between men and women in the pattern of relationships between the carer and the person being cared for. The largest group cared for by both men and women were parents who were non-household members (34 per cent and 38 per cent respectively). Within the household, spouses or civil partners were the most common recipients of care from both men (21 per cent) and women (15 per cent). Around 8 per cent of male and female carers provided care to non-family members, whether within their own household or not. See also 'Measuring National Well-being: What we do' which discusses the hours spent in giving care. (FRS, 2011)

Figure 5: Adult informal carers by relationship to person being cared for, by household type 2009/10
United Kingdom

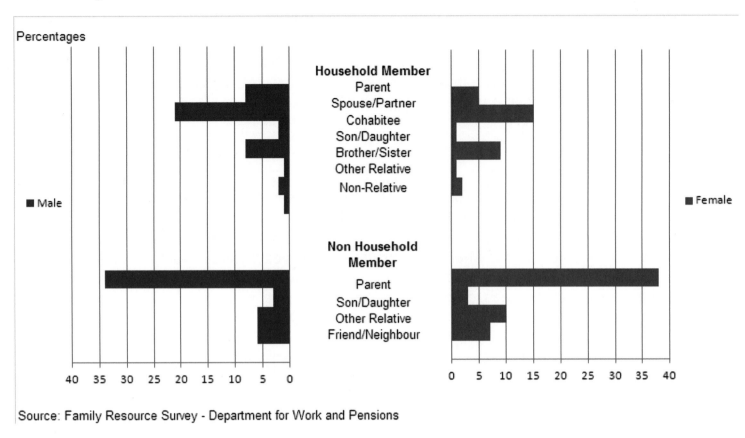

Source: Family Resource Survey - Department for Work and Pensions

About the ONS Measuring National Well-being Programme

NWB logo 2

This article is published as part of the ONS Measuring National Well-being Programme.

The programme aims to produce accepted and trusted measures of the well-being of the nation - how the UK as a whole is doing. It is about looking at 'GDP and beyond' and includes:

- greater analysis of the national economic accounts, especially to understand household income, expenditure and wealth
- further accounts linked to the national accounts, including the UK Environmental Accounts and valuing household production and 'human capital'
- quality of life measures, looking at different areas of national well-being such as health, relationships, job satisfaction, economic security, education environmental conditions
- working with others to include the measurement of the well-being of children and young people as part of national well-being
- measures of 'subjective well-being' - individuals' assessment of their own well-being
- headline indicators to summarise national well-being and the progress we are making as a society

The programme is underpinned by a communication and engagement workstream, providing links with Cabinet Office and policy departments, international developments, the public and other stakeholders. The programme is working closely with Defra on the measurement of 'sustainable development' to provide a complete picture of national well-being, progress and sustainable development.

Find out more on the Measuring National Well-being website pages.

Background notes

1. Details of the policy governing the release of new data are available by visiting www.statisticsauthority.gov.uk/assessment/code-of-practice/index.html or from the Media Relations Office email: media.relations@ons.gsi.gov.uk

Copyright

References

1. Council of Mortgage lenders, 2011 - Number of mortgages

2. FRS, 2011 - Informal carers, Department for Work and Pensions

3. General Register Office for Scotland, 2010 - Live births, numbers and percentages, by marital status of parents and type of registration, Scotland, 1974 to 2009

4. NISRA, 2010a - Additional Tables for Marriages, Divorces and Civil Partnerships in Northern Ireland, 2009

5. NISRA, 2010b - Live births by number of previous children and marital status of parents, 1976 to 2009

6. ONS, 2009 - Historic marriage tables: Previous marital status (146.5 Kb Excel sheet)

7. ONS, 2010a - Civil partnerships formations data (181.5 Kb Excel sheet)

8. ONS, 2010b - Civil partnerships dissolutions data (66.5 Kb Excel sheet)

9. ONS, 2010c - Characteristics of Mother 1 2009: 21/10/10 (141.5 Kb Excel sheet)

10. ONS, 2011a - People living alone. Families and households tables, 2011

11. ONS, 2011b - Subjective well-being for those with or without children.

12. ONS, 2011c - Families and number of people living in families. Families and households tables, 2011

13. Ofsted, 2011 - Numbers of childcare places, England

14. Scottish Government, 2010a - Table 1: Divorces and dissolutions granted, 2000-01 - 2009-10

15. Scottish Government, 2010b - Abortions by place, age, deprivation, gestation, parity, repeat abortions and grounds for termination

Measuring National Well-being, Education and skills

Abstract

This article on 'Education and skills' is the latest in a series which aims to explore in more detail the different aspects that have been considered as important for the measurement of National Well-being. It focuses on education and life-long learning including the stock of human capital in the labour market with some information about levels of educational achievement and skills.

Introduction

A wide variety of studies have investigated the relationship between education and well-being. Some studies identify a positive relationship between education and well-being, while others find that middle-level education is related to the highest levels of well-being (Dolan et al 2008). Previous research has also shown that education and skills are vitally important to an individual's well-being and should be considered when making any assessment of National Well-being.

"Learning encourages social interaction and increases self-esteem and feelings of competency. Behaviour directed by personal goals to achieve something new has been shown to increase reported life satisfaction. While there is often a much greater policy emphasis on learning in the early years of life, psychological research suggests it is a critical aspect of day-to-day living for all age groups. Therefore policies that encourage learning, even in the elderly, will enable individuals to develop new skills, strengthen social networks, and feel more able to deal with life's challenges" (New Economics Foundation 2009).

This was highlighted during the Office for National Statistics (ONS) national debate on Measuring National Well-being. Many people said 'education and skills' were important for the measurement of National Well-being, in addition access to education and its quality were also considered important.

"Underpinning all Government learning and skills policies is the firm conviction that learning is precious because it brings light to all kinds of lives. Whether the learner is a young apprentice looking to gain vocational skills as the basis for a fulfilling career or an older person wanting to remain physically and mentally active by taking part in adult education classes, we know that learning enriches individuals, strengthens communities, and feeds the common good. John Hayes, Minister of State for Further Education, Skills and Lifelong Learning" (BIS, 2012).

This article starts by discussing funding for education services in the UK, followed by a section which gives some information about participation in education at all ages, from the early years to adulthood, and describes some of the formal qualifications obtained. It includes some discussion of disadvantaged groups, the relationship between both qualifications and lifelong learning and individual well-being and there is then a section which describes the value to the economy of the qualifications of those who are active in the labour market.

Key points

- Estimated expenditure on education by central and local government in the UK in 2010–11 was 6.3 per cent of GDP, unchanged from 2009–10 but 1.6 percentage points higher than 1990–91 and higher than the EU-27 average of 5.7 per cent.

Children

- Approximately 97.3 per cent of three and four-year-olds were in early year's placements, 5.6 percentage points higher than the EU-27 average of 91.7 per cent.
- Children who live in relatively poor households, those being looked-after by someone other than their parent or guardian and those with statements of special educational needs all have lower levels of outcome from their education.
- International assessment of pupils aged 15 in the UK show that they achieve about the same standard as the average for all OECD countries in reading, slightly below the average in mathematics and above the average in science.
- The proportion of pupils in the UK gaining the equivalent of five or more GCSEs at grades A* to C, including English and mathematics, continues to increase reaching nearly 53 per cent in 2009/10.

Young people

- Between 2001 and 2011 there was an increase in the percentage of young people aged 16 to 24 in England who were not in employment, education or training, particularly for young men.
- There was a decrease of 3.3 per cent between 2009/10 and 2010/11 in the total number of first year enrolments in higher education institutes in the UK, this was almost entirely because of the fall in the number of part time students.

Adults

- In 2011 employers reported that approximately 1.5 million employees had skills gaps, 3.6 million employees received job-related training with an estimated £49 billion spent by employers on training.
- In the 2012 an estimated one fifth of adults in the UK reported that they were currently engaged in learning, and about two fifths had taken part in some form of learning in the previous three years.
- Adults with an impairment are considerably more likely than those without an impairment to have no formal qualifications.

Qualifications levels and human capital

- Between 1993 and 2011 the proportion of adults aged 16 to 64 without any formal educational qualifications has more than halved from 27 per cent to 11 per cent and the proportion with a degree or equivalent has more than doubled from 11 per cent to 24 per cent.
- The estimated value of qualifications of those in employment was £17,250 billion in 2009 and went down to £17,120 billion in 2010 as the numbers in employment fell during the recession.

Education and subjective well-being

- Higher levels of qualifications and continued formal and informal learning have been found to be associated with greater individual subjective well-being.

Education expenditure

Most countries strive to ensure that young people are able to start their working lives with a minimum level of skill acquired through education. Public financing of provision has been the traditional means of encouraging education. Expenditure on educational services by central and local government in the UK relative to the output of the UK economy measured by Gross Domestic Product (GDP) is shown below (ONS 2012).

Figure 1

Education expenditure as a proportion of GDP (1)

United Kingdom

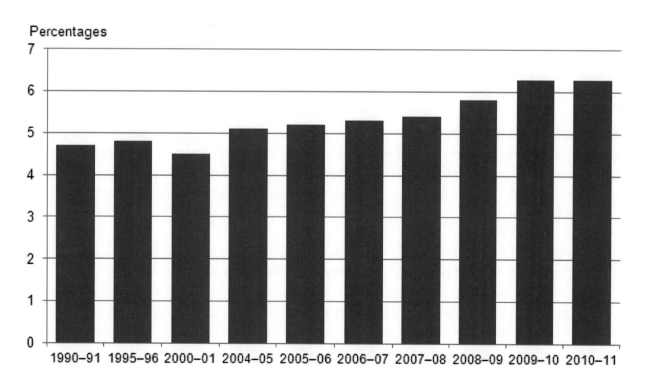

Notes:
1. Data for periods 1995–96 to 2007–08 includes revised data.
2. Source: Department for Education (DfE 2011)

In the UK in 2010–11 expenditure was estimated at £92.5 billion, of which; £4.9 billion was directly on under fives, £24.7 billion was on primary education, £40.2 billion was on secondary education and £15.7 billion was on tertiary education (further and higher education).

Estimated expenditure on education services by central and local government in the UK in 2010–11 was 6.3 per cent of GDP, unchanged from 2009–10 but 1.6 percentage points higher than 1990–91 when the estimated expenditure was 4.7 per cent of GDP (Figure 1).

There are considerable differences between public education expenditure as a proportion of GDP between the 27 European Union countries (EU-27). In 2009 education expenditure was 5.7 per cent of GDP in the UK, just above the EU-27 average of 5.5 per cent. On this measure education expenditure was highest in Denmark at 8.7 per cent, followed by Cyprus at 7.9 per cent and Sweden at 7.3 per cent. Slovakia and Romania had the lowest proportions of expenditure at 4.1 and 4.2 per cent respectively (EU 2012).

Children

Participation in education: early years

In order that individuals may gain the benefits to their well-being of education and learning, they must first participate in the education process. Information about participation levels in education is shown in this section starting with the early years and progressing to adults.

'*We have found overwhelming evidence that children's life chances are most heavily predicted on their development in the first five years of life. It is family background, parental education, good parenting and the opportunities for learning and development in those crucial years that together matter more to children than money, in determining whether their potential is realised in adult life.*' (National Archives 2010)

The foundation years, the first five years of a child's life, are critical. Children's experiences in these years have the biggest impact on how their brains develop. It is also when children grasp the fundamental skills needed to do well at school and develop as happy, confident individuals. For this reason participation in some form of early education can improve a child's chances of achievement and well-being in later years.

Most three and four-year-olds in the UK benefit from early year's placements in educational establishments. Data from Eurostat shows that in 2009 participation rates in early childhood education was universal in France (100 per cent) and nearly universal in the Netherlands (99.5 per cent), Belgium (99.3) per cent and Spain (99.3 per cent). The UK participation rate was 97.3 per cent, 5.6 percentage points higher than the EU-27 average of 91.7 per cent. Participation rates were lowest in Poland (70.9 per cent) and Finland (71.9 per cent) (EU 2012a).

Table 1

Proportion of three and four-year-olds benefiting from early education places: (1) by type of provider and local authority, 2011

England

Percentages

	Nursery schools and classes in primary schools[2]	Infant classes in primary schools[3]	State-funded secondary schools[4]	Other[5]	All providers[6]
England	26.6	31.0	0.2	39.3	97.1
North East	48.3	32.3	0.9	17.5	99.0
North West	31.2	32.2	0.2	34.7	98.3
Yorkshire and the Humber	36.7	32.4	0.2	30.0	99.3
East Midlands	23.8	32.8	0.6	41.6	98.7
West Midlands	31.8	31.7	0.1	33.5	97.2
East of England	20.2	30.0	0.0	47.2	97.5
London	34.8	28.1	0.5	28.8	92.2
South East	12.6	30.8	0.0	54.0	97.4
South West	11.2	31.8	0.2	56.2	99.3

Table notes:

1. Pupils aged three and four at 31 December as a proportion of all the three and four-year-olds in each local authority.
2. Includes primary academies.
3. Includes reception and other classes not designated as nursery classes.
4. Includes maintained secondary schools and secondary academies.
5. Includes private and voluntary providers (including some Local Authority day nurseries registered to receive funding), independent schools and special schools (including general hospital schools and excluding pupils who are also registered elsewhere).
6. Any child attending more than one provider will have only been counted once.
7. Source: Department for Education (DfE 2011a)

In England in January 2011, 97.1 per cent of all three and four -year-olds in England benefited from some free early education (Table 1). Over half of all three and four year olds (57.6 per cent) were in maintained nursery and state-funded primary schools and 31.0 per cent were in infant classes in primary schools. Regionally, participation in education by three and four- year-olds varied between 92.2 per cent in London and 99.3 per cent in the South West.

Participation in education: Disadvantaged groups

In 2010, the Joseph Rowntree Foundation published a report called "Poorer children's educational attainment: how important are attitudes and behaviour" (Joseph Rowntree Foundation 2010). They reported that:

"Children growing up in poorer families emerge from school with substantially lower levels of educational attainment. This is a major contributing factor to patterns of mobility and poverty".

The report found that there are big differences in cognitive development between children at the age of three from rich and poor backgrounds and that this gap had widened by the age of five. Differences in the home learning environment, particularly at the age of three, are shown to be an important explanatory factor with, for example, only 42 per cent of poorer children being read to every day compared to 79 per cent of children from the richest families.

While gaps in educational attainment between children from poor families and those from better-off backgrounds appear early, the report also highlights the gap in educational outcomes between young people from different socio-economic backgrounds at ages 11, 14 and 16. For example, at age 16 only 1 in 5 young people from the poorest families achieved five good GCSEs including English and mathematics compared with three-quarters of young people from the richest families.

Apart from those children from poorer backgrounds there are a number of other groups within the school population that can also be considered as disadvantaged by their personal circumstances. These include those who are looked-after by someone other than their parent or guardian and those with statements of special educational needs (SEN).

Children become looked-after when their parents/guardians are unable to provide on-going care in either a temporary or permanent capacity. This can be by voluntary agreement with their parents or guardians or as the result of a care order.

Table 2

Achievements of looked-after children: (1) by Key Stage, 2011

England

Percentages

	Looked after children	Non looked after children
Key Stage 1[2]		
Number eligible to sit Key Stage 1 tasks & tests	2,230	568,470
Percentage achieving level 2 or above in:		
Reading	*65*	*85*
Writing	*57*	*81*
Mathematics	*71*	*90*
Key Stage 2[3]		
Number eligible to sit Key Stage 2 tests	2,640	552,430
Percentage achieving level 4+ in English & mathematics	*43*	*74*
Key Stage 4[4]		
Number eligible to sit GCSEs	5,680	633,260
Percentage achieving:		
5+ GCSEs inc. A*-C in English & mathematics	*13*	*58*
A*-C in English & mathematics	*14*	*59*

Table notes:

1. Children looked-after for six months, excluding children in respite care.
2. Figures for KS1 are based on teacher assessment. Level 2 is the expected level for the age group.
3. Figures for KS2 are based on tests. Level 4 is the expected level for the age group.
4. Figures for KS4 include GSCEs and other equivalent qualifications approved for use pre 16.
5. Source: Department for Education (DfE 2011b)

As can be seen in Table 2, the number of children who are looked- after at each Key Stage is relatively small however, the average outcome for these children at each of the assessed stages of their education is significantly lower than those for other children. For example, of the 2,230 children looked-after continuously for six months during the year ending March 2011 and who were eligible to sit Key Stage 1[1] tasks and tests, 65 per cent achieved the expected level[2] in reading compared with 85 per cent of other children and a much smaller proportion also achieved the expected levels in writing and mathematics. This relatively low level of outcome for children who are looked-after continues at each Key Stage.

Pupils with special educational needs (SEN)[3] have learning difficulties or disabilities which mean that they need extra assistance in order to make the same progress as other pupils of the same age. In 2011 there were approximately 1.6 million pupils (19.0 per cent of pupils on roll) in England and Wales with statements of SEN. In 2011 boys were two and a half times more likely than girls to have statements at primary school and nearly three times more likely to have statements at secondary school compared with girls. Two per cent of boys (42,000 pupils) at primary schools had statements compared with 0.8 per cent of girls (16,000 pupils). At secondary school, 2.9 per cent of boys (47,400 pupils) had statements compared with 1.0 per cent of girls (16,300 pupils).

Pupils with special education needs (SEN) are more likely than others to experience poor outcomes which may affect their current and future well-being through middle childhood and adolescence. A report from the Centre for Research on Wider Benefits of Learning, Institute of Education (DCSF 2010) estimated that 70.4 per cent of pupils in maintained mainstream schools in England made the expected progress between Key Stages 2 and 4 in English and 62.9 per cent in mathematics. The percentage of pupils with School Action Plus or statements[4] making the expected progress between Key Stages 2 and 4 was generally lower and varied by their impairment.

Figure 2

Proportion of pupils with statements of special educational needs making expected progress in English and mathematics between Key Stage 2 and 4: (1,2) by impairment, 2009/10

England

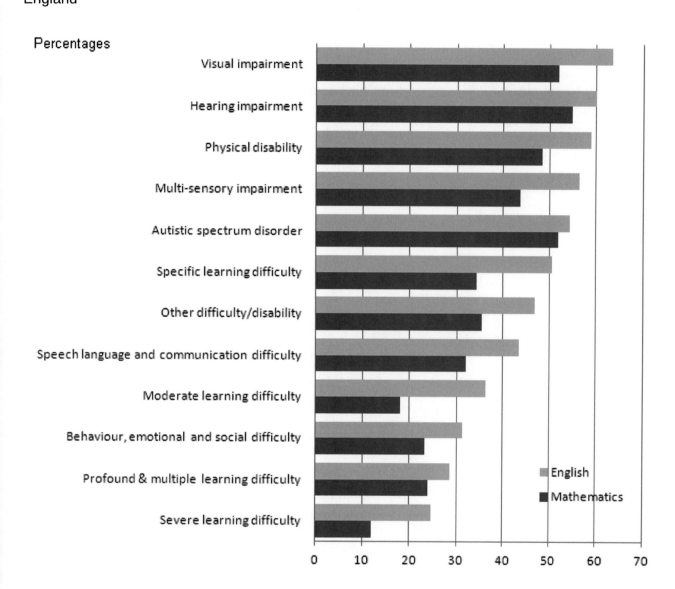

Notes:
1. Maintained mainstream schools only (including academies).
2. Pupils included are those at the end of Key Stage 4 who have valid matched Key Stage 2 result or teacher assessment. Pupils with no prior attainment record are excluded from the calculation unless they are ungraded or have achieved grade B or above at GCSE.
3. Source: Department for Education (DfE 2011c)

Those with visual impairments (63.3 per cent) and hearing impairments (60.1 per cent) were most likely to achieve the expected progress in English (Figure 2). In mathematics, pupils with hearing impairments (54.8 per cent) and autistic spectrum disorder (52.0 per cent) were most likely of all primary need groups to achieve the expected progress.

Participation in education: achievements

The Programme for International Student Assessment (PISA) is a survey of the educational performance of 15-year-olds by the Organisation for Economic Co-operation and Development (OECD). The survey takes place every three years and assesses students in reading, mathematics and science. In each survey one of these is the main focus: in 2009 the main focus was on reading.

Table 3

Programme for International Student Assessment (PISA) in the UK, 2006 and 2009

United Kingdom

Average mean scores

| | United Kingdom | | OECD Average | |
	2006	2009	2006	2009
Reading	492	494	495	493
Science	515	514	500	501
Mathematics	495	492	498	496

Table notes:
1. Source: Organisation for Economic Co-operation and Development (OECD)

Overall there was very little change in the mathematics, reading and science PISA scores between 2006 and 2009 in the UK (Table 3). In this assessment of reading, students in the UK achieved an average score similar to the average for the OECD, while the average score for UK students in mathematics was below the OECD average in both 2006 and 2009. However, average science scores for 15-year-olds in the UK were significantly higher than the OECD average in 2006 and 2009.

Within the UK, achievement at age 16 is generally measured by General Certificate of Secondary Education (GCSE) and equivalent results. The aggregate results have improved in each year since these examinations were introduced in the late 1980s.

Figure 3

Pupils achieving five or more GCSE or equivalent grades A* to C: (1,2) by sex

United Kingdom

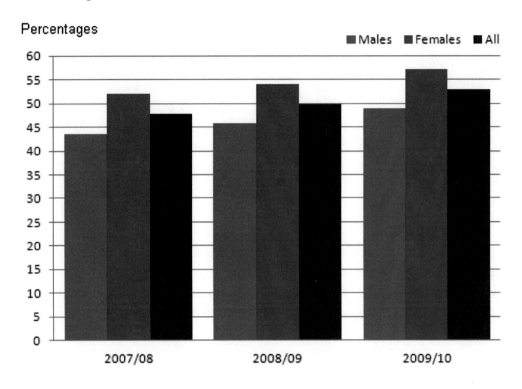

Percentages

Notes:

1.   Including English and mathematics.
2.   For pupils in their last year of compulsory education. Pupils aged 15 at the start of the academic year; pupils in year S4 in Scotland.
3.   Source: Department for Education (DfE 2011)

During the 1950s and 1960s a higher proportion of boys achieved five or more good O-level passes. This situation reversed in the early 1970s and girls have outperformed boys on these measures ever since (HC 2007).

Figure 3 focuses on the combination of core skills with overall GCSE performance. It shows the proportion of pupils achieving at least five or more A* to C grades at GCSE or equivalent including English and mathematics. In 2009/10 52.9 per cent of young people in the UK achieved five or more passes at this standard compared with 49.8 per cent in 2008/09. As in previous years a higher proportion of girls than boys achieved this outcome, with girls also showing a slightly larger increase in achievement between 2008/09 and 2009/10 with a 3.1 percentage point increase compared with 3.0 for boys.

Many students study Advanced Subsidiary (AS) and Advanced (A) level qualifications between the ages of 16 to 18 immediately after completing their GCSE's although adults can take them too. AS and A level qualifications focus on traditional skills and normally take two years to complete full-time, although they are also available to study part-time. AS and A levels are at level 3 on the National Qualifications Framework. Such qualifications and their equivalents are usually a pre-requisite for entry into higher education.

In 2009/10 the number of GCE applied/VCE A/AS and double award passes in England, Wales and Northern Ireland decreased when compared with 2008/09. In 2009/10 there were 34,800 AS level passes, 8,800 (20 per cent lower) than 2008/09 and 33,300 A level passes in 2009/10, 2,500 (7 per cent) lower than 2008/09. The number of A level double awards also decreased from 11,100 in 2008/09 to 9,200 in 2009/10 and the number of AS double awards decreased from 8,600 to 5,800 over the same period.

Notes

1. Key Stage 1 is the legal term for the two years of schooling in maintained schools in England and Wales. Normally known as year 1 and year 2, when pupils are aged between 5 and 7. This Key Stage normally covers pupils during infant school, although in some cases this might form part of a first or primary school. It is also the label used for the third and fourth years of primary education in Northern Ireland.

2. Expected level for age group based on teacher assessments at KS1 and test results at KS2 and KS4.

3. Pupils with special educational needs are currently classified into three distinct provisions of need: School Action, School Action Plus or with statements of special educational needs:

    School Action – where extra or different help is given, from that provided as part of the school's usual curriculum.

    School Action Plus – where the class teacher and the SENCO (Special Educational Needs Coordinator) receive advice or support from outside specialists (the specialist teacher, an educational psychologist, a speech and language therapist or other health professionals).

    Statement – a pupil has a statement of special educational needs when a formal assessment has been made. A document setting out the child's needs and the extra help they should receive is in place.

4. Special educational needs: statements. A statement of special educational need (SEN) sets out a child's needs and the help they should have. It is reviewed annually to ensure that any extra support given continues to meet the child's needs.

Young people

While children up to the age of 16 in the UK are required to be in education, after this age young people can either stay in full-time education at school or college or take employment with or without training. Over the last decade there have been a growing number of young people leaving compulsory education who are not continuing in education and who are also not in employment or training.

Not being in education, employment of training (NEET) can waste young persons potential and reduces their contribution to society. Research shows that disengagement at this age negatively impacts in social terms and those who are disengaged from education and training can cause problems in the community in the form of nuisance and crime. There is also a negative impact on the individual with a tendency towards early criminalisation, drug culture and dependency and teenage pregnancy (LSN, 2009).

Between 2001 and 2011 there was an increase in the number of young people aged 16 to 24 in England not in education, employment or training (NEET) and this was particularly so for young men. There are quarterly variations in the numbers, which peak in the third quarter (July to September) of each year as young people leave compulsory schooling. The total number of young people aged 16 to 24 in England who were NEET in the fourth quarter (October to December) of 2011 was 958,000, 19,000 (2.0 per cent) higher than the same period in the previous year.

Figure 4

Proportion of 16 to 24-year-olds (1) not in employment, education or training (NEET): by sex
England

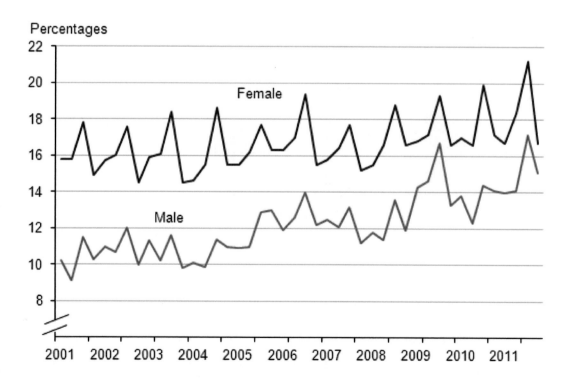

Source: Labour Force Survey - Office for National Statistics

Notes:
1.   Age refers to academic age, which is the respondent's age at the preceding 31 August.

Between 2001 and 2011 there has been a narrowing of the gap in the proportion of females and males who are NEET in any quarter. In the fourth quarter of 2011 the proportion of females aged 16 to 24 in England classed as NEET was 16.7 per cent and males 15.1 per cent (Figure 4). The gap between females and males aged 16 to 24 classed as NEET was at its lowest level in quarter 4 of 2011 with just 1.6 per cent more females being classed as NEET compared with males.

The National Learner Satisfaction Survey (BIS 2011) is the largest survey of the views of post-16 learners ever undertaken in England. It provides an invaluable insight into learners' perceptions of what is already working well in post-16 education and training and what might be improved.

Figure 5

Young people's overall satisfaction with the learning experience (1,2), 2010

England

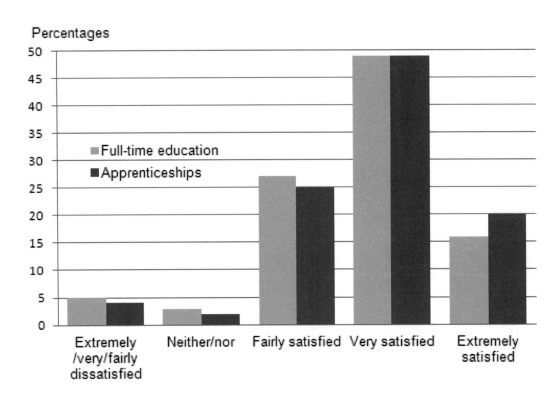

Source: Business, Innovation and Skills

Notes:
1. Based on responses from full-time education and apprenticeship learners aged 16–18 in 2010.
2. Based on responses to the question "how satisfied are you with your current learning experience at college/ provider?"

When asked "how satisfied are you with your current learning experience?" the vast majority of young people aged 16 to18 were satisfied, with over 90 per cent being fairly, very or extremely satisfied (Figure 5). Apprentices were 25 per cent more likely than those in full-time education to be extremely satisfied.

Participation in education: higher and further education

One relatively common response to the National Debate (ONS 2011) was that job security was important to an individual's well-being. According to a report from Statistics Canada, workers with a higher education were more likely to have secure, high-wage, high-benefit jobs. Employees with less than high-school education were more likely to have insecure work, low wages and no benefits (OECD 2007).

Table 4

First year student enrolments on Higher Education (HE) courses: by location and mode of study

United Kingdom

Percentages

	2006/07	2007/08	2008/09	2009/10	2010/11
England					
Full-time	56.2	57.6	58.0	59.7	62.0
Part-Time	43.8	42.4	42.0	40.3	38.0
Total (=100%) (thousands)	877	891	960	996	965
Wales					
Full-time	53.6	54.1	55.3	61.5	61.9
Part-time	46.4	45.9	44.7	38.5	38.1
Total (=100%) (thousands)	63	64	66	66	66
Scotland					
Full-time	64.0	64.7	66.4	68.4	69.6
Part-time	36.0	35.3	33.6	31.6	30.4
Total (=100%) (thousands)	96	93	98	100	92

	2006/07	2007/08	2008/09	2009/10	2010/11
Northern Ireland					
Full-time	*57.4*	*59.7*	*60.8*	*60.8*	*59.0*
Part-time	*42.6*	*40.3*	*39.2*	*39.2*	*41.1*
Total (=100%) (thousands)	21	21	21	23	22
UK					
Full-time	*56.8*	*58.1*	*58.6*	*60.5*	*62.5*
Part-time	*43.2*	*41.9*	*41.4*	*39.5*	*37.5*
Total (=100%) (thousands)	1,057	1,069	1,144	1,185	1,146

Table notes:

1.   Source: Higher Education Statistics Agency

The total number of first year enrolments in HE institutions in the UK was approximately 1.1 million in 2010/11, a decrease of 3.3 per cent compared with 2009/10. The number of full-time enrolments showed little change between 2009/10 and 2010/11, while part-time first year enrolments decreased by 8.2 per cent over the same period (Table 3). The number of applicants in 2010/11 have decreased from all the UK countries; England (9.9 per cent), Northern Ireland (4.4 per cent), Wales (1.9 per cent) and Scotland (1.5 per cent).

Initial data for university and college applications in 2012 shows that the total number of applications by the January deadline (540,000) was approximately 44,000 (7.4 per cent) lower than at the same point in 2011 (584,000). The number of applicants from the UK has decreased by 8.7 per cent overall. The number of applications decreased in England (9.9 per cent), Northern Ireland (4.4 per cent) and Wales (1.9 per cent). Applicants from EU countries have also decreased by 11.2 per cent but there has been an increase of 13.7 per cent in applications from outside the EU.

Figure 6

Qualifications obtained by students at Higher Educational (HE) institutions in the UK: by sex and level of qualification, 2010/11

United Kingdom

Percentages

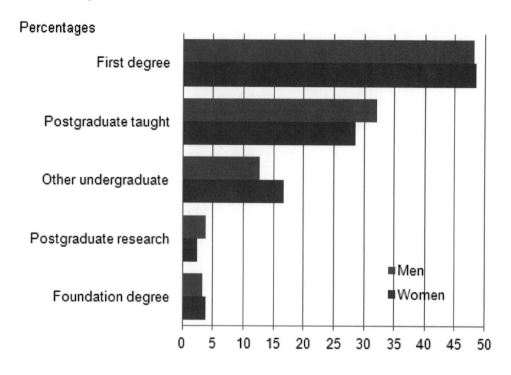

Notes:
1. Source: Higher Education Statistics Agency

In 2010/11, there were 762,540 HE qualifications obtained in the UK compared with 716,940 in 2009/10 an increase of 6 per cent. Of these 369,010 were at first degree level, compared with 350,860 in 2009/10, showing an increase of 5 per cent. First degree qualifications accounted for 48 per cent of all HE qualifications obtained in 2010/11 and other undergraduate qualifications (including foundation degrees and excluding undergraduate PGCE[1]) accounted for 19 per cent (Figure 6). Postgraduate qualifications (excluding postgraduate PGCE) accounted for 30 per cent and PGCE qualifications (at postgraduate and undergraduate level) accounted for the remaining 4 per cent.

Over the last 15 years there has been a drive to increase the proportion of learners who progress to higher education from under-represented sections of the population, particularly those from lower socio-economic groups. This is thought to not only bring private benefits to individuals but also wider socio-economic benefits by promoting social mobility and ensuring employers have the largest possible pool of highly qualified and skilled graduates.

There were approximately 288,800 first degree entrants from under-represented groups in 2010/11. This was an increase of 27,600 (10.6 per cent) compared with 2005/06 when there were approximately 261,000 entrants.

Figure 7

Mature full-time undergraduate entrants: by country (1)

England, Wales & Northern Ireland

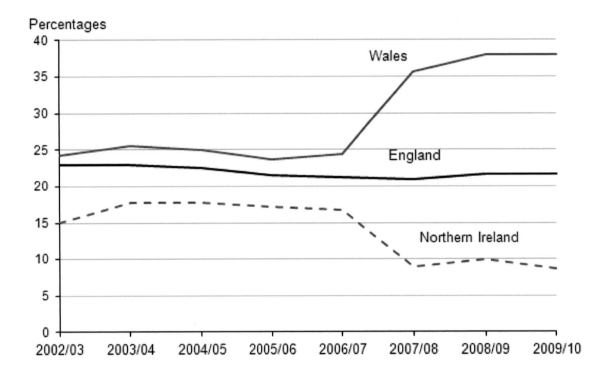

Notes:
1. See note 2.
2. Source: Higher Education Statistics Agency

Not all entrants to higher education are those who have just left school. In 2010/11 nearly a third (32 per cent) of first degree UK resident undergraduate students were over the age of 21.

In 2009/10, there were approximately 73,000 mature full-time first degree entrants in England, Wales and Northern Ireland, 22 per cent of all full-time first degree entrants (Figure 7). This was approximately 3,000 higher than in 2008/09 when there were around 70,000 mature full-time first degree entrants. The proportion of undergraduates entering their first year was slightly higher in Wales at 22.8 per cent (approximately 5,125 students), compared with England at 21.7 per cent (nearly 66,000 students). The Northern Ireland figure was 17.7 per cent, just over 1,700 students.

Apart from those entering higher education there are many adult learners[3] who are still involved in education and training after the end of compulsory education. Gaining new skills or keeping skills up to date is vital to our economy and society. These improvements help businesses succeed and enable individuals to realise their potential.

Figure 8

Summary of further education (FE) and skills participation (1)

England

Thousands

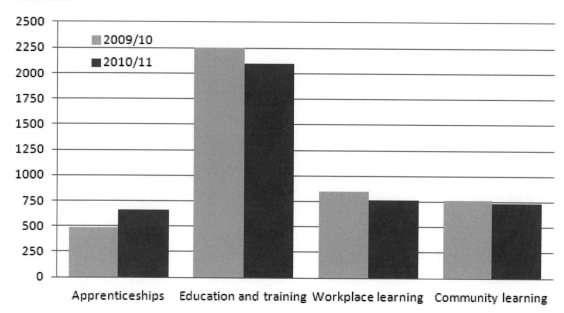

Notes:
1. Item includes apprenticeships, workplace learning, community learning and education and training provision taken at general further education colleges (including tertiary), sixth form colleges (agricultural and horticultural colleges and art and design colleges), specialist colleges an external institutions.
2. Source: The Data Service

Data from the January 2012 Post-16 Education and Skills: Learner Participation, Outcomes and Level of Highest Qualification report (BIS, 2012), shows that 4.3 million learners participated in some form of government-funded further education (excluding schools) in the 2010/11 academic year. This was a decrease in learner participation of 370,600 (8.0 per cent) compared with 2009/10 (Figure 8). Of the 4.3 million learners in 2010/11, nearly half (2.1 million) were participating in further education and training with the remainder learning in the workplace, community or through an apprenticeship.

The report also shows that there was a steady increase in apprenticeship starts between 2006/07 and 2009/10, followed by a large increase between 2009/10 and 2010/11. The total number of learners participating in apprenticeship programs in 2010/11 was 665,900, an increase of 174,600 (36 per cent) compared with 2009/10. Of these there were 415,200 learners in intermediate level apprenticeships, 247,200 learners in advanced level apprenticeships and 3,500 learners in higher apprenticeships[4].

Notes

1. Post grad is Post Graduate Certificate in Education and the undergraduate is Professional Graduate Certificate in Education.

2. The low participation measure used in the figure is based on a UK wide classification of areas into participation bands. The relatively high (in UK terms) participation rate in Scotland coupled with the very high proportion of higher education that occurs in further education colleges means that the figures for Scottish institutions could, when viewed in isolation, misrepresent their contribution to widening participation. Low participation data has therefore not been produced for institutions in Scotland and for students Scottish domiciled.

3. Learning policy tends to treat 'adults' as anyone aged 19 or over and 'learning' includes formal education or training leading to a qualification.

4. There are 3 levels of Apprenticeship for those aged 16 or above:

   Intermediate Level Apprenticeships – Apprentices work towards work-based learning qualifications such as a Level 2 Competence, Functional Skills, and, in most cases, a relevant knowledge based qualification.

   Advanced Level Qualification – Apprentices work towards work-based learning such as Level 3 Competence Qualification, Functional Skills, and, in most cases, a relevant knowledge based qualification.

   Higher Apprentices - Apprentices work towards work-based learning such as Level 4 Competence Qualification, Functional Skills, and, in most cases, a relevant knowledge based qualification.

Adults

Participation in education: training and skills

The importance of training to gain skills while in employment is emphasised in the UK Employer Skills Survey 2011 (UKCES 2011). This is the key UK data source on employer demand for and investment in skills. One of the main findings was that although the majority of establishments have the skills they require, almost 1.5 million employees (5 per cent of all employees) are deemed not fully proficient as they have a skills gap. While skills challenges may not be common, where they do exist their impact can be significant. More than three in five businesses which reported skills gaps (61 per cent) also reported them as impacting on performance. In almost all cases, proficiency problems and skills deficiencies have the effect of increasing the workload of other more proficient staff and they also commonly impact directly on meeting business objectives.

Figure 9

Skills gaps: by occupation, 2011

United Kingdom

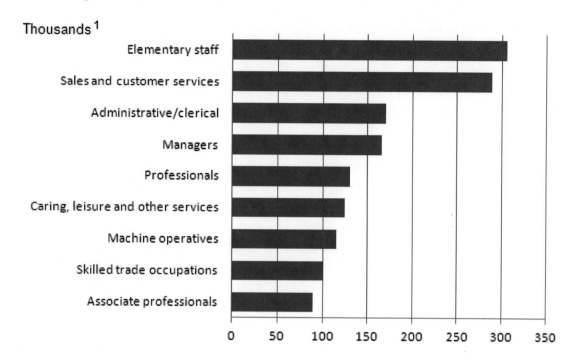

Notes:
1. Rounded to the nearest 50.
2. Source: UK Commission for Employment and Skills (UKCES 2011)

Figure 9 illustrates where skills gaps lie within the existing workforce in the UK. Skills gaps are more commonly reported for elementary staff, 305,000 (8 per cent of all elementary staff) and sales and customer service staff, 289,000 (8 per cent of all sales and customer service staff). Reports of skill gaps were less common for skilled trade occupations, 101,000 (5 per cent of all those in skilled trade occupations) and associate professionals, 90,000 (5 per cent of all associate professionals).

The most common causes of skills gaps are that the employee(s) in question are new to the role (47 per cent) and/or that any training being conducted is currently only partially completed (46 per cent). Other reasons include, staff lacking motivation (32 per cent), staff having been on training but their performance not improving sufficiently (29 per cent), difficulties meeting the quality standards (25 per cent), the introduction of new working practices (23 per cent), and difficulties introducing new working practices (23 per cent).

"Learning can mean practicing, studying or reading about something. It can also mean being taught, instructed or coached. This is so you can develop skills, knowledge, abilities or understanding of something. Learning can also be called education or training. You can do it regularly (each day or month) or you can do it for a short period of time. It can be full time, or part time, done at home, at work, or in another place like a college. Learning does not have to lead to a qualification. We are interested in any learning you have done, whether or not it was finished" (NIACE 2012).

In the 2012 National Institute of Adult Continuing Education (NIACE) Adult Participation in Learning Survey (NIACE 2012), 19 per cent of adults, aged 17 and over, say that they are currently engaged in learning, with around two fifths of the adult population in the UK saying that they have taken part in some form of learning in the previous three years. Neither of these figures has varied greatly since 2010, from 43 per cent of adults who reported learning in the previous three years, down to 38 per cent in 2012. Around a third (36 per cent) of adults say they have not participated in learning since leaving full-time education.

Data from the 2012 NIACE Adult Participation in Learning Survey (NIACE, 2012) estimates that 41 per cent of adults are likely to take up learning in the next three years but 56 per cent are unlikely to learn. Compared to 2011 intentions to learn have increased four percentage points from 37 per cent to 41 per cent, though they remain far short of the record high of 47 per cent in 2010. As in previous years, current participation in learning is a key indicator of future intentions to learn. In the 2012 survey, 80 per cent of current learners say that they are likely to take up learning in the next three years compared with just 17 per cent of those who have done no learning since leaving full-time education.

Formal qualifications are often achieved before entering employment but workers also acquire qualifications once they are working. There is also investment by employers in improving the skills of their employees which may or may not lead to a qualification.

Figure 10

Employees receiving job-related training: by age group (1)

United Kingdom

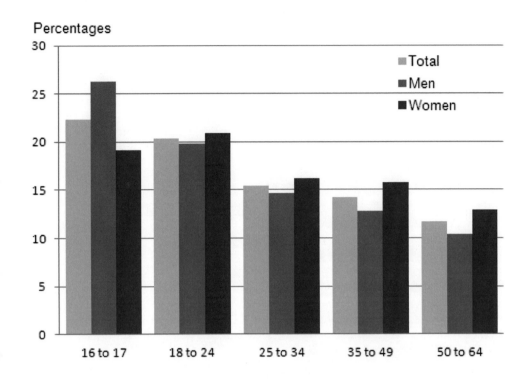

Source: Labour Force Survey - Office for National Statistics

Notes:

1.   Men and women aged 16 to 64.

In 2011 in the UK there were 3.6 million employees receiving job-related training, 90,000 (3 per cent) more than in 2010. Of the 3.6 million employees receiving training in 2011 over half, 1.9 million (53 per cent), were women and 1.7 million (47 per cent) were men. Figure 10 shows that the majority (44 per cent) of employees receiving job-related training were aged 16 to 24 and nearly a third (30 per cent) were aged between 25 and 49. A further 12 per cent were aged between 50 and 64.

Across the UK, total employer expenditure on training in 2011 was an estimated £49 billion[1] , split relatively evenly between training on the job (£25.8 billion) and off the job (£23.2 billion). The bulk of the outlay 'on off the job' training is related to courses taken by the individual (£19.3 billion), with seminars, workshops and open and distance learning forming a far smaller component (£3.9 billion).

Expenditure on training varies by the employment sector. Data from the UK Commission for Employment and Skills shows that the real estate and business activities sector spent the most on training in absolute terms in 2011 at £9.5 million and also spent more than average per trainee at £4,050.

Figure 11

Training expenditure: by sector, 2011

United Kingdom

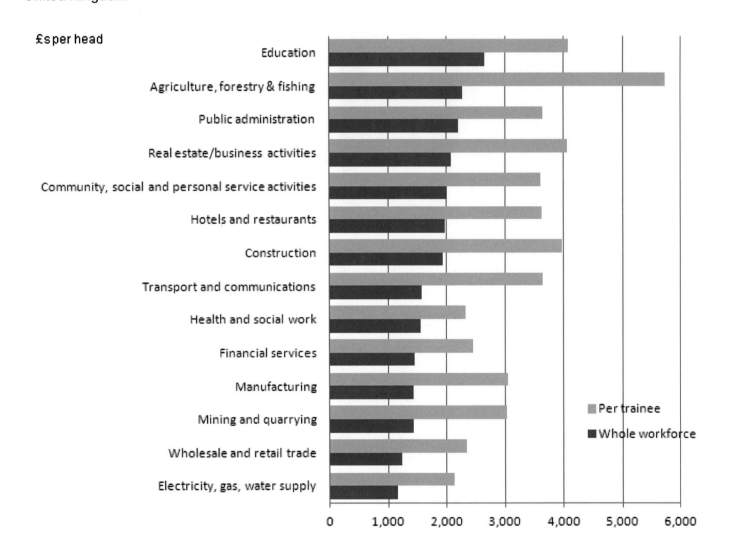

Notes:
1.   Source: UK Commission for Employment and Skills (UKCES 2011)

Per trainee, the agriculture, forestry and fishing sector makes the largest investment per trainee (£5,725), followed by real estate and business activities (£4,050) and public administration (£3,650)

(Figure 11). Conversely, the electricity, gas and water supply sector, and mining and quarrying sector make the smallest investment per trainee (£2,125 and £3,025 respectively).

The education sector makes the largest investment per head of its total workforce (£2,650) followed by agriculture, forestry and fishing (£2,275) and public administration (£2,200). Wholesale and retail, and health and social work on the other hand, both account for a large proportion of the total training expenditure (£5.5 million and £5.4 million respectively) but, because of the relatively large size of their workforce their spend per head is much lower (£1,225 and £1,550 respectively).

Figure 12

Proportion of the population aged 25 to 64 participating in education and training, 2010

EU-27

Percentages

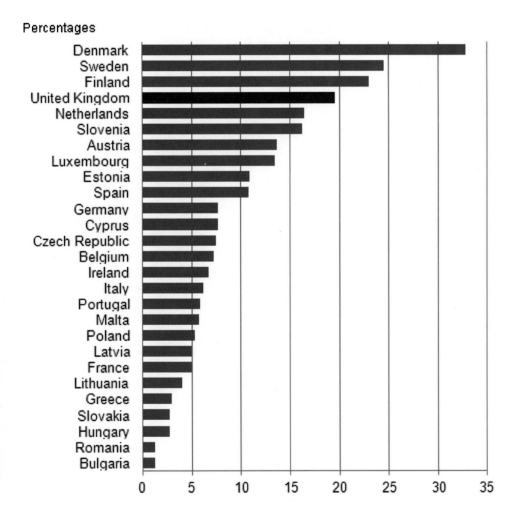

In 2010, the proportion of persons aged 25 to 64 in the EU-27 receiving some form of education or training in the four weeks preceding the labour force survey was 9.1 per cent; a share that was 0.7 percentage points lower than the corresponding share for 2005.

It is noticeable that Denmark, Sweden and Finland have considerably higher proportions of their respective populations who have received education or training in the four weeks before the survey at 32.8 per cent, 24.5 per cent and 23.0 per cent respectively (Figure 12). The UK with 19.0 per cent, the Netherlands with 16.5 per cent and Slovenia with 16.2 per cent were the only other Member States where the participation rate in 2010 already exceeded the 15 per cent target. In contrast, Romania (1.3 per cent) and Bulgaria (1.2 per cent) had learning participation rates of less than 2 per cent.

There are many barriers to learning opportunities for adults. Data from the Life Opportunities Survey 2009/11 (ONS 2012a) show that 11 per cent of all adults in Great Britain reported that they did not have access to all the learning opportunities they wanted. The most common reason given was financial, reported by 55 per cent of those without impairment and 48 per cent of those with impairment. Difficulty with transport, too busy/not enough time and reasons related to health were also cited as barriers to learning opportunities.

Table 5

Adult educational attainment: (2) by impairment status, 2010/11

Great Britain

Percentages

	Without impairment	With impairment	All
Degree level qualification (or equivalent)	26	15	23
Higher educational qualification below degree level	9	8	9
A level or highers	12	7	11
ONC/National level B/Tec	5	5	5
O level or GCSE equivalent[3]	19	18	18
GCSE[4] or standard grade[5]	5	6	6
Other[6]	11	15	12
No formal qualifications	12	26	16

Table source: Office for National Statistics

Table notes:

1.   Life Opportunities Survey (ONS 2012)
2.   Results are for adults aged between 16 and 69.
3.   Grade A to C or O grade/CSE equivalent (grade 1) or standard grade level 1 to 3.
4.   Grade D to G or CSE grades 2 to 5.
5.   Level 4 to 6.
6.   Including foreign qualifications below degree level.

Table 5 shows a breakdown of educational attainment by impairment status[2]. The table summarises the highest level of qualification that adults have received from school, college or since leaving education. Adults without impairment were more likely to have a degree level qualification compared with adults with impairment (26 per cent and 15 per cent respectively). Twenty-six per cent of adults with impairments stated they had no formal qualifications compared with 12 per cent of adults without impairments.

Notes

1.   Please note this figure has been collected across the UK for the first time in this survey and cannot therefore be compared to figures coming out of earlier surveys in the constituent nations.

2.   Impairment relates to the loss of physiological functions of the body such as loss of sight, hearing, mobility or learning capacity. Impairment should be distinguished from medical conditions or loss of bodily structure. For example, glaucoma is a medical condition; loss of vision is the impairment it causes. Activity limitations are restrictions an individual may have in executing physical or mental tasks or actions as a result of their impairment, for example, being unable to read newsprint at arms length without glasses or other aids and adaptations.

Qualification levels and human capital

"*The well-being of modern society is dependent not only on traditional capital and labour but also on the knowledge and ideas possessed and generated by individual workers. Education is the primary source of this human capital.*" (Crocker 2002)

The Organisation for Economic Cooperation and Development (OECD), defines human capital as the knowledge, skills, competencies and attributes embodied in individuals that facilitate the creation of personal, social and economic well-being (OECD 2001). This is a broad definition, encompassing a range of attributes such as the knowledge, skills, competencies and health conditions of individuals. The measurement of human capital has several potential policy applications. First, it can be used as a measure of an economy's future well-being as the empirical work on economic growth suggests that countries with higher levels of human capital, other things being equal, have greater potential output and income in the future. The measures can also be used in the assessment of the impact of an ageing population, changes in retirement ages and in the evolution of the economic benefits of different levels of education. Recent OECD work confirmed the importance of investment in education not just as a determinant of economic growth and also found education to be associated with various non-economic benefits (OECD, 2011).

The qualifications described earlier contribute to the education levels in the workforce within the UK. The level of highest qualification of those aged 16 to 64, the age within which individuals are most likely to be in the workforce, have increased over time.

Table 6

Population aged 16 to 64 with different levels of qualification (1)

United Kingdom

Millions

	1993	1996	1999	2002	2005	2008	2011
Degree or equivalent	3.7	4.2	5.0	5.7	6.6	7.8	9.5
Higher education	2.6	2.9	3.0	3.0	3.2	3.4	3.7
A Level or equivalent	7.5	8.0	8.3	8.8	8.8	8.9	8.7
GCSEs grades A*-C or equivalent	6.6	7.5	7.8	8.0	8.6	8.8	9.3
Other qualifications	4.2	4.9	5.1	5.0	4.7	5.1	4.2
No qualification	9.0	7.7	6.3	5.9	5.4	5.4	4.3
Dont know	0.0	0.2	0.3	0.2	0.3	0.3	0.3
Total[2]	24.5	27.5	29.3	30.5	31.9	33.9	35.4

Table source: Office for National Statistics

Table notes:
1. Highest level of qualification for thosed aged 16-64 using UN ISCED levels for international comparison as returned to Eurostata.
2. Excludes those without qualifications and those who answered 'Don't know'.

Table 6 shows that of the 40 million adults aged 16 to 64 in the UK in 2011, 35.4 million (88 per cent) had some kind of formal educational qualification[1]. Also, 31.2 million (78 per cent) were qualified to GCSE grade A* to C (or equivalent) or above.

Over the last 18 years, the number of adults aged 16 to 64 without any formal educational qualifications has more than halved, decreasing from 9.0 million (27 per cent of all adults of this age) in 1993 to 4.3 million (11 per cent of all adults of this age) in 2011. Over the same time period, the number of adults aged 16 to 64 with a degree or equivalent level qualification has more than doubled. In 1993 there were 3.7 million adults (11 per cent of all adults of this age) in the UK with a degree or equivalent level qualification compared with 9.5 million (24 per cent of all adults of this age) in 2011.

In the UK, the stock of human capital is measured as the value of the qualifications of those in the labour market, so that the qualification levels shown above contribute to human capital for those individuals in employment. Data from ONS shows the estimated value of human capital in the UK has increased from £14,460 billion in 2001 and peaked at £17,250 billion in 2009 before falling to £17,120 billion in 2010.

Figure 13

Human capital stock (1)

United Kingdom

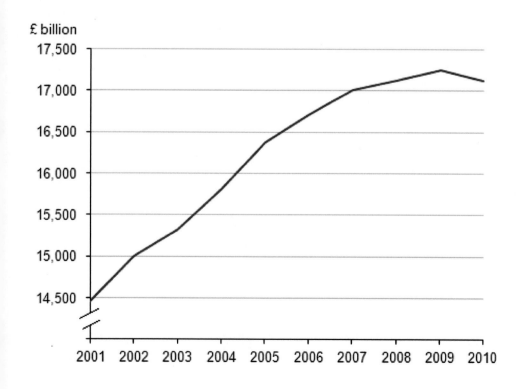

Source: Office for National Statistics

Notes:
1. Figures in 2010 prices, labour productivity growth rate = 2% and discount rate = 3.5%.
2. (ONS 2011a)

Figure 13 illustrates the effect of the economic downturn on the UK's human capital stock as the total number of people employed decreased. The value of the UK's human capital stock increased steadily between 2001 and 2007, averaging annual growth of 2.8 per cent (£425 billion). By 2009 the annual rate of growth had slowed to 0.8 per cent (£130 billion) and its value fell by 0.75 per cent (£130 billion) in 2010.

Notes

1. For further details of the qualifications included in each grouping table:

Degree or equivalent

1. Higher degree

2. NVQ level 5

3. First degree/foundation degree

4. Other degree

Higher education

5. NVQ level 4

6. Diploma in higher education

7. HNC/HND/BTEC higher etc.

8. Teaching – further education

9. Teaching – secondary education

10. Teaching – primary education

11. Teaching – foundation stage

12. Teaching – level not stated

13. Nursing etc.

14. RSA higher diploma

15. Other higher education below degree

A level or equivalent

16. NVQ level 3

17. Advanced Welsh Baccalaureate

18. International Baccalaureate

19. GNVQ/GSVQ advanced

20. A level or equivalent

21. RSA advanced diploma

22. OND/ONC/BTEC/SCOTVEC National etc.

23. City & Guilds Advanced Craft/Part 1

24. Scottish 6 year certificate/CSYS

25. SCE higher or equivalent

26. Access qualification

27. AS-level or equivalent

28. Trade apprenticeship

GCSEs grades A*-C or equivalent

29. NVQ level 2 or equivalent

30. Intermediate Welsh Baccalaureate

31. GNVQ/GSVQ intermediate

32. RSA diploma

33. City & Guilds Craft/Part 2

34. BTEC/SCOTVEC First or General diploma etc.

35. O-level, GCSE grade A*-C or equivalent

Other qualifications

36. NVQ level 1 or equivalent

37. Foundation Welsh Baccalaureate

38. GNVQ/GSVQ foundation level

39. CSE below grade 1, GCSE below grade C

40. BTEC/SCOTVEC First or General certificate

41. SCOTVEC modules

42. City & Guilds foundation/Part 1

43. RSA other

44. YT/YTP certificated

45. Key skills qualification

46. Basic skills qualification

47. Entry level qualification

48. Other qualifications

No qualification

49. No qualification

Education and subjective well-being

Analysis of experimental subjective well-being data collected by ONS between April and October 2011 (ONS 2011) suggests that adults aged 16 and over with higher levels of qualifications are more likely to report having medium or high satisfaction with their lives overall and also to report finding the things they do in their lives to be more worthwhile. It must be remembered that there are also other variables which may affect these results, such as age, income, type of employment, employment status and the individual's health.

Figure 14

Life satisfaction (1) and feeling life is worthwhile (2): by educational attainment

United Kingdom

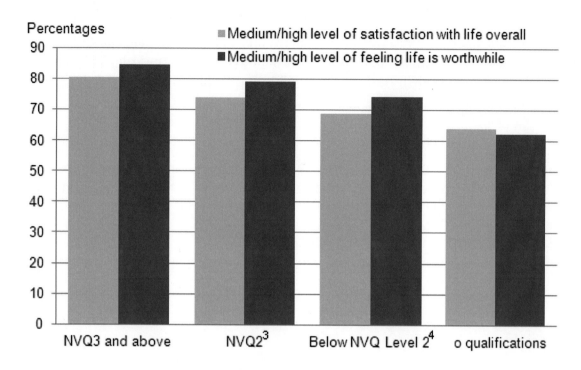

Source: Office for National Statistics

Notes:
1. Adults aged 16 and over were asked 'Overall how satisfied are you with your life?' where 0 was not at all satisfied and 10 was completely satisfied.
2. Adults aged 16 and over were asked 'Overall to what extent do you think the things you do in your life are worthwhile?' where 0 was not at all satisfied and 10 was completely satisfied.
3. Includes those with trade apprenticeships.
4. Includes those with other qualifications.

Of those adults whose highest qualification was a National Vocational Qualification (NVQ) level 3 or above, 81 per cent reported a level of 7 or more when asked about their overall satisfaction with life nowadays (Figure 14). Eighty-five per cent reported a medium/high level (7 to 10 out of 10) when asked how worthwhile the things they did in their lives were (on a scale of 0 to 10 where 0 was not at all worthwhile and 10 was completely worthwhile).

A smaller proportion of those with less than NVQ level 3 qualifications reported medium/ high levels of satisfaction and feelings of the things they do in their lives being worthwhile. For example 64 per cent of those with no qualifications reported a medium/high life satisfaction and 62 per cent reported a medium/high level of when responding to the question about how worthwhile the things they did in their lives were.

Continuing to learn throughout life can also have an effect on individuals' well-being. A study of the British Household Panel Survey used the General Health Questionnaire to analyse well-being of those undertaking and not undertaking lifelong learning. It showed that those in either formal or informal part-time education or who had undertaken part-time education at some point in the previous year reported a greater level of well-being than those who are either not in part-time education or have not recently undertaken part-time education[1] . The study also looked at qualifications and found that those who had a qualification, particularly when it had been obtained at the conventional age (i.e. school leaving age), had greater well-being than those who did not.

Notes

1.   Please note this figure has been collected across the UK for the fist time in this survey and cannot therefore be compared to figures coming out of earlier surveys in the constituent nations.

About the ONS Measuring National Well-being Programme

NWB logo 2

This article is published as part of the ONS Measuring National Well-being Programme.

The programme aims to produce accepted and trusted measures of the well-being of the nation - how the UK as a whole is doing. It is about looking at 'GDP and beyond' and includes:

- greater analysis of the national economic accounts, especially to understand household income, expenditure and wealth
- further accounts linked to the national accounts, including the UK Environmental Accounts and valuing household production and 'human capital'
- quality of life measures, looking at different areas of national well-being such as health, relationships, job satisfaction, economic security, education environmental conditions
- working with others to include the measurement of the well-being of children and young people as part of national well-being
- measures of 'subjective well-being' - individuals' assessment of their own well-being
- headline indicators to summarise national well-being and the progress we are making as a society

The programme is underpinned by a communication and engagement workstream, providing links with Cabinet Office and policy departments, international developments, the public and other stakeholders. The programme is working closely with Defra on the measurement of 'sustainable development' to provide a complete picture of national well-being, progress and sustainable development.

Find out more on the Measuring National Well-being website pages.

Background notes

1. Details of the policy governing the release of new data are available by visiting www.statisticsauthority.gov.uk/assessment/code-of-practice/index.html or from the Media Relations Office email: media.relations@ons.gsi.gov.uk

Copyright

1. BIS 2011   Tu T, Lambert C, Lever Taylor B and Klein A (2011): *National Learner Satisfaction Survey; FE Learners with Learning Difficulties and/or Disabilities*, BIS.

2. BIS 2012   (2012): *Community Learning Trust Pilots: Prospectus*, BIS.

3. Crocker 2002   Crocker R K (2002): *Learning outcomes: A critical review of the state of the field in Canada.*

4. DCSF 2010   Morrison Gutman L, Brown J, Akerman R and Obolenskaya P (2010): *Change in Well being from Childhood to Adolescence: Risk and Resilience*, DCSF.

5. DfE 2011   Askew K (2011): *Education and Training Statistics for the United Kingdom 2011*, DfE.

6. DfE 2011a   Knox G (2011): *Provision for Children Under Five Years of Age in England: January 2011*, DfE.

7. DfE 2011b   Miller J (2011): *Outcomes for Children Looked-after by Local Authorities in England, as at 31st March 2011*, DfE.

8. DfE 2011c   Brook A (2011): *Children with Special Educational Needs: an analysis - 2011*, DfE.

9. Dolan et al, 2008a   Sebates R and Hammond C (2008): *The impact of lifelong learning on happiness and well-being.*

10. EU 2012   Euro stat statistics database (2012): Expenditure on education as % of GDP or public expenditure [educ_figdp], Euro stat.

11. HC 2007   Bolton P (2007): *Education: Historical statistics (SN04252),* House of Commons Library.

12. Joseph Rowntree Foundation 2010   Goodman A and Gregg P (2010): *Poorer Children's Educational Attainment: How Important are Attitudes and Behaviour*, JRF.

13. LSN 2009   *Tackling the NEETs problem: supporting local authorities in reducing young people not in employment, education or training.* ISBN:978-1-84572-881-6.

14. National Archives 2010   Field F (2010): *The Foundation Years: preventing poor children becoming poor adults*, Cabinet Office.

15. New Economics Foundation (2009)   Michaelson J, Abdullah S, Steuer N, Thompson S and Marks N (2009): *National Accounts of Well-being - bringing real wealth onto the balance sheet*, NEF.

16. NIACE 2012   Aldridge F and Hughes D (2012): *Adult participation in learning survey: Headline findings*, NIACE.

17. OECD 2001   Healy T and Cote S (2011): *The Well-being of Nations - The role of human capital and social capital*, OECD, OECD publishing.

18. OECD 2007   Michalos A (2007): *Education, Happiness and Well-being.* Paper written for the International Conference on 'Is happiness measurable and what do those measures mean for

public policy?' at Rome, 2-3 April 2007, University of Rome 'Tor Vergata', organised by the Joint Research Centre of the European Commission, OECD, Centre for Economic and International Studies and the Bank of Italy.

19. OECD 2011   *Education at a Glance 2011*: *OECD indicators*, OECD Publishing.

20. ONS 2011   Evans J (2011): <u>Findings from the National Well-being Debate (1.07 Mb Pdf)</u>, ONS.

21. ONS 2011a   Jones R and Fender V (2011): *Human Capital Estimates, 2010*, ONS.

22. ONS 2012   Quarterly estimates of GDP available at:- <u>Gross Domestic Product: Preliminary Estimate</u>.

23. ONS 2012a   Dawe F (2012): *Life Opportunities Survey - Wave Two Interim Report, 2010/11*, ONS.

24. UKCES 2011   Vivian D, Winterbotham M, Shury J and Davies B (2011): *UK Employer Skills Survey 2011: First findings*, UKCES.

this page is intentionally blank

Measuring National Well-being - Where we Live, 2012

Author Name(s): Chris Randall Office for National Statistics

Abstract

This article is published as part of the Office for National Statistics (ONS) Measuring National Well-being Programme. The programme aims to produce accepted and trusted measures of the well-being of the nation - how the UK as a whole is doing. This article on 'Where we Live' is part of a series which aims to explore in more detail the different domains that have been considered as important for the measurement of National Well-being. Where we live can have a significant impact on our sense of well-being. Homes which meet our individual needs and provide us with shelter and security are made all the better by having easy access to local shops and services, and green spaces to walk or play in, which in turn can help people to live healthier and happier lives.

Key points

Satisfaction with living accommodation

- In October 2011 and February 2012, 84 per cent of adults aged 16 and over in Great Britain reported a medium/high satisfaction (7 to 10 out of 10) with their living accommodation.

Importance of services and amenities

- In 2008, adults aged 18 and over in England reported levels of crime (61 per cent), clean streets (45 per cent) and health services (44 per cent) as the most important factors in making somewhere a good place to live.

Tenure and housing stock

- A higher proportion of adults aged 16 and over who owned their property, either outright or with a mortgage, reported a medium/high level of life satisfaction (7 to 10 out of 10) than those with other tenures in the UK in 2011/12.

Housing conditions

- In 2010 5.7 per cent of the EU-27 population lived in households that experienced severe housing deprivation, compared with 2.8 per cent in the UK.

Housing market

- In the 12 months to May 2012, UK house prices increased by 2.3 per cent. The average UK mix-adjusted house price was £228,000 (not seasonally adjusted).

Satisfaction with local area

- Of adults aged 16 and over in Great Britain in 2011-12 who reported a medium/high satisfaction (7 to 10 out of 10) with their local area, 19 per cent reported a low satisfaction (0 to 6 out of 10) with their life. Of those who reported a low satisfaction with their local area, 42 per cent reported a low satisfaction with their life.
- In 2010/11 just under 6 in 10 (59.9 per cent) adults aged 16 and over reported that there was a little more or a lot more crime in England and Wales as a whole than two years ago, compared with under 3 in 10 (27.9 per cent) who reported more crime in their local area.

Access to the local environment

- In 2010/11, a third (33 per cent) of adults aged 16 and over in England reported that they visited the outdoors, away from home, several times a week or more often in the 12 months prior to interview.

Access to local services

- In 2011, 5 per cent of adults aged 18 and over in Great Britain reported feeling a sense of isolation due to difficulties accessing local shops and services, while 22 per cent reported that they knew someone who felt a sense of isolation due to difficulties accessing local shops and services.

Introduction

An individual's dwelling, access to local services and the local environment in which they live can contribute to a person's well-being. This was highlighted in the ONS National Debate on Measuring National Well-being. When people were asked what mattered most for the measurement of National Well-being, 'where we live' was one aspect that people considered as most important.

The quality and affordability of housing were identified as gaps in the headline measures of national well-being during the recent consultation. There is no single measure across the UK which can assess the number of dwellings which are not of suitable standard for their occupants. Information is collected to different criteria in the constituent nations of the UK. A different issue arises with affordability of housing. There are three main types of tenure: owner occupation, social renters and those rented from the private sector. While we can make some assessment of affordability, or at least the costs of each of these types of tenure these cannot be aggregated to a single measure. It is therefore more appropriate that these issues be addressed in this background analysis of the 'Where we Live' domain.

Previous research has also shown that where we live is vitally important to an individual's well-being and should be considered when making any assessment of National Well-being.

'We spend much of our lives in the home, our primary emotional connections are shaped in the domestic arena of the home; where we live and how we live are important determinants of our social position, physical health and individual well-being' (Rennie Short, 1999)

'....neighbourhood features do affect life satisfaction, but through the mediating effects of community satisfaction, housing satisfaction and home satisfaction...' (Sirgy and Cornwell, 2002).

Satisfaction with living accommodation

There is an old maxim that an 'Englishman's home is his castle', but how satisfied are we with our living accommodation and does this relate to our overall life satisfaction? Adults aged 16 and over in Great Britain were asked on the ONS Opinions Survey how satisfied they were overall with their living accommodation, where 0 was not satisfied at all and 10 was completely satisfied. In October 2011 and February 2012, 84 per cent people reported a medium/high satisfaction (7 to 10 out of 10) with their living accommodation, while the remaining 16 per cent reported a low satisfaction (0 to 6 out of 10).

Figure 1. Satisfaction with living accommodation compared with life satisfaction (1), 2011–12 (2)

Great Britain

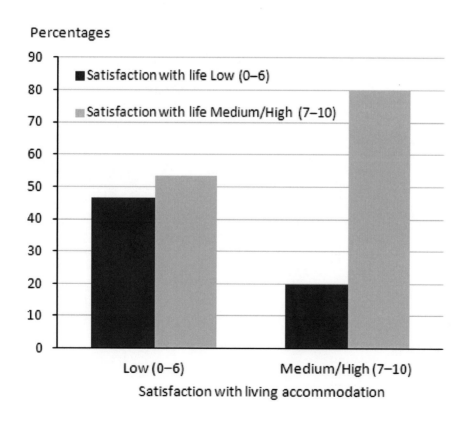

Source: Opinions (Omnibus) Survey - Office for National Statistics

Notes:

1. Adults aged 16 and over were asked 'Overall, how satisfied are you with your life nowadays?' and 'Overall, how satisfied are you with your living accommodation (that is the property that you live in)?' where nought is 'not at all satisfied' and 10 is 'completely satisfied' .
2. Data are for October 2011 and February 2012.

Satisfaction with living accommodation and life satisfaction are related. Of adults aged 16 and over in Great Britain who reported a medium/high satisfaction (7 to 10 out of 10) with their accommodation, a fifth (20 per cent) reported a low satisfaction (0 to 6 out of 10) with their life (Figure 1). However, of those reporting a low satisfaction with their accommodation, nearly half (47 per cent) reported a low satisfaction with their life. However, it must be noted that 53 per cent reported a medium/high satisfaction with their life, despite a low satisfaction with their accommodation, which indicates that there are factors other than living accommodation that impact on overall individual well-being.

Importance of services and amenities

The area in which we live in and the availability of local services and amenities can also contribute to our sense of life satisfaction and well-being.

Figure 2. Selected services and amenities regarded as important in making somewhere a good place to live (1), 2008 (2)

England

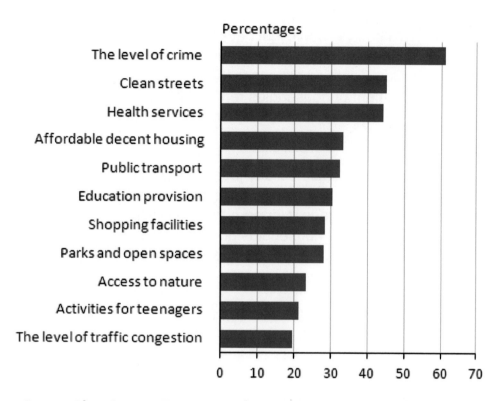

Source: Place Survey, Department for Communities and Local Government

Notes:
1. Adults aged 18 and over were asked 'Which of these things would you say are the most important in making somewhere a good place to live?'
2. Data are for September to December 2008.

The 2008 Place Survey (the latest data available), run by the Department for Communities and Local Government (DCLG), asked adults aged 18 and over in England to select up to five priorities that would be important in making somewhere a good place to live. Among the most important factors were the level of crime (61 per cent), clean streets (45 per cent), health services (44 per cent), affordable decent housing (33 per cent) and public transport (32 per cent) (Figure 2) (DCLG, 2008).

Tenure and housing stock

Housing tenure describes the legal status under which people have the right to occupy their accommodation. The most common forms of tenure are home-ownership and renting.

Home ownership, either outright or through a mortgage, is the most common form of tenure in the UK. According to the 2010 General Lifestyle Survey just over two-thirds (68 per cent) of households in Great Britain owned their own homes: with just under a third (32 per cent) owning outright and 36 per cent owning with a mortgage. Social renting describes those who rent from a local authority or housing association. In 2010, 10 per cent of households rented from a council and 8 per cent from a housing association. The remaining 13 per cent of households rented from the private sector (ONS, 2010).

According to the 2010/11 Continuous Household Survey just over two-thirds (68 per cent) of households in Northern Ireland owned their own homes: with just over a third (35 per cent) owning outright and 33 per cent owning with a mortgage. Northern Ireland Housing Executive (NIHE) rented accommodation accounted for 12 per cent of households and the remaining 19 per cent consisted of housing association and privately rented dwellings. Rent free, which includes squatting, accounted for the final 1 per cent of housing.

Table 1. Life satisfaction (1): by selected housing tenure (2), 2011/12

United Kingdom (Percentages)

	Satisfaction with life	
	Low (0–6)	Medium/High (7–10)
Owned outright	19.0	81.0
Bought with mortgage or loan	20.1	79.9
Rented	32.2	67.8

Table source: Office for National Statistics

Table notes:
1. Adults aged 16 and over were asked ' Overall, how satisfied are you with your life nowadays? where 0 is 'not at all satisfied' and 10 is 'completely satisfied' .
2. Those who stated they were 'part renting/part mortgage', 'rent free' and 'squatting' are not included in the table due to small sample sizes.

An individual's housing tenure and the level of their overall satisfaction with life are linked. According to the 2011/12 Subjective Well-being Annual Population Survey dataset (which are experimental data), a higher proportion of those who owned their property, either outright or with a mortgage, reported a medium/high level of life satisfaction (7 to 10 out of 10) than those with other tenures in the UK in 2011/12 (Table 1). Conversely, nearly a third (32 per cent) of those who rented reported a low satisfaction with life (0 to 6 out of 10) compared with just under a fifth (19 per cent) of those who owned their accommodation outright and a fifth (20 per cent) of those who owned their accommodation with a mortgage.

The availability of different tenures and types of accommodation in a local area may contribute to a person's overall satisfaction with the area in which they live. In 2010, adults aged 18 and over in Great Britain were asked in the British Social Attitudes Survey which type of tenure they thought was most needed if new homes were to be built in their local area. Nearly 4 in 10 (39 per cent) considered that social housing for rent was the priority, while 27 per cent thought the housing tenure most needed locally was homes to buy, with a similar level of support for part-own/part-rent homes (25 per cent). Private rental housing was considered a priority by less than 1 in 10 (8 per cent). Two-thirds (66 per cent) of those who were already tenants in social housing considered social housing as a priority compared with just under a third (32 per cent) of home owners (BSAS, 2010).

Respondents to this survey were also asked what types of dwelling were needed in their local area: 35 per cent stated 1 to 2 bedroom houses and 37 per cent stated 3 to 4 bedroom houses. However there was relatively little support for more flats or maisonettes (14 per cent), even though the proportion of flats built in some areas has risen rapidly in recent years (BSAS, 2010).

In England in 2010/11, 35 per cent of all permanent dwellings that were completed were flats, while 13 per cent were 1 to 2 bedroom houses, 30 per cent were 3 bedroom houses and 22 per cent were 4 or more bedroom houses (DCLG 2010-11). In Wales in 2010/11, 24 per cent of all permanent dwellings that were completed were flats, while 16 per cent were 1 to 2 bedroom houses, 38 per cent were 3 bedroom houses and 22 per cent were 4 or more bedroom houses.

Figure 3. Dwelling stock (1) and households (2,3)

Great Britain

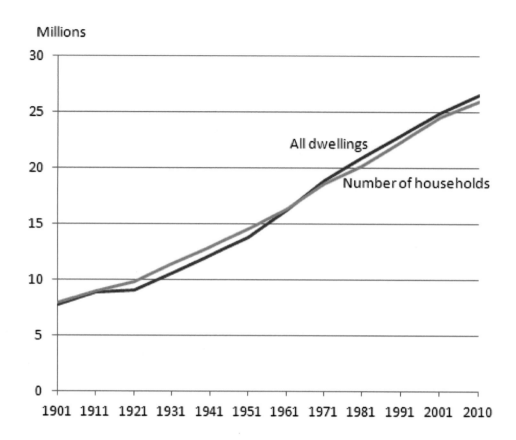

Source: Labour Force Survey, Census - Communities and Local Government, Office for National Statistics

Notes:

1. See note 1.
2. Data for number of households for 2001 and 2010 are Q2 (April to June) Labour Force Survey data and are not seasonally adjusted.
3. No census was undertaken in 1941 , so data for this year is plotted as the mid-point between 1931 and 1951.

The increase in population over the past century has increased demand for accommodation.

Dwelling stock[1] in Great Britain has increased substantially from 7.7 million at the start of the 20th century to 26.5 million in 2010 (Figure 3). In 1901, and all subsequent censuses up to and including 1961, there were fewer dwellings than households, therefore some dwellings accommodated more than one household. Between 1971 and 2010 there was a 40.8 per cent increase in the number of dwellings which exceeded the 39.8 per cent increase in the number of households. More recently, between 2008 and 2010, the increase in the number of dwellings was 1.3 per cent. It must be noted that the dwelling count includes empty dwellings and second homes so does not equate directly to households.

As of March 2008 there were around 22.4 million dwellings in England, of which more than four-fifths (82 per cent) were houses or bungalows. This was based on a three-year average (2006-07 and 2007-08 from the English House Condition Survey, and 2008-09 from the dwelling sample of the English Housing Survey). The remaining 18 per cent were either converted or purpose-built flats. Just under 3 in 10 (29 per cent) were terraced housing and 27 per cent were semi-detached (DCLG, 2008a).

Across the regions of England there are variations in the types of dwellings. For example, 92 per cent of homes in the East Midlands were houses or bungalows, compared with 52 per cent in London. Semi-detached homes were the most common type of accommodation in all regions, with the exception of London where flats were the most common (47 per cent), and the South West where detached homes were as common (22 per cent) (DCLG 2008a).

According to the 2010 Scottish House Condition Survey, semi-detached and detached houses made up 42 per cent of dwelling stock, while terraced housing made up 21 per cent. The remainder (37 per cent) were tenement flats and other flats. According to the 2008 Living in Wales survey (the latest data available), nearly a third (32 per cent) of the dwelling stock consisted of terraced housing. Semi-detached and detached houses or bungalows made up 30 per cent and 27 per cent of the dwelling stock respectively. In 2010–11 in Northern Ireland around 92 per cent of homes were either houses or bungalows: of which 39 per cent were detached, 25 per cent were semi-detached and 28 per cent were terraced. The remaining 7 per cent were either flats or maisonettes (purpose-built or other) (SG, 2010a, WG, 2008).

Access to affordable housing[2] can be an important factor in improving some people's life satisfaction and well-being.

Figure 4. Gross supply of affordable housing (1)

England

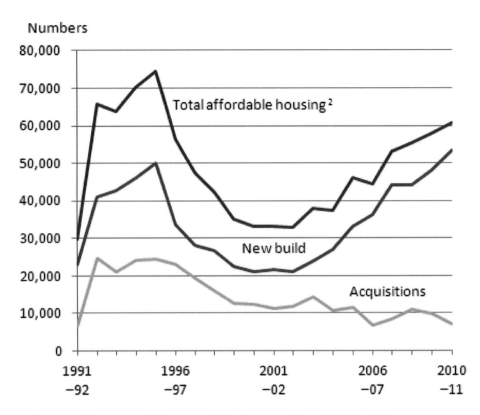

Source: Homes and Communities Agency; Local Authorities

Notes:

1.   Affordable housing is the sum of social rent, intermediate rent and low cost home ownership.

2.   Also includes Recycled Capital Grant Fund, Disposal Proceeds Fund, and remodelled units

A total of 60,640 additional affordable homes were supplied for rent or low-cost ownership in England in 2010–11, the highest number since 1995–96. Just under 9 in 10 (88 per cent) of all affordable homes provided in England in 2010–11 were newly built homes: about 53,340 homes (Figure 4). This was a 10.9 per cent increase from the 48,090 newly built homes in 2009–10, and more than one and a half times more than were built in 2000–01. See note 2 for definition of affordable housing (DCLG, 2011).

A proportion of the affordable homes provided are by acquisition. This is an existing private sector property that has been purchased for use as an affordable home. After remaining broadly level over the previous three years, acquisitions decreased slightly in 2010–11 at 7,050, equivalent to 12 per cent of all affordable homes. This was half the amount of affordable housing acquisitions in 2003–04 (14,180) (DCLG, 2011).

According to the Affordable Housing Securing Planning Consent Survey 2010/11, in Scotland (not including the Highlands) an estimated 5,624 affordable housing units were granted planning consent during 2010/11. This was a 16 per cent reduction from 2009/10. Additionally in 2010/11 there were 7,231 units completed which were funded by the Affordable Housing Investment Programme (AHIP) - this figure is 11 per cent down on the previous year, however it is the second highest figure in the series. In Wales during 2010–11, 2,486 additional affordable housing units were delivered, representing just over 1 per cent of all socially rented dwellings as at 31 March 2010. Over 9 in 10 additional affordable housing units in Wales during 2010-11 were delivered by Registered Social Landlords. For more information on affordable housing in Scotland and Wales see note 2. (SG, 2010/11a & WG, 2010/11).

Notes

1. The definition of a dwelling follows the census definition applicable at that time. Currently the 2001 Census definition is used, which defines a dwelling as 'structurally separate accommodation'. This was determined primarily by considering the type of accommodation, as well as separate and shared access to multi-occupied properties. In all dwelling stock figures, vacant dwellings are included but non-permanent dwellings are generally excluded. For house building statistics, only data on permanent dwellings are collected.

   Estimates of the total dwelling stock, stock changes and the tenure distribution in the UK are made by the Department for Communities and Local Government for England, the Scottish Government, the Welsh Government, and the Northern Ireland Department for Social Development. These are primarily based on census output data for the number of dwellings (or households converted to dwellings) from the censuses of population for the UK. Adjustments are carried out if there are specific reasons to do so. Census year figures are based on outputs from the censuses. For years between censuses, the total figures are obtained by applying gains and losses for each successive year. The increment is based on the annual total number of completions plus the annual total net gain from other housing statistics, that is, conversions, demolitions and changes of use. More information on dwelling stock is available here: DCLG - Dwelling stock

2. England - Affordable housing in England includes social rented and intermediate housing, provided to specified eligible households whose needs are not met by the market.

   Affordable housing should:

   • meet the needs of eligible households including availability at a cost low enough for them to afford, determined with regard to local incomes and local house prices,
   • include provision for the home to remain at an affordable price for future eligible households or, if these restrictions are lifted, for the subsidy to be recycled for alternative affordable housing provision.

   More information on affordable housing is available on the DCLG website.

   Scotland - Affordable housing In Scotland is defined in Scottish Planning Policy as housing of a reasonable quality that is affordable to people on modest incomes. Local authorities, registered social landlords (RSLs) and developers need to consider the full range of tenure types that can contribute to affordable housing and apply them as appropriate. The range of tenures that contribute to affordable housing are social rented housing, subsidised low cost sale, subsidised and unsubsidised shared ownership, shared equity, entry level housing for sale, and mid-market (or intermediate) rent. The requirements for affordable housing will be set out in local authority development plans, based on Housing Need and Demand Assessment (HNDA) and the Local Housing Strategy (LHS). More information is available on the Scottish Government website.

Wales - Affordable housing in Wales applies to housing where there are secure mechanisms in place to ensure that it is accessible to those who cannot afford market housing, both on first occupation and for subsequent occupiers as defined in Technical Advice Note (TAN) 2. The figures published in this release cover all additional affordable housing units (including general needs, supported housing, sheltered accommodation and extra care units), whether through new build, purchase, acquisition, leasing or conversion of existing dwellings. They do not take account of any loss of affordable housing stock through demolitions or sales during the year. In the case of conversions only the net gain will be included. More information is available on the Welsh Government website.

Northern Ireland - Affordable Housing in Northern Ireland comprises the social rented sector, housing benefit funded private rented and that part of the low cost owner occupation market which can be purchased utilising 30 per cent or less of gross household income (Department for Regional Development, 2012, Regional Development Strategy: RDS 2035, p.105).

Housing conditions

Living in poor quality or badly maintained accommodation can put people's well-being at risk. Each of the devolved administrations across the UK has a national housing quality standard in place - the Decent Homes Standard in England and Northern Ireland, the Scottish Housing Quality Standard (SHQS) and the Welsh Housing Quality Standard (WHQS). Each standard differs in a number of ways, reflecting the choices and priorities of each devolved administration[1].

In 2010 around 5.9 million dwellings (26.5 per cent) failed to meet the decent homes standard in England (DCLG, 2010).

Table 2. Homes failing decent homes criteria (1): by tenure, 2010

England (Percentages)

	Minimum standard (HHSRS)[2]	Thermal comfort	Repair	Modern facilities	All non-decent
Owner occupied	17.6	9.1	5.1	2.0	25.4
Private rented	23.1	16.4	8.7	3.3	37.4
Private sector	18.7	10.6	5.8	2.2	27.8
Local authority	10.9	6.2	5.7	4.0	22.0
Housing association	7.8	7.5	3.1	*	18.2
Social sector	9.3	6.9	4.3	3.0	20.0
All tenures	17.1	9.9	5.6	2.3	26.5

Source: English Housing Survey 2010, dwelling sample, Department for Communities and Local Government

Table notes:
1. Using SAP 05, see note 2.
2. The 'minimum standard' is based on 15 HHSRS hazards to maintain consistency with previous years' decent homes reporting. Minimum standard (HHSRS) is calculated using SAP09 methodology.

Privately rented homes were the most likely of all tenure types to fail at least one of the four decent homes criteria, with 37.4 per cent rated as non-decent compared with 22.0 per cent and 18.2 per cent for those rented from local authorities and housing associations respectively (Table 2). Nearly a quarter (23 per cent) of privately rented homes failed the HHSRS compared with under a fifth (18 per cent) of owner-occupied homes. Failure to meet the HHSRS was also the most common reason for failing the decent home standard among local authority homes, with 10.9 per cent not meeting the criteria. (DCLG, 2010)

According to the 2010 Scottish Housing Condition Survey (which is based on occupied dwellings only), just over 6 in 10 (61 per cent of all housing) failed the SHQS; about 1.4 million dwellings. Just under half (48 per cent) of dwellings that failed the SHQS failed on the energy efficiency criterion. In Wales, just over a quarter of all social housing (26 per cent) met the WHQS in full, as at 31 March 2010, according to a pilot study. However, a larger proportion of homes met some elements of the WHQS, with the greatest shortfall being in standards of bathrooms and kitchens. In Northern Ireland in 2009 (the latest data available), 15 per cent of all dwellings failed to meet the Decent Home Standard, this was equivalent to 111,800 homes.

Figure 5. Housing deprivation (1) rate (2), 2010

EU-27 comparison

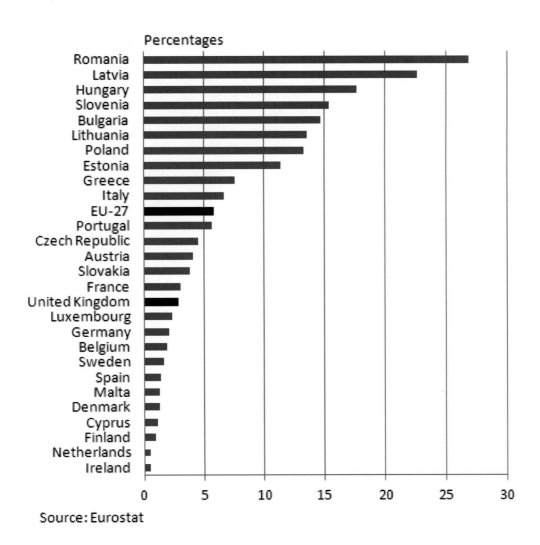

Source: Eurostat

Notes:
1. The housing deprivation is defined as the percentage of the population living in a dwelling which is considered to be overcrowded, and with at least one of the following three housing situations: 1) a leaking roof, or damp walls, floors, foundations, or rot in window frames or floor (referred afterwards as 'leaking roof'), 2) neither a bath, nor a shower, nor an indoor flushing toilet, or 3) too dark.
2. Percentage of population.

In 2010, 5.7 per cent of the EU-27 population (around 30 million) lived in households that experienced severe housing deprivation[3]. This compares with just 2.8 per cent in the UK (Figure 5).

Over a quarter (26.9 per cent) of the population of Romania and 22.6 per cent of the population of Latvia were living in severe housing deprivation. The Republic of Ireland and the Netherlands had the lowest proportion of their population living in severe housing deprivation (both at 0.5 per cent).

Notes

1. The definition of a decent home in England is one that meets all of the following criteria:

    *   meets the statutory minimum standard for housing. This was the Fitness Standard up to April 2006 when it was replaced by the Housing Health and Safety Rating System (HHSRS). More information is available on the DCLG website - Housing Health and Safety Rating System,
    *   it is in reasonable state of repair,
    *   has reasonably modern facilities and services,
    *   provides a reasonable degree of thermal comfort (adequate heating and effective thermal insulation).

    In Scotland housing quality is defined by the Scottish Housing Quality Standard (SHQS). The five higher-level criteria are that the dwelling must be above the statutory Tolerable standard; free from serious disrepair; energy efficient; have modern facilities and services; and be healthy, safe and secure. More information is available on the Scottish Government website - Scottish Housing Quality Standard.

    The Welsh Housing Quality Standard (WHQS) was published in 2002. The Assembly Government expected all social landlords in Wales to adopt the standard, to devise realistic programmes for bringing all their homes up to it by the end of 2012 and to maintain into the future. The WHQS means homes must:

    *   be in a good condition and structurally stable,
    *   be safe and secure,
    *   have proper heating and be fuel efficient and well insulated,
    *   contain up-to-date kitchens and bathrooms,
    *   be well managed,
    *   be in attractive and safe environments,
    *   meet the needs of the people living in them as far as possible.

    In Northern Ireland the Fitness Standard is used as a component to the Decent Homes standard. The Northern Ireland House Condition Survey measures:

    *   Decent Homes,
    *   Standard Assessment Procedure (SAP),
    *   Fuel Poverty,
    *   HHSRS,
    *   Repair Costs,
    *   Fitness.

More information is available on <u>the Northern Ireland Housing Executive website - Northern Ireland House Condition Survey</u>.

2.   The Government's Standard Assessment Procedure (SAP) is an index based on calculated costs per m^2 of floor area for space and water heating, ventilation and lighting, less cost savings from energy generation technologies based on a standard heating regime for a dwelling. It is expressed on a scale of 1 (highly energy inefficient) to 100 (highly energy efficient, with 100 representing zero energy cost). The detailed methodology for calculating the SAP to monitor the energy efficiency is periodically updated to reflect developments in the energy efficiency technologies and knowledge of dwelling performance. The rating scale underpinning figures reported here are based on the SAP 2005 methodology.

More information on SAP is available <u>on the DCLG website - Standard Assessment Procedure</u>.

3.   Severe housing deprivation rate is defined as the percentage of population living in the dwelling which is considered as overcrowded, while also exhibiting at least one of the housing deprivation measures.

Housing deprivation is a measure of poor amenities and is calculated by referring to those households with a leaking roof, no bath/shower and no indoor toilet, or a dwelling considered too dark.

More information on the severe housing deprivation rate and overcrowding is available <u>on the Eurostat website - Severe housing deprivation rate and overcrowding</u>.

Housing market

The state of the housing market affects an individual's housing mobility, and is closely linked to conditions in the wider economy. This, in addition to falling house prices which raise the possibility of homeowners falling into negative equity, may have an effect on some people's sense of well-being.

As already stated in this article most people in the UK are owner-occupiers. However, Table 3 shows that they acknowledge that renting can also have practical advantages.

Table 3. Main advantages of renting a home (1): by tenure, 2010

Great Britain (Percentages)

	Owners	Social renters	Private renters	All
Flexibility to move at short notice	28	14	28	25
Someone else is responsible for repairs and maintenance	23	37	22	25
Greater choice where to live	9	9	12	10
Don't have to worry about taking on a mortgage	8	13	11	10
Less risky than owning a home	7	11	9	8
Less responsibility than owning a home	9	6	6	8
Less upfront costs	3	4	4	4
No advantage	11	4	7	9

Source: British Social Attitudes Survey, NatCen Social Research

Table notes:
1. Adults aged 18 and over were asked ' what is the main advantage of renting a home rather than owning it?'

Just over 1 in 10 (11 per cent) owner-occupiers in Great Britain in 2010 reported that there was no advantage to renting (Table 3). Conversely nearly 3 in 10 (28 per cent) stated that renting gave more flexibility to move at short notice, while 23 per cent reported the advantage of lack of personal responsibility for repairs and maintenance. While less than 1 in 10 (9 per cent) owner-occupiers reported having greater choice over where to live, private renters were slightly more likely to choose this as an advantage (12 per cent). Social renters were more likely than the other two groups to state that it is less risky than owning a home, while owners were slightly more likely to suggest that renting carries a lower level of responsibility than owning a home (BSAS, 2010).

From the same survey, respondents were also asked about the main advantages of owning a home rather than renting it. The main advantage cited by just over a quarter (26 per cent) of all adults was that owning a home represented a good investment, with current home owners more likely than those who were renting to share this opinion. The next most popular advantages were that home ownership was more secure in the long-term than renting (23 per cent) and that it gave people the freedom to do what they wanted with a property (21 per cent) (BSAS, 2010).

Figure 6. Residential property transactions (1)

United Kingdom

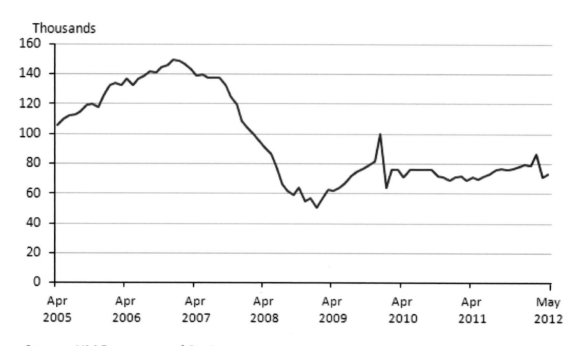

Source: HM Revenue and Customs

Notes:
1.   Data are seasonally adjusted. Number of residential property transactions with a value of £40,000 or more. Transactions are allocated to the month in which the transaction was completed. Data for April and May 2012 are provisional.

There were 1.7 million residential property transactions in the UK in 2006. Although the number of transactions remained high in 2007, at 1.6 million, the count in December 2007 was 27 per cent lower than in December 2006 (Figure 6). A sharp decline in the number of property transactions continued throughout most of 2008 with the overall number of transactions for that year around 0.9 million. The number of transactions in early 2009 dropped to a low of 51,000 in January, but then there were monthly increases to a total of 100,000 in December. This was due to December being the final month before the end of the Stamp Duty 'holiday', which exempted residential properties worth less than £175,000 from Stamp Duty Land Tax (SDLT). Overall in 2009 there were 0.8 million transactions. Since the start of 2010 the numbers of transactions have been relatively stable each month. However, the number of transactions rose to 87,000 in March 2012 but decreased to 71,000 in April and 73,000 in May 2012. This was probably due to the First Time Buyers relief coming to an end in March 2012, where homebuyers rushed to get their transactions through while they were still free of SDLT (HMRC, 2012).

House prices may have an effect on some people's confidence in the economy and their own financial circumstances, which in turn may have an effect on their overall well-being. The average UK mix-adjusted house price is a weighted average of prices for a standard mix of dwellings[1]. The latest data available shows that in the 12 months to May 2012, UK house prices increased by 2.3 per cent. The average UK mix-adjusted house price was £228,000 (not seasonally adjusted). The year on year increase reflected 2.6 per cent growth in England and 3.5 per cent growth in Wales, which was offset by declines in Scotland and Northern Ireland of 1.0 per cent and 10.3 per cent respectively (ONS, 2012a).

Figure 7. Mix-adjusted house prices index (1,2)

United Kingdom

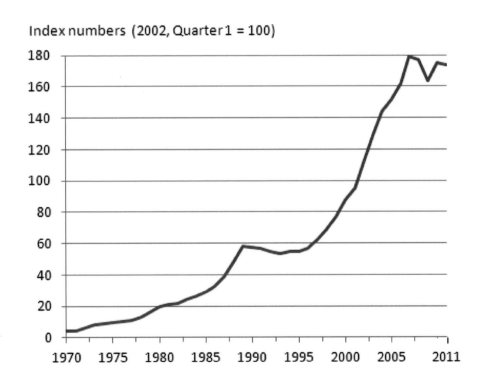

Index numbers (2002, Quarter 1 = 100)

Source: Office for National Statistics

Notes:

1. Based on mortgages completed and adjusted for the mix of dwellings sold.
2. Data up to and including 2002 is from 5 per cent sample. Data from 2003 is based on a significantly enhanced sample size. Data from September 2005 is collected via the Regulated Mortgage Survey. Data from 2005 is based on combined data from the Survey of Mortgage Lenders and the Regulated Mortgage Survey. The data are not seasonally adjusted.

Large decreases in house prices were not seen until 2009. Between 2008 and 2009, the annual house price in the UK had dropped by 7.6 per cent, the largest annual decline since the series began in 1969 (Figure 7). This followed a 0.8 per cent decrease between 2007 and 2008. This decrease was the first time house prices had experienced annual negative growth since the recession of the early 1990s, during which annual house prices declined in each year between 1990 and 1993 (ONS, 2012a).

Table 4. Average weekly rents: by region

United Kingdom (£ per week)

	Local authority[1]			Private registered provider[2]		
	1998–99	2011–12	Per cent change	1997	2011	Per cent change
England	42.25	72.30	71.1	46.81	78.28	67.2
North East	35.28	59.38	68.3	39.56	65.78	66.3
North West	39.49	62.63	58.6	38.61	68.65	77.8
Yorkshire and The Humber	33.64	60.55	80.0	41.69	66.20	58.8
East Midlands	36.67	62.94	71.6	45.43	72.08	58.7
West Midlands	38.83	67.40	73.6	43.57	72.47	66.3
East of England	44.20	75.26	70.3	46.81	81.87	74.9
London	55.25	89.17	61.4	53.12	97.46	83.5
South East	48.36	78.70	62.7	51.64	89.94	74.2
South West	42.48	67.06	57.9	48.52	76.04	56.7
Wales	39.13	66.32	69.5	..	..	..
Scotland	35.36	56.94	60.6	..	..	..
Northern Ireland	35.93	54.73	52.3	..	..	..
United Kingdom	40.64	69.13	70.1	..	..	..

Table source: Communities and Local Government

Table notes:
1. Figures for 2011-12 are provisional. Average rents for Wales, Scotland and Northern Ireland are calculated by the respective departments and methodologies may differ. Not all figures are audited.
2. Data is collected by the Tenant Services Authority via the annual Regulatory and Statistical Return (RSR) based on general needs stock only. Figures are based on only the larger Private Registered Provider (PRPs) completing the long form. Up until 2006 the threshold for completing the long formwas that the PRP owned/ managed at least 250 units/bedspaces. From 2007 this increased to 1,000 units/bedspaces. Averages are calculated for self-contained units only. As at 31 March each year.

Local authority average weekly rents in the UK increased between 1998-99 and 2011-12 by 70.1 per cent (Table 4). The highest proportional rate rise was in Yorkshire and The Humber (80.0 per cent), while the lowest proportional rise was in Northern Ireland (52.3 per cent). However, in monetary terms the largest average weekly rate was in London (£89.17). In England the largest proportional average weekly rate rise for accommodation provided by private registered providers was in London (83.5 per cent), while the lowest was in the South West (56.7 per cent). London had the largest weekly rate at £97.46 (DCLG, 2011-12).

Notes

1. The mix-adjusted house price index is a weighted average of prices for a standard mix of dwellings.

   More information on the mix-adjusted house price index is available on the DCLG website - Mix-adjusted house price index.

Satisfaction with the local area

'Those who are satisfied with life are more likely to feel satisfied with their local area and feel strongly about it compared with those who are not' (What influences wellbeing? NHS North West, 2011).

Adults aged 16 and over in Great Britain were asked on the ONS Opinions Survey how satisfied they were overall with their local area (15 to 20 minutes walking distance from home), where 0 was not satisfied at all and 10 was completely satisfied. In October 2011 and February 2012, nearly 8 in 10 (79 per cent) people reported a medium/high satisfaction (7 to 10 out of 10) with their local area, while the remaining 21 per cent reported a low satisfaction (0 to 6 out of 10).

Figure 8. Satisfaction with local area compared with life satisfaction (1), 2011–12 (2)

Great Britain

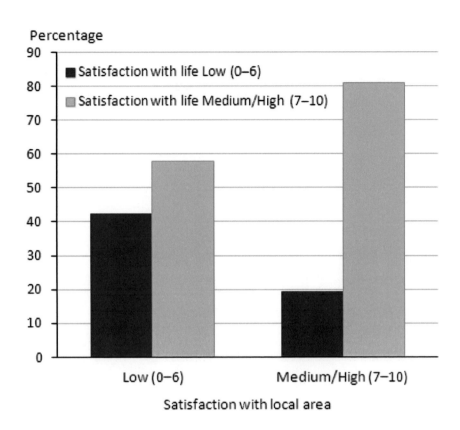

Source: Opinions (Omnibus) Survey - Office for National Statistics

Notes:
1.   Adults aged 16 and over were asked 'Overall, how satisfied are you with your life nowadays?' and 'Overall, how satisfied are you with the local area where you live? (When answering, please consider the area to be within 15 to 20 minutes walking distance from your home)' where nought is 'not at all satisfied' and 10 is 'completely satisfied' .
2.   Data are for October 2011 and February 2012.

Figure 8 shows that there is some relationship with local area satisfaction and life satisfaction. Of those who reported a medium/high satisfaction (7 to 10 out of 10) with their local area, 19 per cent reported a low satisfaction (0 to 6 out of 10) with their life. However, of those who reported a low satisfaction with their local area, 42 per cent reported a low satisfaction with their life. However it must be noted that 58 per cent who reported a low satisfaction with their local area also reported a medium/high satisfaction with life.

Figure 9. Belonging and involvement with the local area (1) 2011–12 (2)

Great Britain

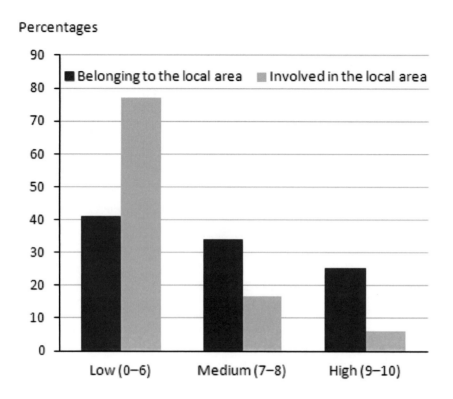

Source: Opinions (Omnibus) Survey - Office for National Statistics

Notes:
1. Adults aged 16 and over were asked 'To what extent do you feel you belong in the local area where you live?', 'To what extent do you feel you belong in the local area where you live?'
2. Data are September 2011 and January 2012.

Adults in Great Britain were also asked on the ONS Opinions Survey to what extent they felt involved with or belonged to the local area. Over three-quarters (77.2 per cent) of people reported that the extent of their involvement in the local area as low (0 to 6 out of 10) (Figure 9). Just under three-quarters reported the extent of their sense of belonging in the local area was either low (0 to 6 out of 10) or medium (7 to 8 out of 10) at 41.1 per cent and 33.8 per cent respectively.

Trusting the people that live locally may have an impact on a person's satisfaction with the area around them and in turn their well-being. According to the 2009–10 Citizenship Survey (the latest data available) run by the Department for Communities and Local Government around half (49.5 per cent) of adults aged 16 and over in England reported that many of the people in their neighbourhood could be trusted. Around a third (33.9 per cent) reported that some people could be trusted and 14.2 per cent reported a few could be trusted. Just 2.4 per cent stated that no-one in their neighbourhood could be trusted (DCLG, 2009-10)

Living in an area which is continually exposed to unacceptable levels of noise can be associated with a wide range of adverse impacts on health, quality of life and well-being. Conversely, a quiet area with an absence of unnecessary or inappropriate sounds can benefit well-being and may improve creativity, problem solving, mental health, concentration and undisturbed sleep.

Figure 10. Satisfaction that the area lived in is a quiet environment (1): by region, 2011

England

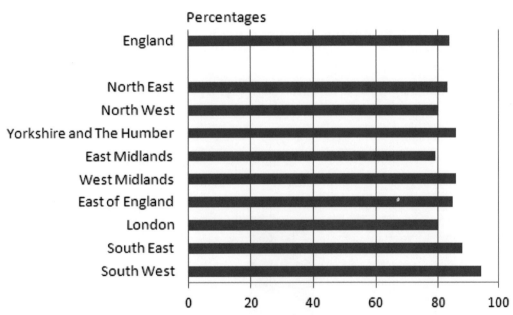

Source: Survey of public attitudes and behaviours towards the environment, Department for the Environment and Rural Affairs

Notes:
1.   Adults aged 16 and over were asked 'How satisfied are you that where you live is a quiet environment?'

The 2011 Survey of public attitudes and behaviours towards the environment, run by Department for Environment, Food and Rural Affairs (Defra), shows that over 8 in 10 (84 per cent) of adults aged 16 and over in England were satisfied that the place where they live was a quiet environment (Figure 10). However there was some regional variations; a lower proportion of people in the East Midlands (79 per cent) and the North West and London (both 80 per cent) reported being satisfied that the place where they live was a quiet environment, compared with the South West (94 per cent) (DEFRA, 2011).

Noise nuisance complaints for England and Wales are compiled by the Chartered Institute of Environmental Health. In 2010/11 there were 137,977 noise complaints across the 152 local authorities who responded to the survey. The vast majority of complaints were recorded in the domestic sector (95,245) followed by the commercial and leisure sector (17,110) (CIEH, 2010/11).

According to the 1999/2000 National Survey of Attitudes to Environmental Noise (the latest data available), 40 per cent of adults in the UK reported being bothered, annoyed or disturbed to some extent by road traffic noise, while 37 per cent of respondents reported being bothered, annoyed or disturbed to some extent by noise from neighbours and/or other people nearby (BRE 2002).

Feeling safe in a local area can be an important factor for a person's sense of satisfaction in the area around them. A good indicator of this is to find out whether a person feels safe walking in their local area after dark.

Figure 11. Feeling safe walking alone in local area after dark (1): by sex, 2011–12 (2)

Great Britain

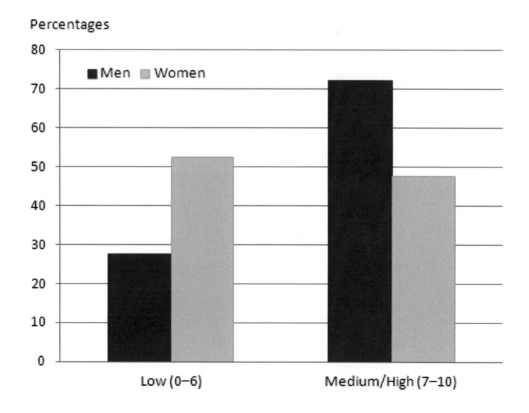

Source: Opinions (Omnibus) Survey - Office for National Statistics

Notes:

1. Adults aged 16 and over were asked 'How safe would you feel walking alone in this local area after dark?'
2. Data are at September 2011 and January 2012.

The Opinions Survey asked adults aged 16 and over in Great Britain in September 2011 and January 2012, how safe they would feel walking alone in their local area after dark, where 0 was not safe at all and 10 was completely safe. There was a marked difference between men and women's sense of security. Over half (52 per cent) of women reported that they had a low feeling of safety (0 to 6 out of 10) when walking alone after dark in their local area compared with 28 per cent of men (Figure 11). Conversely, under half (48 per cent) of women had a medium/high feeling of safety compared with 72 per cent of men. According to the 2010/11 Northern Ireland Crime Survey 9 per cent of adults aged 16 and over reported feeling very unsafe walking alone after dark.

Crime and antisocial behaviour also have an impact on local area satisfaction and can have a negative impact on people's lives and their sense of well-being: it can have an adverse impact on relationships and communities.

Figure 12. Police recorded crime: by offence, 2011 (1)

England and Wales

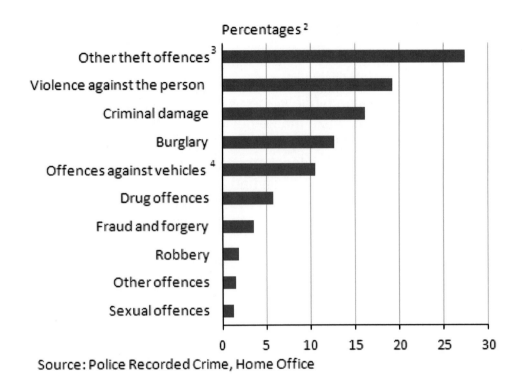

Source: Police Recorded Crime, Home Office

Notes:

1.   In the 12 months to December 2011.
2.   As a percentage of the 4,043,339 crimes recorded.
3.   Covers a range of offences, including shoplifting, theft from the person and theft of a bicycle.
4.   Includes theft of motor vehicle, theft from a vehicle, aggravated vehicle taking and interfering with a motor vehicle.

In the 12 months to December 2011 there were 4.04 million police recorded crimes in England and Wales. Almost 3 in 10 (27.4 per cent) of these crimes were for 'other theft offences' which includes theft from the person, shoplifting, bicycle theft, and theft of unattended property (including both offences against individuals and against organisations) (Figure 12). Around 2 in 10 crimes (19.2 per cent) were violence against the person and 16.1 per cent of crimes were criminal damage. Burglary accounted for 12.7 per cent of police recorded crime (ONS, 2012b).

In Scotland in 2010-11, the Scottish police recorded 323,247 crimes. Nearly half of all crimes (48.2 per cent) were 'crimes of dishonesty' such as housebreaking and theft, while fire-raising or vandalism accounted for just over a quarter (25.4 per cent) of crime. The total number of crimes recorded in Northern Ireland in 2010/11 was 105,040, the lowest level since 1998/99. This was equivalent to a crime rate of 58 per 1,000 population. Property crime accounted for 62 per cent of all recorded crime in Northern Ireland (SG, 2010-11b & NI, 2010/11a).

'Residential burglary can be regarded as one of the most important crimes, since as well as being one of the most common forms of criminal behaviour, it also intrudes into the home and damages feelings of personal security, peace of mind and well-being' (Coupe and Griffiths 1998).

According to the 2010 European Social Survey (ESS), just over 7 in 10 (70.4 per cent) of adults aged 15 and over in the UK agreed that the phrase 'It is important to live in secure and safe surroundings' was 'either very much like them' or 'like them'. Two-thirds (66.0 per cent) of respondents stated that they worried either a lot, sometimes or just occasionally about their house being burgled. Of these respondents who did worry about being burgled, three-quarters (75 per cent) claimed it had no real effect on their quality of life (ESS, 2010).

Many people may be victims of some form of property or other crime, or anti-social behaviour, at some point in their lives and a lot of people may know someone who has been a victim. People could also be indirectly exposed to crime and anti-social behaviour through other things such as the media. This could mean that individuals perceive crime rates as higher than they are and this can have a negative impact on an individual's well-being and their quality of life.

Since 1996, the Crime Survey for England and Wales (CSEW) (previously known as the British Crime Survey), has asked adults aged 16 and over how much they think the level of crime has changed in their local area and in the country as a whole in the two years prior to interview.

Figure 13. Perceptions of changing crime levels (1)

England and Wales

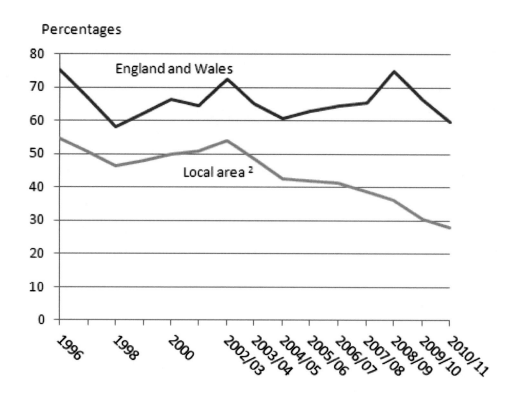

Source: Crime Survey for England and Wales - Office for National Statistics

Notes:

1. Respondents were asked if they thought there was more or less crime than two years ago and given the following options: 'A lot more'; 'A little more'; 'About the same'; 'A little less'; 'A lot less'. Data are the proportion of people who answered 'A lot more' or 'A little more'.
2. Questions were asked of respondents who had lived in their area for three years or more.

For all iterations of the survey, the proportion of adults in England and Wales who thought that crime had increased nationally is higher than the proportion who thought that crime had increased in their local area. In 2010/11 just under 6 in 10 (59.9 per cent) people reported that there was a little more or a lot more crime in England and Wales as a whole than two years ago, compared to under 3 in 10 (27.9 per cent) who reported more crime in their local area (Figure 13). The gap between perceptions of change in national and local crime levels widened between 2003/04 and 2008/09. It then narrowed slightly in 2009/10 and 2010/11, following a sharp increase in the proportion of adults who thought that crime had gone up nationally in 2008/09 and a decrease in the proportion who thought it had gone up locally (ONS, 2012b).

According to the 2010–11 Scottish Crime and Justice Survey, 23 per cent of adults aged 16 and over in Scotland perceived that there had been an increase in the crime rate over the previous two years in their local area, while 9 per cent perceived there had been a decrease in the crime rate in their local area. According to the 2010-11 Northern Ireland Crime Survey, over a third of respondents (35 per cent) felt that crime levels in their local area had increased in the preceding two years; just under a quarter (24 per cent) felt there was 'a little more crime', while 11 per cent felt there was 'a lot more crime' (SG, 2010-11b & NI, 2010/11b).

Figure 14. Anti-social behaviour indicators, 2010/11 (1)

England and Wales

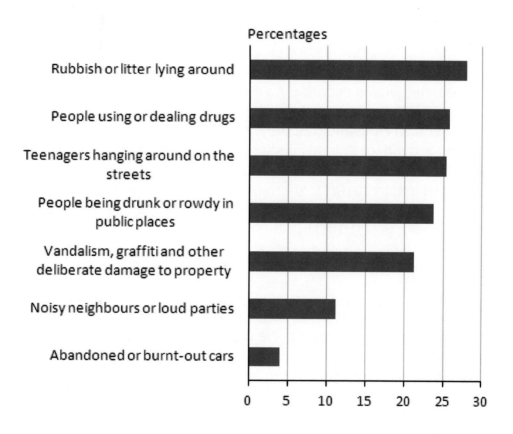

Source: Crime Survey for England and Wales - Office for National Statistics

Notes:

1. Respondents were asked how much of a problem each of the anti-social behaviour indicators were in their local area and given the following options: 'A very big problem'; 'A fairly big problem'; 'Not a very big problem'; 'Not a problem at all'. Data are the proportion of people who answered 'A very big problem' or ' A fairly big problem'.

The CSEW also asks about people's perceptions of different types of anti-social behaviour in their local area. In 2010/11, 13.7 per cent of adults in England and Wales perceived there to be a high level of anti-social behaviour in their local area. Around 3 in 10 (28.0 per cent) people reported rubbish or litter lying around was a problem (Figure 14). Just over a quarter of respondents reported that people using or dealing drugs and teenagers hanging around on the streets were a problem at 25.7 per cent and 25.4 per cent respectively (ONS, 2012b).

The Local Environmental Quality Survey for England, carried out each year by Keep Britain Tidy, involves physical surveys of 10,000 sites in a rolling sample of 54 English local authorities. In 2010/11, 15 per cent of sites fell below an acceptable standard for litter. Graffiti was considered an issue for 6 per cent of sites, and 7 per cent of sites were affected by dog-fouling (KBT, 2012

Fly-tipping of waste may also have an impact on the local area and in turn affect a person's satisfaction in their local area. In 2010/11 local authorities in England dealt with nearly 820,000 incidents of fly-tipping. Over 6 in 10 (63 per cent) of fly-tips dealt with by local authorities involved household waste; 8 per cent commercial waste; and a range of categories where waste could be derived from either households or businesses, for example construction, demolition and excavation waste; green waste; white goods; electrical items; tyres; and asbestos. Over 4 in 10 (44 per cent) of all fly-tipping cleared by local authorities occurred on the highway (DEFRA, 2010/11).

According to the 2009–10 Scottish Household Survey, around a quarter of adults aged 16 and over felt that rubbish or litter lying around, or animal nuisance such as noise or dog fouling, was a very or fairly common neighbourhood problem (25 per cent and 24 per cent respectively). The Northern Ireland Crime Survey reported that in 2010/11, 'teenagers hanging around on streets' and 'rubbish or litter lying around' (19 per cent and 18 per cent respectively) were most commonly cited as the biggest problems in the local area (NI 2010/11b).

Access to the local environment

Having access to green space such as public gardens or parks can improve the quality of life for many people. It was mentioned by respondents to the national debate and also by some of those who commented on the discussion paper about proposed domains and measures for measuring national well-being. More information is in Measuring National Well-being - Discussion paper on domains and measures.

'Access to a park or green space can have wide-ranging benefits for our health and wellbeing. A safe, natural environment can be a break from our busy lives - a place to get some fresh air, to exercise or play – a place to go and relax' (Faculty of Public Health, 2010).

According to the 2011 Survey of public attitudes and behaviour towards the environment, run by the Department for the Environment and Rural Affairs, over 9 in 10 (92 per cent) of adults aged 16 and over in England reported that it was very or fairly important to have public gardens, parks, commons or other green spaces nearby. Those who had visited public gardens, parks, commons or other green spaces were asked what their three most important reasons for visiting were. Just under three-quarters (74 per cent) reported that fresh air was an important reason, followed by open space (46 per cent), scenery (36 per cent) and tranquillity (27 per cent) (DEFRA, 2011).

Figure 15. Frequency of visiting the natural environment (1) 2010/11

England

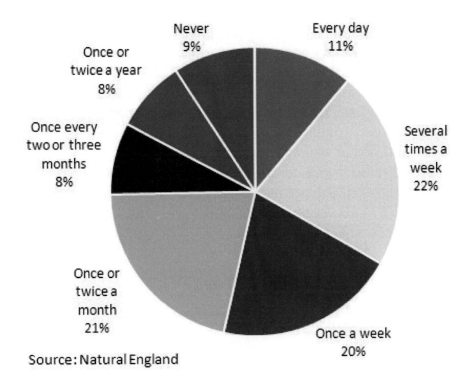

Source: Natural England

Notes:
1.   Adults aged 16 and over were asked 'Thinking about the last 12 months, how often on average have you spent your leisure time out of doors, away from home?' Percentages do not add to 100 per cent due to rounding.

In 2010/11, a third (33 per cent) of adults aged 16 and over in England reported that they visited the outdoors, away from home, several times a week or more often, in the 12 months prior to interview (Figure 15). While 11 per cent reported that they visited on a daily basis, just under 1 in 10 (9 per cent) stated that they had not visited in the previous 12 months. Walking was the most popular activity on visits to the natural environment and was a selected activity on just over three-quarters of all visits (77 per cent). Walking with a dog was undertaken on 51 per cent of all visits and walking without a dog on 26 per cent of all visits (NE, 2011).

According to the 2011 Scottish Recreational Survey, over 8 in 10 (83 per cent) adults aged 16 and over visited the outdoors for leisure or recreation at least once in the 12 months prior to interview. Just under half (49 per cent) of all outdoor recreation visits were made to the countryside. Walking was reported as the main activity on just under three-quarters (74 per cent) of visits to the outdoors. According to the 2008 Welsh Outdoor Recreation Survey (the latest data available), 94 per cent of adults resident in Wales had visited the outdoors at least once in the 12 months prior to interview. The most commonly undertaken activities were walking (86 per cent) and sightseeing (71 per cent) (SRS, 2011 & WORS, 2008).

The 2009 Scottish Social Attitudes Survey asked adults aged 16 and over 'what makes somewhere a good public park or local green space?' The most frequently chosen factor was 'that it is well-maintained' chosen by nearly half (48 per cent) of people as either a first or second choice. The next most popular response was 'having good play facilities for children' (34 per cent as a first or second choice) (SG, 2010b).

In October 2011 and February 2012 the ONS Opinions Survey asked people in Great Britain how satisfied they were with the public gardens, parks, commons or other green spaces in the local area where they lived. The local area is defined as within 15 to 20 minutes walking distance from the respondent's home. Satisfaction was rated from 0 to 10, where 0 represented not at all satisfied and 10 completely satisfied. Just under 7 in 10 (69.7 per cent) adults aged 16 and over in Great Britain reported a medium/high satisfaction (7 to 10 out of 10) with their local green space, while 3 in 10 (30.3 per cent) reported a low satisfaction (0 to 6 out of 10).

Figure 16. Satisfaction with local green space (1): by region, 2011–2012 (2)

Great Britain

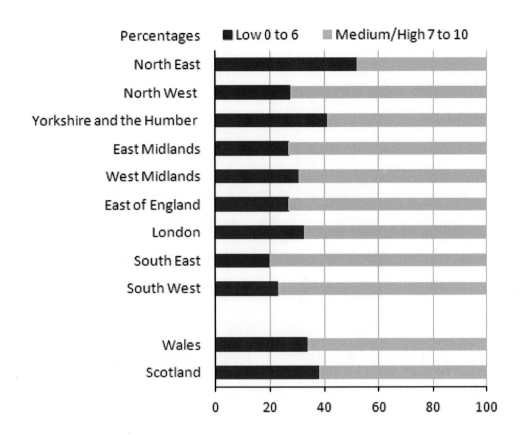

Source: Opinions (Omnibus) Survey - Office for National Statistics

Notes:
1. Adults aged 16 and over were asked 'Overall, how satisfied are you with the public gardens, parks, commons or other green spaces in the local area where you live?' When answering please consider the local area to be the area within 15 to 20 minutes walking distance from your home. Satisfaction was rated from 0 to 10 where 0 represented not at all satisfied and 10 completely satisfied.

Satisfaction rates varied between English regions and Great Britain countries in 2011-12. Just over 8 in 10 (80 per cent) people in the South East and 77 per cent of people in the South West had a medium/high satisfaction (7 to 10 out of 10) with public gardens, parks, commons or other green spaces in the local area where they lived (Figure 16). This compares with under a half (48 per cent) in the North East.

Access to local services

Ideally the local environment surrounding the area where people live would contain the type of services and amenities that would be needed on a regular basis, and would help towards people's satisfaction with the area and in turn their overall well-being.

Figure 17. Satisfaction with local services, 2008 (1)

England

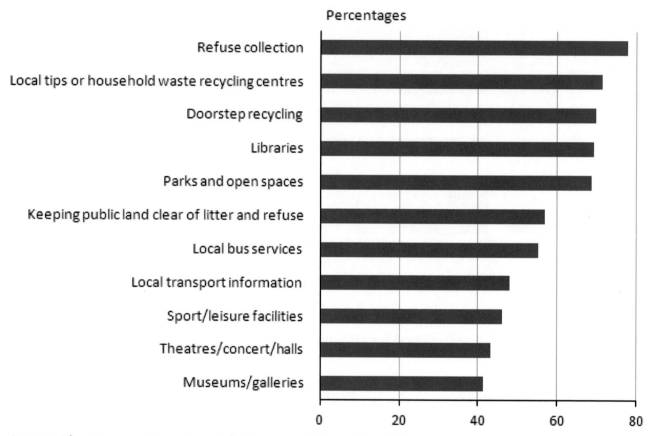

Source: Place Survey, Department for Communities and Local Government

Notes:
1.   1 Data are at September to December 2008.

According to the 2008 Place Survey (the latest data available), levels of satisfaction for adults aged 18 and over in England varied between local services. For most services associated with the local environment, satisfaction was above 70 per cent (Figure 17). For example, 77.6 per cent of people aged 18 and over were very or fairly satisfied with their refuse collection and 71.2 per cent their local tips or household recycling centres. However, satisfaction levels for sports, leisure and cultural services apart from libraries were below 50 per cent (DCLG, 2008).

According to the Scottish Household Survey, just under two-thirds (64.0 per cent) of adults aged 16 and over were very or fairly satisfied with a combination of three local services (health services, schools and public transport) in 2010. Looking at the services individually, people were most satisfied with local health services (86.4 per cent), followed by local schools (83.3 per cent) and public transport (74.3 per cent).

Reasonable access to local services is an important consideration in looking at the correlation of local service provision and well-being.

'Location is an important consideration . . . Access to local shops, post offices, places of entertainment and community activity all contribute to well-being' (Harding 1997).

The Department for Transport measures access to eight key services in England (employment centres; primary schools;, secondary schools; further education institutions; GPs; hospitals; food stores; and town centres) by public transport and walking. Unsurprisingly a higher proportion of people in urban areas had 'reasonable' access by public transport and/or walking than those who lived in a rural area (see DFT, 2010 for a definition of 'reasonable'). The largest variation between the number of people in urban and rural areas in 2010 was for further education institutes (16 percentage points), while the smallest variation was for primary schools (5 percentage points) (DFT, 2010).

The proximity of housing to a range of employment, services and facilities, as well as the public transport infrastructure determines how far and how long people have to travel. This could have a bearing on the satisfaction level with the area in which they live. According to the Department for Transport, the average minimum travel time to a selection of key services in England (employment centres, primary schools, secondary schools, further education, GPs, hospitals and food stores) in 2010 by public transport or walking was 14 minutes. By cycle the average minimum time was 9 minutes and by car 6 minutes. However, it must be noted that there will be considerable variation in these times between those living in rural areas and those living in urban areas (DFT, 2010).

Figure 18. Average minimum travel time by public transport or walking to reach the nearest key services: by mode of travel, 2010

England

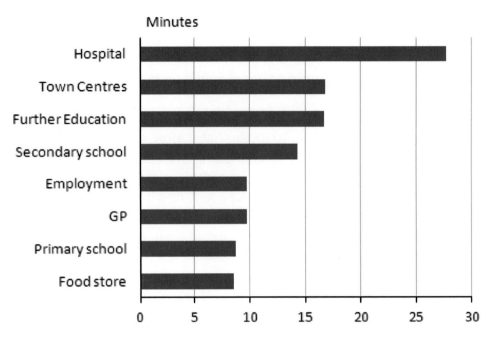

Source: Department for Transport

Looking at trips by public transport or walking in more detail, a trip to the hospital recorded the longest average minimum time at 28 minutes (Figure 18). This was followed by trips to further education establishments and town centres (17 minutes). The shortest average minimum time was to primary schools and local food stores at nine minutes (DFT 2010).

A survey by YouGov in 2011 gives further evidence of the importance of easy access to local services for some people. Adults aged 18 and over in Great Britain were asked how willing they would be to pay more to live somewhere they could easily access shops and services by foot. Just under a quarter (24 per cent) said they were very or fairly willing to do this. However, it must be noted that 42 per cent stated that they already lived somewhere where they could easily walk to local services (YouGov, 2011).

Difficulty accessing local shops and services can also give some people a feeling of isolation. From the same YouGov survey, 5 per cent of people reported feeling a sense of isolation, while 22 per cent reported that they knew someone who felt a sense of isolation due to difficulty accessing local shops and services (YouGov 2011).

The extent to which people feel that they can influence local decisions can relate to the way people are able to shape the local services they use and influence the way these services are delivered.

Figure 19. Whether people feel able to influence decisions in their local area (1)

England

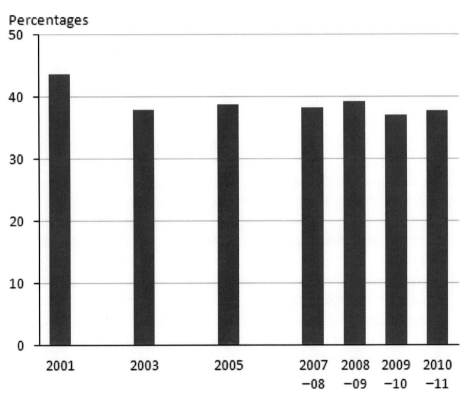

Source: Citizenship Survey,
Department for Communities and Local Government

Notes:
1. Adults aged 16 and over were asked 'Do you agree or disagree that you can influence decisions affecting your local area (within a 15-20 minute walk from your home)?' Includes those who 'definitely agree' and 'tend to agree' that they can influence decisions.

According to the Citizenship Survey, 37.8 per cent of adults aged 16 and over in England in 2010–11 said that they felt able to influence decisions affecting their local area (Figure 19). This was slightly up from the 37.0 per cent in 2009-10 which was the lowest percentage recorded for this measure since the Citizenship Survey began in 2001. Nearly three-quarters (73.9 per cent) of people reported in 2010–11 that it was important for them personally to feel that they could influence decisions in their local area (DCLG, 2010-11).

About the ONS Measuring National Well-being Programme

NWB logo 2

This article is published as part of the ONS Measuring National Well-being Programme.

The programme aims to produce accepted and trusted measures of the well-being of the nation - how the UK as a whole is doing. It is about looking at 'GDP and beyond' and includes:

- greater analysis of the national economic accounts, especially to understand household income, expenditure and wealth,
- further accounts linked to the national accounts, including the UK Environmental Accounts and valuing household production and 'human capital',
- quality of life measures, looking at different areas of national well-being such as health, relationships, job satisfaction, economic security, education environmental conditions,
- working with others to include the measurement of the well-being of children and young people as part of national well-being,
- measures of 'subjective well-being' - individuals' assessment of their own well-being,
- headline indicators to summarise national well-being and the progress we are making as a society.

The programme is underpinned by a communication and engagement workstream, providing links with Cabinet Office and policy departments, international developments, the public and other stakeholders. The programme is working closely with Defra on the measurement of 'sustainable development' to provide a complete picture of national well-being, progress and sustainable development.

Find out more about <u>Measuring National Well-being</u> on the ONS website.

Background notes

1. Details of the policy governing the release of new data are available by visiting
    www.statisticsauthority.gov.uk/assessment/code-of-practice/index.html or from the Media
    Relations Office email: media.relations@ons.gsi.gov.uk

Copyright

References

1. BRE, 2002 - The UK National Noise Attitude Survey 1999/2000, C.J. Grimwood, C.J. Skinner & G.J. Raw.

2. BSAS, 2010 – British Social Attitudes Survey 28 NatCen Social Research – British Social Attitudes Survey 28.

3. CIEH, 2010/11 - Annual Survey of Local Authority Noise Enforcement Activity CIEH - Annual Survey of Local Authority Noise Enforcement Activity.

4. DCLG, 2008 – Place Survey DCLG – Place Survey.

5. DCLG, 2008a – Survey of English Housing Survey of English Housing.

6. DCLG, 2009-10 – Citizenship Survey DCLG - Citizenship Survey.

7. DCLG 2010 – Survey of English Housing Survey of English Housing.

8. DCLG, 2010-11 – House building statistics DCLG – House building statistics.

9. DCLG, 2011 – Affordable Housing Supply DCLG - Affordable housing in England.

10. DCLG, 2011-12 - Live tables on rents, lettings and tenancies DCLG - Live tables on rents, lettings and tenancies.

11. DEFRA, 2010/11 - Fly-tipping in England – annual statistics DEFRA - Fly-tipping in England – annual statistics.

12. DEFRA, 2011 Survey of public attitudes and behaviours towards the environment DEFRA Survey of public attitudes and behaviours towards the environment.

13. DFT, 2010 – Transport statistics DfT: Transport statistics.

14. ESS, 2010 – European Social Survey European Social Survey.

15. HMRC, 2012 - Property transactions in the United Kingdom HMRC - Property transactions in the United Kingdom.

16. KBT, 2012 – Local Environmental Quality Surveys of England Keep Britain Tidy – Local Environmental Quality Surveys of England.

17. NE, 2011 - Monitor of Engagement with the Natural Environment: The national survey on people and the natural environment - Annual Report from the 2010–11 survey Natural England.

18. NI, 2009 – Northern Ireland House Condition Survey Northern Ireland Housing Executive- Northern Ireland House Condition Survey.

19. NI, 2010/11a – Police Service of Northern Ireland Statistics Police Service of Northern Ireland Statistics.

20. NI, 2010-11b 'Perceptions of Crime': Findings from the 2010/11 Northern Ireland Crime Survey' NI - Perceptions of Crime: Findings from the 2010/11 Northern Ireland Crime Survey.

Measuring National Well-being - Health

Author Name(s): Jen Beaumont Jennifer Thomas

Abstract

During the national debate about Measuring National Well-being, when asked what affected their well-being, health was the most common response from individuals. Following the national debate one of the proposed domains for Measuring National Well-being is health. In the most recent consultation there was strong support for the domain and for most of the proposed experimental headline measures within it. These currently include healthy life expectancy, self-reported health and a measure of mental illness. This article explores the headline measures in more detail and puts them into the context of other objective and subjective measures of health and well-being. It starts with self-reported health and its relationship to the Office for National Statistics measures of subjective well-being, which indicate how people think and feel about their lives. The subsequent sections will examine life expectancy, mortality, disease and physical ill health, mental health and some lifestyles which can affect health. There is also a short section on social care which covers those with specific needs.

Key points

Key points

Self-reported health and subjective well-being

- In 2011/12, adults aged 16 and over in the UK who report that they have health problems do not always report low levels of life satisfaction: about two in five of those who report bad or very bad health report a medium or high level of life satisfaction
- In 2011/12, adults aged 16 and over in the UK who report good health do not always report high levels of satisfaction with their lives: about one in five of those who report good or very good health report a low or very low level of life satisfaction

Life expectancy, mortality, illness and disease

- Between 1930 and 2010 life expectancy at birth in the UK (that is the length of time that an individual born in a specific year can expect to live) increased by around a third for both sexes from 58.7 to 78.2 years for men and from 63.0 to 82.3 for women
- Death rates in the UK have decreased over time but the prevalence of negative lifestyle behaviours such as obesity, heavy drinking and binge drinking has increased
- Cancer was still the most common cause of death in the UK in 2011, followed by heart disease, diseases of the respiratory system and cerebrovascular diseases, which includes stroke

- While cancer rates increased considerably between 1971 and 2010 in the UK, survival rates have improved: half of people with cancer now survive their disease for five years after diagnosis
- About half of adults in the UK who stated they have both a Disability Discrimination Act (DDA) disability and a work limiting disability, report low or very low levels of life satisfaction compared to less than one in five of those with neither a DDA disability and a work limiting disability

Mental ill health and mental well-being

- The GHQ-12 measure of psychosocial illness shows little change between 2002/03 and 2008/09: about 20 per cent of adults in the UK showed some evidence of psychological distress in each year (scoring 4 or more on a scale from 0 to 12)
- In England in 2007, around one in six adults had a common mental disorder such as anxiety or depression

Health and life satisfaction

This section explores the relationship between individuals' views of their own health and their feelings about their well-being.

People's own assessment of their health is associated with their assessment of their overall life satisfaction. However, it should be remembered that health is only one determinant of life satisfaction. When asked about their satisfaction with their lives, not everyone who reported that their health was good or very good reported high levels of life satisfaction, nor did all those who reported bad or very bad health report that their life satisfaction was low. Analysis of ONS data shows that nearly 1 in 5 (18 per cent) of those who reported good or very good health reported low satisfaction with life overall. Nearly 2 in 5 (38 per cent) of those who reported bad or very bad health reported high or medium levels of satisfaction with life overall (Figure 1). Similar patterns emerge when the questions about how worthwhile the things they do are, and how happy and anxious they felt yesterday are analysed for these two self reported health categories.

Figure 1. Self-reported health (1) and satisfaction with life overall (2), 2011/12

United Kingdom

Source: SWB experimental APS dataset, ONS(April 2011–March 2012)

Notes:
1. Individuals are asked to say whether their general health is very good, good, fair, bad or very bad.
2. Individuals were asked to rate how satisfied they were with their lives overall on a scale of 0 to 10 where 0 was 'not at all satisfied' and 10 was 'completely satisfied'.
3. For more detail on grouping please refer to ONS 2012b.

While this analysis shows that those who feel that they have good health are much more likely to report higher levels of subjective well-being and, conversely, that those who report poor health are much more likely to report lower subjective well-being; it also supports the view that individuals' well-being depends on additional aspects of their lives. For example, different levels of well-being are shown when data are analysed by age, marital status, tenure of dwelling, level of volunteering, continued learning and employment status[1]. More information about these relationships can be found in other Measuring National Well-being domain publications[2].

Notes

1. ART First ONS Annual Experimental Subjective Well-being Results

2. Measuring National Well-being index

Life expectancy

This section discusses various life expectancy measures. Between 1930 and 2010, there have been considerable improvements in life expectancy in the UK. During this period, life expectancy at birth (that is the length of time that an individual born in the specific year can expect to live) in the UK increased by around 20 years (or a third) for both sexes. In 1930 life expectancy at birth was 58.7 years for males and 63.0 years for females, increasing to 78.2 years for males and 82.3 years for females in 2010 (ONS, 2011b). Such increases in life expectancy are a clear indication of improvements in the health of individuals as a result of better lifestyles, enhanced health care, increases in prosperity and public health regulation (for example, the Clean Air Act 1956). The more recent improvements are shown in Table 1: in the years between 2000-2002 and 2008-2010, life expectancy at birth has increased by 2.5 years for males and 1.9 years for females.

As those who report good health are more likely to also report higher levels of well-being, it is important to measure not only the total life expectancy but also how many years of life can be expected to be lived in good general health. This can be examined by looking at Disability Free Life Eexpectancy (DFLE) and Healthy Life Expectancy (HLE), both of which measure the length of time an individual can expect to live free of activity restricting long-lasting illness and in very good or good health respectively[1]. Their calculation uses mortality data combined with measures of health quality. Over the period 2000–02[2] to 2007–09 HLE for males at birth in the UK increased from 60.7 years to 63.0 years and from 62.4 years to 65.0 years for females. Disability-free life expectancy has also risen for both males and females at birth in the UK over this time period. So at birth about four-fifths of life is expected to be spent in good health or disability-free and this proportion remains similar for data analysed for the years 2000–02 to 2006–07 (Table 1).

RFT HEALTH TAB 1 (30 Kb Excel sheet)

Life expectancy and disability-free life expectancy are also available at age 65: for example, based on data for 2007-09, a male at age 65 can expect to live another 17.8 years with just under 10 of those years in good health and a female at age 65 can expect to live another 20.4 more years with 11.5 of those years in good health[3]. However, sub-national breakdowns in the form of Local Authorities (LAs), small areas and by socioeconomic position reveal sizeable variation in the levels of health expectancy and in the proportion of life spent in favourable health states. Sub UK geographical variation in life expectancy over time is available and can be seen on the ONS website in the ONS Interactive Content[4].

The World Bank[5] published data about life expectancy at birth for all residents as well as for males and females for a large number of countries. Of the 193 countries for which they provide figures for 2010, the UK was ranked 20th with a life expectancy at birth of 80.4 years. Of these countries; San Marino, Japan, Hong Kong SAR, and Switzerland had the highest life expectancies (between 82.2 years and 83.2 years) in 2010. Lesotho and Sierra Leone had the lowest with life expectancies at birth of 47 years.

Notes

1. Healthy life expectancy (HLE) and disability-free life expectancy (DFLE) are summary measures of population health that combine mortality and self-reports of health status. In contrast to life expectancy, these two indicators measure both the quality and quantity of life. Essentially they partition life expectancy into the following two components:

    • years lived free from activity restricting ill health or disability (DFLE) or in a good state of general health (HLE)
    • years lived with activity restricting ill health or disability and years lived in a not good state or poor state or general health

    Period life expectancy for the UK is the average number of additional years a person would live if he or she experienced the age-specific mortality rates of the given UK population during the observed time period for the rest of their life. Therefore, it is not the number of years someone in the UK population in that time-period would actually be likely to live, because the death rates in the population are likely to change.

    HLE at birth is defined as the number of years that a newly born baby can expect to live in good or fairly good health if he or she experienced current mortality rates and 'good' or 'very good' health rates, based on self-assessed general health for different age-groups during their lifespan.

    Disability-free life expectancy, defined as expected years lived without a limiting long-standing illness, is calculated in the same way as HLE, except that is uses age-sex specific rates of 'without limiting long-standing illness' instead of rates of 'good/very good' health.

2. 2000–02 estimate is based on synthetic extrapolation because of a change in data definition from 2005.

3. Health Expectancies at birth and at age 65 in the United Kingdom, 2007-09, Office for National Statistics available at Health Expectancies at birth and age 65 in the United Kingdom index.

4. Neighbourhood Statistics - Find statistics for an area

5. World bank, (2010): life expectancy figures

Mortality and cause of death

Increases in life expectancy are linked to changes in lifestyles and improvements in both access to and quality of health care which have contributed to a reduction in early deaths for adults and to increases in the proportion of children who survive beyond infancy. Improvements in preventative measures such as immunisation and screening have also had a positive effect on life expectancy and will be discussed later in this article. This section will investigate mortality over time and causes of death.

Mortality over time

In order to compare mortality over time, death rates have to be standardised by age to take into consideration the changes in the age structure of the population. These adjusted data are described as age standardised. Those shown for England and Wales in Figure 2 illustrate change in mortality by setting the rate in 1950–52 to 100, and comparing other years with this, so that index numbers higher than 100 will indicate a higher rate than that in 1950–52 and those lower than 100 will show a rate lower than that in 1950-52. Age-standardised death rates have shown a steady decrease over the time period shown in Figure 2: in the period 1931–35 rates were more than one and a half times as high as those in 2012.

Figure 2. Age-standardised mortality ratios (1), 1931–2010

England and Wales

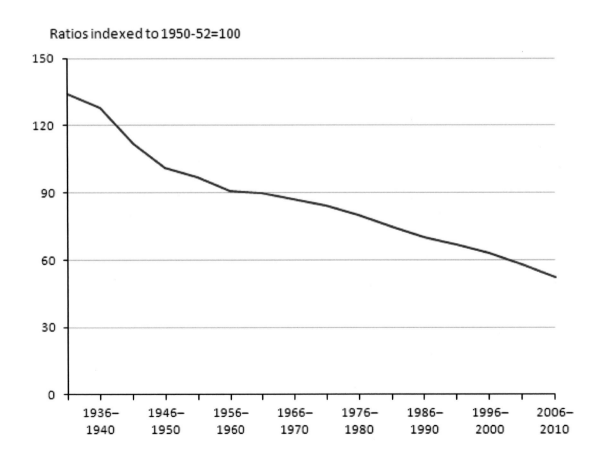

Source: Office for National Statistics

Notes:

1. Figures include deaths of non-residents. Figures are for deaths registered in each calendar year.Age-standardised mortality ratios are standardised to the European Standard Population. Age-standardised rates are used to allow comparison between populations which may contain different proportions of people of different ages, and so also allow comparisons over time.

Information about mortality rates at local authority level in England and Wales is provided as an interactive map of age standardised mortality rates by gender[1].

Infant mortality has also reduced in recent years and has contributed to the reduction in overall mortality rates and the increases in life expectancy discussed above. Infant mortality is calculated as the rate of death in those aged less than one year old per 1,000 live births so that the change in the number of births does not affect the rate[2]. Between 1980 and 2010 infant death rates in England and Wales decreased from 12.0 per 1,000 live births to 4.3 per 1,000 live births and the number of infant deaths decreased from nearly 7,900 to nearly 3,100. For England and Wales there have also been considerable decreases in all the age-specific mortality rates over the last 10 years. For example, in 2000 the age specific mortality rates for those aged 70-74 were 38.4 per 1,000 population for males and 23.2 for females per 1,000 population. By 2010 these rates had reduced by almost a third to 26.0 per 1,000 population for males and 16.8 per 1,000 population for females (ONS, 2010a).

Causes of death
In 2001 there were just over 604,000 deaths in the UK, the number of deaths decreased to just over 561,000 in 2010. Of these, 493,242 deaths were in England and Wales, a rise of 0.4 per cent compared with 2009 (491,348) (ONS, 2010b).

Figure 3 shows the most common causes of death which were cancer, heart disease, diseases of the respiratory system and cerebrovascular disease (which includes strokes) respectively. Men are more likely than women to die of the more common causes of death in all instances. Each of these causes can be linked, in part, to the lifestyles which are discussed later in this article.

Figure 3. Age-standardised death rates (1) per 100,000 population for selected underlying causes: by sex, 2008

United Kingdom

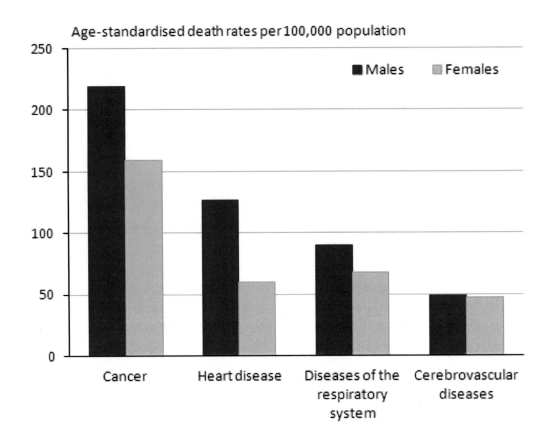

Source: Office for National Statistics, Scottish Government, Northern Ireland Statistics and Research Agency

Notes:

1.   Rates are based on the European Standard Population and include those aged under one.

Notes

1. Neighbourhood Statistics - Find statistics for an area

2. For more information about births see Measuring National Well-being - Population Social Trends 42 - Population and for more information about childhood mortality see Gestation-specific infant mortality in England and Wales.

Disability, disease and ill health

Physical health has a strong association with individual well-being. As reported in the section describing health and life satisfaction, those who report very bad or bad health are much more likely to report lower levels of well-being. This section will discuss self-reported disability, disease and ill health, and will include information about changes in the prevalence and survival following a diagnosis of cancer.

Reported Disability

Nearly one in five (18 per cent) adults aged 16 and over report a current disability[1]. Figure 4 shows the variations in proportions of disabled and non-disabled people reporting medium to high (7 to 10 on a scale of 0 to 10 where 0 is not at all and 10 is completely) and low (0 to 6) ratings for 'life satisfaction'.

Figure 4. Current disability and low satisfaction (1) with life overall (2,3): by sex, 2011/12

United Kingdom

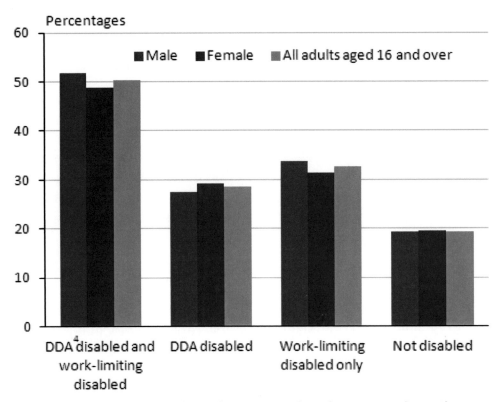

Source: SWB experimental APS dataset, ONS (April 2011–March 2012)

Notes:
1. Adults aged 16 and over were asked 'Overall, how satisfied are you with your life nowadays?' where 0 is 'not at all satisfied' and 10 is 'completely satisfied'.
2. All data weighted.
3. Non-respondents not included.
4. Disability Discrimination Act.

People who report having a disability are a very wide ranging group. The group includes those who have a disability which substantially limits their day-to-day activities, referred to in Figure 4 as 'DDA disabled'. This is because their reported disability fits the description of disability in the Disability Discrimination Act (DDA). There is a second group who have a disability which limits the work they can do. From these two groups a third can be constructed which is those with both DDA and work-limiting disability. This analysis looks at the three separate groups: those who are DDA disabled only (about 11 per cent of those aged 16 and over), those who are work-limiting disabled only (about 3 per cent of those aged 16 and over) and those who are both DDA disabled and work-limited disabled (about 11 per cent of those aged 16 and over). The subjective well-being of these three groups is compared with those who are neither DDA nor work-limiting disabled (the remaining 75 per cent).

Nearly 2 in 10 of those with no disability reported low overall life satisfaction (19 per cent). This compares to around 3 in 10 of those classed as DDA disabled only or having a work-limiting disability only (29 and 33 per cent respectively), and half of those classed as both DDA disabled and work-limiting disabled. This pattern is similar for responses about feeling that things in life are worthwhile or being happy yesterday. Also those who do not report to being DDA disabled or having a work-limiting disability are much more likely to report high anxiety yesterday. Life satisfaction seems to be most affected by being DDA disabled only or having a work-limiting disability followed by happiness, worthlessness and anxiety respectively.

Ill health

Apart from the measures of self-reported illness in the Annual Population Survey[2] and similar measures in the Census and other surveys, there is no single source of objective data from which the number of people who are in good health or who have an illness at any one time can be estimated. However, changes in the use of health care can be taken as an indication of the numbers who have conditions which need treatment. For example, hospital admissions, particularly admissions for elective treatment or surgery, can give some indication of changes in the frequency of the need for inpatient care. However, it should be remembered that individuals can be admitted more than once during a year for the same or a different condition and improvements in treatment and screening and their availability and resourcing level can lead to more admissions. Between 2000/01 and 2010/11 hospital admissions in England increased by over a third per cent from just over 11 million to nearly 15 million. In 2010/11, 1 in 9 admissions were related to cancer (that is for neoplasms) an illness for which multiple admissions are more likely. Other diagnoses which accounted for relatively high proportions of admissions in England in 2010/11 were diseases of the digestive system (11.6 per cent) and additional admissions from pregnancy and childbirth (9.1 per cent) (HES, 2011).

Disease prevention and low birth weight

In the UK, there are several disease prevention measures to improve our health and protect individuals and the community from serious diseases. Throughout the UK, young people and adults can receive screening for abdominal aortic aneurisms, diabetes, several cancers and receive various antenatal and newborn diagnostic tests. In addition to this, immunisations and vaccinations are available including Flu prevention, Measles, Mumps and Rubella, Meningitis and Tetanus.

One issue which has been shown to affect the future health of individuals is being born at a low birth weight. This is also a measure of possible poor maternal health. Reduction in the number of low birth weight babies is an important public health issue. Low birth weight babies face immediate and life-long risks to their health and development, including poor health in the first four weeks of life, and a higher risk of infant mortality. In the longer term, low birth weight has a higher association with premature death from coronary artery disease, and delayed physical and cognitive development in early childhood and adolescence (Department of Health, 2012). Of all live deliveries in England and Wales in 2009, 7.2 per cent of the babies had a birth weight of less than 2,500 grams (5 pounds 8 ounces) which is considered low for a full term baby. However, many of these babies had a low birth weight because they were born earlier than would normally be expected. When gestational age (the estimated time from conception) is considered, a much smaller proportion of babies born full term had a low birth weight. Of those babies whose gestational age was known and who were considered to be born at full term or after, only 3.0 per cent had a birth weight of less than 2,500 grams (ONS, 2009).

Cancer

Cancer is both the leading cause of death and the most frequent reason for being admitted to hospital as an inpatient in the UK. It is estimated that 1 in 3 people will develop some form of cancer during their lifetime (Cancer Research UK, 2010a). The UK is widely acknowledged as having one of the most comprehensive cancer registration systems in the world. There are currently 11 cancer registries in the UK, each covering populations of between approximately 1.7 and 13.8 million people[3].

The number of newly diagnosed cases of cancer recorded each year has increased considerably from around 150,000 in 1971 to over 250,000 in 2001 and to nearly 290,000 in 2010 (ONS, 2010d). Cancer can develop at any age but is most common in older people. Figure 5 shows a considerable increase in the number of cancer patients in the older groups. For example in 2010 more than 6 in 10 newly diagnosed cases of cancer were for those aged 65 and over. Figure 5 shows wide differences between the sexes and across the age groups. Following a small decrease in rates after early childhood, rates increased continuously across the age range for both males and females. From the 20 to 24 age group up to the 55 to 59 age group, rates of cancer were higher in females than in males, ranging from 30 to 671 per 100,000 population for men and 32 to 694 per 100,000 of the population for women. In the 40 to 44 age group, the rate in females was more than double that for males (251 compared to 117 per 100,000 population). This can be partially explained by the prevalence of cervical and breast cancer in these age groups. Rates of cancer were higher in males than females from the 60 to 64 age group onwards, with an increasing difference in rates between the sexes with age up to 85 years and over, ranging from 1,130 to 3,248 per 100,000 population for men and 979 to 2,028 per 100,000 population for women. Rates of cancer were 40 per cent higher for males than for females in the 65 to 69 age group, but were 65 per cent higher in those aged 70 to 74 and over (ONS, 2010d). Around 1 per cent of cancers occur in children, teenagers and young adults (up to age 24) (Cancer Research UK, 2010a).

Figure 5. Cancer incidence rates (1): by sex and age-group, England, 2010

England

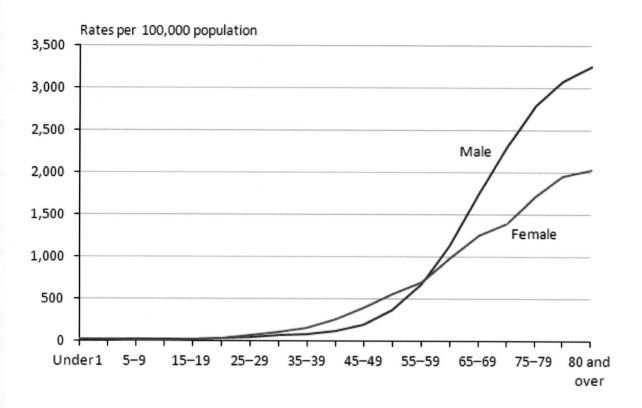

Source: Office for National Statistics

Notes:

1. All malignant neoplasm's (excluding non-melanoma skin cancer).

As some of the increase in diagnosed cases of cancer can be accounted for by the change in the distribution of ages within the population[4], annual cancer rates are standardised to the age distribution of the population so that comparisons over time can be made. Between 2001 and 2010 there was an increase in the age standardised rate for all cancer[5], from 417.1 to 422.6 per 100,000 population for males and 349.3 to 369.6 per 100,000 population for females of all ages (ONS, 2010d).

While cancer rates have risen, survival rates from cancer have also improved. Half of people diagnosed with cancer now survive their disease for at least five years (Cancer Research UK,

2010a). Table 2 shows that cancer patients diagnosed between the years 2005 and 2009 are more likely to have survived five years after diagnosis than those diagnosed between 1993 and 2003 for all types of cancer (ONS, 2010e). The largest improvement in survival rate was for patients with Lymphoma, where men are 10 percentage points more likely and women 9 percentage points more likely to survive than those diagnosed between 1993–2003.

Table 2. Five-year age-standardised (1) relative survival for adults (aged 15–99 years)

England and Wales (Percentages (2))

Cancer[3]		Diagnosis 1993–2003, follow up 2004	Diagnosis 2005–2009, follow up 2010
Lung	Men	7	8
	Women	8	9
Colon	Men	50	54
	Women	51	55
Non-Hodgkin lymphoma	Men	51	61
	Women	57	66
Prostate	Men	74	81
Testis	Men	97	97
Breast	Women	81	85
Ovary	Women	39	43
Cervix	Women	63	67

Source: Office for National Statistics, London School of Hygiene and Tropical Medicine

Table notes:

1. Age-standardisation requires the estimation of survival for each age group. Age-specific estimates may not be obtained if there are too few events (deaths) in a given age group; this can happen because survival is very high (there are very few deaths) or because it is very low (most of the patients die early in the five-year period of follow-up). When age-standardisation was not possible, un-standardised estimates are reported instead, italicised and underlined.
2. Relative survival is an estimate of the probability of survival from the cancer alone. For convenience, it is expressed as a percentage in the range 0–100 per cent. It can be interpreted as the survival of cancer patients after taking into account the background mortality that the patients would have experienced had they not had cancer. Background mortality is derived from life tables of all-cause mortality rates in the general population.
Relative survival varies with age, and the age profile of cancer patients can vary with time and between geographical areas, so the estimates are age-standardised to facilitate comparison.
3. Cancers were defined by codes in the International Classification of Diseases, Tenth Revision (ICD-10) and International Classification of Diseases for Oncology, Second Edition (ICD-02)

Some cases of cancers are diagnosed for the first time as the result of screening. This is designed to diagnose cancer early and give the patient a greater chance of survival. The UK has several screening initiatives that are nationally coordinated, including the NHS breast, cervical, and bowel cancer screening programmes.

Notes

1. Includes those classified as having a limiting long standing illness or disability which would be classified as a disability under the Disability discrimination Act The Disability Discrimination Act (DDA) defines a disabled person as someone who has a physical or mental impairment that has a substantial and long-term adverse effect on his or her ability to carry out normal day-to-day activities.

2. Annual Population Survey (APS)

3. How is cancer registration organised in the UK?
    The UK is widely acknowledged as having one of the most comprehensive cancer registration systems in the world. There are currently 11 cancer registries in the UK, each covering populations of between approximately 1.65 and 13.8 million people. Cancer registration in England is conducted by eight regional registries, which also submit a standard dataset of information to the Office for National Statistics (ONS), for the collation of national cancer incidence data. Northern Ireland, Scotland and Wales each have one, national, cancer registry.

    Although changes in health geography, including the introduction of cancer networks in response to the Calman Hine report for commissioning cancer services, have led to some cross-boundary issues for the English registries, the registries still provide complete coverage of the UK for the collection of population-based cancer data.

    Commissioning for the provision of the cancer registration system in the UK is now shared between the Department of Health in England, the National Assembly for Wales Department of Health and Social Care, the Scottish Executive Health Department, and the Department of Health, Social Services and Public Safety in Northern Ireland. Consequently, the UKACR has an essential role in providing a focus for cancer registration in the UK, especially by ensuring that registries are fully aware of any cross-national issues or relevant legislation.

4. For more information see Social Trends 42 - Population

5. Apart from non-melanoma skin cancer which is believed to be greatly under-registered.

Mental health

'Mental health and well-being are fundamental to quality of life, enabling people to experience life as meaningful and to be creative and active citizens. Mental health is an essential component of social cohesion, productivity and peace and stability in the living environment, contributing to social capital and economic development in societies' (WHO, 2005).

Positive mental health is people thinking and feeling good about themselves and feeling able to cope with their problems and such positivity is very important to an individual's well-being. The term is used to distinguish mental health from mental illness. Mental illness covers a range of mental health problems which can cause marked emotional distress and interfere with daily function and include different types of depression and anxiety. These types of problems can also have a significant effect on an individual's well-being.

Several ways of measuring those with some degree of mental health problems are in use in the UK such as the General Health Questionnaire (GHQ-12) and those based on diagnosis such as the Adult Psychiatric Morbidity Survey (APMS). The ONS Measuring National Well-being Programme set of domains and measures currently uses the General Health Questionnaire (GHQ-12) as a headline measure of mental illness. The GHQ-12 measure has been used regularly on the British Household Panel Survey in the UK and therefore allows some measurement of change over time.

GHQ-12 asks 12 questions which relate to an individual's state of mind and returns a score for the individual of between 0 and 12. High scores are an indication of conditions such as anxiety and depression although they do not provide a diagnosis of specific psychiatric problems. Between 2002/03 and 2008/09 around a fifth of GHQ-12 respondents had a score of four or more[1], which indicates some element of psychological distress. For the same period, between 3.0 and 3.5 per cent had a score of eleven or twelve, indicating a much higher level of distress (Table 3).

RFT HEALTH TAB3 (29.5 Kb Excel sheet)

The Adult Psychiatric Morbidity Survey[2] (APMS) estimates the number of adults suffering from common mental disorders (CMDs) such as anxiety and depression. Results showed that in England in 2007 around 1 in 6 adults (17.6 per cent) met the diagnostic criteria for at least one CMD in the week prior to interview (Table 4). Between the surveys conducted in 1993 and 2000 there had been an increase in the prevalence of both mixed anxiety and depressive disorders and a slight increase in generalised anxiety disorders (from 7.5 to 9.4 per cent and 4.4 to 4.7 percent respectively) , but there were only small changes between 2000 and 2007 (HSCIC, 2009).

Table 4. Prevalence of a common mental disorder (CMD) in past week (1)

England (Percentages)

	1993	2000	2007
Mixed anxiety and depressive disorder	7.5	9.4	9.7
Generalised anxiety disorder	4.4	4.7	4.7
Depressive episode	2.2	2.8	2.6
All phobias	2.2	2.8	2.6
Obsessive compulsive disorder	1.4	1.2	1.3
Panic disorder	1.0	0.7	1.2
Any CMD	15.5	17.5	17.6

Source: The NHS Information Centre for Health and Social Care

Table notes:

1.   An individual can have more than one CMD. Adults aged 16 to 64 and living in England.

The Welsh Health Survey 2010 showed that in Wales, 9 per cent of adults over 16 reported currently being treated for depression, 6 per cent for anxiety and 10 per cent for any mental illness (Welsh Government 2011).

There are a number of other measures which assess mental and psychological well-being which are also available. For example the Health Survey for England 2010 included EQ-5D and the Warwick-Edinburgh Mental Well-being Scale[3] (WEMWBS) as well as GHQ-12. WEMWBS was developed to capture a broad concept of positive mental well-being and includes psychological functioning, cognitive-evaluative dimensions and affective-emotional aspects of well-being. The scale is based on 14 statements and the responses are aggregated so that the result ranges from 14 (those who answer 'rarely' on every statement) to 70 (those who answer 'All of the time' to all statements), so that the higher the score the greater the individual's positive mental well-being. In the Health Survey for England in 2010 the average score for all adults was 51.0, with very little difference between men and women. While most scores (77 per cent) were in the 40-62 range 11 per cent of the population had a score of 39 or less and. There was a U-shape in the relationship between age and WEMWBS score with the lowest scores for both men and women in the middle age groups (49.9 for men aged 35-44, 49.7 for women aged 45-54), while scores were highest in the 65-74 age group (53.3 and 52.4 respectively). (HSCIC, 2011a). In the Scottish Health Survey in 2010 the average WEMWBS score for adults was 49.9 which was little changed from the previous two years and showed a similar distribution by age as the data for England (Scottish Government, 2010).

Analysis of this survey and of similar surveys which use both GHQ-12 and WEMWBS have shown a very strong negative correlation between WEMWBS and GHQ12. In other words, respondents with below average mental well-being tended to have high GHQ-12 scores while those with above average mental well-being tended to have low GHQ-12 scores (a score of four or more). For example see the analysis of the 2008 Scottish Survey of Public Attitudes to Mental Wellbeing and Mental Health Problems (Scottish Government, 2008).

The Attitudes to Mental Illness (HSCIC, 2011b) report shows that there is an increasingly positive response to mental illness. In England in 2011 those with a mental illness were less commonly viewed as a burden on society (a reduction from 10 per cent of respondents in 1994 to 6 per cent in 2011). There also appears to be less of a stigma attached to mental illness. The percentage of people agreeing that 'Mental illness is an illness like any other' increased from 71 per cent in 1994 to 77 per cent in 2011 and the percentage of people saying they would be comfortable talking to a friend or family member about their mental health increased from 66 per cent in 2009 to 70 per cent in 2011.

Notes

1. The GHQ-12 questionnaire concentrates on the broader components of psychological morbidity and consists of twelve items measuring general levels of happiness; depression and anxiety; sleep disturbance; and ability to cope over the last few weeks. The twelve items are rated on a four-point response scale, where a score of 0 is given to responses such as that the symptom is present 'not at all' or 'no more than usual' and a score of 1 is given to responses symptom is present 'not at all' or 'no more than usual' and a score of 1 is given to responses such as 'rather more than usual' or 'much more than usual'. Consistent with analysis of other surveys, a GHQ12 score of 4 or more is referred to as a 'high GHQ12 score', indicating probable psychological disturbance or mental ill health.

2. The Adult Psychiatric Morbidity Survey (APMS) series provides data on the prevalence of both treated and untreated psychiatric disorder in the English adult population (aged 16 and over).

3. The WEMWBS scale is based on 14 statements, for each of which participants are asked to tick the box that best describes their experience over the previous two weeks. They can answer on a 5-point scale: 'None of the time', 'Rarely', 'Some of the time', 'Often', or 'All of the time'. The statements are all expressed positively – for example, 'I've been feeling optimistic about the future'. The responses, numbered 1 to 5, are aggregated to form an Index which ranges from 14 to 70.

Lifestyles

This section discusses some lifestyles which may have a negative effect on a person's health, such as the use of tobacco, alcohol and drugs and the growing levels of obesity. More information about the more positive aspects of individuals' lifestyles, such as physical activity and engagement in other leisure activities, is available in the Measuring National Well-being article 'What we do[1].

Figure 6 shows that, for England, there has been a decrease in the number of smokers over the last 20 years but a considerable increase in other lifestyle behaviours which may have a negative impact on health. Those drinking more than the Department of Health's daily alcohol guidelines (3–4 units for men, 2–3 units for women) and those considered binge drinkers (drinking double the recommended daily guideline on at least one occasion over the week prior to interview), in addition to those classed as obese have increased over the last two decades. Each of these behaviours, in addition to drug use, is discussed in more detail in below.

Figure 6. Obesity, smoking and drinking over time (1)

England

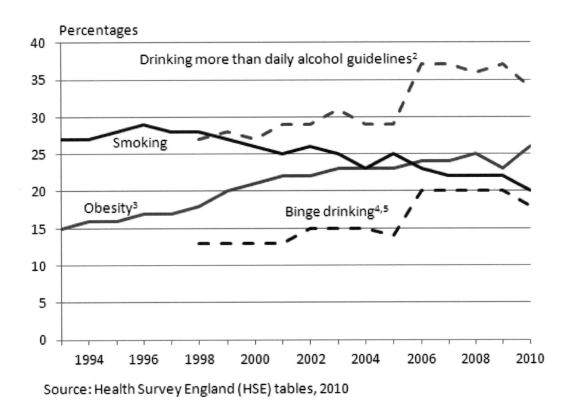

Source: Health Survey England (HSE) tables, 2010

Notes:
1.   Data up to 2002 are unweighted; from 2003 onwards data have been weighted for non-response.
2.   Includes those who drunk 3 units for women and 4 units for men on at least one day in the week prior to interview.
3.   Obese = BMI 30 or more (includes morbidly obese = BMI 40 or more).
4.   Includes those who drunk 6 units for women and 8 units for men on at least one day in the week prior to interview.
5.   Results from 2006 include longitudinal data. From 2006, figures produced using the updated methodology for converting volumes of alcohol to units assuming an average wine glass size.

Tobacco

The causal link between smoking and lung cancer was established over 50 years ago. In the UK, tobacco consumption is now recognised as the single greatest cause of preventable illness. Early death from smoking-related disease was responsible for more than 102,000 deaths in 2009 (Cancer Research UK, 2010b).

In 2010, around one in five (22 per cent of men and 18 per cent of women in England) smoked regularly. Over the last 20 years the proportion of the population who use tobacco has declined by 7 percentage points in England (HSE, 2010). According to the 2008/2009 Opinions Survey, around two-thirds (67 per cent) of smokers in Great Britain reported that they would like to stop smoking: the most common reason given was "at least one health reason" (ONS, 2009b).

The European Commission 'Attitudes of Europeans towards Tobacco Survey' in 2012 showed that 28 per cent of the EU population smoke, a decrease of 1 per cent since 2009. In the same survey the UK was just below the EU average (at 27%) although the methodology differed from the HSE Survey above. Since the late 1980s, the European Union has worked to encourage the trend towards fewer people starting to smoke, more people quitting smoking and more citizens living and working in smoke-free environments. EU legislation on the control of tobacco regulates the marketing of tobacco products for public health reasons and ensures appropriate consumer information.

Alcohol

The World Health Organisation has estimated that alcohol consumption accounts for 4.5 per cent of all disease burden[2] worldwide although this excludes many of the indirect effects of alcohol (WHO, 2011). Alcohol consumption can lead to an increased likelihood of developing health problems such as high blood pressure, cancer and cirrhosis of the liver. Alcohol has been identified as a causal factor in more than 60 medical conditions including mouth, throat, stomach, liver and breast cancers; hypertensive disease (high blood pressure); cirrhosis; and depression (HSCIC, 2010).

The excessive consumption of alcohol is a major preventable cause of premature mortality with alcohol-related deaths accounting for almost 1.5 per cent of all deaths in England and Wales in 2010 (ONS, 2010f). In 2008, the Department of Health published a report titled 'The cost of alcohol harm to the NHS in England' (Department of Health, 2008) which estimated that the cost of alcohol harm to the National Health Service (NHS) in England is £2.7 billion each year (2006/07 prices).

In 2010 there were 8,790 alcohol-related deaths[3] in the UK, 126 more than in 2009 (8,664). The age-standardised rate has increased from 6.9 per 100,000 in 1991 to 12.9 per 100,000 in 2010 but this is lower than a peak of 13.6 per 100,000 in 2008 (ONS, 2010f).

The proportion of men and women who drank more than the Department of Health's daily alcohol guidelines on at least one occasion during the week prior to interview (3-4 units for men, 2-3 units for women) increased by 5 percentage points for men (36 to 41 per cent) and 8 percentage points (20 to 28 per cent) for women between 1998 and 2010.Those considered binge drinkers, i.e. drinking double the recommended daily guideline, increased by 3 percentage points for men (20 to 23 per cent) and 7 percentage points (7 to 14 per cent) for women in the same time period (HSE, 2010).

Drugs

According to the British Crime Survey, 12 million people (36.3 per cent or more than 1 in 3) in England and Wales reported that they had used drugs at least once in their lifetime and 5 million (15.2 per cent or 1 in 6) had used a class A drug (Home Office 2011). Cannabis was the most frequently used drug in almost a third (30.7 per cent) of all cases reported by drug users.

Between 1993 and 2009, deaths related to drug misuse[4] in England and Wales more than doubled, from 831-1,784 deaths. Males were more considerably more likely than females to die from drug misuse in all years. In 2010, men were almost 3.5 times more likely to die from drug misuse than women. Although there was an increase in deaths overall, the number of deaths fell among the youngest and oldest adult population. Among those aged under 20 numbers have fallen 30 per cent to 35 deaths. For those over 70, numbers have fallen 23 per cent to 68 deaths (ONS, 2010g).

Obesity

Another area which is related to lifestyle is obesity. Obesity can lead to heart disease, Type-2 diabetes and hypertension. It can reduce the quality of a person's life, contribute to feelings of low self-esteem, increase the risk of premature death and create a strain on health services. In 2010, just over a quarter of adults (26 per cent of both men and women aged 16 or over) were classified as obese[5].This has increased considerably since 1993 from 13.2 per cent and 16.4 per cent for men and women respectively. In 2010, 17 per cent of boys and 15 per cent of girls (aged 2 to 15) were classed as obese, an increase from 11 per cent and 12 per cent respectively since 1995 (HSCIC, 2012).

An indication of the increase in health problems associated with obesity is the total number of hospital admissions related to obesity. The total number of admissions in England increased from just over 2,000 in 2004/05 to about 5,000 in 2007/08 and over 11,500 in 2010/11 (although it should be noted that some individuals may have been admitted more than once in a given year) (HSCIC, 2012).

Further information for healthy lifestyles across England can be found from the network of Public Health Observatories Health Profiles.

Notes

1. Measuring National Well-being - What we do

2. Global Burden of Disease analysis provides a comprehensive and comparable assessment of mortality and loss of health due to diseases, injuries and risk factors for all regions of the world. The overall burden of disease is assessed using the disability-adjusted life year (DALY), a time-

based measure that combines years of life lost due to premature mortality and years of life lost due to time lived in states of less than full health.

3.   Alcohol-related deaths in the United Kingdom index

4.   These figures represent the number of deaths where the underlying cause of death is regarded as poisoning, drug abuse or drug dependence and where any substances controlled under the Misuse of Drug Act (1971) was mentioned on the death certificate. The data on drug misuse deaths do not include deaths from other causes that may have been related to drug taking (for example, road traffic accidents or HIV/AIDS).

5.   Individual's that had a Body Mass Index (BMI) 30 {i.e. weight in kg/ height in metres squared} or over).

Social care

Information about life expectancy and potential need for health intervention and social care is very important for future planning of healthcare and expenditure, as is the role of caring which is discussed in the Measuring National Well-being article 'What we do'[1] . Social care is one area which can help maintain and improve the quality of life of the individuals who need it. This section discusses social care provision, trends in demand and services, and satisfaction with care received.

In England, in July 2011, there were 2,500 independent hospitals; around 4,600 care homes with nursing; nearly 13,500 care homes without nursing; and around 5,900 home care agencies. Nearly half (45 per cent) of care home places are occupied by people who are self funding rather than paid for by the state (CQC, 2011).

In England during 2010/11 over 1.3 million adults received caring services: of these 885,000 received community-based services, such as meals on wheels, house cleaners, housing modifications for the elderly or those with disabilities, or day-care centres. The largest users of services, around two-thirds of the total, were the 873,000 clients aged 65 and over. There were also more than 467,000 clients aged 18 to 64 (HSCIC, 2011c). Recently there has been a rise in demand for services. The Care Quality Commission (2011) report indicated a 4 per cent increase in new contacts for councils responsible for providing social care.

Figure 7 shows the total number of contact hours of home care in England increased between 2005-06 and 2008-09 from 176.9 to 200.2 million hours and the total number of hours recorded in 2010-11 was very similar to 2008-09 (200.3 million hours). Data for 2009-10 indicated a fall in the total number of hours of contact time to 183.2 million hours, but this may have been because of errors in data recording. In contrast the hours provided by councils with social services responsibilities (CASSR) has gone down from 48.7 to 25.6 million hours a year. This may be due to a higher reliance on informal care-giving due to both cuts in services and new types of provision developed which enable people to live at home for longer. For example, residential care services fell by 10 per cent between 2004 and 2010 (CQC, 2011).

Figure 7. Actual number of contact hours of home care provided during the year: by sector England

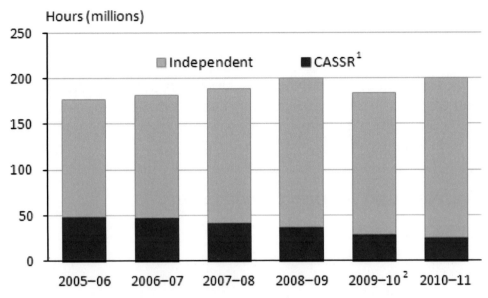

Source: The NHS Information Centre for health and social care,
Community Care Statistics 2009–10: Social Services Activity Report, England

Notes:
1. CASSR - Councils with social services responsibilities.
2. The 2009–10 data should be treated with caution as it looks out of line with the trend from previous years. This may be because some councils under recorded those receiving home care via a personal budget to tie in with changes made to the RAP return and although the definitions were not changed, it is possible some councils may have recorded home care hours differently. The change was reverted back to 2008-09 definitions so the 2010-11 figures are unaffected.

Responses to the Personal Social Services Adult Social Care Survey in England indicate that nine out of ten users who responded to the survey in 2010/11 reported that their quality of life was very good, good or alright[2]. Nine out of ten also reported that they were very satisfied, satisfied or fairly satisfied with the care and support services they had received (HSCIC, 2011d). Further, the Care Quality Commission, 2011 found that of 17,000 respondents to the 2011 survey of people who use community mental health services, 29 per cent rated their received care as excellent, 30 per cent as very good and 20 per cent as good. Respondents also felt they were listened to and had trust in their care providers and social workers.

Notes

1. <u>Measuring National Well-being - What we do</u>

2. The User Experience Survey Programme of Adult Social Services in England seeks opinions over a range of outcome areas to gain an understanding of service users' views rather than measuring quantities of care delivered. The survey asks all service users aged 18 and over receiving services funded wholly or in part by Social Services. It aims to learn more about whether or not the services are helping them to live safely and independently in their own home and what is the impact on their quality of life.

About the ONS Measuring National Well-being Programme

Nat_well-being general logo

This article is published as part of the ONS Measuring National Well-being Programme.

The programme aims to produce accepted and trusted measures of well-being of the nation - how the UK as a whole is doing. It is about looking at 'GDP and beyond' and includes:

*   greater analysis of the national economic accounts, especially to understand household income, expenditure and wealth
*   further accounts linked to the national accounts, including the UK Environmental Accounts and valuing household production and 'human capital'
*   quality of life measures, looking at different areas of national well-being such as health, relationships, job satisfaction, economic security, education and environmental conditions
*   working with others to include the measurement of well-being of children and young people as part of national well-being
*   measures of 'subjective well-being' - individuals' assessment of their own well-being
*   headline indicators to summarise national well-being and the progress we are making as a society

The programme is underpinned by a communication and engagement workstream, providing links with Cabinet Office and policy departments, international developments, the public and other stakeholders. The programme is working closely with Defra on the measurement of 'sustainable developmemnt' to provide a complete picture of national well-being, progress and sustainable development.

Find out more on the Measuring National Well-being web site pages.

Background notes

1. Details of the policy governing the release of new data are available by visiting www.statisticsauthority.gov.uk/assessment/code-of-practice/index.html or from the Media Relations Office email: media.relations@ons.gsi.gov.uk

Copyright

This document is also available on our website at www.ons.gov.uk.

Table 1
Life expectancy, healthy life expectancy and disability-free life expectancy at birth[1]

United Kingdom						Years
		Life Expectancy	Healthy Life Expectancy	Disability-free Life Expectancy	Healthy Life Expectancy as a proportion of Life Expectancy	Disability-free Life Expectancy as a proportion of Life Expectancy
Males	2000–02	75.7	60.7	60.3	80.2	79.7
	2001–03	75.9	60.6	60.9	79.8	80.2
	2002–04	76.2	61.0	61.5	80.0	80.6
	2003–05	76.6	61.5	62.3	80.2	81.3
	2004–06	77.0	62.0	62.4	80.6	81.2
	2005–07	77.3	61.4	62.5	79.6	81.0
	2006–08	77.5	62.5	63.4	80.8	81.9
	2007–09	77.9	63.0	63.4	81.1	81.6
	2008–10	78.2	..	..	..	..
Females	2000–02	80.4	62.4	62.8	77.6	78.1
	2001–03	80.5	62.2	63.0	77.2	78.2
	2002–04	80.7	62.5	63.3	77.4	78.4
	2003–05	80.9	62.9	63.9	77.7	79.0
	2004–06	81.3	63.7	63.9	78.3	78.6
	2005–07	81.5	62.9	63.7	77.2	78.2
	2006–08	81.7	64.2	64.3	78.7	78.8
	2007–09	82.0	65.0	65.1	79.4	79.5
	2008–10	82.3	..	..	..	..

1 Estimates are based on a three year moving average.
Source: Office for National Statistics

References

1. Cancer Research UK (2010a). Cancer Stats – Key Facts. Available at <u>Cancer Research UK (2010a). Cancer Stats – Key Facts</u>

2. Cancer Research UK (2010b). Smoking Statistics – Smoking and Cancer.' Available at <u>Cancer Research UK (2010b). Smoking Statistics – Smoking and Cancer</u>

3. CQC (2011) Care Quality Commission The state of health care and adult social care in England. Available at <u>CQC (2011) Care Quality Commission: The state of health care and adult social care in England</u>

4. Department of Health (2008). The cost of alcohol harm to the NHS in England. Available at <u>Department of Health (2008). The cost of alcohol harm to the NHS in England</u>

5. Department of Health (2012).'Healthy lives, healthy people: Improving outcomes and supporting transparency'. Available at <u>DH: Healthy lives, healthy people: Improving outcomes and supporting transparency</u>

6. European Commission, 2012, Attitudes of Europeans Towards Tobacco. Available at <u>European Commission: Attitudes of Europeans Towards Tobacco</u>

7. HES, (2011). Health Episode Statistics. Available at <u>HES: Health Episode Statistics</u>

8. HSE (2010) Health Survey for England 2010 trend tables. Available at <u>HSE: Health Survey for England 2010 trend tables</u>

9. Home Office (2011) Drug Misuse Declared: Findings from the 2010/11 British Crime Survey. Available at: <u>Home Office: Drugs misuse</u>

10. HSCIC, (2009). Health and Social Care Information Centre: Adult Psychiatric Morbidity Survey 2007. Available at <u>HSCIC: Adult Psychiatric Morbidity Survey 2007</u>

11. HSCIC (2010). Health and Social Care Information Centre: Health Survey for England, 2009. Available at <u>HSCIC: Health and Social Care Information Centre: Health Survey for England, 2009</u>

12. HSCIC (2011a) Health and Social Care Information Centre: HSE 2010 Annual Report, Well-being, Health and Work Chapter. Available at <u>HSCIC: Health and Social Care Information Centre: HSE 2010 Annual Report, Well-being, Health and Work Chapter</u>

13. HSCIC 2011b) Health and Social Care Information Centre: Attitudes to Mental Illness - 2011 survey report. Available at <u>HSCIC: Attitudes to Mental Illness - 2011 survey report</u>

14. HSCIC (2011c) Health and Social Care Information Centre: Community Care Statistics: Social Services Activity, England 2010-2011. Available at <u>HSCIC: Community Care Statistics: Social Services Activity, England 2010-2011</u>

15. HSCIC (2011d) Health and Social Care Information Centre: Personal Social Services Adult Social Care Survey, England 2010-11 (Final Release). Available at <u>HSCIC: Personal Social Services Adult Social Care Survey, England 2010-11</u>

16. ONS, (2009a). Gestation Specific Infant Mortality for England and Wales, 2009. Available at <u>Gestation-specific infant mortality in England and Wales</u>

Measuring National Well-being - Personal Finance, 2012

Author Name(s): Carla Seddon Office for National Statistics

Abstract

This article is published as part of the Office for National Statistics (ONS) Measuring National Well-being programme. The programme aims to produce accepted and trusted measures of the well-being of the nation - how the UK as a whole is doing. This article on personal finance is part of a series which aims to explore in more detail the different domains that are considered important for the measurement of National Well-being. Personal finance can have a significant impact on people's sense of well-being and the financial situation of the population is an important aspect of National Well-being. This article examines different aspects of household income, expenditure and wealth, including financial poverty as well looking at peoples own views about their own financial situation.

Introduction

Personal finance refers to individuals and household consumption possibilities, both now and in the future, and is therefore driven by both income and wealth.

A range of studies have investigated the relationships between people's financial situation and well-being. Joo (1998) conceptualised financial wellness as 'a level of financial health. It includes satisfaction with material and non-material aspects of one's financial situation, perception (or subjective assessment) of financial stability including adequacy of financial resources, and the objective amount of material and non-material financial resources that each individual possesses'.

This was highlighted in the National Debate on Measuring National Well-being and illustrated by one response that stated 'It's not about having millions of pounds, but working and earning a good amount to keep myself and any future family I have safe and well'. (ONS 2011)

In the recent Office for National Statistics (ONS) report on the Consultation on Proposed Domains and Measures (788 Kb Pdf) the scope of the domain 'Personal finance' is described as intending to include income and wealth and its distribution.

In this same report the four headline measures proposed to Measure National Well-being within this domain are:

- percentage of individuals living in households where income was less than 60 per cent of median income after housing costs,
- median wealth per household including pension wealth,
- percentage who were somewhat, mostly or completely satisfied with the income of their household,
- percentage who report it quite or very difficult to get by financially.

The analysis of these measures will be used to address the concepts of poverty, inequality of income and assets which were mentioned in the national debate responses. This article explores these headline measures in more detail and puts them into the context of other objective and subjective measures of personal finance.

It starts by looking at household income and poverty before moving onto satisfaction with income, satisfaction with financial situation, income and life satisfaction and how people are managing financially. The article then moves on to look at household expenditure, fuel poverty, household wealth and household debt.

Macroeconomic measures and their effects on households will be reported in the domain analysis of 'The economy' which will also be published by the Measuring National Well-being Programme in October 2012. All publications and further information about the programme can be found on the Well-being page.

Key points

Household income

- In 2010/11 median income after housing costs in the UK was £359 per week, a rise since the £277 per week in 1994/95 but a fall from £373 per week in 2009/10.

Poverty

- In the UK in 2010/11, 16 per cent of individuals lived in households with an income less than 60 per cent the median household income before housing costs.

Poverty: characteristics

- In the UK in 2009, 64 per cent of households with above average poverty rates included large families, 64 per cent were entirely workless households and 47 per cent were headed by a lone parent.
- In 2010, 76 per cent of weekly household income was from social security benefits for UK households in the lowest income quintile, while for those in the highest quintile 76 per cent of weekly income came from wages and salaries
- In the UK in 2010/11 those in the top income quintile group had an average original income of £81,500 per year before taxes and benefits compared to £5,100 for those in the lowest: a ratio of 16 to 1; the inequality was reduced once the effects of taxes and benefits were taken into account.

Satisfaction with income

- In 2008/09, 8.5 per cent of people in the UK reported being completely satisfied with the income of their household compared to 11.1 per cent in 2002/03

Satisfaction with financial situation

- In 2011/12, 47.4 per cent of adults aged 16 and over in Great Britain reported relatively low satisfaction with their financial situation compared to 19.6 who had high satisfaction.

Income and life satisfaction

- In Great Britain in 2011/12 adults aged 16 and over with a personal income between £4,159 and £11,439 had a mean score of 7.2 out of 10 for life satisfaction.

Managing financially

- In 2008/09, 7.5 per cent of people in the UK reported they were finding it quite or very difficult to manage financially compared to 6.0 per cent in 2001/02.
- In April 2012, 28 per cent of respondents in Great Britain thought their personal financial situation would worsen over the next 6 months compared to 22 per cent who thought it would improve.

Household expenditure

- In 2010, housing, fuel and power became the second highest category of household expenditure (£60.40 per week), behind transport (£64.90 per week) replacing recreation and culture (£58.10) which was second in previous years.

Household expenditure: housing

- In 2009 in the UK, 17 per cent of the population were living in households where housing costs were 40 per cent or more of their disposable income compared to the EU average of 10 per cent.
- In 2011 mortgage re-possessions in the UK fell to 37,000 from 48,000 in 2009; mortgage re-possessions were at their highest in 1991 with 76,000 re-possessions.

Fuel poverty

- In the UK in 2010, 4.8 million households (approximately 19 per cent of all UK households) were in fuel poverty, a fall of 0.7 million since 2009.

Household wealth

- In Great Britain in 2008/10 the median household wealth, including pension wealth, was estimated to be £235,500 and excluding pension wealth was £149,500.

Household wealth: savings ratio

- In 2011 the savings ratio in the UK stood at 6.6 per cent, up from 2.2 per cent in 2008.

Household debt

- In Great Britain in 2008/10 the mean value of non-mortgage borrowing was £7,300.

Household income

'I do not aspire to be wealthy, however I do want to be able to work and earn a fair wage for the work that I do'. Response to the National Debate. (ONS, 2011)

There are a number of measures of the income of households in use. Household equivalised median income from the Family Resources Survey (FRS) is used to examine the changes in household income over time and to estimate its distribution. This Survey is also analysed to estimate the number of individuals who live in households with different relative levels of income, in particular those who live in relative poverty.

Figure 1: Household Median Income (1), 1994/95 - 2010/11

United Kingdom (2)

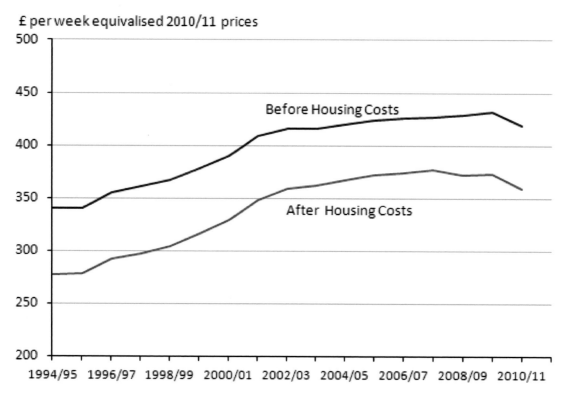

Source: Family Resource Survey, Department for Work and Penions

Notes:

1. Small changes in estimates from year to year may not be significant in view of data uncertainties.
2. Data is for the United Kingdom for 2002/03 onwards, prior to this it covers Great Britain.

Data from the FRS shows weekly net (disposable) equivalised household median income[1]. The median income before housing costs gradually increased between 1994/95 to 2009/10 from a median of £340 per week to £432 per week respectively at equivalised 2010/11 prices (note that 1994/95 data are for Great Britain and 2009/10 data are for the UK). However, median income fell in 2010/11 to £419 per week (Figure 1).

For median income after housing costs the same general pattern applied, rising from £277 in 1994/95 to £377 in 2007/08. In 2008/09 it fell slightly to £372 and stayed fairly stable at £373 in 2009/10. However, in 2010/11 it fell further to £359 per week. This fall in median income between 2009/10 and 2010/11 was mainly due to earnings increasing by less than the relatively high inflation rate over the period.

Increases in inflation have outweighed the rise in income, effectively resulting in lower incomes and higher costs as the income buys less due to higher prices. This in real terms has put a further squeeze on the finances of many, highlighting the extent to which households continued to face difficult financial circumstances.

The proportion of income used for housing costs also increased in 2010/11 to 14.3 per cent, since its lowest level of 11.7 per cent in 2007/08, but it has not reached the levels seen in 1994/95 when 18.5 per cent of income was housing costs. (DWP, 2012.

Notes

1. In the FRS survey income is adjusted for household size and composition by means of equivalence scales, which reflect the extent to which households of different size and composition require a different level of income to achieve the same standard of living.

Poverty

A response to the National Debate suggested that financial well-being was 'A sense that everybody has access to a good standard of living'. (ONS, 2011)

Although looking at median income is useful, it is only an average measure and it is important to also look at those who have lower than average incomes as a way of understanding what percentage of the population are in 'poverty'.

In 2009 the British Social Attitudes survey found that, 58 per cent of respondents aged 18 and over living in private households in Great Britain believed that there was quite a lot of poverty in Britain, compared with 39 per cent who thought there was very little poverty.

These figures contrast with the 52 per cent who thought there was quite a lot of poverty in 2006 and 45 per cent who thought there was very little poverty. In 1986, 41 per cent thought there was very little poverty compared with 55 per cent who thought there was quite a lot. (BSA, 2010)

Figure 2: Income distribution for the total population (After Housing Costs) (1), (2), 2010/11

United Kingdom

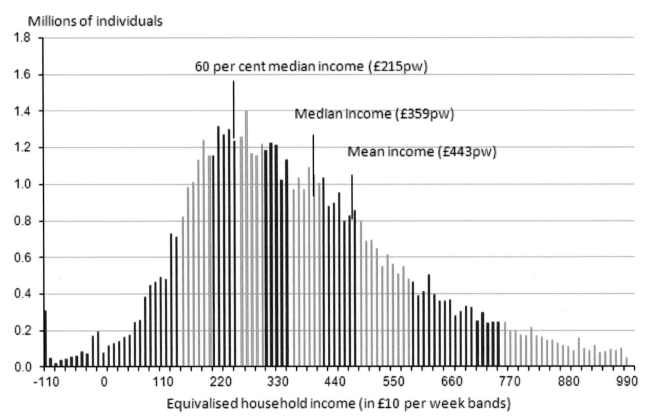

Source: Households Below Average Income, Department for Work and Pensions

Notes:
1. Equivalised household disposable income before deduction of housing costs (in £10 bands), using OECD equivalisation scale. The £10 bands are grouped into decile groups in alternating colours. See Appendix, Part 5: Households Below Average Income (HBAI).
2. Negative incomes BHC are reset to zero, but negative AHC incomes calculated from the adjusted BHC incomes are possible. Where incomes have been adjusted to zero BHC, income AHC is derived from the adjusted BHC income.

Figure 2 illustrates the distribution of equivalised incomes after housing costs have been accounted for and shows how such incomes are distributed for households in the UK in 2010/11. The data show that the income distribution for 2010/11 disposable incomes after housing cost deduction are not distributed evenly. (DWP, 2012a)

There is a much greater concentration of people at lower levels of weekly income, with nearly two-thirds of individuals living in households with a disposable weekly income lower than the mean. There is a long 'tail' of people at the higher end of the distribution which results in a higher mean[1] income per week, £443 compared with the median[2] of £359.

A household is currently described as in poverty if its income is less than 60 per cent of the median (average) net household income, before and after housing costs[3]. Data from the FRS show that between 1998/99 and 2010/11 there have been some small changes in the proportion of individuals living in households where the income falls below 60 per cent of contemporary median income, either before or after housing costs (note that data prior to 2002/03 are for Great Britain and more recent data are for the UK).

When looking at before housing costs, 19 per cent of individuals lived in such households in 1998/99 but by 2010/11 this had decreased to 16 per cent. When focusing on income after housing costs 24 per cent were considered to be in poverty in 1998/99, falling to 21 per cent in 2010/11.

The reduction in the percentage below the poverty rate between 2009/10 and 2010/11 is in part attributable to the fall in median income (see Figure 1) rather than any substantial improvement of the financial situation of the people at the bottom of the distribution. Before then reductions in poverty were driven by incomes at the bottom of the distribution growing faster than incomes in the middle of the distribution.

The inequality of incomes can be illustrated further by calculating the ratio between the incomes at different points in the distribution: For example, those who have incomes which are 90 per cent from the bottom of the distribution (90th percentile) have about five times as much income as those who have incomes which are 10 per cent from the bottom of the distribution (10th percentile) and those at the 75th percentile have about twice the income of those at the 25th percentile. (DWP, 2012a)

For further information see Households Below Average Income (HBAI).

Notes

1. The mean is equal to the sum of the values divided by the number of values. The mean is the arithmetic average of a set of values, or distribution.

2. The median is the numerical value separating the higher half of a sample. The median of a finite list of numbers can be found by arranging all the observations from lowest value to highest value and picking the middle one.

3. This value of a specific income or 'poverty' depends on the number of individuals in the household, as larger households need more money (although not proportionately more) than smaller ones in order to achieve the same standard of living.

Poverty: characteristics

Income data from the first wave of the Understanding Society Survey in 2009 have been analysed using a truncated measure of income, where the lowest and highest incomes were excluded from analysis. This measure results in an estimate of about 18 per cent of all households in the UK being in poverty. The results show some of the household characteristics which are associated with higher levels of poverty. (US, 2009)

Table 1: Estimated poverty rates, 2009 (1)

United Kingdom

		Percentages
	Poverty rate	Sample size (General Population sample Wave 1 Year 1)
All households	18	13,505
Households including someone over pension age	23	4,362
Households including someone over 75	30	1,652
Among non-pensioner households		
Households with children	20	4,521
Households with four or more children	64	187
Lone parent households	47	770
Households with no worker	64	1,708
Households whose members have no qualifications	41	934
Households renting their accommodation	31	3,563
Households including a disabled person	22	2,061
Households including a severely disabled person	31	755
Households containing an Indian person	14	250
Households including a Pakistani or Bangladeshi person	40	184
Households including a Caribbean person	22	233
Households including an African person	30	244
Households in England	15	7,585
Households in Wales	20	442
Households in Scotland	17	823

Table 1: Estimated poverty rates, 2009 (1)

United Kingdom

Percentages

	Poverty rate	Sample size (General Population sample Wave 1 Year 1)
Households in Northern Ireland	20	891

Source: Understanding Society

Table notes:
1. Derived from Understanding Society Wave 1 Year 1, 2009.

Households with above average poverty rates include large families (with four or more children) and workless households, both at 64 per cent (Table 1). This is followed by lone parents (47 per cent), those without educational qualifications (41 per cent), and Pakistanis and Bangladeshis (40 per cent). Poverty is also above average for households containing older pensioners, tenants, severely disabled people, Africans and for households in Wales and Northern Ireland.

A 2011 report by the Joseph Rowntree Foundation found that two age groups had worrying poverty rates, a very high proportion of 16 to 19-year-olds in the UK who were not in full-time education were in poverty. At the other end of the age scale, those approaching retirement (aged 55 to 64) contained high proportions of both poor and rich in comparison with older age groups.(JRF, 2011)

For further information see 'Monitoring poverty and social exclusion, 2011'

The next section focuses on sources of income.

Table 2: Sources of income by gross income quintile group, 2010

United Kingdom

Percentages

Gross income quintile group	Wages and salaries	Self employment	Investments	Annuities and pensions[1]	Social security benefits[2]	Other sources
	Percentage of gross weekly household income					
Lowest 20 per cent	8	3	2	10	76	2
Second quintile group	27	4	2	16	48	2
Third quintile group	53	7	2	15	22	1
Fourth quintile group	73	7	2	8	8	1
Highest 20 per cent	76	13	3	5	2	1

Source: Living Costs and Food Survey, Office for National Statistics

Table notes:

1. Other than social security benefits
2. Excluding housing benefit and council tax benefit (rates rebate in Northern Ireland).

According to results from the Living Costs and Food Survey (LCF) adults aged 16 and over who were in the lowest fifth of the income distribution in the UK obtained about three-quarters of their income from social security benefits, this reduced to about half of the income in the next highest fifth and to about a fifth of those in the middle fifth of the income distribution (Table 2). In contrast, those in the highest two-fifths of the income distribution obtained over four-fifths of their income from wages or self employment. (ONS, 2011a)

Many of those whose main source of income is from social security benefits, especially those in the lowest quintile group, are living in workless households. Data from the Labour Force Survey (LFS) in the UK show that there was a slight reduction in both the number and the percentage of workless households (households in which no adult aged 16 to 64 was working) between April to June 1996 and April to June 2012. Since 1996, when there were 3.9 million UK workless households representing 20.9 per cent of all households, the lowest estimate for both the number and percentage of workless households was in 2006, two years before the economic downturn hit the UK in 2008 (3.4 million, representing 17.3 per cent of all households).

In April to June 2012 there were 3.7 million UK households with at least one member aged 16 to 64 where no-one was currently working, representing 17.9 per cent of all households, down 0.8 percentage points (or 153,000 households) from a year earlier. In comparison over the same period, the percentage of households where all adults were working was 53.0 per cent (10.9 million households), down 0.3 percentage points (36,000 households) from a year earlier. (ONS, 2012)

For more information see 'Work and Workless households'.

'The effects of taxes and benefits on household income, 2010/11' published by the ONS in 2012 reports that cash benefits and direct taxes have the impact of redistributing income from richer households to those with lower incomes, thereby reducing income inequality. (ONS, 2012a)

Figure 3: The effects of taxes and benefits on household income quintile groups (1), 2010/11

United Kingdom

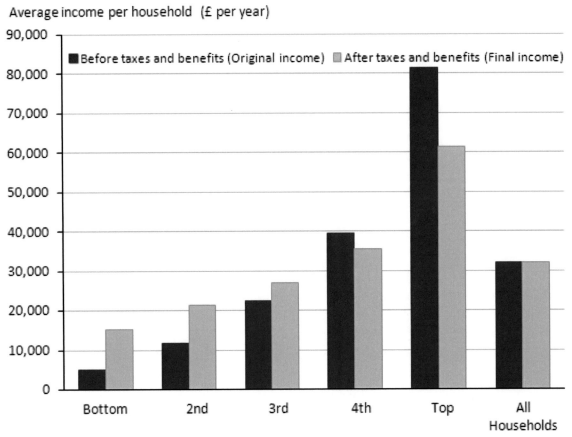

Average income per household (£ per year)

Source: The effects of taxes and benefits on household income 2010/11, Office for National Statistics

Notes:
1. Households are ranked by their equivalised disposable incomes, using the modified-OECD scale.

In 2010/11 the richest fifth (those in the top income quintile group) in the UK had an average[1] original income of £81,500[2] per year before taxes and benefits, compared with £5,100 for the poorest fifth – a ratio of 16 to 1 (Figure 3). This ratio was also 16 to 1 in 2009/10, indicating that inequality of original income has not changed between the two years according to this measure.

Original income includes earnings, private pensions and investments. After benefits were added and taxes subtracted, the richest fifth had income that was four times that of the poorest fifth (final incomes of £61,400 per year compared with £15,200, respectively).

The largest cash benefits[3] were received by households in the second quintile group at £8,300 per year, compared with £7,000 for households in the bottom group. This is largely because more retired households are located in the second quintile group, compared with the bottom group, and in this analysis the state pension is classified as a cash benefit. Cash benefits therefore reduced the inequality of income.

Notes

1. Data are the average for the quintile.

2. Effects of taxes and benefits estimates are produced using the Living Costs and Food Survey together with a variety of other sources. The estimates of income used earlier in this article are from the Households Below Average Income (HBAI) publication which is published each year by the Department for Work and Pensions (DWP). This provides analysis of the income and income distribution based on data from the Family Resources Survey. Due to HBAI being based on a different survey, and some methodological differences (for example HBAI measures inequality on an individual basis whereas Effects of Taxes and Benefits (ETB) measures inequality on a household basis), HBAI and ETB estimates differ slightly. However, historical trends are similar.

3. Cash benefits such as tax credits, housing benefit and income support.

Satisfaction with income

Table 3: Satisfaction with income of household (1)

United Kingdom

Percentages2

Responses[3]	2002/03	2003/04	2004/05	2005/06	2006/07	2007/08	2008/09
Completely satisfied	11.1	11.2	10.1	9.7	9.7	9.6	8.5
Mostly satisfied	19.9	21.8	22.0	18.3	20.7	22.4	20.4
Somewhat satisfied	27.4	29.0	27.5	26.6	28.0	28.2	29.5
Neither satisfied nor dissatisfied	19.9	19.2	20.1	20.9	20.2	20.1	20.8
Somewhat dissatisfied	11.7	10.7	11.8	12.7	12.0	11.3	11.9
Mostly dissatisfied	5.9	5.0	5.1	6.9	5.6	5.2	5.3
Completely dissatisfied	4.1	3.1	3.4	5.0	3.7	3.2	3.6
Somewhat, mostly or completely satisfied	58.4	61.9	59.6	54.6	58.4	60.2	58.5

Source: British Panel Household Survey

Table notes:
1. Responses to "How dissatisfied or satisfied are you with.........The income of your household ?"
2. The percentages are of those who responded. Estimated percentages are based on the full sample adjusted to UK figures using cross-sectional weights.
3. Responses to earlier waves of the BHPS differ. However, they have always been on a 7 point scale varying from completely (or very) satisfied to completely (or very) dissatisfied.

Between 2002/03 and 2008/09 there have been some variations in the proportion of individuals aged 16 and over in the UK who report that they are somewhat, mostly or completely satisfied with the income of their household, ranging between 54.6 per cent and 61.9 per cent according to the British Panel Household Survey (BPHS) (Table 3). However, over this period there has been a decrease in the proportion who reported that they are completely satisfied from just over 11 per cent to less than 9 per cent and an increase in those reporting that they are somewhat or mostly satisfied with their income. About one in five respondents were neither satisfied nor dissatisfied with their income in each year. (BPHS, 2009)

Satisfaction with financial situation

Responses to the National Debate included:

'I am financially well off but I would hate for someone to be worrying about whether they will have something to eat or a roof over their head. Also doing other things including recreation activities improves your mental well-being which in turn affects your general well-being but you can only do those things if you are in a good financial position'. (ONS, 2011)

Figure 4: Satisfaction with financial situation (1), (2), April 2011 to February 2012

Great Britain

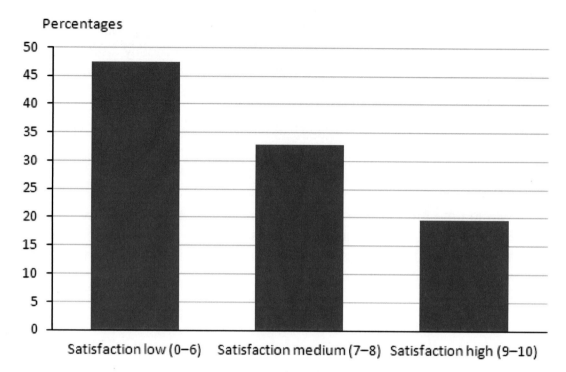

Source: Opinions Survey, Office for National Statistics

Notes:

1. Respondents were asked 'Overall, how satisfied are you with your financial situation'? where 0 is 'not at all' and 10 is 'completely satisfied'.
2. Data collected in April, June and October 2011 and February 2012. February 2012 data collected also used show cards which could have a slight impact on the data.

In the Opinions Survey when the question 'Overall, how satisfied are you with your financial situation?' was asked of adults aged 16 and over in Great Britain, nearly half of those surveyed (47.4 per cent) in 2011/12 reported low levels of satisfaction with their financial situation (between 0 and 6 on a scale of 0 to 10 where 0 is 'not at all' and 10 is 'completely') (Figure 4). A further 33.0 per cent had medium levels of satisfaction (between 7 and 8 on the scale) with their financial situation while 19.6 per cent had high levels of satisfaction (9 to 10 on the scale). (ONS, 2012b).

Income and life satisfaction

Figure 5: Average (mean) Life Satisfaction, Worthwhile, Happy Yesterday and Anxious Yesterday Rating: by income group

Great Britain

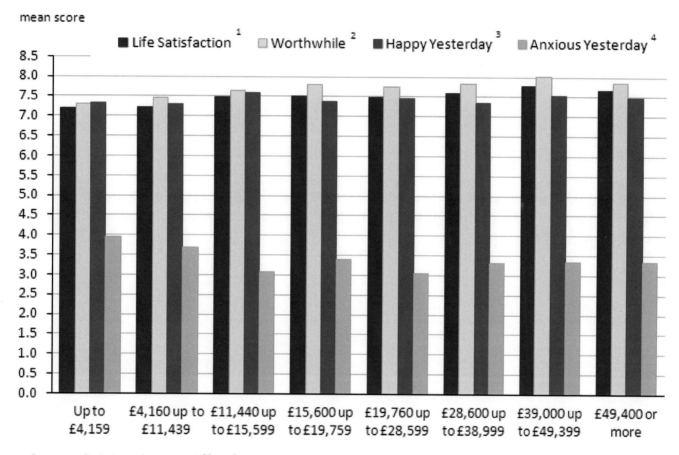

Source: Opinions Survey, Office for National Statistics

Notes:

1. Respondents were asked 'Overall, how satisfied are you with your life nowadays? where 0 is 'not at all' and 10 is 'completely satisfied'.
2. Respondents were asked 'Overall, to what extent do you feel that things you do in your life are worthwhile? where 0 is 'not at all' and 10 is 'completely worthwhile'.
3. Respondents were asked 'Overall, how happy did you feel yesterday? where 0 is 'not at all' and 10 is 'completely happy'.
4. Respondents were asked 'Overall, how anxious did you feel yesterday? where 0 is 'not at all' and 10 is 'completely anxious'.

These data from the Opinions Survey are published as experimental. The observed differences between the subjective well-being measures for the income groups are from a relatively small sample and should be interpreted carefully. ONS plan to do further analysis to better understand these data and related determinants of individual well-being.

Those in the lowest two personal income groups had the lowest mean scores for life satisfaction (both at 7.2) worthwhile (7.3 and 7.5 respectively) and happy yesterday (both at 7.3): these income groups also recorded the highest mean scores for anxious yesterday (4.0 and 3.7) (Figure 5). (ONS, 2012b).

Managing financially

During the National Well-being Debate respondents were asked 'what things in life matter to you?' 45 per cent of respondents highlighted the importance of having adequate income or wealth to cover basic needs. (ONS, 2011)

Table 4: Managing financially (1)

United Kingdom

Percentages2

Responses[3]	2001/02	2002/03	2003/04	2004/05	2005/06	2006/07	2007/08	2008/09
Living comfortably	33.8	32.9	34.2	33.4	31.4	32.4	32.4	28.4
Doing alright	38.4	39.8	39.7	39.5	40.0	39.7	39.8	38.2
Just about getting by	21.9	21.7	21.3	21.5	22.7	21.8	21.8	25.8
Finding it quite difficult	4.3	4.1	3.5	4.1	4.1	4.2	4.3	5.4
Finding it very difficult	1.7	1.5	1.4	1.5	1.8	2.0	1.7	2.1
Finding it quite/very difficult	6.0	5.6	4.9	5.6	5.9	6.2	6.0	7.5

Source: British Panel Household Survey

Table notes:
1. Responses to "How well would you say you yourself are managing financially these days? Would you say you are.... ?"
2. The percentages are of those who responded. Estimated percentages are based on the full sample adjusted to UK figures using cross-sectional weights.
3. Responses to earlier waves of the BHPS differ. However, they have always been on a 7 point scale varying from completely (or very) satisfied to completely (or very) dissatisfied.

Adults aged 16 and over in the UK where asked 'How well would you say you yourself are managing financially these days?' on the British Panel Household Survey. In 2008/09, 7.5 per cent reported that they were finding it either quite or very difficult to manage financially (Table 4). This is higher than previously recorded for any of the years since 2001/02. Between 2001/02 and 2008/09 there was also a reduction to 28.4 per cent in the proportion who reported that they were living comfortably, the lowest for any of the years shown.

An estimated 25.8 per cent said they were 'Just about getting by' in 2008/09 higher than in each of the preceding years. As 2008/09 was the first year of the most recent recession, it is likely that these changes are the result of the economic downturn affecting individual's ability or feelings about their ability to manage financially. (BPHS, 2009).

Figure 6: Financial Outlook (1)

Great Britain

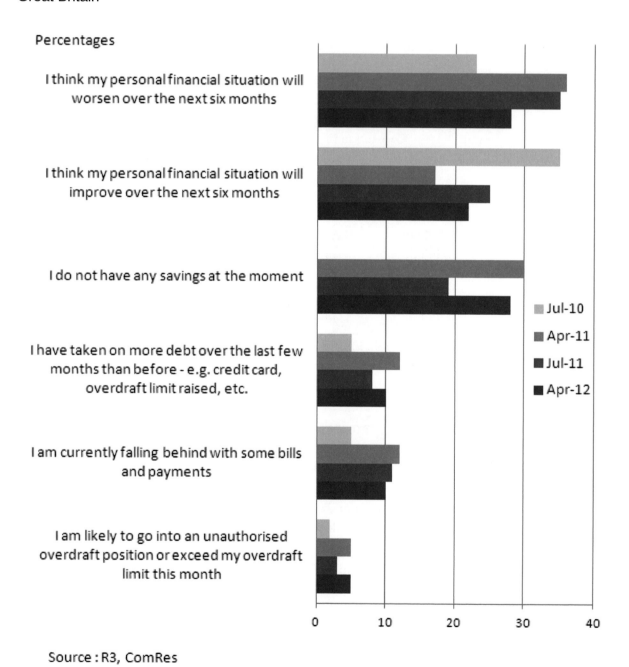

Source : R3, ComRes

Notes:
1. Where data not shown, data is unavailable.

A survey conducted by ComRes on behalf of R3: Association of Business Recovery Professionals (Rescue, Recovery, Renewal) looked at individuals' financial outlook for the next six months. The results found that there is still more pessimism than optimism. Overall, in April 2012, 28 per cent of individuals aged 18 and over in Great Britain think that their personal financial situation will worsen over the next six months, while only 22 per cent think it will improve (Figure 6).

This was a decrease from 35 per cent and 25 per cent respectively since July 2011. In April 2011, 30 per cent stated that they did not have any savings at the moment, although this fell to 19 per cent in July 2011. It has since risen again to 28 per cent in April 2012. (R3, 2012).

Household expenditure

Household expenditure is another area that has implications for personal finance. Data from the Living Costs and Food survey shows total weekly household expenditure in the UK by the 12 Classification of Individual Consumption by Purpose (COICOP) categories. These figures are given in 2010 prices so that differences in expenditure between years have been adjusted to remove the effects of inflation. (ONS, 2011a)

Table 5: Total household expenditure based on COICOP classification, 2006 to 2010, at 2010 prices (1)

United Kingdom

£'s

COICOP commodity	2006	2007	2008	2009	2010
Food & non–alcoholic drinks	52.30	52.10	52.80	54.60	53.20
Alcoholic drinks, tobacco & narcotics	12.50	12.10	11.20	11.70	11.80
Clothing & footwear	25.90	23.80	22.50	21.90	23.40
Housing(net)^2, fuel & power	53.60	56.10	55.20	60.00	60.40
Household goods & services	33.80	33.30	31.40	29.20	31.40
Health	6.60	6.20	5.30	5.50	5.00
Transport	68.70	66.70	66.00	61.10	64.90
Communication	13.10	12.90	12.40	12.20	13.00
Recreation & culture	65.00	62.10	62.50	60.50	58.10
Education	7.90	7.30	6.40	7.30	10.00
Restaurants & hotels	42.40	40.30	39.30	40.20	39.20
Miscellaneous goods & services	40.20	38.20	37.10	36.70	35.90
Other expenditure items	84.80	85.90	88.10	75.10	67.30
Total expenditure	506.70	496.90	490.30	476.00	473.60
Average weekly expenditure per person (£)					
Total expenditure	216.70	210.90	208.00	203.40	203.10

Source: Living Costs and Food survey, Office for National Statistics

Table notes:

1. Figures have been deflated to 2010 prices using the RPI all items index.
2. Excluding mortgage interest payments, council tax and Northern Ireland rates.

Spending levels were greatest in 2006, with households spending £506.70 per week at 2010 prices, they subsequently fell every year to reach £473.60 in 2010, £2.40 less than in 2009, and £33.10 less than in 2006 (Table 5).

The largest categories for household expenditure per week in each year, apart from 'other expenditure items', were transport (£64.90 in 2010), housing, fuel & power (£60.40), recreation and culture (£58.10), and food & non-alcoholic drinks (£53.20). Spending in these four categories accounted for half of total household expenditure in 2010. Between 2006 and 2010, spending on housing, fuel and power increased by nearly 13 per cent while food and non-alcoholic drinks had shown an increase of less than 2 per cent at 2010 prices.

Over the same time period these increases were offset by reductions in expenditure of over 10 per cent on recreation and culture and over 5 per cent on transport. There were also decreases in spending on restaurants and hotels, miscellaneous goods and service and other expenditure items. From this data it appears that households are making ends meet by increasing their expenditure on basics such as food, housing and utilities and reducing expenditure on items which are not essential such as travel, recreation and eating out.

Household expenditure: housing

As has already been seen housing, fuel & power1 form a major component of expenditure for households in the UK. According to European Union Statistics on Income and Living Conditions, housing costs2 also represents the largest component of expenditure for many households in Europe.

Figure 7: Housing cost overburden rate in European countries (1), 2009

Europe

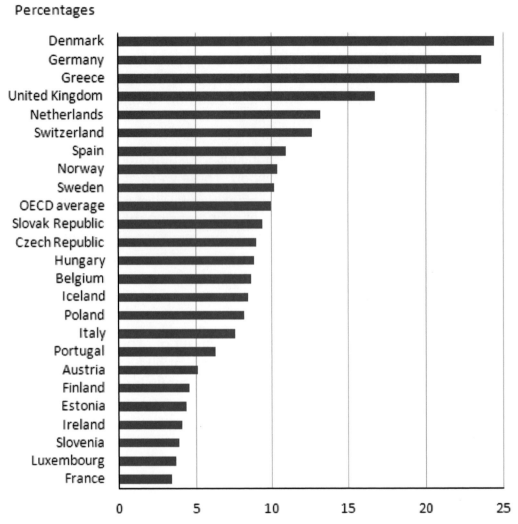

Source: European Union Statistics on Income and Living Conditions (EU-SILC)

Notes:

1. Data refer to people living in households where the total housing costs ("net" of housing allowances) represent 40 per cent or more of their disposable income.

In 2009, about 10 per cent of the population in the 24 Organisation for Economic Co-operation and Development (OECD) countries surveyed by EU-SILC lived in households that spent 40 per cent or more of their equivalised disposable income on housing. The OECD 50, How's life? Measuring Well-being report continues to explain that there were, however large cross-country differences.

The share of the population where housing costs are equal to or greater than 40 per cent of their equivalised disposable income is small in France, Luxembourg, Slovenia and Ireland but very high in

Denmark, Germany and Greece (Figure 7). To some extent this may reflect public housing policies and in particular social housing or housing subsidies provided by governments. Also, this indicator has to be interpreted with caution because it does not factor in essential housing allowances (such as tax benefits for renters or investment grants for owners). (OECD, 2011)

The UK is above the OECD average, with 17 per cent of the people aged 16 and over living in households where housing costs are 40 per cent or more of their equivalised disposable income.

Housing affordability is evaluated according to other standards in Australia, Canada and the United States. In 2009, more than 38 per cent of households in the United States spent 30 per cent of their current income on housing costs, while this share was around 25 per cent in Canada in 2006. In 2008, 36 per cent of low income renter households in Australia were classified as being in a condition of rental stress.

For those buying their own property with the aid of a mortgage, inability to meet mortgage repayments can lead to re-possession of their dwelling.

Figure 8: Mortgage repossessions (1)

United Kingdom

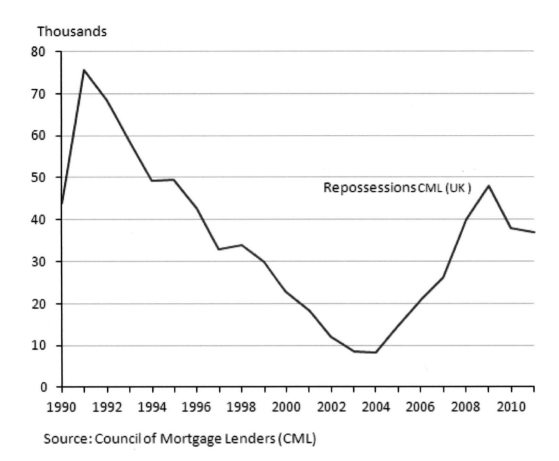

Source: Council of Mortgage Lenders (CML)

Notes:
1. Data on repossessions are based on first-charge loans data supplied by CML members. CML estimates that their lenders currently account for over 95 per cent of all first-charge mortgage lending.

According to the Council of Mortgage Lenders, mortgage re-possessions in the UK peaked in 1991 with 76,000 re-possessions and then declined steadily to 8,000 in 2004 (Figure 8). However mortgage re-possessions then rose sharply between 2004 and 2009, they rose to 15,000 in 2005 and then to 48,000 in 2009, before falling back somewhat in 2010 (to 38,000).

In 2011 mortgage re-possessions fell again slightly to 37,000. Mortgage re-possessions are currently similar to the levels of the mid-1990s. According to Ministry of Justice data for England and Wales, repossession claims issued and claims leading to an order for repossessions followed a similar pattern. (CML, 2012).

Notes

1. COICOP classification of housing, fuel and power includes actual rentals for housing, maintenance and repair of dwelling, water supply and miscellaneous services relating to the dwelling and electricity, gas and other fuels. The housing-related costs, mortgage interest payments, mortgage protection premiums, council tax, and domestic rates are included under the other expenditure items category.

2. Housing costs in the EU-SILC definition refer to monthly costs and include actual rents paid, the costs of utilities (water, gas, electricity and heating), housing taxes and compulsory insurance, as well mortgage interest payments and regular maintenance and repairs by home owners while excluding the repayments of principal on mortgages.

Fuel poverty

There are certain costs that affect all household income groups but have a larger effect on the budgets of those in low income households. For example, the rise in energy bills may result in many households in the lowest income distribution groups suffering from fuel poverty[1]. For the years for which data are available, the largest number of households in fuel poverty was about 6.5 million in 1996.

Figure 9: Fuel poverty in the UK, 1996 to 2010 (1), (2)

United Kingdom

Households (millions)

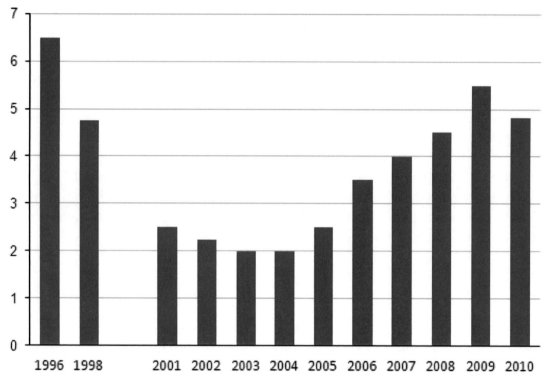

Source: Annual Report on Fuel Poverty Statistics, Department of Energy and Climate Change

Notes:
1.   Fuel poverty was not calculated in 1997, 1999 and 2000.
2.   Wales figure estimated for 2009 and 2010. Northern Ireland figure estimated for 2010.

In 2010 the number of households in fuel poverty in the UK was about 4.8 million households (representing approximately 19 per cent of all UK households), a fall of 0.7 million since 2009 (Figure 9). However, there had been an increase of about 1 million households between 2008 and 2009, continuing an upward trend since 2004. After a period between 1996 and 2004 when fuel prices fell and incomes rose, prices started rising in 2004 and the effect of these price rises outweighed the impact of increasing incomes and improved energy efficiency.

According to the Department of Energy and Climate Change the reduction in the numbers in fuel poverty in between 2009 and 2010 was due to stable energy prices between these years, a small rise in incomes and the installation of energy efficiency measures, particularly more efficient boilers which resulted in using less fuel. The fuel poverty level of each UK country has followed the same trend. (DECC, 2012)

In January 2012 the Citizens Advice Bureau (CAB) reported that 43 per cent of respondents in Great Britain were worried they couldn't afford their next fuel bill and one in two said energy bills would put a strain on their finances this year[2]. In November 2011 eight times as many people used Citizens Advice for online advice on cutting their fuel bills compared with the previous November[3]. In 2011 the Citizens Advice Bureau helped clients with over 96,000 fuel debt problems[4]. (CAB, 201).

Notes

1. A household is considered to be in fuel poverty if it needs to spend more than 10 per cent of its income on fuel for adequate heating (usually 21 degrees for the main living area, and 18 degrees for other occupied rooms). Living in cold homes can damage people's health and affect their quality of life. The elderly, children and those with a disability or long-term illness are especially vulnerable.

2. This data comes from TNS OnLineBus who interviewed 2069 GB adults aged 16 to 64 between 20th and 28th December 2011.

3. This data is from Citizens Advice web stats.

4. The source of this data is CAB stats on client enquiries.

Household wealth

Wealth is an important component of the economic well-being of households as it can be used to fund future consumption and can provide a 'safety net' against loss of income. Therefore, when looking at financial well-being it is necessary to look further than just a measure of household income. Home ownership, investment schemes, the ownership of shares and the accumulation of wealth, for instance through pensions, all contribute to the changing composition of wealth.

The Wealth and Assets Survey (WAS) is a longitudinal survey that aims to address gaps identified in data about the economic well-being of households. It gathers information on financial and physical assets and liabilities, long term savings and investments, the distribution of wealth among households or individuals and other factors that affect financial planning.

Figure 10: Total household wealth (1), 2008/10

Great Britain

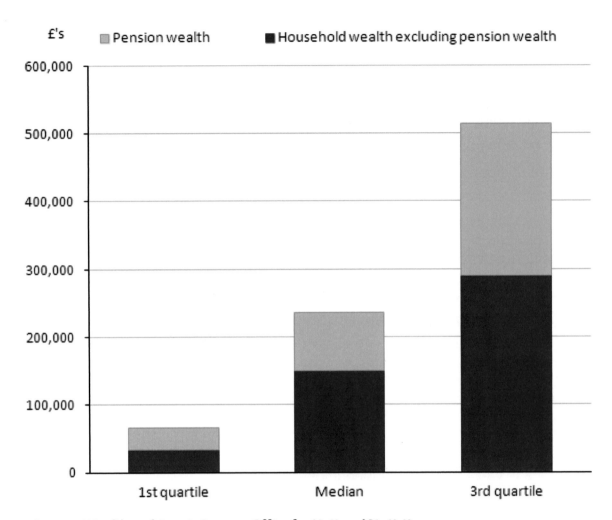

Source: Wealth and Assets Survey, Office for National Statistics

Notes:
1.   Excludes assets held in Trusts (except Child Trust Funds) and any business assets held by households.

In 2008/10 the WAS estimated the median household wealth for Great Britain, including pension wealth, to be £235,500 while the median household wealth, excluding pension wealth, to be £149,500 (Figure 10). The median value of household wealth masks considerable variation in wealth for households. For example, in 2008/10 households a quarter of the way from the top of the distribution of all wealth (at the 75th percentile) had about eight times more wealth than those households a quarter of the way up the distribution from the bottom (at the 25th percentile). (ONS, 2012c)

Wealth inequality seems to be much greater than income inequality and therefore may be of greater concern for well-being.

Household wealth: savings ratio

Savings form part of the wealth and assets of individuals and households and can provide a buffer against changes in economic circumstances. The savings ratio shows the percentage of income that households and non-profit organisations serving households (NPISH) save in relation to their available resources.

Figure 11: Household Saving ratio

United Kingdom

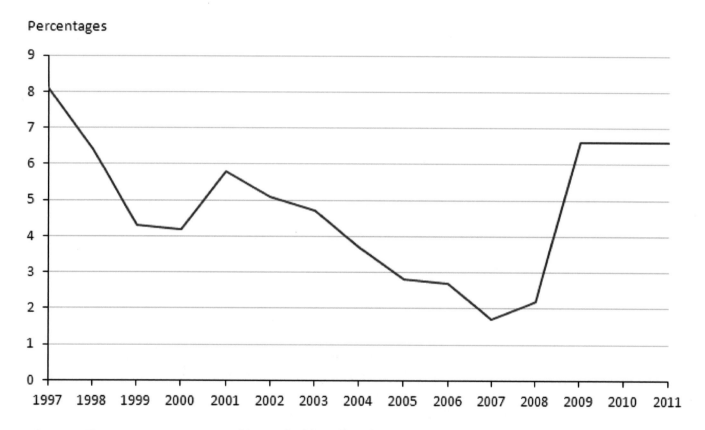

Source: The economic position of households, Office for National Statistics

'The economic position of households' published by ONS in 2012 shows the changes in the household saving ratio over the past few years. Decisions about the amount of savings reflect the economic conditions that households have been facing. Before the financial crisis in 2008 the saving ratio had been on a downwards trend (Figure 11).

This was driven by high levels of household spending and the more widespread use of credit. However, between 2008 and 2009 the saving ratio in the UK increased from 2.2 per cent to 6.6 per cent in 2009. Following this, the saving ratio has stayed stable at 6.6 per cent in 2010 and 2011. These changes suggest that with the financial crisis households are paying down debts, borrowing less and saving a higher proportion of their income despite decreases in income. (ONS, 2012d).

For further information see 'the economic position of households'.

Household debt

According to Credit Action[1] an estimate for the average household debt in June 2012 in the UK was £7,854 excluding mortgages and £55,448 including mortgages. They also report that average consumer borrowing (including credit cards, motor and retail finance deals, overdrafts and unsecured loans) per UK adult during that month was £4,205. (CA, 2012).

Data from the insolvency service shows the rate of total individual insolvencies in England and Wales (including bankruptcy orders, debt relief orders [DROs] and individual voluntary arrangements [IVAs]) fell to 27.3 per 10,000 adults in 2011 (119,941 new cases).This followed a generally increasing trend from 7.5 per 100,000 adults (30,587 new cases) in 2002 to the peak of 31.1 per 100,000 adults (134,142 new cases) reached in 2009 (some of the increase between 2008 and 2009 was driven by the introduction of DROs from April 2009).

The rise up to 2009 occurred as the number of insolvencies grew faster over this period than the underlying population growth. The fall in the total individual insolvency rate from 2009 through to 2011 is attributable to the reduction in numbers of bankruptcy orders from a rate of 17.3 to 9.5 per 10,000 adults over the same period. The reduction in the number of individual insolvencies has itself been driven by the fall in consumer bankruptcies as opposed to trader bankruptcies. Some of the fall in bankruptcies can also be attributed to DRO's which by contrast, have continued to rise since their introduction in April 2009 while the rate per 10,000 adults has increased each year, to 6.6 in quarter 4[2] 2011 from 5.8 in quarter 4 2010. (IS, 2012).

Insolvency service regional statistics[3] show that from 2008, the North East has seen the highest total individual insolvency rate in England and Wales (35.2 per 10,000 adults in 2011), followed by the South West and the East Midlands (both 30.4 in 2011). The North East also showed the largest increase in the rate between 2000 and the peak in 2009, up by 30.9 per 10,000 adults. London had the lowest insolvency rate (17.5 in 2011). As a whole in 2011, England had an insolvency rate of 26.7 (111,073 new cases) while Wales had an insolvency rate of 28.9 (6,968 new cases).

The Consumer Credit Counselling Service reported that since January 2009 there has been a six-fold increase in the number of people approaching them for advice about payday loan debts. By

December 2011 the charity was counselling close to 1,500 clients a month with this form of high cost credit. Overall in 2011, they helped 17,414 clients with payday loan debts, with more than £22 million outstanding. The total average amount owed in payday loans was £1,267, which is some four and a half times the average size of a loan (around £275). This suggests clients with payday loans are often struggling to keep control of the spiralling costs of this type of credit. (CCCS, 2012)

Respondents to the European Social Survey were asked in 2010 'to what extent they. had to draw on savings or get into debt to cover ordinary living expenses in the last 3 years'. For the UK, 41.3 per cent of respondents aged 15 and over, reported that they didn't have to draw on savings or get into debt at all while 11.6 per cent stated that they had to draw on savings or get into debt a great deal over the last 3 years. (ESS, 2010).

Data from the WAS show that there has been a rise in the proportion of households who have non-mortgage borrowing. Non-mortgage borrowing includes credit and store cards that are not settled each month, overdrafts and all forms of fixed term loans. In 2006/08, 48.2 per cent of households in Great Britain had some form of non-mortgage borrowing; this increased to 49.2 per cent in 2008/10.

There were increases in households with personal loans (formal and informal) and loans from student loan companies. The proportion of households with most other forms of non-mortgage borrowing was more stable or decreased between the two time periods. (ONS, 2012c)

Table 6: Distribution of amounts outstanding for household non-mortgage borrowing: by type of borrowing (1)

Great Britain

£'s

	Mean			Median	
	2006/08	2008/10		2006/08	2008/10
Formal loans	8,600	8,200		4,500	4,600
Informal Loans	3,900	3,900		1,500	1,300
Loans from the Student Loan Company	9,500	9,200		8,000	8,500
Hire purchase	5,200	4,200		2,600	2,400
Credit and charge cards	3,200	3,400		1,500	1,600
Overdrafts	1,100	1,200		500	500
Store cards and charge accounts	500	400		200	200
Mail order	400	600		100	200
Any non-mortgage borrowing (excluding new loans)	7,100	7,300		2,800	3,200
Excluding overdrafts	7,300	7,400		3,100	3,500
Excluding loans from the Student Loans Company	6,600	6,800		2,500	2,900

Source: Wealth and Assets Survey, Office for National Statistics

Table notes:
1. Includes only households with each type of borrowing.

The WAS provides mean and median values for the level of borrowing for households in Great Britain who have non-mortgage borrowing. There was little difference in the overall level of borrowing between 2006/08 and 2008/10, with the mean value of non-mortgage borrowing being £7,100 in 2006/08 and £7,300 in 2008/10, while the median value increased from £2,800 to £3,200 over the same period (Table 6).

The large difference between the mean and median occurs because the mean average was influenced by a small minority of households who owed very large sums. As such, it is particularly appropriate to consider both the mean and median alongside each other when considering the average amounts owed in non-mortgage borrowing, the mean providing the arithmetic average and the median providing a better indication of the typical amounts owed.

Table 6 includes examples of large differences between the mean and median values of non-mortgage borrowing. In 2008/10 the differences between the mean and median values for non-mortgage borrowing of between £1,800 and £3,600 were seen for formal loans, informal loans, hire purchase and credit and charge cards.

For further information see 'Wealth in Great Britain Wave 2'.

In October 2011, 60 per cent of adults aged 18 and over in Great Britain reported in a ComRes survey that they were worried about their current levels of debt, up 21 percentage points on the previous year. In October 2011, 40 per cent reported that they were saving less at the time than they usually did, while 29 per cent were putting off making any big financial decisions. (R3, 2012)

Notes

1. Household debt and consumer borrowing figures provided by Credit Action are calculated using a combination of data from the Bank of England and the ONS. While these were best estimates at the time of publication it should be noted that the numbers they are based on can change afterwards, either due to historical revision or more up-to-date data becoming available and are therefore subject to change.

2. Quarter 4 consists of October to December.

3. Regional data is taken from the insolvency service regional statistics as opposed to their quarterly release which provide headline figures (used in previous paragraph). For data taken from the regional statistical release numbers presented are new cases and are not consistent with the official, headline National Statistics published as they have been extracted from a live database at a different point in time and on a different basis'.

About the ONS Measuring National Well-being Programme

NWB logo 2

This article is published as part of the ONS Measuring National Well-being Programme.

The programme aims to produce accepted and trusted measures of the well-being of the nation - how the UK as a whole is doing. It is about looking at 'GDP and beyond' and includes:

- greater analysis of the national economic accounts, especially to understand household income, expenditure and wealth,
- further accounts linked to the national accounts, including the UK Environmental Accounts and valuing household production and 'human capital',
- quality of life measures, looking at different areas of national well-being such as health, relationships, job satisfaction, economic security, education environmental conditions,
- working with others to include the measurement of the well-being of children and young people as part of national well-being,
- measures of 'subjective well-being' - individuals' assessment of their own well-being,
- headline indicators to summarise national well-being and the progress we are making as a society.

The programme is underpinned by a communication and engagement workstream, providing links with Cabinet Office and policy departments, international developments, the public and other stakeholders. The programme is working closely with Defra on the measurement of 'sustainable development' to provide a complete picture of national well-being, progress and sustainable development.

Find out more on the Measuring National Well-being website pages.

Background notes

1. Details of the policy governing the release of new data are available by visiting www.statisticsauthority.gov.uk/assessment/code-of-practice/index.html or from the Media Relations Office email: media.relations@ons.gsi.gov.uk

Copyright

References

1. BSA, 2010 - British Social Attitudes

2. BPHS, 2009 – British Panel Household Survey

3. CA, 2012 – Debt statistics, Credit Action

4. CAB, 2012 – Citizens Advice Bureau

5. CCCS, 2012 – CCCS statistical yearbook 2011, Consumer Credit Counselling Service

6. CML, 2012 - Council of Mortgage Lenders

7. DECC, 2012 – Fuel poverty statistics, Department of Energy, and Climate Change

8. DWP, 2012 - Family Resources Survey, Department for Work and Pensions

9. DWP, 2012a - Households Below Average Income, Department for Work and Pensions

10. ESS, 2010 – European Social Survey

11. JRF, 2011 - Monitoring poverty and social exclusion 2011, Joseph Rowntree Foundation

12. IS, 2012 – The Insolvency Service

13. Joo, 1998 – Joo. S, Garman.E.T (1998), Personal Financial Wellness May be the Missing Factor in Understanding and Reducing Worker Absenteeism

14. OECD, 2011 – How's Life? Measuring Well-being

15. ONS, 2011 - Findings from the National well-being debate, Office for National Statistics (1.07 Mb Pdf)

16. ONS, 2011a - Living Costs and Food Survey, Family Spending, Office for National Statistics

17. ONS, 2012 - Working and workless households 2012, Office for National Statistics

18. ONS, 2012a - The effects of taxes and benefits on household income 2010/11, Office for National Statistics

19. ONS, 2012b - Opinions Survey, Office for National Statistics

20. ONS, 2012c – Wealth and Assets Survey, Office for National Statistics

21. ONS, 2012d – The Economic position of households, Office for National Statistics

22. R3, 2012 – Personal Debt Snapshot, R3

23. US, 2009 - Understanding Society

Measuring National Well-being - Measuring young people's well-being, 2012

Author Name(s): Angela Potter-Collins:ONS Jen Beaumont:ONS

Abstract

This article is published as part of the Office for National Statistics (ONS) Measuring National Well-being Programme and aims to examine some aspects of well-being for young people aged 16 to 24. The Programme aims to produce accepted and trusted measures of the well-being of the nation - how the United Kingdom as a whole is doing. In addition to the set of experimental domains and measures, a series of articles have been published which aim to explore in some detail the different domains that are considered important for the measurement of National Well-being.

Introduction

The currently proposed 10 Measuring National Well-being domains and the measures within them which are proposed for measuring national well-being are of relevance to young people just as they are to other age groups (these can be seen in the appendix). This article does not cover all these domains for young people but concentrates on specific areas within three domains and, where possible, what young people think and feel about their lives in relation to them. The three domains are 'Where we live', 'What we do' and 'Individual well-being'. More information about these domains and others has been published in articles which can be found on the National Well-being publications page.

As young people aged 16-24 make their transition into adulthood there are many factors that can have a significant impact on their overall well-being. These include:

- That a relatively high proportion of young people remain living in the parental home, although the proportion is not increasing over time
- The evidence that more young people are students now than in the past and a smaller proportion are economically active
- The use of leisure time for sport and cultural activities

This article reports that, on average, young people are more likely than other age groups to be highly satisfied with their lives and the use of their leisure time. They are also more likely to be optimistic about the future.

Further information about other areas of importance to young people can be found in previously published analyses of the domains proposed for Measuring National Well-being. In particular, more detail of levels of educational attainment, access to higher education, and those young people not in education, employment or training can be found in the analysis of 'Education and skills'.

Key points

Where we live: Living with parents

- In the UK an estimated 63 per cent (4.6 million) of all those aged 16-24 were living in the parental home in 2012

- In the UK, in 2012, there were more men than women aged 16-24 living with their parents at 69 per cent and 57 per cent respectively

What we do: Labour market

- There has been a decrease between 2002 and 2012 in the percentage of young people who were active in the labour market: from 54 per cent to 37 per cent for those aged 16 to 17 and from 75 per cent to 72 per cent of those aged 18-24
- The unemployment rate for those aged 16 or 17 has increased from 19 per cent in 2002 to 37per cent in 2012: over the same time period the rate for 18-24 year olds increased from 11 per cent to 20 per cent
- In 2012 a smaller percentage of those in full-time education were also in employment than in 2002 in both the 16-17 and 18-24 age groups

What we do: Leisure time

- Around three quarters of 16-17 year olds and 18-19 year olds (77 per cent and 72 per cent respectively) in Great Britain in 2011/12 reported medium to high levels of satisfaction with the amount of time to do the things they like, compared with just over half (55 per cent) of 20-24 year olds
- There was a reduction in participation in moderate intensity sport by 16-19 year olds in England between 2005/06 and 2011/12:for example, 63 per cent of 16-19 year olds participated in sport once a week in 2011/12 compared with 67 per cent in 2005/06
- In 2012 in England there was a significant increase (6.6 percentage points) in young adults who visited a museum or gallery compared with a year earlier
- Between 2005/06 and 2011/12 in England there was an increase of 3.6 percentage points in the number of 16-24 year olds who had volunteered in the last twelve months

Individual well-being

- In 2012 in the UK, young people aged 16-24 rated their satisfaction with their lives at a higher level than the average for all ages
- Highest ratings for life satisfaction were in the 16-17 and 18-19 age groups with slightly lower ratings for those in their twenties: a similar pattern for the age groups emerges in response to questions about how worthwhile the things in their lives are and how happy they were yesterday

- Young people in the UK in 2012 reported the lowest levels of anxiety for the previous day compared with the average for all other age groups
- In 2012 young people in Great Britain reported that they were very optimistic about the next 12 months: between 80 and 85 per cent reported a medium to high level of optimism

Where we live: Living with parents

Where you live can have a significant impact on your well-being. For young people leaving the parental home, it enables them to practise essential life skills, gain confidence and become independent, all of which mark the transition into adulthood contributing to a sense of worth and well-being. However, the transition to independent living has become more protracted and more diverse than in previous generations. This section looks at some of the contributing socio-economic and health factors of young people who remain in the parental home.

There are many factors that contribute to young people living with a parent or parents such as:

- The need for support from their parents while in education
- The financial security of incurring less debt and having the opportunity to save money
- Support when out of work or before entering the labour market: 34 per cent of those aged 16-24 living with parents in 2011 were economically inactive (not in employment or actively looking for a job)
- Additional help when in work, as young people have lower earnings at around 42 per cent less than the rest of the workforce aged 25 and above
- The availability and affordability of separate housing for those trying to set up home: Shelter reported that there is currently a shortage of affordable housing, and the public sector deficit means that there has been a reduction in funding for new affordable housing (Shelter, 2011)
- Some young people living with parents have dependent children of their own and need support to look after them

Unlike previous generations young people's experiences are very different and they are more subject to 'boomeranging' between leaving home and independence (Kneale et al, 2010 cited Joseph Rowntree, 2010). Recent estimates from the Labour Force Survey (LFS) show that 4.6 million, or 63 per cent of all those aged 16-24 were living in the parental home at the time of the survey in 2012. Figure 1 shows that there was no change in the percentage of the overall 16-24 age band living in the parental home, however, there had been slight increases for those in their twenties between 2004 and 2012. In 2012, there were more young men than young women living in the parental home, at 69 per cent and 57 per cent respectively (ONS, 2012).

Those aged 16 and 17 are most likely to remain living in the parental home which is understandable as many are still studying and need the support of their parents to continue education. More than 90 per cent of both men and women aged 16-17 were living with their parents. A higher percentage of men (82 per cent) than women (72 per cent) lived with parents at the age of 18 and 19, and likewise for the 20-24 year old men (56 per cent) and women (39 per cent).

Figure 1: Young adults aged 16 -24 living with their parents by age, 2004 and 2012 (1,2)

United Kingdom

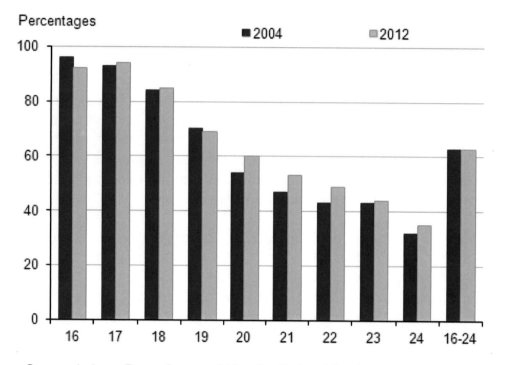

Source: Labour Force Survey, Office for National Statistics

Source: Labour Force Survey - Office for National Statistics

Notes:

1. The Labour Force Survey is a household survey of people in the UK. It includes those resident at private addresses, but does not cover most communal establishments.
2. All data weighted.

The percentage of both men and women living at home declines steadily with age. As individuals get older they are more likely to move away from their parental home as their average earnings increase and there is a higher likelihood of living with a partner: having both a higher income and a partner make moving out of the parental home more likely and more affordable. The difference between the sexes may in part be explained by women being more likely to participate in higher education and therefore need to move away from the parental home, and by women on average forming partnerships at a younger age than men.

There are some differences between the regions and countries of the UK in the percentage of those aged 16-24 who are living in the parental home. In 2012 there was a 16 percentage point difference between the lowest in the Yorkshire and the Humber at 56 per cent and the highest in Northern Ireland at 72 per cent. Between 2004 and 2012 there have been slight decreases in the percentage of those living in the parental home in the northern regions and slight increases for those living further south.

Poor physical or mental health may be a contributing factor to young people continuing to live in the parental home. According to LFS (2012) there were about 900,000 young people aged 16-24 who were living with their parents and reporting a health problem in 2012. Chest and breathing problems were the most common health problem that was reported, with about one in twenty of all those still living at home and nearly a quarter of all those with a health problem reporting this condition. The next most common health problems were learning difficulties and other problems which included some disabilities; both these were reported by about one in forty of those with a health problem.

At a time when young people are making the transition into adulthood, some young people have children of their own and pressures of parenthood may have a significant impact on their well-being. Some young people continue to live in the parental home while others live in their own residence. Some are lone parents. while others have partners.

The total number of lone parents is estimated to be nearly 2 million in 2012. Figure 2 shows that the estimated number of lone parents aged 16-24 has varied between 2004 and 2012, but has always been over 200,000. In 2012, 75 per cent of lone parents in the 16-24 age group have one child and 25 per cent reported to have two children or more. Estimates show that there is slight variation from year to year in the numbers with one child but the pattern remains consistent. The number that have two or more children has remained very similar between 2004 and 2012.

Figure 2: Lone parents aged 16–24 with dependent children, 2004 to 2012 (1,2,3)

United Kingdom

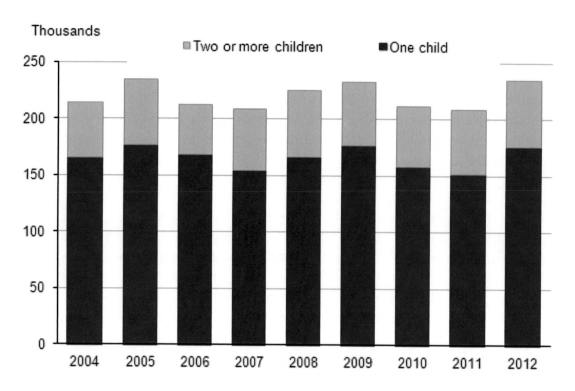

Source: Labour Force Survey, Office for National Statistics

Notes:

1. The LFS is a household survey of people in the UK. It includes those resident at private addresses, but does not cover most communal establishments.
2. Dependent children are those living with their parent(s) and either (a) aged under 16, or (b) aged 16 to 18 in full-time education, excluding children aged 16 to 18 who have a spouse, partner or child living in the household.
3. All data weighted.

What we do: Labour market

Previous research has consistently shown that unemployment has a negative effect on subjective well-being (ONS, 2012a).

Up to the age of 16 individuals are required to be in full-time education. After this age some stay in education while others may be active in the labour market. Recent data from the Labour Force Survey (May-July 2012) shows about 37 per cent of those aged 16 or 17 and 72 per cent of those aged 18-24 were economically active (that is, in employment or actively looking for a job). This is a decrease when compared with ten years earlier (May-July 2002) when the rates were 54 and 75 per cent respectively (ONS 2012).

For all age groups there have been increases in the unemployment rate since 2008. In 2002, the rate for those aged 16-17 was 4.9 times that for those aged 25-64; by 2007 it had risen to 7.8 times and by 2012 it had decreased to 5.7 times as much. Comparing the rates for those aged 18-24, in 2002 the unemployment was 2.7 times that for those aged 25-64, by 2007 it had risen to 3.4 times and by 2012 the rate had decreased to 3.3 times as much (Figure 3).

Figure 3: Unemployment rates (1) for selected age groups, 2002 to 2012 (2)

United Kingdom

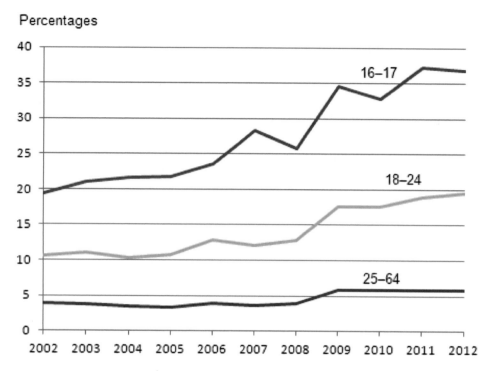

Source: Labour Force Survey, Office for National Statistics

Notes:

1.   The unemployment rate is calculated as the percentage of those who are economically active (that is employed) in the relevant age group.
2.   May to July each year, Seasonally adjusted.

There are also differences between the rates of employment between age groups. There was a considerable reduction in the percentage of those aged 16 or 17 who were in employment from over 43 per cent in 2002, to about 24 per cent in 2012. Over the same period the percentage of those aged 16 or 17 who were unemployed (that is those who were economically active and also seeking employment) had nearly doubled from about 19 per cent to 37 per cent. For those aged 18 to 24 the change in the employment rate was less marked: from about 67 per cent in 2002 to about 58 per cent in 2012. The unemployment rate had increased over this time period from nearly 11 per cent to just less than 20 per cent of the economically active (Table 1).

Many of those who either had or were looking for a job were also in full-time education and, therefore, would be in or seeking part-time employment. Between 2002 and 2012 LFS estimates showed there had been an increase in the proportion of those who were in full-time education: from 73 per cent in 2002, to 83 per cent in 2012 for those aged 16- 17 and from 26 per cent in 2002 to 31 per cent in 2012 for those aged 18-24.

There is a difference between these age groups in the rates of employment and unemployment for those who were in full-time education and those who were not. Those in full-time education in both younger age groups were more likely to be employed in 2002 than in 2012, and less likely to be unemployed in 2002 than in 2012. Employment rates for those in full-time education were 38 per cent of those aged 16 or 17 in 2002, compared with 21 per cent in 2012 and 41per cent of those aged 18-24 in 2002 compared with 35 per cent in 2012 . Unemployment rates for those in full-time education were 14 per cent of those aged 16 or 17 in 2002 compared with 35 per cent in 2012 and 11 per cent of those aged 18-24 in 2002 compared with 20 per cent in 2012.

Those not in full-time education in both younger age groups were more likely to be employed in 2002 than in 2012 and less likely to be unemployed in 2002 than in 2012. Unemployment rates for those not in full-time education were 57per cent of those aged 16 or 17 in 2002 compared with 36 per cent in 2012 and 77 per cent of those aged 18-24 in 2002 compared with 68 per cent in 2012 . Unemployment rates for those not in full-time education were 27 per cent of those aged 16 or 17 in 2002 compared with 40 per cent in 2012 and 11per cent of those aged 18-24 in 2002 compared with 19 per cent in 2012.

Table 1: Employment and Unemployment rates for those aged 16–24 by education status

United Kingdom

Percentages

	In full-time education (FTE)		Not in full-time education (FTE)[1]		All	
	16–17	18–24	16–17	18–24	16–17	18–24
Employed[2] 2002	38.3	40.8	57.4	76.6	43.4	67.3
Employed[2] 2012	21.0	34.6	36.3	68.3	23.6	57.7
Unemployed[2] 2002	14.2	10.5	27.3	10.6	19.4	10.6
Unemployed[2] 2012	35.4	20.3	40.3	19.4	36.8	19.6
Economically inactive 2002	55.3	54.4	21.0	14.4	46.1	24.8
Economically inactive 2012	67.4	56.5	39.3	15.3	62.7	28.2

Source: Labour Force Survey, Office for National Statistics

Table notes:

1. May to July each year seasonally adjusted.
2. People in full–time education are employed if they have a part-time job or unemployed if they are looking for part-time.

When young people who were economically inactive were asked why they were not looking for a job, nearly eight in ten (78 per cent) said it was because they were a student. This proportion varied by age group with nearly 95 per cent of the economically inactive aged 16 or 17, nearly 86 per cent of those aged 18 or 19 and about 61 per cent of those aged 20-24 giving their reason as being a student (Table 2).

The next most frequent response was that individuals were not looking for a job because they were looking after their family or home. Overall about 12 per cent of the economically inactive aged 16-24 gave this as the reason for not seeking work, with less than one per cent of those aged 16 or 17, about 5 per cent of those aged 18 or 19 and 24 per cent of those aged 20-24. The third and fourth most common reasons were concerned with individuals' sickness or disability. These also became increasingly more common as age increased.

Table 2: Reasons for not looking for a job by age 16–24 (1,2)

United Kingdom

Percentages

	Student	Looking after family or home	Long–term sick or disabled	Temporarily sick or injured	Any other reason
16–17	94.6	0.9	1.2	0.3	3.1
18–19	85.6	5.3	3.3	1.1	4.7
20–24	60.6	24.2	7.6	1.4	6.2
Total aged 16–24	78.3	11.6	4.4	1.0	4.7

Source: Labour Force Survey (LFS) January– December 2011 Office for National Statistics

Table notes:

1. The LFS is a household survey of people in the UK. It includes those resident at private addresses, but does not cover most communal establishments.
2. Figures may not add up to 100 per cent due to rounding.

For more information about the labour market in this age group see:

Young people in work, 2012

Graduates in the Labour Market, 2012

What we do: Leisure Time

During the National Debate, leisure time was highlighted as an important factor for individual's wellbeing. Leisure time (or free time) is considered as a period of time spent doing non-compulsory activities, when people are able to do the things they like according to their preferences and lifestyles. The extent to which young people engage in leisure activities is very important, recent discussions (ONS yet to be published) with young people revealed that they saw leisure time as being part of their identity. They said that:
'what we do with our time helps to define us'.

Having leisure time is crucial as young people make the transition into adulthood. It is vital for their personal and social development, helps in achieving a balanced and healthy lifestyle and their overall well-being. Studies on participation in leisure activities have shown improvements in self esteem and life satisfaction which help in reducing depression and anxiety and enhance a person's sense of well-being (Haworth, 2010). This is important as young people mentioned that not having enough leisure time:

'*could make you feel stressed and down'*.

Young people who are satisfied with their leisure time are more likely to be well-rounded and content (NZ, 2006).

Satisfaction with the amount of leisure time varies with age. In the opinions survey in Great Britain when respondents were asked if they were satisfied with the amount of time they had to do the things that they like doing a higher proportion of younger and older people reported high levels of satisfaction (ONS 2012b) (Figure 4).

Figure 4: Satisfaction with time to do things by age band 2012 (1,2,3,4)

Great Britain

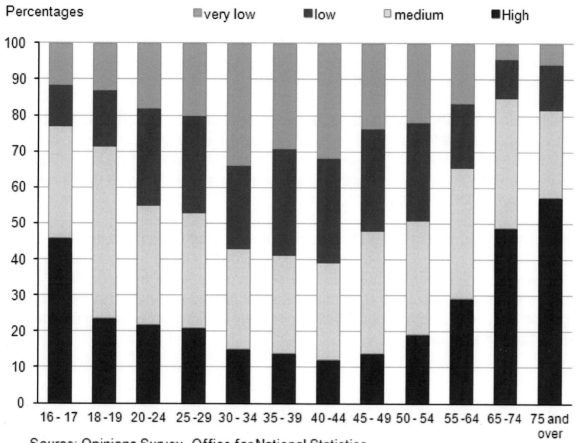

Percentages   ▦very low   ■low   ▢ medium   ■High

Source: Opinions Survey, Office for National Statistics

Notes:

1. Respondents were asked 'if they were satisfied with the amount of time to do the things that they like doing' and responded on a scale where nought is 'not at all' and 10 is 'completely'.
2. Data collected in October 2011, February and June 2012. February 2012 data collected also used show cards which could have a slight impact on the data.
3. All data weighted.
4. Non-respondents not included.

More than three quarters (77 per cent) of those aged 16 or 17 and nearly three quarters (72 per cent) of 18-19 year olds reported medium or high levels of satisfaction with the amount of time to do the things that they like doing (rating their satisfaction at a level of 7-10 on a scale of 0-10 where 0 was not at all and 10 was completely). The over 65's were the only age group to report higher levels of satisfaction. There was a decrease in reported levels of satisfaction with the amount of time to do the things they like doing for 20-24 year olds with just over half (55 per cent) reporting medium to high levels of satisfaction.

Participation in sport and cultural activities has been shown to be positively associated with better well-being. The Taking Part Survey in England by the Department for Culture, Media and Sport (DCMS) examined engagement in sport and cultural activities.

In the run-up to the Olympic and Paralympic Games (between April 2011 to March 2012), estimates of overall participation in sport and active recreation for 16-24 year olds showed that there had been no change since 2005/06. Participation in moderate intensity sport (MIS) was analysed at different levels of frequency: one session in the last four weeks, one session in the last week and three or more sessions in the last week (DCMS, 2012).

However, further analysis showed that in 2010/11 there has been a drop in percentage of 16-19 year olds participating at each of the reported frequencies since 2005/06 but there has been an increase in participation for 20-24 year olds in one or three or more sessions per week between 2005/06 and 2011/12. A new youth sport strategy 'creating a sporting habit for life' was launched in January 2012 aimed at promoting sport for young people and DCMS is currently working on adapting measures to be able to consistently track this group.

Table 3: Participation in sport by age 16–24, 2005/06 and 2011/12

England

Percentages

	2005/06	2011/12
1x30 moderate intensity sport per week		
16-19 year old	62	55.4
20-24 year old	55.3	56.3
3 x 30 moderate intensity sport per week		
16-19 year old	39.2	36.6
20-24 year old	31.3	34
Once in the last 4 weeks		
16-19 year old	67	62.5
20-24 year old	59.7	56.9

Source: Taking Part Survey (2011/12 quarter 4), Department for Culture, Media and Sport

Results from the same survey showed that there had been a significant increase in the number of young adults who had visited a museum or gallery in the last year at 44 per cent in 2011/12, an increase of 7 per cent since 2010/11. It was also reported that there has been major investment in museums via the Arts Council's Renaissance programme in an attempt to increase visitors. Free entry is also an incentive for young people (ACRP).

In the National Debate (1.07 Mb Pdf) (1.07 Mb Pdf), when people were asked 'what things in life mattered most to them', personal and cultural activities that included volunteering came high on the list, above income and wealth and the effects of crime. Volunteering gives young people the opportunity to make a difference in the community, to widen their social skills and improve their job prospects (ONS 2011). An evaluation of independent charity 'v' found that:

'volunteering opportunities helped young people to develop 'soft' skills linked to well-being, such as confidence and self-esteem, raised aspirations, enhanced social skills and networks, amongst others' (BLF UK)

According to the Taking Part Survey the percentage of young people aged 16-24 who had volunteered in the last 12 months had increased by 3.6 percentage points between 2005/06 and 2011/12. Interestingly, a higher percentage of young people were volunteering compared with any other age group in both 2010/11 and 2011/12, overtaking the percentage of 65-74 year olds who had previously had the highest percentage of volunteers (DCMS 2012).

Figure 5: Volunteering in the last 12 months by age, 2005/06 to 2011/12 (1,2)

England

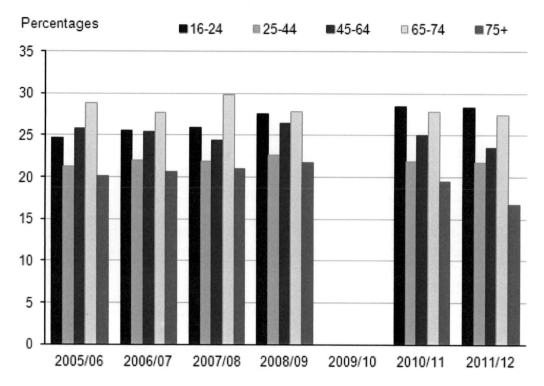

Source: Taking Part Survey Annual Report, Department for Culture, Media and Sport

Notes:
1. No data for 2009/10.
2. Taking Part Survey Annual Report, March 2011 to April 2012.

These findings paint a positive picture of young people's engagement with volunteering. There are many volunteering projects spread across the UK that encourage young people to actively engage and volunteer, these and the recent 'London 2012 Olympic and Paralympic Games Maker Programme' looks set to further inspire a new generation of volunteers.

The Taking Part Survey also asks individuals 'How happy are you?' and results showed that there was a significant association between volunteering, sport participation and cultural engagement and positive responses to this question. This lends support to the views that either such activities can have a positive effect on individual's subjective well-being or that those who report that they are happy are more likely to engage in volunteering, sport and cultural activities (DCMS, 2012)

Leisure time for some young people can mean indulging in risky behaviour such as the use of recreational drugs. The proportion of young people reporting the use of drugs has decreased considerably over the last 15 years. Almost half of young people in 1996 (49 per cent) admitted to using drugs during their lifetime. This included using chemicals such as cannabis and anabolic steroids along with the class A drugs and stimulants such as cocaine and ecstasy. Reported use of these drugs by young people decreased by 8.5 percentage points to 40 per cent in 2010/11 (ONS, 2012c).

The proportion of young people reporting the use of drugs in the last year had also decreased from almost a third to a fifth (30 per cent to 20 per cent) between 1996 and 2010/11. Those who reported frequently taking drugs over the last year decreased by 4 percentage points (from 12 to 7 per cent) between 2002/03 (the first year that this was collected) to 2009/10.

Individual Well-being

Individual well-being includes individual's feelings of satisfaction with life, whether they feel their life is worthwhile and their positive and negative emotions on the previous day. All of these things matter a great deal to young people, and in recent discussions young people summed up how important well-being was to them. They said that:

'At the end of the day that's all that matters, your own well-being'

'It's your life'

Young people acknowledged that an individual's well-being could vary considerably amongst different groups of people and how young people view their own well-being can also vary. For some in this group it meant 'how you feel about yourself and your image:

'Whether you like yourself as a person".....and your "self image'

'Social status really matters to young people'

'A lot of people only feel about themselves what other people think about them'

Talking about life satisfaction for some, it meant an urge to do better, while for others an aspiration of this kind did not matter. For example:

'I think some people are just satisfied with whatever'

Young people talked a lot about having 'choice' and being able to do what they wanted to do, not in an egotistical way but in a way that perhaps suggested that having a particular job might not necessarily make you happy, for example:

'You might not be happy being a doctor'

'You might want to work in McDonalds'

The recently published 'First Annual Report on Subjective Well-being (2012)' and previous research by ONS reported a U shaped relationship between subjective well-being ratings and age groups with overall higher ratings reported by younger and older people (ONS, 2012a).

The four questions asked, for which responses were made on a scale of 0 to 10 where 0 was 'not at all' and 10 was 'completely', were:

'Overall, how satisfied are you with your life, nowadays?' (life satisfaction)

'Overall, to what extent do you feel the things you do in your life are worthwhile?' (worthwhileness)

'Overall, how happy did you feel yesterday?' (happy yesterday)

'Overall, how anxious did you feel yesterday?' (anxious yesterday)

Analysis of the younger age groups reveals that those aged 16-17 rated their life satisfaction at a higher level (on average) than all other age groups. A higher than above average rating was also recorded for those aged 18-19. Life satisfaction ratings in general dropped from the twenties onwards. A similar pattern is seen for responses to the question about worthwhileness (ONS, 2012d). (Figure 6)

Figure 6: Average (mean) life satisfaction and worthwhile ratings by age, April 2011 to March 2012 (1,2,3)

United Kingdom

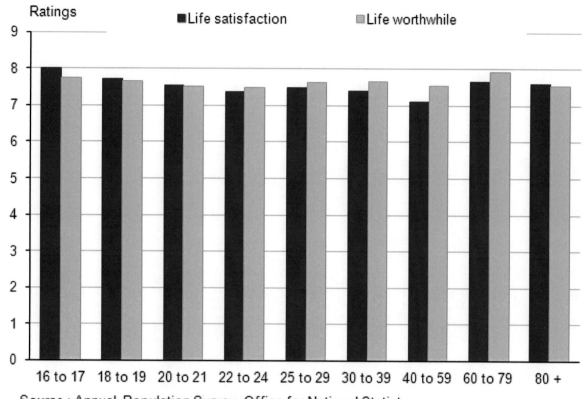

Source : Annual Population Survey, Office for National Statistcs

Notes:
1. Adults aged 16 and over were asked 'Overall, how satisfied are you with your life nowadays?', 'Overall, to what extent do you feel the things you do in your life are worthwhile?', 'Overall, how happy did you feel yesterday?' and 'Overall, how anxious did you feel yesterday?' where nought is 'not at all' and 10 is 'completely'.
2. All data weighted.
3. Non-respondents not included.

The pattern for the younger and older groups is also apparent for responses to the questions about happiness and anxiety yesterday, with a gradual decrease in average ratings as age increases between the 16-17 age group and those aged 22-24. For responses to the question about anxiety yesterday, average ratings for young people in all the age groups from 16-17 to 22-24 were lower than the average for all ages indicating that young people are less likely to report anxiety.

Figure 7: Average (mean) happy and anxious yesterday, ratings by age (1,2,3,4)

United Kingdom

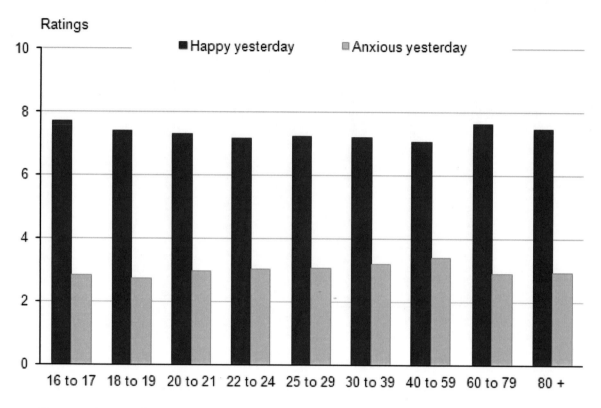

Source: Annual Population Survey, Office for National Statistics

Notes:
1. Adults aged 16 and over were asked 'Overall, how satisfied are you with your life nowadays?', 'Overall, to what extent do you feel the things you do in your life are worthwhile?', 'Overall, how happy did you feel yesterday?' and 'Overall, how anxious did you feel yesterday?' where nought is 'not at all' and 10 is 'completely'.
2. Data from Annual Population Survey, April 2011 to March 2012.
3. All data weighted.
4. Non-respondents not included.

The Opinions Survey asked people, 'how optimistic they felt about the next twelve months', and responses have shown (see Figure 8 below) that young people are very optimistic, with those aged 16-19 reporting the highest levels of optimism: 85 per cent reported medium to high levels of optimism about the next 12 months. On the whole, medium to high levels of optimism decrease with age up to the 50-54 age group. However, even some increases at older age groups in levels of medium to high optimism never reach the levels seen in the youngest group (ONS, 2012b).

Figure 8: Level of medium to high optimism for the next twelve months by age, April 2011 to March 2012 (1,2,3,4)

United Kingdom

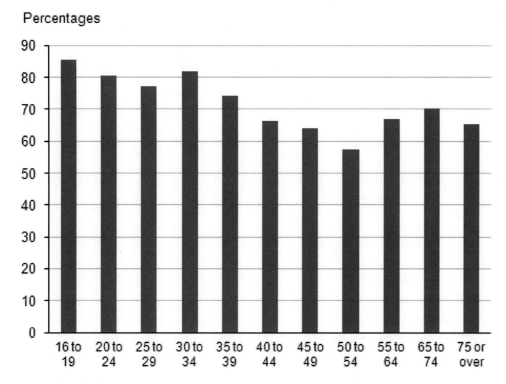

Source: Opinions Survey, Office for National Statistics

Notes:
1. Respondents were asked 'Overall, how optimistic they felt about the next twelve months'? where 0 is 'not at all' and 10 is 'completely satisfied'.
2. Data collected in June and October 2011 and February 2012. February 2012 data collected also used show cards which could have a slight impact on the data.
3. All data weighted.
4. Non-respondents not included.

About the ONS Measuring National Well-being Programme

NWB logo 2

This article is published as part of the ONS Measuring National Well-being Programme.

The programme aims to produce accepted and trusted measures of the well-being of the nation - how the UK as a whole is doing. It is about looking at 'GDP and beyond' and includes:

- greater analysis of the national economic accounts, especially to understand household income, expenditure and wealth
- further accounts linked to the national accounts, including the UK Environmental Accounts and valuing household production and 'human capital'
- quality of life measures, looking at different areas of national well-being such as health, relationships, job satisfaction, economic security, education environmental conditions
- working with others to include the measurement of the well-being of children and young people as part of national well-being
- measures of 'subjective well-being' - individuals' assessment of their own well-being
- headline indicators to summarise national well-being and the progress we are making as a society

The programme is underpinned by a communication and engagement workstream, providing links with Cabinet Office and policy departments, international developments, the public and other stakeholders. The programme is working closely with Defra on the measurement of 'sustainable development' to provide a complete picture of national well-being, progress and sustainable development.

Find out more on the Measuring National Well-being website pages.

Background notes

1. Details of the policy governing the release of new data are available by visiting
    www.statisticsauthority.gov.uk/assessment/code-of-practice/index.html or from the Media
    Relations Office email: media.relations@ons.gsi.gov.uk

Copyright

References

1. Haworth, John T. (2010), LIFE, WORK, LEISURE, AND ENJOYMENT: the role of social institutions.

2. ACRP, Art's Councils Renaissance Programme

3. BLF UK - Well-being: the impact of volunteering, Big Lottery Fund UK

4. DCMS, 2012 - Taking Part Survey, Department for Culture, Media and Sport

5. DCMS, 2012a- Youth Sports Stategy, Department for Culture, Media and Sport

6. Joseph Rowntree, 2010 - Young People Housing Charter Summary, Joseph Rowntree Foundation

7. ONS, 2011 - Findings from the National Well-being debate (1.07 Mb Pdf), Office for National Statisitcs

8. ONS, 2012 - Labour Force Survey, Office for National Statistics

9. ONS, 2012a - First Annual ONS Experimental Subjective Well-being Results, Office for National Statistics

10. ONS, 2012b - Opinions Survey, (October 2011, February and June 2012), Office for National Statistics

11. ONS, 2012c - Crime Survey for England and Wales, Office for National Statistics

12. ONS, 2012d - Annual Population Survey, Office for National Statistics

13. Shelter, 2011 - Shelter Private Rent Watch, Report one: Analysis of local rent levels and affordability.

14. NZ, 2006 - Quality of Life Survey (2006) Youth statistics, a statistical profile of young people in New Zealand. Ministry of Youth Development

Proposed domains and measures for Measuring National Well-being

More information about these proposed domains and measures can be found in Measuring National Well-being summmary of proposed domains and measures. Most of the measures in this table are of direct or indirect relevance to young people. In particular, measures in the three more contextual domains, 'The economy', 'Governance' and 'The natural environment', are applicable to the whole population. More information, some of which is of direct relevance to young people, is already available in the domain publications for 'Our relationships' 'Health', 'Education and skills', Where we live' and 'Personal finance' which can be found on the Measuing National Well-being publications page.

The ONS has produced a table which lists the proposed domains and measures.

Proposed domains and measures for Measuring National Well-being
United Kingdom

Proposed domain and measure	Source
Individual Well-being	
Percentage with medium and high rating of satisfaction with their lives overall	ONS/SWB APS UK
Percentage with medium and high rating of how worthwhile the things they do are	ONS/SWB APS UK
Percentage who rated their happiness yesterday as medium or high	ONS/SWB APS UK
Percentage who rated how anxious they were yesterday as low or very low	ONS/SWB APS UK
Our Relationships	
Average rating of satisfaction with family life out of 10	Eurofound UK
Percentage who were somewhat, mostly or completely satisfied with their social life	BHPS UK
Percentage who said they had one or more people they could really count on in a crisis	BHPS UK
Health	
Healthy life expectancy at birth	ONS UK
Percentage who reported a long term illness and a disability	ONS/APS UK
Percentage who were somewhat, mostly or completely satisfied with their health	BHPS UK
Percentage with some evidence indicating probable psychological disturbance or mental ill health	BHPS UK
What we do	
Unemployment rate	ONS/LFS
Percentage who were somewhat, mostly or completely satisfied with their job	BHPS UK
Percentage who were somewhat, mostly or completely satisfied with their amount of leisure time	BHPS UK
Percentage who were somewhat, mostly or completely satisfied with their leisure time	BHPS UK
Percentage who volunteered in the last 12 months	BHPS UK
Where we live	
Crimes against the person (per 1,000 adults)	ONS/CSEW England and Wales
Percentage who felt very or fairly safe and walking alone after dark	ONS/CSEW England and Wales
Percentage who accessed green spaces at least once a week in England	Natural England; England
Percentage who agreed or agreed strongly that they felt they belonged to their neighbourhood	BHPS UK
Personal finance	
Percentage of individuals living in households with less than 60 per cent of median income after housing costs	FRS, DWP UK ONS/WAS GB
Mean wealth per household, including pension wealth	BHPS UK
Percentage who were somewhat, mostly or completely satisfied with their income of their household	BHPS UK
Percentage who report finding it quite or very difficult to get by financially	BHPS UK
Education and skills	
Human capital – the value of individuals' skills, knowledge and competences in the labour market	ONS UK
Percentage with 5 or more grades A*–C incl English and Maths	DfE; WG;SG; NIDoE
Percentage ok UK residents aged 16 to 64 with no qualifications	ONS/LFS UK
The economy	
Real household income per head	ONS UK
Net National Income of the UK (£ million)	ONS UK
UK Net National debt as a percentage of Gross Domestic Product	ONS UK
Consumer Price Inflation index (2005=100)	ONS UK

this page is intentionally blank

Measuring National Well-being - The Economy

Author Name(s): Gerard Carolan, Valerie Fender, Sue Punt and Damian Whittard, Office for National Statistics

Abstract

This article is published as part of the ONS Measuring National Well-being Programme. The programme aims to produce accepted and trusted measures of the well-being of the nation - how the UK as a whole is doing. This article focuses on one aspect of well-being, the economy, and is part of a series which aims to explore in more detail the different domains that have been considered as important for the measurement of national well-being. The article describes how economic well-being has evolved over the last decade and focuses on the period beginning with the 2008 recession.

Introduction

The economy is the set of activities related to the production and distribution of goods and services. Its performance will impact on all of us financially and therefore affect our personal well-being.

The article does not focus on gross domestic product (GDP), but rather uses GDP as a reference point before explaining, and then analysing, economic indicators that give a better insight into the material well-being of the UK and its households.

In the recent ONS Report on the Consultation on Proposed Domains and Measures (788 Kb Pdf) the domain 'The economy' is described as an important contextual domain for measurement of national well-being. The scope of the domain is given as including measures of economic output and stock. These measures will reflect the household perspective as was recommended in the Stiglitz, Sen, Fitoussi Report published in 2009.

In the ONS report the four headline indicators proposed to measure the economy domain of national well-being were:

- Real net national income per head
- Real household actual income per head
- Inflation rate (as measured by the Consumer Prices Index)
- UK public sector net debt[1] as a percentage of GDP

The article describes how the economic well-being of the UK and the household sectors has developed by focussing on changes over the past decade, and paying particular attention to changes since the start of the recession in 2008.

The recent data generally describe a stagnant economy. After a period of sustained growth during the beginning and middle part of the last decade, since the recession, real national and household incomes have been under pressure, the rate of inflation has been relatively high, national and household wealth have been squeezed, and public sector net debt (PSND) has risen substantially.

Notes

1. PSND is defined as total gross financial liabilities less liquid financial assets, where liquid assets are cash and short term assets which can be realised for cash at short notice and without significant loss. The version of PSND used in this bulletin is the PSND excluding temporary effects of financial interventions.

Key points

- In the second quarter of 2012 net national income per head in real terms was 13.2 per cent below its level in the first quarter of 2008; a sharper fall in economic well-being than the GDP data alone indicate
- In the second quarter of 2012, real household actual income per head was 2.9 per cent below its peak in quarter three 2009
- Household income has been put under pressure from price inflation, for example in September 2011 inflation peaked at 5.2 per cent whereas the annual change in household actual income per head rose by 1.9 per cent in the third quarter of 2011
- At the end of 2011 public sector net debt was in excess of one trillion pounds, the first time on record, equivalent to 65.7 per cent of annual GDP

Economic well-being

'Material living standards are more closely associated with measures of NNI and consumption than with GDP' (Stiglitz, Sen and Fitoussi, 2009).

GDP is the most high profile macroeconomic indicator, and can be considered as either the total of income, expenditure or production within an economy. It can be defined as the value of all the goods and services produced within the economic territory of a country, in other words its entire output, during a given period. Equivalently, it is the income during that period from the production of these goods and services to those directly involved, the workers, their employers, and the self-employed; and to government in the form of taxes on goods and services, for example VAT. GDP is also the total expenditure on goods and services within the economy, by individuals, businesses, and government, including both imports and exports.

GDP is often used for judging how well an economy is doing. A country with a higher figure for GDP is said to have a 'bigger economy'. When GDP is increasing, the economy is said to be growing. The term 'recession' is often defined as two consecutive quarters of declining GDP.

GDP, however, was not designed as a measure of individual or national well-being (although it is sometimes used for these purposes).[1] GDP measures production and not material well-being. Living standards are more closely aligned with net national income (NNI) (the total income available to residents of that country) as GDP can expand at the same time as incomes decrease and vice versa. For example, if the sum of net income paid abroad and the depreciation of capital is greater than the increase in production, the overall effect will be an increase in GDP but a decline in NNI. It was for this reason that NNI was chosen as the first economy headline indicator for measuring economic aspects of National Well-being.

With this in mind, it is worth outlining the connection between GDP and gross national income (GNI), and then the difference between GNI and NNI. Loosely speaking, GNI includes the income from UK production (in other words, the share of GDP) that can be claimed by organisations and individuals resident in the UK plus the income that these residents can claim from the GDP of other countries. They are part of the UK's income but not generated by production within its national boundaries.

The incomes that stem directly from the productive process are known as primary incomes.[2] Typical examples of primary income that forms part of the UK's GDP but is not a part of its GNI include:

- a non-UK resident receiving wages for seasonal work undertaken in this country
- the profits of a UK based subsidiary that are repatriated to its parent company in another country
- a pensioner resident abroad receiving dividends on shares held in a British business

In measures such as GNI (and for that matter, GDP), the 'gross' refers to the fact capital depreciation - that is to say the day-to-day wear and tear on vehicles, machinery, buildings and other fixed capital used in the productive process - has not been taken into account. A truer estimate of the UK's income for a given period can be made by subtracting the cost of this capital depreciation from GNI to give NNI. Figure 1 graphically represents how GDP is adjusted to take account of depreciation and net income from abroad to derive NNI.

Figure 1: Deriving net national income from gross domestic product

Figure 1: Deriving net national income from gross domestic product

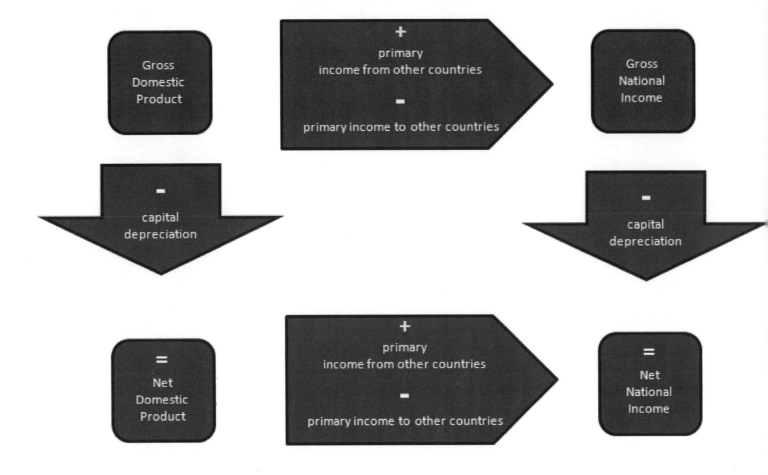

Notes

1. See, for example, Vanoli, 2005 for a discussion of the development of national accounts.

2. More formally, primary incomes are those received in return for involvement in the process of production or the ownership of assets that may be needed for the purposes of production. They also include net income to government from production, which is taxes on production and products such as VAT, less subsides.

National income

Figure 2 shows the annual values of both GDP and NNI per head in the ten years to 2011. To aid comparisons of different years, 2009 prices have been used throughout to remove the effects of inflation.

Figure 2: UK gross domestic product and net national income per head

United Kingdom

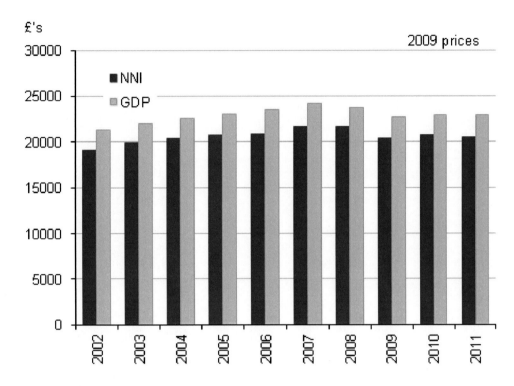

Source: Office for National Statistics

Prior to the recession, both GDP per head and NNI per head grew steadily up until 2007. During the recessionary years of 2008 and 2009, both GDP and NNI per head fell. The fall in NNI per head was less pronounced in 2008, 0.3 per cent compared to a 1.6 per cent fall in GDP per head. In 2009, NNI per head fell by 5.8 per cent, greater than the GDP fall of 4.6 per cent. This suggests that in the initial phase of the recession material living standards fell less sharply than output but then fell more sharply as the recession continued. In the latest two years, both NNI and GDP per head have remained relatively flat.

Over the entire period GDP has been higher than NNI. This difference was driven by capital depreciation – it had varied between 10.5 per cent and 12.5 per cent of GDP in the decade described. The difference also included net primary income flows to and from the rest of the world, but these were relatively small and were, in fact, a net gain to the UK for each of the years. The highest of these was 2.5 per cent of GDP recorded in 2004. This net gain to the UK economy stood at 2.3 per cent in 2008 and explains, at least partially, why NNI per head did not fall as much as GDP per head during this period. Subsequently, however, the net gain from income from abroad decreased year on year and by 2011 it was just 0.2 per cent. In other words, the income of UK residents from overseas activities has grown more slowly than the corresponding income flow in the opposite direction.

In order to get a fuller understanding of how the 2008 recession has affected the economic well-being of the UK, Table 1 details the growth rates for four indicators; GDP, NNI, GDP per head and NNI per head [1] [2].

Table 1: Volume comparison of indicators since the first quarter of 2008

United Kingdom

	Peak to 2009 Q2 trough	2009 Q2 trough to latest	Peak to 2012 Q2
GDP	-6.3%	2.4%	-4.1%
NNI	-11.2%	0.8%	-10.4%
GDP per head	-7.0%	0.0%	-7.0%
NNI per head	-11.9%	-1.5%	-13.2%

Table source: Office for National Statistics

None of the four indicators have returned to the level they experienced prior to the recession, ranging from a fall of 4.1 per cent for GDP to -13.2 per cent for NNI per head.

Both GDP and NNI were at their lowest in the fifth quarter of the recession, the second quarter of 2009, but the fall was considerably sharper for NNI which contracted by 11.2 per cent compared with a fall of 6.3 per cent for GDP. This indicates that the fall in the economic well-being was sharper than the GDP data alone indicate. Given that the UK's population increased steadily throughout the period and is the denominator used in the per head calculation, the falls on a per head basis are even greater – a peak to 2009 Q2 trough fall of 11.9 per cent in NNI, compared to a fall of 7.0 per cent for GDP. However, this should not be taken to mean that living standards and well-being have been reduced by population growth, as both GDP and NNI are likely to have grown faster than they would in the absence of an increase to the population.

The trough to latest growth rates shows how the economy has recovered since the 2009 Q2 trough of the recession. NNI has recovered at a slower rate than GDP. However, after taking in to account population growth, GDP growth has remained flat but NNI per head has fallen further, falling to its lowest point in the most recent quarter.

Notes

1. Quarterly data for NNI are not available at present, and therefore the analysis presented here estimates NNI using the following methodology. Deduct capital depreciation from GNI giving

NNI at current market prices. This is then deflated by the GDP (expenditure) deflator to give real NNI.

2. GNI data for pre-1987 are consistent with Blue book 2010.

Net national income during the recessions

The following analysis concentrates on movements in NNI per head as it is the preferred measure of income in terms of economic well-being. In Figure 3, indices are used to compare NNI per head during the recession that began in the second quarter of 2008, with the two recessions that preceded it; those that began in the first quarter of 1980 and in the third quarter of 1990. For each of the three recessions, the value of NNI per head in the last quarter before the beginning of the downturn has been used as a reference point to index its values for the following seventeen quarters.

Figure 3: net national income per head during three recessions

United Kingdom

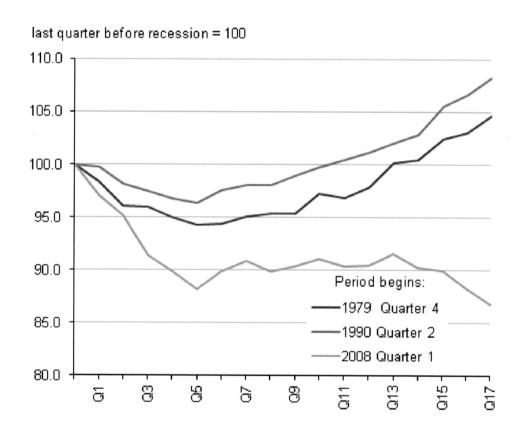

Source: Office for National Statistics

In all three recessions NNI per head declined quarter on quarter for five consecutive periods. The recession that began in 2008 in the wake of the financial crisis has, however, two distinguishing features as regards NNI per head:

- During this recession, the fall in NNI per head was markedly more pronounced. It fell quarter on quarter throughout the recession and, by the second quarter of 2009 (the fifth quarter of the recession), was 11.9 per cent below its pre-recession level. Coincidently, both the other recessions also lasted five quarters and, for both, the fifth quarter saw NNI per head at its lowest for the entire recessionary period; down 5.7 per cent on its pre-recession level in the 1980s and 3.6 per cent in the 1990s
- Immediately following this, there was a short recovery in NNI per head, although the recovery was to a lesser extent than the previous recessions, and was not sustained. The economy returned to recession in the final quarter of 2011, following a period of slow recovery. By the second quarter of 2012 NNI per head was 13.2 per cent below its pre-recession level. In the 1980s, NNI per head had recovered to its pre-recession value three years after the beginning of the recession. The equivalent recovery came earlier in the recession of the 1990s; it took two and a half years

Household income

Having considered the income of the economy as a whole on a per head basis, an obvious consideration in any discussion of individual well-being is the proportion of this income that goes to the household sector. Most householders, however, would not focus on their share of NNI in describing how well off they feel. Their concern is much more likely to be how much cash they have left after deductions such as tax and pension contributions.

'…the re-distribution of economic flows between sectors needs to be taken into account. For example, some of the income of citizens is taken away in the form of taxes: this is money that is not at their disposal. Conversely, households receive payments from governments and this must be added to their income. Households also receive and pay property income, for instance dividends paid out by corporations and mortgage interest paid to banks. When all these monetary flows are taken into account, one ends up with a measure of household disposable income' (Stiglitz, Sen and Fitoussi, 2009).

If two individuals whose disposable incomes provide equal levels of purchasing power are compared in the knowledge that one enjoys free education and healthcare while the other has to pay full market price for these services, the likely conclusion is that they do not have equal living standards. The data discussed in this section are adjusted to include the extra benefit to households of goods and services that are free or subsidised, for example healthcare in the UK, thus allowing better international comparisons of material well-being. This adjusted income is known as real household actual income (RHAI).

Real household actual income during the recessions

Figure 4 uses the same method as Figure 3 to compare RHAI[1] per head during the 1990s recession and the recession that began in 2008. The 1980s recession has not been included in this analysis as no data were available.

Figure 4: Real household actual income per head during two recessions

United Kingdom

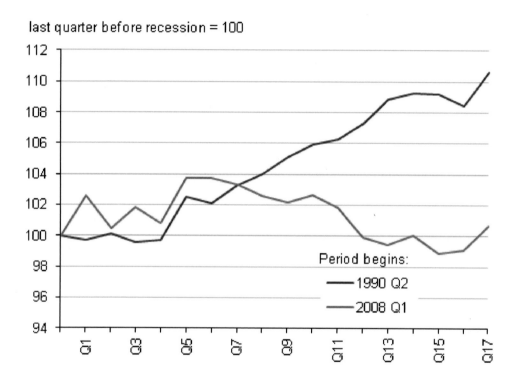

Source: Office for National Statistics

We see differences between the behaviour of RHAI per head. In the early stages of the 1990s recession RHAI per head remained relatively flat. During the more recent recession, although the paths are similar, RHAI held up better and initially experienced a small overall increase. However, following this, the behaviour of income in the two recessions begin to diverge considerably. In the 1990s recession RHAI began a sustained period of growth from Q6. This is contrasted with the 2008 recession which saw a general period of decline from Q6. The decline was mainly driven by relatively high rates of inflation.

Following the onset of the 2008 recession the economy made a stuttering return to growth in the third quarter of 2009. The average household's real actual income for that quarter had increased by £167 pounds per head compared to its pre-recession level. This happened against a backdrop of toughening economic conditions, falling employment and rising unemployment.

A substantial proportion of household income comes from earnings from employment. We would therefore expect any deterioration in this to have a negative impact on income growth. However, employment did not fall, and unemployment did not rise, to the same extent as previous recessions, or to the extent expected given the size of the fall in GDP. This helped to support RHAI per head in the initial stages of the recession. In addition to reducing RHAI per head, unemployment also has a direct, and strongly negative, impact on individual well-being (OECD, 2012). ONS Experimental Subjective Well-being results showed that forty-five per cent of unemployed people rated their life satisfaction as 'low' or 'very low'; over twice the proportion reported by employed people.

Figure 5: UK quarterly unemployment rate

United Kingdom

Source: Office for National Statistics

The International Labour Organisation (ILO) classifies someone who is unemployed as an individual who is without a job and, available to start a job within two weeks and has either looked for a job in the last four weeks or is waiting to start a job that has already been obtained.

Figure 5 shows the quarterly unemployment rate from 1990 to 2012. Prior to the 2008 recession, the unemployment rate moved around a broadly flat trend, never below 4.7 per cent and never above 5.5 per cent. It climbed steeply throughout the recession, reaching 7.9 per cent as the economy returned to growth in the third quarter of 2009. There followed another broadly flat period. By the fourth quarter of 2011 as the economy returned to recession, the rate stood at 8.4 per cent.

The subdued extent of the rise in unemployment relative to the fall in output (and income) has been the focus of much discussion. There are a number of aspects that can help explain this conundrum:

- A gradual movement from full-time to part-time employment
- Firms cutting the hours worked by employees rather than making people unemployed
- Evidence that cash flow of many businesses remained stronger than in previous recessions, thus making it easier to retain staff
- The number of self employed has experienced an upward trend since the last quarter of 2008. The flat unemployment trend may have been be partly driven by an increased tendency of those who are made redundant to become self-employed

However, this does not completely account for the growth in real household actual income per head during the recession that began in the second quarter of 2008. Additionally, there were two other factors acting against any fall in income that would be expected from the lower levels of employment associated with the recession:

- Interest rates reached historic lows and therefore many people's mortgage interest payments fell. This meant many householders' disposable incomes rose as a result of lower mortgage payments
- More significantly, as employment fell and unemployment rose, people paid less in the way of taxes and claimed more in the way of benefits. The result was that real household actual incomes were supported by rising social security benefits and reduced taxes

The 1990s recession saw a remarkably small fall in RHAI per head. It fell marginally over the first four quarters of the recession before starting a period of general growth during the fifth and final quarter.

It is after this point, as the economy began to recover, that the two recessions really begin to differ. After the 2008 recession as the economy emerged from the first period of contraction, real household actual income began to fall. In the fourth quarter of 2011, real household actual income per head was slightly lower (about £50 in 2009 prices) than it had been in the first quarter of 2008.

This fall in household actual income per head was primarily due to prices going up at an increasing rate over most of the period. Figure 6 shows that, by 2011, consumer price inflation was markedly stronger than it had been in recent years. Inflation hit a peak of 5.2 per cent in September of that year whereas the annual change in household actual income per head rose by 1.9 per cent in the third quarter of 2011. This peak equalled the September 2008 inflation rate and was otherwise the highest for almost twenty years. During 2011 high inflation was driven by rises in food prices, utility bills and fuel prices.

Figure 6: Rate of inflation

United Kingdom

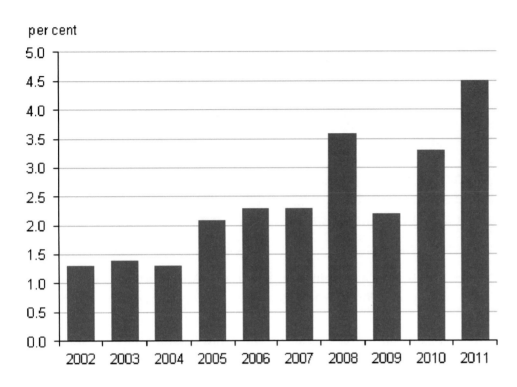

Source: Office for National Statistics

The increase in prices eroded the growth of household incomes, meaning real household actual incomes fell. This means that prices were rising at a faster rate than people's incomes, and therefore over time, people have found their income purchased a lower quantity of goods and services. Furthermore, the growth of household actual incomes (ie. without taking account of inflation) also weakened over the period. This was because the impact of the factors initially providing a boost to income (lower mortgage interest payments and taxes and higher benefits) had worn off – i.e. these factors become part of a new baseline. However, in the latest periods, the first two quarters of 2012, real household actual income has recovered somewhat to return to its pre-recession level, although it remains 2.9 per cent below its peak in the third quarter of 2009.

The analysis on household actual income shows that average real income levels have been under pressure, however averages do not tell the whole story. In terms of economic well-being it is useful to look at median measures, as these provide a better measure of what is happening to the "typical" individual or household, and to examine the effect on different parts of the income distribution. This analysis is out of scope of this economy domain article as it has previously been covered in detail in the Measuring National Well-being – Personal Finance 2012 domain article published by ONS on 20 September 2012.

Notes

1. Real household actual income = Real household actual gross disposable income.

European Union comparisons of household income

Although real household actual incomes per head have generally fallen since 2009, it is useful to compare the position of the UK internationally. Figure 7 compares household actual income per head in the different Member States of the European Union.

Figure 7: 2010 EU household actual income per head

European Union

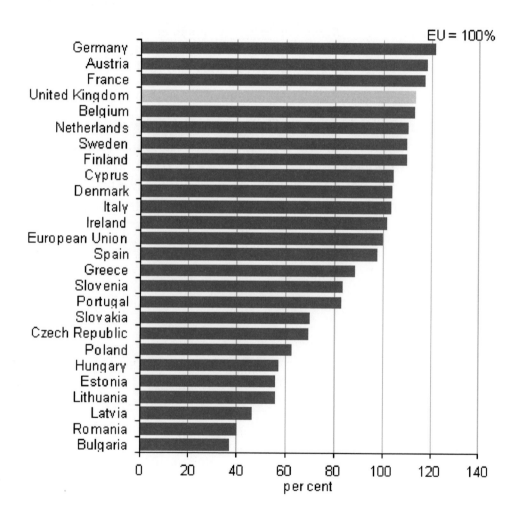

Source: Eurostat

Notes:
1. This analysis excludes Luxembourg and Malta due to data availability.
2. Purchasing Power Parities.

In 2010 the UK was ranked fourth amongst the EU Member States listed, up from fifth place in 2009 after leapfrogging Belgium. The UK's actual income per head was 13.2 per cent above the EU average.

German residents came first enjoying adjusted disposable income that is 21.9 per cent above the average. Three countries – Bulgaria, Romania and Latvia - were below 50 per cent of the EU average at 37.1 per cent, 40.3 per cent and 46.5 per cent respectively.

Household saving ratio

Households have a choice as to what they do with their disposable income - they can either spend it on current consumption or save it. The household saving ratio shows the proportion of disposable income households save. This is of interest to economists, not least because it may give an indication of household sentiment. Generally speaking, people save more when they are worried about their future prosperity and may spend more and save less when they are feeling optimistic about the future.

Figure 8 shows the UK household saving ratio from 1987 to 2011. It reached a peak of 11.0 per cent in 1992, a year when unemployment rose above ten per cent for the first time in five years. The trend in the saving ratio was broadly downward until a low of 1.7 per cent was reached in 2007. It remained low the following year but shot up to 6.6 per cent in 2009 as households cut their spending in response to the deteriorating economic environment. It maintained this level for the following year before dropping to 6.0 per cent in 2011.

Figure 8: Household saving ratio

United Kingdom

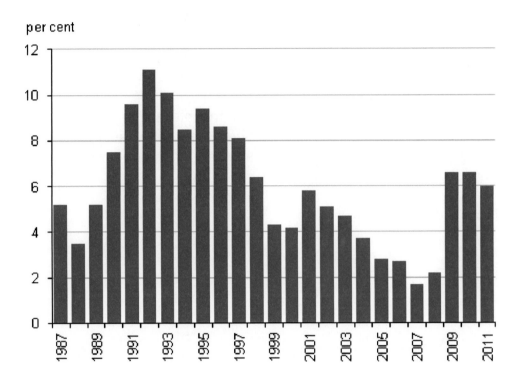

Source: Office for National Statistics

In 2011, the household saving ratio remained relatively high against a background of the first annual fall in real household income since 1981. This, coupled with low returns on deposits, may be indicative of increased levels of financial insecurity.

Inflation

As part of the consultation on the proposed domains and measures, the inflation rate, as measured by CPI, was identified as an important indicator of economic well-being. This article has already highlighted the impact of high inflation on household income. However, the rate of inflation also has a considerable impact on net wealth, and hence the distribution of economic well-being.

A high rate of inflation reduces the real value of wealth held in cash terms - the higher the rate of inflation the greater the reduction in the real value of wealth held in cash. In addition, if inflation is above the interest rate, the value of wealth in the form of savings also falls in real terms. The opposite is true for debtors as this scenario results in a fall of the real value of debt. Therefore the rate of inflation relative to the rate of interest has an important impact on the distributional effects of economic well-being; a relatively high inflation rate redistributes net wealth from savers to debtors and vice versa.

This redistribution can have implications between generational groups. For example older people are more likely to be net savers having paid off a mortgage and saved for their pension, whereas the younger generation are more likely to be debtors as they take out mortgages and unsecured loans to fund other living expenses. Therefore, a relatively high inflation rate can redistribute wealth from the older to the younger generation. Although this scenario may apply to some it is certainly not true for all. For example some older people's savings will deliver a fixed income indexed to a price index and therefore their real income remains unaltered.

Figure 9 compares the UK's inflation rate, as measured by the CPI, to the interest being paid on individual savings accounts (ISAs) and time deposits (savings accounts where the saver does not have instant access). It shows that since August 2008 inflation has exceeded interest rates resulting in a redistribution of net wealth from savers to debtors.

Figure 9: Inflation and interest rates paid on savings

United Kingdom

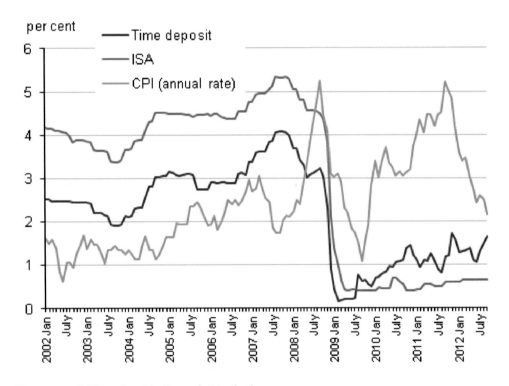

Source: Office for National Statistics

In general, up until May 2008 the CPI remained between one and three per cent, and the interest paid on savings higher. However, through 2008 inflation continued to climb month on month until reaching a peak of 5.2 per cent in September 2008. Meanwhile, the Bank of England cut the official bank rate (base rate) to an unprecedented low of 0.5 per cent, resulting in interest rates paid on savings falling.

By mid to late 2008, the average saver's deposit was earning a rate of interest below that of inflation. This real terms loss to savers was at its most pronounced in September 2011 when the CPI reached its joint peak of 5.2 per cent.

It should be noted that the historically low base rate set by the Bank of England coupled with higher inflation has been beneficial to some debtors. A prime example is those who took out a tracker mortgage, where the interest paid is directly linked to the record low 0.5 per cent base rate.

Wealth

Household income and consumption tell us much about a country's standard of living, but a more complete picture can be afforded by also considering wealth:

Income flows are an important gauge for the standard of living, but in the end it is consumption and consumption possibilities over time that matter. The time dimension brings in wealth. A low income household with above-average wealth is better off than a low-income household without wealth. The existence of wealth is also one reason why income and consumption are not necessarily equal: for a given income, consumption can be raised by running down assets or by increasing debt, and consumption can be reduced by saving and adding to assets. For this reason, wealth is an important indicator of the sustainability of actual consumption.' (Stiglitz, Sen and Fitoussi, 2009).

Figure 10 details the net worth (wealth) of the UK and shows the contribution of the household, corporate and government sectors to the overall wealth of the nation - price effects have not been removed.

Figure 10: Net worth of the UK by sector

United Kingdom

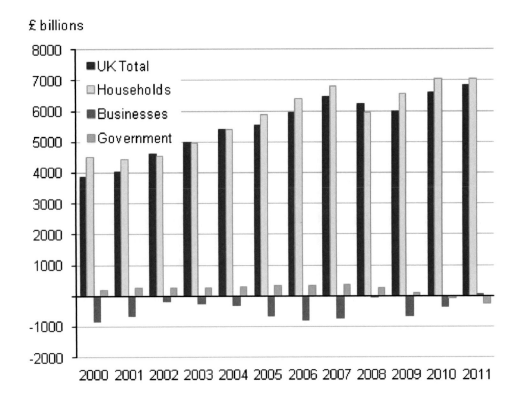

Source: Office for National Statistics

The estimates show that net worth of the UK, in current prices, grew consistently from 2000 to 2007. During the recessionary years of 2008 and 2009, the wealth of the nation declined. In 2010, growth in current prices was 10.7 per cent, this growth has slowed in 2011 to just 3.3 per cent.

Figure 10 reveals that household wealth exceeds that of the UK as a whole in most years. This is explained by the fact that the average household's assets – mainly the houses themselves – exceed its liabilities, whereas other sectors may owe more than the total worth of their assets.

Household net wealth

Figure 11 shows household net worth since the year 2000[1], all figures are in current prices (i.e. not adjusted for price effects). Other non-financial assets are made up of physical assets; such as vehicles (including cars). Net financial assets include stocks, shares and savings taking account of any debt attributed to households.

Figure 11: Household net wealth

United Kingdom

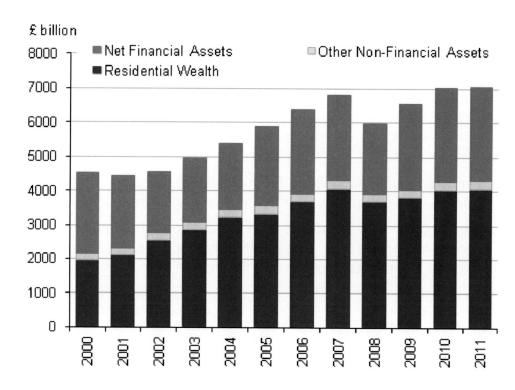

£ billion

Legend: ■ Net Financial Assets | □ Other Non-Financial Assets | ■ Residential Wealth

Source: Office for National Statistics

After a flat start to the decade, there was an increase in household wealth from 2003 to 2007, driven mainly by rising house prices. However, the onset of the recession in 2008 saw the net worth of households drop 12.4 per cent, leaving a final worth of just under £6 trillion, driven by falls in both residential wealth and other assets. During this period house prices fell and there was a reduction in the number of new mortgages and an increase in repossessions as the financial crisis deepened. Data from the Department for Communities and Local Government show that the total number of mortgages peaked in 2007 and has fallen since, and repossessions reached a high in 2009. As the constraints on mortgage lending eased and repossessions slowed, the residential wealth of households began to grow again in 2009 and 2010. However, the annual House Price Index shows house prices in 2011 were 0.9 per cent lower than in 2010. In line with this fall in house prices, growth in the total value of residential wealth also slowed in 2011, and as a result the level remains around its pre-recession peak.

In terms of financial assets, the value of shares and other equities held by the household sector fell sharply in 2008. This fall in the value of assets is the first reduction since 2002 following the burst of the dot com bubble at the start of the century. The fall in 2008 was caused partly by a sell off of assets but mainly by falling prices, as stock exchanges around the world reacted to the ongoing financial crisis. The equity households had tied up in life assurance schemes and pension funds also fell sharply in 2008, again as a result of falling markets. By the end of the year the value of the household sector's net financial assets had fallen almost half a trillion pounds - a drop of 17.5 per cent. However these returned to levels broadly similar to their 2007 levels in 2009.

Notes

1. The household wealth data used in this section are consistent with data published in Blue Book 2012.

Economic sustainability

Debt and investment are important indicators of sustainability. Debt effectively transfers the burden of paying for current consumption from the present to the future. Personal debt remains the liability of the individual (at least until their death); however, PSND[1], is government debt and can be transferred from one generation of tax payers to the next. Investment increases future economic well-being as the assets created are used to generate income over its lifetime.

Notes

1. The public sector consists of the government sector and other units under public control, for example, Royal Mail is included within the public sector.

UK public sector net debt

Whereas net worth is calculated by subtracting total liabilities from total assets, PSND is calculated by subtracting the sector's liquid assets from its liabilities. Liquid assets consist of deposits and short term securities which are easily converted into cash[1].

Figure 12 shows net public sector debt as a percentage of GDP, a comparison that is often used as it gives an indication of the sustainability of the debt. There is no precise ratio as to what level of debt is sustainable, this depends on a variety of country specific risks. Growth in GDP, however, is seen as a critical element in reducing the risks. Ultimately debt sustainability is decided by the financial markets. Greece is a recent example of where the financial markets created a vicious circle of increasing government debt refinancing costs and therefore furthered their debt sustainability risk.

Figure 12: Public sector net debt as a percentage of gross domestic product

United Kingdom

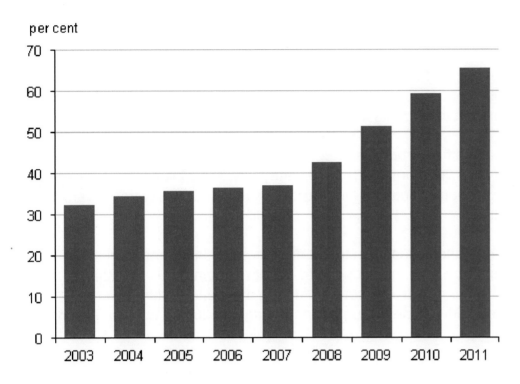

Source: Office for National Statistics

Notes:
1. Excluding the temporary effects of financial interventions

Up until 2007, the year the financial crisis began, the UK debt to GDP ratio grew but at a decelerating rate. From 2008, as the recession took hold and the public sector finances began to deteriorate, the ratio grew and reached 42.8 per cent of GDP that year. This was an increase from 37 per cent from the previous year. By 2009, PSND rose to over half the value of annual GDP. By 2011, it was close to two thirds of the annual value of GDP, and exceeded one trillion pounds for the first time in history, equivalent to 65.7 per cent of GDP.

Notes

1. More precisely, net public sector debt is defined as total gross financial liabilities less liquid financial assets, where liquid assets are cash and short term assets which can be realised for cash at short notice and without significant loss. These liquid assets mainly comprise foreign exchange reserves and bank deposits. This is further elaborated on in The Public Sector Balance Sheet – 2009 (239.6 Kb Pdf) (Jim O'Donoghue).

Gross fixed capital formation

Figure 13 illustrates gross fixed capital formation as a percentage of GDP. Gross fixed capital formation consists of acquisitions less disposal of fixed assets. Fixed assets are tangible or intangible produced assets that can be used repeatedly in the productive process.

Between 2000 and 2007, the proportion of fixed assets to GDP was broadly flat, varying between 16.4 and 17.7 per cent. From 2007 to 2011 fixed assets as a percentage of GDP fell, dropping by 3.5 percentage points to 14.2 per cent in 2011, its lowest point for the entire period.

Throughout this period, building and other structures was the largest component, increasing as a percentage of GDP every year from 2000 until 2007, when they reached 11.4 per cent. As the financial crisis took hold in 2008, property prices fell and buildings and other structures shrank as a percentage of GDP. In 2011 it fell to 8.7 per cent.

The second largest component throughout was investment in other machinery and equipment. In 2000 it accounted for 6.4 per cent of GDP, this reduced to 3.7 per cent in 2011. Investment in transport equipment fell from 1.4 per cent to 0.6 per cent during the same period, whereas investment in intangibles remained fairly stable throughout the period; in 2011 it was equivalent to 1.1 per cent of GDP.

Figure 13: Gross fixed capital formation as a percentage of gross domestic product

United Kingdom

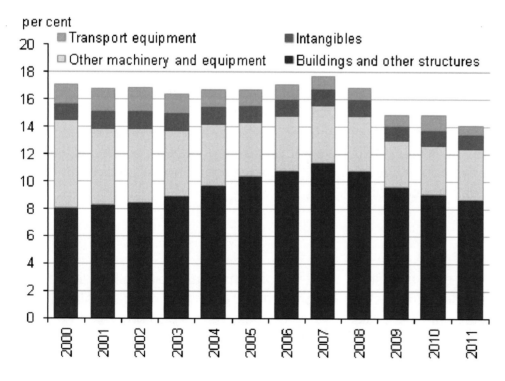

Source: Office for National Statistics

Research and development

In terms of sustainability, the level of expenditure in research and development (R&D) influences the future economic well-being of a country. R&D spending is similar to ordinary investment in that expenditure is undertaken today to secure returns in the future. The main difference from ordinary investment is that the investment is a driver of innovation in the economy, which has a direct bearing on the rate of productivity growth and hence is a critical element in generating a dynamic and competitive economy.

Figure 14 shows the levels of investment in R&D as a percentage of GDP. From 2001 to 2004, R&D spend as a percentage of GDP fell as GDP growth outstripped growth in spending on R&D; spending on R&D in this period grew in real terms in every year except 2004 when spending was virtually unchanged from the previous year.

In 2004, the R&D to GDP ratio recorded a low of 1.67 per cent. There followed a broadly upward trend until a peak of 1.84 per cent was reached in 2009. The percentage fell back in 2010 to 1.78 per cent; this equated to just over £26 billion in real terms. Expenditure on R&D, in real terms, has declined every year since its £27 billion peak in 2007. In 2010, R&D was mainly carried out by business enterprises (61 per cent of the total) and higher education (27 per cent of the total). The remainder was carried out by government, research councils and non-profit making institutes.

Figure 14: Expenditure on research and development as a percentage of gross domestic product

United Kingdom

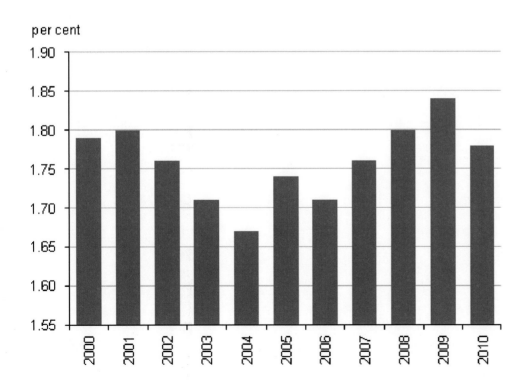

Source: Office for National Statistics

Human capital

Stocks are an important measure of sustainability as they give an estimate of how much resource can be carried forward into the future, rather than how much has been consumed. Human capital has been defined as the stock of 'knowledge, skills, competencies and attributes embodied in individuals that facilitate the creation of personal, social and economic well-being'[1].

Human capital is recognised as having important economic impacts. At a macroeconomic level, the accumulation of human capital is thought to be an important driver of output growth; those countries with higher levels of human capital have greater potential for future growth, other things being equal. At the microeconomic level, individuals' labour market outcomes are linked to their individual level of human capital. Generally speaking individuals with low skills or levels of education are more likely to be unemployed[2].

The Office for National Statistics has produced experimental statistics using a 'lifetime labour income approach' to estimate the stock of the UK's human capital.[3] In 2010 the UK's human capital stock was estimated to be worth over £17 trillion, more than two and a half times the value of the UK's tangible assets – its buildings, vehicles, plant, machinery etc.

Figure 15 illustrates the effect of the economic downturn on the UK's human capital stock in real terms. Prior to the recession the value of the UK's human capital stock rose steadily, averaging annual growth of 2.75 per cent (£425 billion). The annual rate of growth then slowed to 0.7 per cent (£120 billion), for 2008 and 2009, before falling by 0.8 per cent (£130 billion) in 2010.

Figure 15: UK human capital stock

United Kingdom

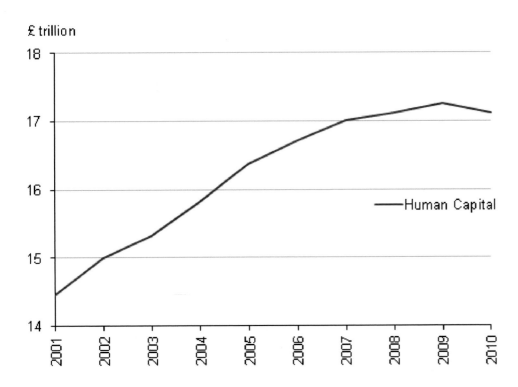

£ trillion

Source: Office for National Statistics

The fall in the level of Human Capital stock was primarily due to a fall in the real average earnings (most notably for those with degrees) combined with a fall in the percentage of those in employment.

Using a 'lifetime labour income approach' the stock of human capital is directly affected by employment rates (e.g. human capital falls as people leave the labour market). Indirectly it is also affected; research has shown that if individuals are away from the labour market for any length of time they face a wage penalty, hence their lifetime income and stock of human capital falls. The effect is thought to be particularly problematic for the young as long-term unemployment not only comes with a wage penalty but can have a scarring effect leading to an increased probability of being unemployed later in life. During the recession unemployment has not been distributed equally across the age bands. The youngest of the age bands have seen the greatest percentage point increase in unemployment.

In the three years before the recession of 2008, the percentage of those in the 16 to 24 age group who were unemployed and not in full time education followed a relatively flat quarterly path averaging 13.4 per cent. This is just over two and a half times the rate for the entire workforce over the same period. By the time the economy emerged from recession in the third quarter of 2009, youth unemployment had climbed sharply to reach 18.8 per cent, at that time it was the highest proportion since records began in 1992. There followed an upward trend and, in the third quarter of 2011, two years after the economy had emerged from the 2008 recession, one in every five people in this age group were unemployed and not in full time education. Youth unemployment has remained broadly similar since (to the second quarter of 2012).[4]

Notes

1. Organisation for Economic cooperation and Development (OECD) (2001)

2. Steedman, H. (1996) Measuring the quality of educational outputs: a note. CEPDP, 302. Centre for Economic Performance, London School of Economics and Political Science, London, UK

3. Jones, R. and Fender V. (2011)

4. Labour Force Survey (LFS), seasonally adjusted quarterly data.

Background notes

1. Details of the policy governing the release of new data are available by visiting www.statisticsauthority.gov.uk/assessment/code-of-practice/index.html or from the Media Relations Office email: media.relations@ons.gsi.gov.uk

Copyright

References

1. Bank of England statistical interactive database – http://www.bankofengland.co.uk/boeapps/iadb/newintermed.asp

2. Blue Book (ONS 2012) – http://www.ons.gov.uk/ons/rel/naa1-rd/united-kingdom-national-accounts/index.html

3. Consumer price index (ONS 2012) – http://www.ons.gov.uk/ons/rel/cpi/consumer-price-indices/index.html

4. First ONS annual experimental subjective well-being results – http://www.ons.gov.uk/ons/rel/wellbeing/measuring-subjective-wellbeing-in-the-uk/first-annual-ons-experimental-subjective-well-being-results/first-ons-annual-experimental-subjective-well-being-results.html

5. Gross domestic expenditure on research and development – http://www.ons.gov.uk/ons/rel/rdit1/gross-domestic-expenditure-on-research-and-development/index.html

6. Human Capital Estimates – 2010 (Jones, R. and Fender V. 2011) http://www.ons.gov.uk/ons/rel/mro/news-release/human-capital-estimates-nr/index.html

7. Labour market statistics, October 2012 (ONS) – http://www.ons.gov.uk/ons/taxonomy/index.html?nscl=Labour+Market

8. Measuring national well-being: report on consultation responses on proposed domains and measures - http://www.ons.gov.uk/ons/guide-method/user-guidance/well-being/publications/index.html

9. Measuring the quality of educational outputs: a note. CEPDP, 302. (London School of Economics 1996) http://eprints.lse.ac.uk/20662/

10. Real adjusted gross disposable income of households per capita (Eurostat 2011) – http://epp.eurostat.ec.europa.eu/tgm/table.do?tab=table&init=1&plugin=1&language=en&pcode=tec00113

11. Report by the Commission on the Measurement of Economic Performance and Social Progress by Stiglitz, Sen and Fitoussi (2009) – http://www.stiglitz-sen-fitoussi.fr/documents/rapport_anglais.pdf

12. Steedman, H. (1996) Measuring the quality of educational outputs: a note. CEPDP, 302. Centre for Economic Performance, London School of Economics and Political Science, London, UK.

13. The economic position of households – http://www.ons.gov.uk/ons/rel/hsa/the-economic-position-of-households/index.html

14. The well-being of nations: the role of human and social capital, (OECD 2001) http://www.oecd.org/site/worldforum/33703702.pdf

15. United Kingdom Economic Accounts (ONS 2012) – http://www.ons.gov.uk/ons/rel/hsa/the-economic-position-of-households/index.html

16. Vanoli A (2005) 'A history of national accounting', IOS Press, Amsterdam

this page is intentionally blank

Measuring National Well-being - Children's Well-being, 2012

Author Name(s): Theodore Joloza Office for National Statistics

Abstract

This article is published as part of the Office for National Statistics (ONS) Measuring National Well-being Programme and discusses the well-being of children aged 0 to 15. The Programme aims to produce accepted and trusted measures of the well-being of the nation - how the UK as a whole is doing. The article will cover both objective and subjective measures of well-being. Areas covered will include infant mortality, birth weight, satisfaction with relationships and access to and use of technology.

Introduction

During the Measuring National Well-being national debate many respondents told us of the importance of children's well-being. It is now largely accepted that what children become in their adult life is to a great extent a product of their experiences in the early stages of their lives (Aldgate et al, 2010). Particularly important are issues such as health and safety, material and emotional security, education and socialisation.

The ten domains currently proposed to measure the well-being of the UK and many of the measures within them are of relevance to children just as they are to other age groups. The domains and measures can be seen in Proposed domains and measures for Measuring National Well-being. This article does not cover all of these domains for children aged 0 to 15 but examines some specific aspects. These include circumstances in which they live, what they feel about their relationships, what they do and also decisions that adults make on their behalf. This article specifically examines these different aspects and measures and presents where possible what children think and feel about their lives and focuses on:

- How many children there are in England and Wales
- Children's health
- Poverty and its relationship with parental economic activity
- Education and skills
- Children's relationships and their well-being
- Use of technology and social media
- Where children live

Key Points

- In 1911, one in three of the population in England and Wales were children aged 0 to 15 years, by 2011 this proportion had fallen to one in five
- In 1911, 130 out of every 1,000 children born in England and Wales would die before their first birthday but in 2010 this had decreased to 8 in every 1,000 children
- Boys born between 2008 and 2010 in the UK might expect to live for 78 years and girls for 82 years. They can expect to spend about 80 per cent of their lives in good health
- About 27 per cent of children in the UK were living in households where the income was less than 60 per cent of median income in 2010/11 compared with 34 per cent in 1998/99
- In 2011, about 16 per cent of children in the UK lived in households where no adult was working
- There was a strong association with children's reported feelings about their family, friends, school, school work and appearance and their overall feelings about their lives in 2010
- Children aged 10 to 15 who reported being bullied the least were also happiest with their lives
- In the UK in 2009/10 boys aged 10 to 15 were more likely than girls to spend over an hour on a school day using a games consoles. Girls are more likely than boys to spend over an hour chatting on the internet
- In 2012, a considerably higher percentage of children aged 10 to 15 in England and Wales thought that crime had increased nationally than that it had increased in their local area

Population change

According to the 2011 Census there were just over 10.5 million children aged 0 to 15 in England and Wales - about one in five of the population compared with one in three in 1911. Figure 1 shows that there has been a steady decline in the proportion of children in the population while the proportion of the more elderly has risen. The reasons for this change over the last 100 years are the reduction in family size and improvements in medicine, health services and care of the elderly.

Over the same period there has been a change in attitudes to children which has arguably improved their well-being. For example, in 2012 all children are expected to be in compulsory education until they are at least 16 years old. In 1911, a child was only required to be in education until they were 12 years old.

Figure 1: The percentage of children aged 0 to 5 and adults aged 60 and over, selected Census years

England and Wales

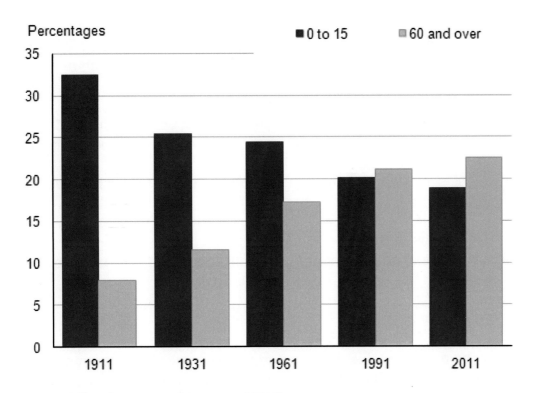

Source: Office for National Statistics (ONS)

Health

During the national debate respondents reported that their health was one of the most important areas which affected their well-being. Good health is also very important for children.

Some aspects of children's health are beyond children's control yet can have a large influence on whether they will survive infancy and may determine the quality of life they enjoy in adulthood. Examples include smoking and drinking during pregnancy, preterm births and low birth weight.

Smoking is known to adversely affect development of the central nervous system in babies of smoking mothers. This is because nicotine restricts blood flow and the amount of oxygen available to the foetus (Key et al, 2007).

Preterm children (those born before 37 weeks of pregnancy) are at a higher risk of having low birth weight. According to the World Health Organisation (WHO) a child's weight at birth is healthy if it is 2,500 grams or higher and 1 in every 10 children born in the world is born before full term (WHO, 2012). Birth weight is an important indicator of overall health and is influenced by a number of factors including smoking and drinking during pregnancy , low parental socio-economic status, education levels, low income and inadequate living conditions. In the UK nearly 8 per cent of births are preterm and they occur most frequently for mothers with obesity or diabetes or those who are older. This is similar to the average of the 24 European member countries of the OECD (Organisation for Economic Corporation and Development (OECD) 2007 – Health at a Glance 2007: OECD Indicators).

In England and Wales, around 700,000 babies were born in 2009 of which about 50,000 were born at a low birth weight. Of all those babies who were born with a low weight, 62 per cent were preterm.

Having a healthy birth weight is important to children's well-being because low birth weights are associated with:

- Death within the first 24 months of life
- Delayed physical and intellectual development in early childhood and adolescence
- Cerebral palsy
- Sight and hearing defects
- Hernias

While low birth weight can be a result of the life style and living conditions of parents it can also be because of other factors including birth by caesarean section, increase in incidences of multiple birth and some mothers having children young or later in life (OECD, 2007).

Figure 2 shows that the proportion of children born at a low birth weight in the UK is similar to the OECD average of 7 per cent and is higher than of other countries including Slovenia, Poland, Australia and Canada.

Figure 2: Percentage of children born with a low birth weight for selected OECD countries, 2011

International

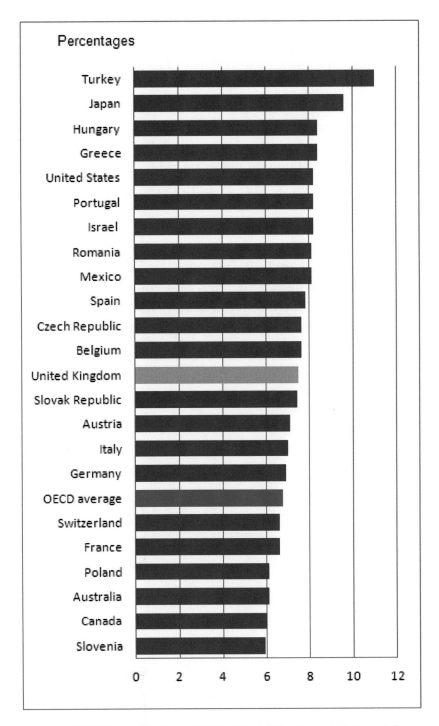

Percentages

Source: OECD Health Data 2011; World Bank and National Sources from non-OECD countries

The infant mortality rate is the number of children who die aged less than one year old per 1,000 births. A lower infant mortality rate can indicate that better care is being taken of children and is linked to several factors including access to health care services for pregnant mothers and infants, socio-economic status of the child's parents, the health of the mother, low birth weight and preterm birth. In April 2012, ONS reported that:

- In 2010, the infant mortality rate was 4 deaths per 1,000 live births, the lowest ever recorded in England and Wales, and compares with an infant mortality rate of 12 deaths per 1,000 live births in 1980 and 5 deaths per 1,000 live births in 2009
- Infant mortality rates in 2010 were lowest among babies of mothers aged 30 to 34 years (4 deaths per 1,000 live births) and highest among babies of mothers aged 40 years and over (6 deaths per 1,000 live births)
- In 2010, the infant mortality rates for very low birth weight babies (under 1,500 grams) and low birth weight babies (under 2,500 grams) were 165 and 37 deaths per 1,000 live births respectively

In 1911, 130 out of every 1,000 children born in England and Wales would die before their first birthday. The decrease in infant deaths between 1911 and 2010 is because of considerable improvements in health care, including the control of infectious diseases and public health infrastructure over this time period. For the UK as a whole infant mortality has been declining and is now only about a quarter of what it was in 1970. The infant mortality rate is currently similar to the OECD average (Figure 3).

Figure 3: UK infant mortality rates compared to the OECD average, 2011

United Kingdom/OECD

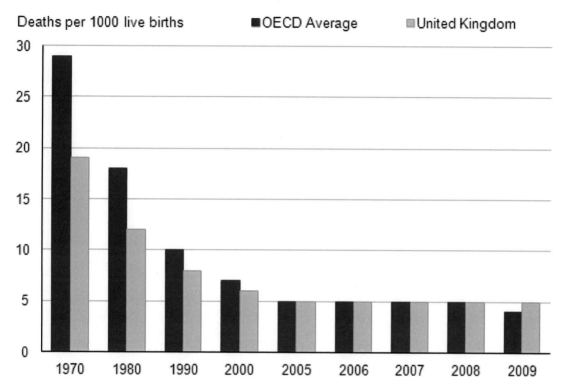

Source: OECD Factbook 2011

Another reflection of good health care is the length of life that children in the UK can expect at birth. Based on data for 2008-10, males at birth can expect to live for 78 years and females for 82 years. Over 80 per cent of this time is expected to be spent in good health by both sexes if the 2008-10 levels of self-reported health are maintained.

One area which may affect the future well-being of a child is the age of its mother. Older mothers are more at risk of delivering their child early and encountering the associated risks. However, being the child of a young mother or being a young mother can also affect your well-being. In 2010, there were 1,063 births to mothers under 16 years old in England and Wales (ONS, October 2011). Some of the problems associated with becoming a mother at that age include disrupted schooling which may lead to the mother and child living in relative poverty and becoming a low socio-economic household. In addition, children born to teenage mothers are twice as likely to become teenage parents themselves (Rendall, 2003).

There are a number of risky behaviours children can undertake that can affect their health including the use of alcohol and smoking.

Alcohol

Drinking alcohol remains a risky behaviour that can have detrimental effects on a child's health and well-being. In general, the proportion of children who have ever had an alcoholic drink has declined over recent years as has the amount of alcohol that they drink. Boys are more likely to report being drunk than girls in Great Britain (Bradshaw, 2011).

The Survey of Smoking, Drinking and Drug Use among Young People in England (SDDS) found that 45 per cent of 11 to 15 year old pupils had drunk alcohol at least once. Table 1 shows that although there was very little change between 2010 and 2011 the proportion of pupils ever having had a drink has been decreasing since 2005.

Table 1: Proportion of pupils who have ever had an alcoholic drink by sex, 2005 to 2011

England

Percentages

	2005	2006	2007	2008	2009	2010	2011
Boys	57	56	54	53	53	46	46
Girls	60	55	54	52	50	45	44
Total	58	55	54	52	51	45	45

Source: Health and Social Information Centre, 2011

There was also a decline between 2009 and 2011 in the proportion of pupils in England who report having alcohol in the last week. Figure 4 shows that 12 per cent of pupils reported drinking alcohol in the last week in 2011 compared to 18 per cent in 2009. There was no significant change between 2010 (13 per cent) and 2011.

Figure 4: When pupils last had an alcoholic drink

England

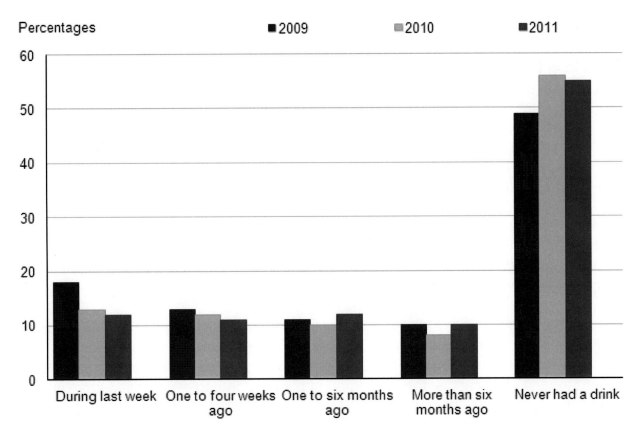

Source: Health and Social Care Information Centre 2011

The survey also found that only 7 per cent of pupils in England in 2011 said they had drunk alcohol every week: down from 20 per cent in 2001. The proportion of pupils who had never used alcohol has gone up in recent years, from 39 per cent in 2003 to 55 per cent in 2011.

This decreasing trend in regular alcohol use is similar to findings from The Health Behaviours of School-age Children Survey (HBSC). The proportion of 15 year olds in England reporting drinking alcohol at least once a week has decreased over the years from just over 50 per cent in 2002 to around 30 per cent in 2010. However, the study found that the level of drunkenness at this age has not shown a corresponding decline (HBSC England, 2010). In Scotland, the proportion of 15 year old pupils who said they drink alcohol at least once a week has gone down from around 43 per cent in 2002 to 27 per cent in 2010 and the level of drunkenness among 15 year olds was lower in 2010 (44 per cent) than it was in 2002 (52 per cent). Data for Wales also show a similar trend with 33 per cent of 15 year olds reporting drinking alcohol once a week or more in 2009/10 compared to 56 per cent in 2002.

Smoking

Another behaviour which can be detrimental to children's health is smoking. Tobacco use, particularly cigarette smoking is the most preventable cause of death in the UK and in the world today (WHO, 2008). In the UK around 100,000 deaths per year are due to smoking related diseases. It has a long lasting impact on the well-being of individuals including the risk of developing smoking related diseases.

Children whose parents smoke are at risk of developing respiratory diseases including asthma and also likely to die prematurely. Children who smoke themselves are at risk of dying prematurely from diseases such as lung cancer and Chronic Obstructive Pulmonary Disease - COPD (U.S. Department of Health and Human Services, 2006).

Nearly 65 per cent of all current smokers and ex-smokers started smoking when they were below 18 years old (ONS, 2009). Among children who smoke a quarter had their first cigarette before they reached the age of 10 (WHO). Smoking is also strongly linked with the likelihood of the use of alcohol and drugs (Bradshaw, 2011).

Overall, studies are showing that in the UK smoking by children is declining over time. Findings from the Survey of Smoking, Drinking and Drug Use among Young People in England (SDDS), Health Behaviours in School age Children (HBSC) and the Young Person's Behaviours and Attitudes Survey in Northern Ireland all show that the proportion of pupils reporting ever having smoked cigarettes or smoking regularly has been decreasing over time.

Data from SDDS show that the proportion of pupils who had ever smoked was about 25 per cent in 2011 compared to 53 per cent in 1980 (SDDS, 2011). Figure 5 shows that lower proportions of younger than older pupils are likely to report smoking in the last week. These findings were similar to those in the HBSC Survey in England.

Figure 5: Proportion of pupils who smoked in the last week, by age and sex, 2011
England

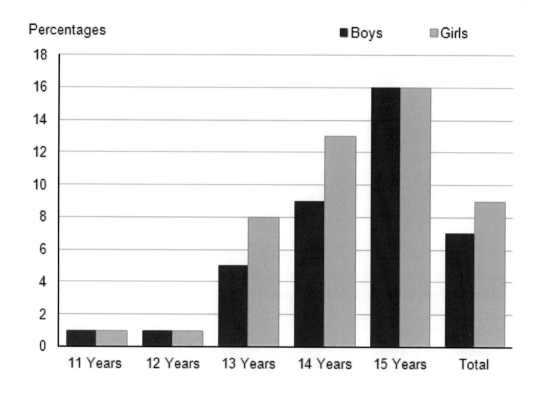

Source: Health and Social Care Information Centre 2011

The most recently available data that allows comparison with other countries shows that the proportion of 15 year olds who reported smoking at least once a week in 2010 was lower in Great Britain (14 per cent) than the average for all countries that took part in the HBSC Survey (18 per cent). It was also lower when compared to other countries like France (20 per cent), Germany (15 per cent) and Italy (23 per cent) (Currie et al, 2012).

Poverty and Parental Economic Activity

Parents' employment status has implications for children's well-being. Children whose parents are in employment are at a reduced risk of poverty and its implications. Having an income can lead to more access to available resources and services and improvements in children's well-being.

Poverty

A recent paper from the Institute of Economic Research (Knies, 2012) explored whether child life satisfaction is associated with household income using interviews with about 4,900 children aged 10 to 15 from Wave 1 of the Understanding Society Survey. The results suggest that family income and income-based measures of poverty are not associated with child life satisfaction as perceived by children themselves. However, a range of other indicators of material well-being show some association with child life satisfaction. Reported life satisfaction was lower for those children who lived in households where adults experience material deprivation and the association was more marked if the children themselves are deprived of things other children enjoy. The associations also held when differences in other aspects of children's lives such as the quality of the schools they go to, the number of friends they have, their health and levels of physical activity.

While on average children living in low income families do not report low levels of well-being, poverty in childhood has very strong associations with children's outcomes in life. Bradshaw (2011) asserts that one of the best measures of a country's success is how it protects its children from poverty and its effects. This makes poverty one of the important factors for both children's and overall national well-being.

A review of evidence of children's views on poverty revealed that experiences of poverty in childhood can be damaging and its effects disruptive. Children living in poverty mentioned several areas of concern that covered most of the areas of well-being that the ONS is using to measure for national well-being (Ridge 2009). These include:

- Being anxious that money coming into their households would not be enough to meet needs
- Material deprivation including toys, games, and essentials like food
- Restricted opportunities to make and sustain friendships
- Restricted opportunities at school due to inability to buy study materials or pay for social trips
- Not fitting in due to lack of possessions or clothes similar to those of well off children
- Taking on additional chores in the home when parents had to work long hours
- Poor quality housing and homelessness
- Perceiving neighbourhoods as insecure and sometimes dangerous

The accepted current measure of poverty for individuals is that they are living in a household with an income below 60 per cent of the contemporary median income (for this analysis we are using this measure after housing costs have been deducted). Data from the Family Resources Survey (Figure 6) show that in 2010/11 27 per cent of children lived in households where the income was below 60 per cent of the current median after housing costs had been accounted for. This is a reduction since 1998/99 when 34 per cent of children were living in these circumstances.

Figure 6: Children in households with income below 60 per cent of contemporary median income after housing costs, 1998/99 to 2010/11

United Kingdom

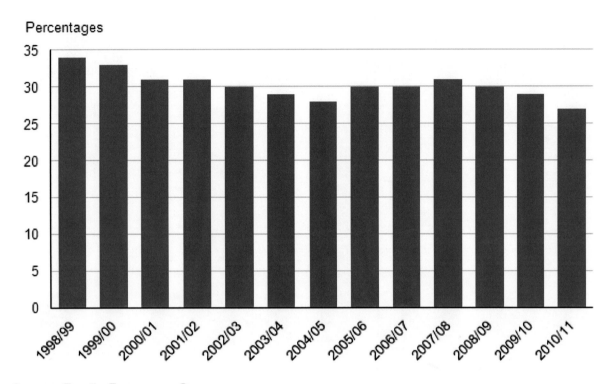

Source: Family Resources Survey

As is reported in the article on 'Personal finance' published by the Measuring National Well-being Programme in September 2012, 76 per cent of weekly household income was from social security benefits for UK households in the lowest fifth of the income distribution in 2010, while for those in the highest fifth 76 per cent of weekly income came from wages and salaries. Therefore, children in the poorest households are also more likely to be living in households where adults are not working and are receiving benefits of some kind.

Parental Economic Activity

Figure 7 shows that in the United Kingdom the majority of children (51 per cent) live in households where both parents work and nearly 16 per cent of children are in households where both parents do not work. Northern Ireland has the highest proportion of children living in working households (57 per cent) followed by Scotland (56 per cent), Wales (52 per cent) and England (51 per cent). Wales had the highest proportion of children living in workless households (20 per cent) compared to England, Scotland and Northern Ireland (all with approximately 16 per cent).

Figure 7: Percentage of children(1) by economic activity status of adults in their household(2), October to December 2011

United Kingdom

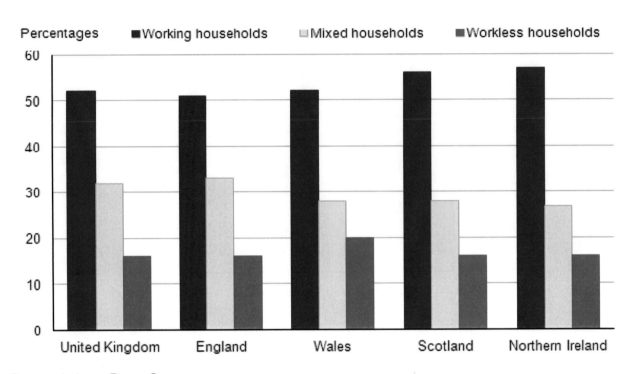

Source: Labour Force Survey

Notes:
1.   Children are those under 16 years old
2.   Mixed households contain both working and workless members

Education and Skills

Children's education and development of skills are important for their well-being and for that of the nation as a whole. A child's knowledge, skills and competencies will contribute to future human capital once the individual enters the labour market. Human capital is one of the important measures of a nation's well-being as its accumulation is an important driver of output growth (Durlauf et al, 2005).

Children's future labour market outcomes can also be linked to how much knowledge, skills and competencies they acquire. In the UK adult population, individuals with low skills or levels of education are more likely to be unemployed and face social exclusion. There is also evidence that better-educated people have better health status, more social connections, and greater engagement in civic and political life. Education brings a range of benefits (monetary and non-monetary) to both the person investing in the education and the community in which they live (Stiglitz, 2008).

The early years

As was reported in the article on <u>Education and skills</u> the foundation years, the first five years of a child's life, are critical. Children's experiences in these years have the biggest impact on how their brains develop. It is also when children grasp the fundamental skills needed to do well at school and develop as happy and confident individuals. For this reason, participation in some form of early education can improve a child's chances of achievement and well-being in later years.

Many children spend time during the day with childcare providers. In 2010, the use of child care varied depending on the age of the children in England. It was lowest from birth to two years old at 59 per cent of children and highest among three to four year olds at 89 per cent while uptake for 12 to 14 year olds was 50 per cent. The high uptake for three to four year olds is likely to be due to the cost of care being offset by the universal free early education that children are entitled to after their third birthday (Smith, 2012).

The article on Education and skills reported that: 'Most three and four year olds in the UK benefit from early year's placements in educational establishments. Data from Eurostat shows that in 2009 participation rates in early childhood education was universal in France (100 per cent) and nearly universal in the Netherlands, Belgium and Spain (all just above 99 per cent). The UK participation rate was 97 per cent, 6 percentage points higher than the EU-27 average of 92 per cent. Participation rates were lowest in Poland (71 per cent) and Finland (72 per cent).'

Research has shown that among children starting primary school those that have had pre-school education tend to be more confident, more sociable and have more developed cognitive function than those who have not had pre-school education exposure. Children from disadvantaged backgrounds have also been found to have benefitted significantly from good quality child care and early learning as it allows mixing children from different social backgrounds. (Sylva, 2004)

Poverty as described above and the associated disadvantages have an effect on children's achievement at school. A study commissioned by the Joseph Rowntree Foundation found that by age 11 around 75 per cent of boys from the poorest fifth of families reach the expected government level at Key Stage 2 compared to 97 per cent of children from the richest fifth of families.

A study analysing the Millennium Cohort Study of siblings of children born around 2000 (Goodman and Gregg, 2010) found that several other factors which affected a child's cognitive development;

- Children who go to nursery and private school tend to have higher cognitive test scores than those who do not
- Children whose parents think they are very or fairly likely to go to university tend to have higher test scores than those whose parents are pessimistic
- Children who read for enjoyment also tend to have higher cognitive test scores than those who do not

Achievements at the end of compulsory schooling

In the UK, achievement at the school leaving age is generally measured by General Certificate of Secondary Education (GCSE) and equivalent results.

Figure 8 shows that the percentage of pupils aged 16 achieving 5 or more grades A* to C or the equivalent have improved in each year. This has been the case since these examinations were introduced in the late 1980s. The figure also shows that for a long time girls have performed better than boys.

Figure 8: Pupils achieving five or more GCSE or equivalent grades A* to C (1,2) by sex
United Kingdom

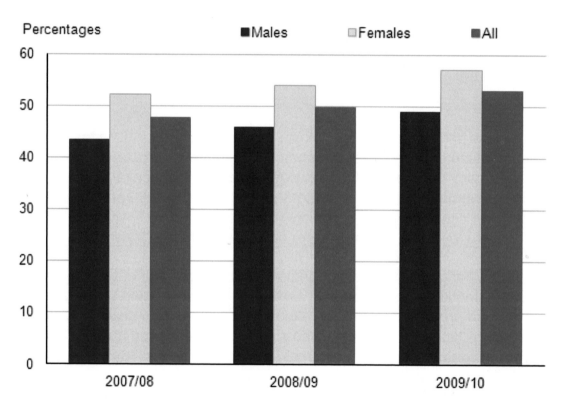

Source: Department for Education (DfE, 2011)

Notes:
1. Including English and mathematics
2. For pupils in their last year of compulsory education. Pupils aged 15 at the start of the academic year; pupils in year S4 in Scotland.

Children's circumstances affect how well a child does in school and examinations. In England, data released by the Department for Education shows that in 2011:

- 35 per cent of pupils eligible for free school meals (FSM) achieved 5 or more A* to C grades at GCSE or equivalent including English and mathematics GCSEs, compared to 62 per cent of all other pupils
- 34 per cent of disadvantaged pupils (pupils eligible for FSM or looked after children) achieved 5 or more A* to C grades at GCSE or equivalent including English and mathematics GCSEs, compared to 62 per cent of all other pupils
- The proportion of pupils with Special Educational Needs (SEN) without a statement achieving 5 or more A* to C grades at GCSE or equivalent including English and mathematics GCSEs is 25 per cent. For pupils with SEN with a statement is 9 per cent while pupils with no identified SEN is 70 per cent

Children who are persistently absent from school lose out on learning and may fail to catch up with their peers. This absence can be for several reasons but one problem is bullying. Studies have shown that bullying contributes to unauthorised absence although this relationship is not necessarily causal but more of a trend. Whatever the cause of unauthorised absence, it is a big indicator of whether children will be involved in crime, whether as a juvenile or as an adult and also the likelihood of experiencing mental problems (Reid, 1999).

Some children speak languages at home other than the medium used in school. While coming from such households has some benefits for children for others it can also present difficulties once children enter education. Data for all school age children show that the proportion of children speaking another language at home is higher among primary school children than those in secondary school. The total proportion of children whose main language at home is other than English has increased from 12 per cent in 2006 to 16 per cent in 2012. This is probably due to recent increases in immigration. It should be noted that some parents have deliberately chosen to bring up their children using an extra language and that English not being the main language at home does not necessarily mean that children are not proficient in English.

Children's Relationships and their Subjective Well-being

During the national debate on measuring national well-being children reported that aspects of their life such as family, friends, school and appearance were very important to their own well-being. Other relationships that matter to children are relationships with teachers and other members of their community at large. In particular, children in primary school said they were most happy when shown physical affection by parents and siblings.

Understanding Society, the UK Household Longitudinal Study (UKHLS) asked children aged 10 to 15 years old how they feel about some of these aspects of their lives. In this analysis 'happy' refers to those who reported their happiness with life as a whole to be at a level of 1 to 3 on a range of scores from 1 being 'completely happy' to 7 being 'not at all happy'. Nearly 90 per cent of children were completely happy, somewhat happy or happy with their life as a whole.

When asked about other aspects of their lives the highest proportion of children reported being happy to completely happy with family and friends (94 and 96 per cent respectively). Lower percentages of 10 to 15 year olds reported being happy to completely happy with school (82 per cent), school work (79 per cent) and appearance (76 per cent). Further analysis of these findings indicates that there is a significant association between how children feel about these important aspects of their life and how they feel about life as a whole.

Figure 9: Percentage of children aged 10 to 15 who were happy to completely happy about aspects of their lives

United Kingdom

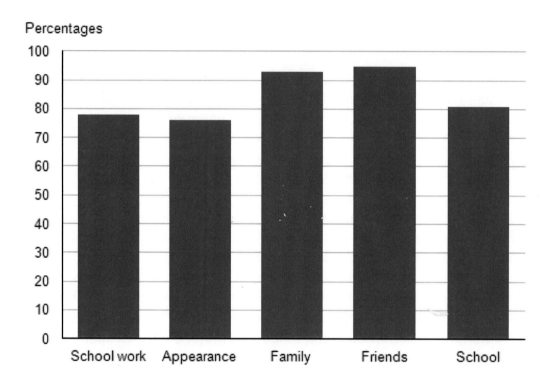

Source: Understanding Society, Wave 1, 2009 – 2010

These findings are similar to those in research by the Children's Society which found a significant association between a child's well-being and the 10 aspects of children's life including family, friends and school covered in the Good Childhood Index (The Good Childhood Report, 2012).

While the majority of children report being happy with their relationships with family and friends and with their lives overall, it is important not to overlook the small proportion of children who are not. Children who report low levels of subjective well-being do so for several reasons including feeling that they are not listened to by parents (Children's Society, 2012) or because they are being bullied by friends or siblings (Wolke, 2010).

Bullying

Bullying occurs in different settings and for children it can affect both what they do and their feelings about where they live. In schools bullying is not a new phenomenon but it is only in the last two decades that it has been openly discussed and placed on the educational agenda. It is a key issue and been recognised as a serious problem both for those who are bullied and for the bullies themselves. There are several reasons for bullying which may include differences in culture, ethnicity, age, ability or disability, religion, body size, physical appearance, personality, sexual orientation or economic status (Rigby, 2011). Bullying also takes many forms such as verbal abuse, spreading rumours, physical beatings or excluding victims from activities. More recently cyber bullying has emerged where bullies victimise others via the internet and use of mobile phones. It is compulsory for schools to take steps to ensure that all forms of bullying are prevented. There are also some initiatives aimed at parents and families. It is important to note that the bullies need help as much as their victims in order to effectively control bullying.

Bullying has a number of negative consequences including increased absence levels for victims, lower academic achievement, anxiety and social problems. Bullying can also negatively affect children's self esteem and general life satisfaction (Gobina, 2008). Data from Understanding Society show that 85 per cent of all children who reported that they had never been bullied at all selected the highest level of happiness with life in general. Nearly 55 per cent of children who reported the lowest satisfaction with life in general had been bullied at least once in the last six months prior to completion of the survey (Figure 10).

Figure 10: Happiness with life as a whole by frequency of bullying

United Kingdom

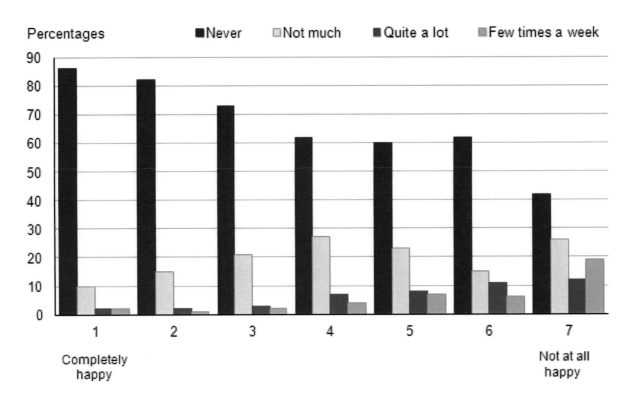

Source: Understanding Society, Wave 1, 2009 – 2010

Technology and Social Media

Data from Understanding Society showed that in the UK 96 per cent of children aged 10 to 15 years had computer access at home. Computer use for educational purposes in the home was also found to be high, with just over 80 per cent of children using a computer at least once a month for homework or course work. The same survey, collected between 2009 and 2010, showed that a higher proportion of boys (96 per cent) than girls (89 per cent) had at least one games console in their home[1]. Girls on the other hand are more likely (90 per cent) to have their own mobile phone than boys (84 per cent).

The use of technology and social networking by children has advantages which include:

- Catching up with family and friends
- Sending messages instantly to several friends at once

- Ability to engage in play even if external weather conditions do not allow outside play
- Able to play video games with people who are thousands of miles away
- Easier communication for shy individuals
- Enhance existing friendships, happiness and well-being (Valkenburg and Peter, 2009)

Too much time spent playing or chatting on line may also have disadvantages including:

- The possibility of cyber bullying
- Being preyed on by perverted individuals
- Addictive in rare cases
- Risk of obesity because of lack of physical activity

For children there is a connection between the length of time for which they use media and their well-being. Research in 2011 from the Institute for Social and Economic Research (ISER) reported that children in the UK who had access to computer games, games consoles and internet use at home for less than an hour on a normal school day also reported better well-being than those who used these facilities for four hours or more. Children who spend too much time chatting on line may also be at risk of unwanted attention and harassment (Skew et al, 2011).

While playing on games consoles and chatting on social media sites can enhance children's recreational and networking experiences there are risks with excessive usage. Figure 11 shows that 6 per cent of children chat online for four hours or more on a school day compared to 26 per cent and 30 per cent who spend less than one hour and up to 3 hours chatting on line. The figure also shows proportions of children playing on games consoles on a school day; 33 per cent playing for less than an hour, 29 per cent playing for up to three hours and 6 per cent playing for four hours or more.

Figure 11: Use of technology and social media on a school day by 10 to 15 year olds

United Kingdom

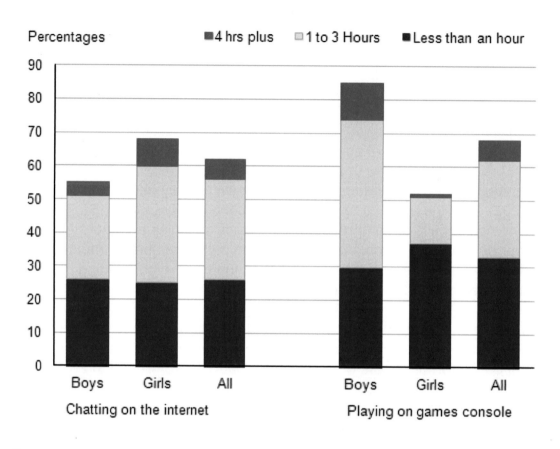

Source: Understanding Society, Wave 1, 2009 – 2010

Data from the Millennium Cohort Study[2] also show that:

- Nearly 85 per cent of children born in 2000-2001 have access to a computer and the internet at home but only three quarters of them use it
- 12 per cent of these children have their own computer and another 12 per cent have their own mobile phone
- A high proportion of 11 to 12 year olds (83 per cent) have rules about how long they can watch TV on a school day

Notes

1. All differences are statistically significant at 95 per cent Confidence Interval

2. MCS is a longitudinal study of children born in the New Millennium (2000-2001) and their siblings.

Where we live

Where a child lives can have an impact on their life. Availability of facilities for leisure activities as well as green open spaces was highlighted as important for children's well-being during the national debate. A child's or their parent's perception of the area they live in is important as it affects participation in activities in the area. Children who live in an area they consider safe will be confident to go outside and play. If they consider the neighbourhood to be friendly they will also be able to go and make friends with other children in the neighbourhood.

The perception of parents of crime and safety in the neighbourhood is also important to well-being. Studies have shown that parents will restrict outside play if they have concerns over crime and safety (Kalish et al, 2010). Some young people fear for their safety walking home from school citing as reasons bullies, gangs and paedophiles. In winter this fear is increased due to poor lighting and may lead to children avoiding use of certain routes or use of available facilities all together (Audit Commission).

In order to understand this aspect of well-being it is important to know what children think about crime in relation to where they live. The 2011/12 Crime Survey for England and Wales (CSEW, previously named the British Crime Survey) asked 10 to 15 year olds living in England and Wales if they thought that that their local area was a friendly place to live. Nearly 80 per cent agreed that it was, while 7 per cent said that it was not (Table 2).

Table 2 shows that children experience violence or thefts more in or around their school and in the neighbourhood of their dwelling than in parks and other public places. This does not necessarily imply that parks and open spaces are low risk areas. Some children may not be allowed to take valuable items to these places and may only visit these places in the company of an adult.

Table 2: Where incidents experienced by children aged 10 to 15 years old took place

England and Wales (1)

Percentages

	Violence[2,3]	Thefts[4]
School	56	46
Home/neighbourhood	16	27
Park/open space	13	7
Other public place	9	9
Elsewhere	6	10

Source: Home Office, Crime Survey of England and Wales

Table notes:
1. These are experimental statistics based on the Crime Survey of England and Wales, 2011
2. The CSEW 10-15s survey used two measures of crime for 10-15 year olds, a 'Broad measure' and a 'Preferred measure' The 'Preferred measure' takes into account factors identified as important in determining the severity of an incidence (such as relationship to the offender, level of injury, value of item stolen or damaged) while the 'Broad measure' also includes minor offences between children and family members that would not normally be treated as criminal matters. The figures presented in this table use the 'Preferred measure'.
3. 'Violence' includes the offence types of wounding, robbery, assault with minor injury and assault with injury. 'All thefts' includes theft from the person and other theft of personal property but also theft from inside and outside a dwelling and theft of bicycles where the property stolen or damaged belonged solely to the child respondent
4. 'Thefts' includes theft from the person and other theft of personal property but also theft from inside and outside a dwelling and theft of bicycles where the property stolen or damaged belonged solely to the child respondent

The survey results also show that most children think that crime has gone up at the national level but stayed the same at the local level. When asked about how crime has changed in the country in past few years, 55 per cent of the children thought that crime had gone up, 35 per cent thought it had stayed the same while 10 per cent thought it had gone down. (Figure 12) When asked whether crime had gone up, stayed the same or gone down in their local area, the proportions were 17 per cent, 63 per cent and 19 per cent respectively.

Figure 12: Perceptions of 10 to 15 year old children of the changes in crime levels over the past few years in their local area and the country as a whole

England and Wales

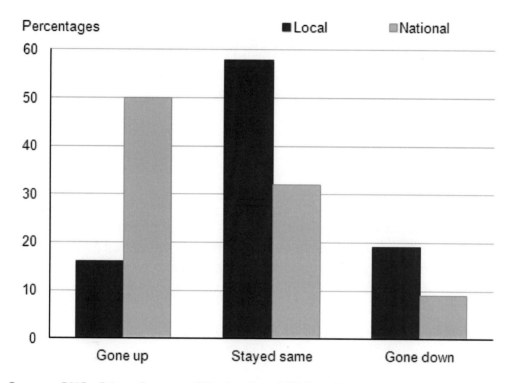

Source: ONS, Crime Survey of England and Wales, 2012

Availability and access to facilities and activities is also important for well-being. A survey of 10 to 15 year olds in England and Wales found that 37 per cent of this age group did not feel that there were enough activities for children in their local area (ONS, CSEW, 2011/12).

Several studies have shown that young people consider availability of facilities for leisure activities as being very important to their well-being. The Audit Commision has reviewed a number of pieces of research on what issues affect children's behaviour. This found that children who have no access to suitable activities after school are left bored and blame boredom for engagement in anti social behaviour. Children also said that even in local areas with adequate activities and facilities personal safety is an important consideration.

Studies have also shown that there is a link between the type of neighbourhood a child lives in and their well-being. Children in deprived areas are likely to show significantly worse levels of concentration, are likely to feel sad, worried or fearful, and have significantly more problems with their peers than children living in more affluent neighbourhoods. The studies have also shown that initiatives to build social cohesion in a community can play a role in closing the gap between children living in advantaged and disadvantaged areas (Edwards and Bromfield, 2010).

Background notes

1. Details of the policy governing the release of new data are available by visiting www.statisticsauthority.gov.uk/assessment/code-of-practice/index.html or from the Media Relations Office email: media.relations@ons.gsi.gov.uk

Copyright

References

1. 1. Adams, N., Carr, J., Collins, J., Johnson, G., Matejic, P. (eds). (2012). Households Below Average Income; An analysis of the income distribution 1994/95 – 2010/11 June 2012 (United Kingdom). London: DWP
2. Aldgate, J., Jones, D., Rose, W., and Jeffery, C. (Eds), (2006) The Developing World of the Child London: Jessica Kingsley Publishers.
3. Benefits of childcare and early learning accessed at http://www.daycaretrust.org.uk/pages/benefits-of-childcare-and-early-learning.html
4. Bradshaw, J. (2011) Child poverty and deprivation, in J. Bradshaw (ed.) The Well-being of Children in the UK, 3rd ed., The Policy Press, Bristol, pp.27-52.
5. Brooks, F et al, (2011) England National Report, Health Behaviour in School-aged Children (HBSC): World Health Organisation Collaborative Cross National Study, Accessed at http://www.hbscengland.com/reports/
6. Census Factsheet :1911 Census – A window to the past accessed at http://media.1911census.co.uk/census-factsheet
7. Crime Survey for England and Wales, Home Office,http://www.homeoffice.gov.uk/publications/science-research-statistics/research-statistics/crime-research/hosb0612/hosb0612?view=Binary

8. Currie, C et al., (2011) Scotland National Report Health Behaviour in School-aged Children (HBSC): World Health Organisation Collaborative Cross National Study. Accessed at http://www.st-andrews.ac.uk/cahru/research/hbscscotland/publications.php.html

9. Currie, C et al., eds. Social determinants of health and well-being among young people. Health Behaviour in School-aged Children (HBSC) study: international report from the 2009/2010 survey. Copenhagen, WHO Regional Office for Europe, 2012 (Health Policy for Children and Adolescents, No. 6). Accessed at http://www.hbsc.org/

10. Department for Education, GCSE and Equivalent Attainment by Pupil Characteristics in England, 2010/11, Statistical First Release, 2012 accessed at http://www.education.gov.uk/researchandstatistics/datasets?f_contentType=Statistics&page=1&f_publication_category=Performance+and+achievement

11. Department for Work and Pensions (2012). Households Below Average Income; An analysis of the income distribution 1994/95 – 2010/11, June 2012 (United Kingdom). London: DWP.Accessed at http://research.dwp.gov.uk/asd/hbai/hbai2011/index.php?page=contents

12. Durlauf, S. N., Johnson, P.A. and Temple, J. R. W. (2005) 'Growth econometrics'. In P. Aghion and S. N. Durlauf (eds.) Handbook of Economic Growth, Volume 1A Amsterdam: North-Holland, 555-677.

13. Edwards, B and Bromfield, L. (2010) Neighbourhood influences on young children's emotional and behavioural problems accessed on http://www.aifs.gov.au/institute/pubs/fm2010/fm84/fm84a.html

14. Gobina, I., et al. (2008) Bullying and subjective health among adolescents at schools in Latvia and Lithuania: International Journal of Public Health, 2008, Volume 53, Number 5, Pages 272-276

15. Goodman, A. and Gregg.P. (2010). Poorer children's educational attainment: how important are attitudes and behaviour. Joseph Rowntree Foundation. Accessed at http://www.jrf.org.uk/search/site/goodman%20A%20and%20gregg%20p

16. Human Services, Centers for Disease Control and Prevention, National Center for Chronic Disease Prevention and Health Promotion, Office on Smoking and Health, 2006 [accessed August 2012) http://www.surgeongeneral.gov/library/reports/secondhandsmoke/

17. Kalish, M., Banco, L., Burke, G. and Lapidus,G. (2010) .Outdoor play: A survey of parent's perceptions of their child's safety. Accessed at http://www.ncbi.nlm.nih.gov/pubmed/20938312

18. Key, A.P., Ferguson, M., Molfese, D.L., Peach ,K., Lehman, C., and Molfese, V.J. (2007) Smoking during pregnancy affects speech-processing ability in newborn infants. Environmental Health Perspectives. Accessed at http://www.ncbi.nlm.nih.gov/pubmed/17450234

19. Knies , G. (2012) Life satisfaction and material well-being of children in the UK ,ISER Working Paper Series: 2012-15 . Accessed at https://www.iser.essex.ac.uk/publications/working-papers/iser/2012-15

20. Lader, D., Hoare,J. and Lau,I. (2012) Hate crime, cyber security and the experience of crime among children: Findings from the 2010/11 British Crime Survey: Supplementary Volume 3 to Crime in England and Wales 2010/11 Accessed at http://homeoffice.gov.uk/science-research/research-statistics/crime/crime-statistics/british-crime-survey/

21. OECD, (2007), Health at a glance: 2007 OECD indicators Accessed at http://www.oecd-ilibrary.org/social-issues-migration-health/health-at-a-glance-2007_health_glance-2007-en

22. Office for National Statistics,(2011) 'Work and Worklessness among Households 2010', ONS Statistical Bulletin. Accessed at http://www.ons.gov.uk/ons/rel/lmac/working-and-workless-households/2011/stb-working-and-workless-2011.html

23. ONS: 100 years of Census; England and Wales 1911 – 2011. Accessed at http://www.ons.gov.uk/ons/interactive/vp1-story-of-the-census/index.html

24. ONS: Measuring National Well-being –Personal finance 2012. Accessed at http://www.ons.gov.uk/ons/rel/wellbeing/measuring-national-well-being/personal-finance/art-personal-finance.html

25. ONS: Statistical Bulletin: Childhood, Infants and Perinatal Mortality in England and Wales 2010. Accessed at http://www.ons.gov.uk/ons/rel/vsob1/child-mortality-statistics--childhood--infant-and-perinatal/2010/stb-cms-2010.html

26. Rees, G., Goswami, H. and Bradshaw, J.(2010) Developing an index of children's subjective well-being in England .The Children Society . Accessed at http://www.childrenssociety.org.uk/what-we-do/research/research-publications

27. Rees, G., Haridhan, G. and Pople, L., Bradshaw, J., Keung, A. and Main, G.(2012). The Good Childhood Report 2012: A review of our children's well-being, London: Children's Society. Accessed at http://www.childrenssociety.org.uk/what-we-do/research/research-publications

28. Reid, K (1999) *Truancy and Schools*, London: Routledge

29. Rendall 2003 – How important are inter-generational cycles of teenage motherhood in England and Wales? A comparison with France, Population Trends 111 Spring. Accessed at http://www.ncbi.nlm.nih.gov/pubmed/12743896

30. Rendall, M. (2003) How important are intergenerational cycles of teenage

31. Report by the Commission on the Measurement of Economic Performance and Social Progress by Stiglitz, Sen and Fitoussi (2009) – http://www.stiglitz-sen-fitoussi.fr/documents/rapport_anglais.pdf

32. Rigby, K. (2011) Bullying in schools and what to do about it. Accessed at http://www.kenrigby.net

33. Skew, A, et al, (2011) : Young People and Well-Being, Presentation to children and young people as part of the 2011 Festival of Social Science, London, 3 November 2011

34. Smith, P. et al, (2010) Childcare and early years survey of parents, London: Department for Education; https://www.education.gov.uk/publications/

35. Smoking, drinking and drug use among young people in England in 2011. Health and Social Care Information Centre, 2012. Accessed at http://www.ic.nhs.uk/statistics-and-data-collections/health-and-lifestyles-related-surveys/smoking-drinking-and-drug-use-among-young-people-in-england/smoking-drinking-and-drug-use-among-young-people-in-england-in-2011

36. Sylva, K, (2004) Effective Provision of Pre-School Education (EPPE) Project: Final Report - A Longitudinal Study, 1997-2004 DfES Publication, Accessed at http://www.childcareresearch.org/childcare/resources/7215?classifCode=1.2&type=Fact+Sheets+%26+Briefs&paging.startRow=1&author=Siraj-Blatchford%2C+Iram

37. University of Essex. Institute for Social and Economic Research and National Centre for Social Research, Understanding Society: Wave 1, 2009-2010 [computer file]. 2nd Edition. Colchester, Essex: UK Data Archive [distributor], September 2011. SN: 6614.

38. Valkenburg, P.M, & Peter, J (2009). Social consequences of the Internet for adolescents: a decade of research. *Current Directions in Psychological Science, 18*, 1-5.

39. Welsh Government (2011). Children and Young People's Well-being Monitor, 2011. Available at http://wales.gov.uk/about/aboutresearch/social/latestresearch/cypwell-beingmonitor/?lang=en

40. WHO (2008) Report on the global Tobacco epidemic. Accessed at http://www.who.int/tobacco/publications/surveillance/en/index.html

41. Wolke, D., & Skew, A. (2012). Bullying among siblings. International Journal of Adolescent Medicine & Health, 24(1), 17-26. Accessed at http://dx.doi.org/10.1515/ijamh.2012.004

Proposed domains and measures for Measuring National Well-being

More information about these proposed domains and measures can be found in *Measuring National Well-being, Summary of Proposed Domains and Measures*. Most of the measures in this table are of direct or indirect relevance to young people. In particular, measures in the three more contextual domains, 'The economy', 'Governance' and 'The natural environment', are applicable to the whole population. More information, some of which is of direct relevance to young people, is already available in the domain publications for 'Our relationships' 'Health', 'Education and skills', Where we live', 'Personal finance' and *'Young people's well-being'* which can be found *http://www.ons.gov.uk/ons/guide-method/user-guidance/well-being/publications/index.html*).

PRT - Domains and measures (24.5 Kb Excel sheet)

Proposed domains and measures for Measuring National Well-being
United Kingdom

Proposed domain and measure	Source
Individual Well-being	
Percentage with medium and high rating of satisfaction with their lives overall	ONS/SWB APS UK
Percentage with medium and high rating of how worthwhile the things they do are	ONS/SWB APS UK
Percentage who rated their happiness yesterday as medium or high	ONS/SWB APS UK
Percentage who rated how anxious they were yesterday as low or very low	ONS/SWB APS UK
Our Relationships	
Average rating of satisfaction with family life out of 10	Eurofound UK
Percentage who were somewhat, mostly or completely satisfied with their social life	BHPS UK
Percentage who said they had one or more people they could really count on in a crisis	BHPS UK
Health	
Healthy life expectancy at birth	ONS UK
Percentage who reported a long term illness and a disability	ONS/APS UK
Percentage who were somewhat, mostly or completely satisfied with their health	BHPS UK
Percentage with some evidence indicating probable psychological disturbance or mental ill health	BHPS UK
What we do	
Unemployment rate	ONS/LFS
Percentage who were somewhat, mostly or completely satisfied with their job	BHPS UK
Percentage who were somewhat, mostly or completely satisfied with their amount of leisure time	BHPS UK
Percentage who were somewhat, mostly or completely satisfied with their leisure time	BHPS UK
Percentage who volunteered in the last 12 months	BHPS UK
Where we live	
Crimes against the person (per 1,000 adults)	ONS/CSEW England and Wales
Percentage who felt very or fairly safe and walking alone after dark	ONS/CSEW England and Wales
Percentage who accessed green spaces at least once a week in England	Natural England; England
Percentage who agreed or agreed strongly that they felt they belonged to their neighbourhood	BHPS UK
Personal finance	
Percentage of individuals living in households with less than 60 per cent of median income after housing costs	FRS, DWP UK ONS/WAS GB
Mean wealth per household, including pension wealth	BHPS UK
Percentage who were somewhat, mostly or completely satisfied with their income of their household	BHPS UK
Percentage who report finding it quite or very difficult to get by financially	BHPS UK
Education and skills	
Human capital – the value of individuals' skills, knowledge and competences in the labour market	ONS UK
Percentage with 5 or more grades A*–C incl English and Maths	DfE; WG;SG; NIDoE
Percentage ok UK residents aged 16 to 64 with no qualifications	ONS/LFS UK
The economy	
Real household income per head	ONS UK
Net National Income of the UK (£ million)	ONS UK
UK Net National debt as a percentage of Gross Domestic Product	ONS UK
Consumer Price Inflation index (2005=100)	ONS UK

Measuring National Well-being - Governance, 2012

Author Name(s): Chris Randall Office for National Statistics

Abstract

This article is published as part of the Office for National Statistics (ONS) Measuring National Well-being Programme. The programme aims to produce accepted and trusted measures of the well-being of the nation – how the UK as a whole is doing. This article explores in more detail aspects of governance considered important for understanding National Well-being. It considers information on the involvement in democracy and trust in how the UK is run including statistics on the percentage of registered voters who voted, percentage who trust in parliament and in national government.

Introduction

This article is published as part of the Office for National Statistics (ONS) Measuring National Well-being programme. It includes information on one aspect of National Well-being: Governance.

Governance is one of the ten domains which the Programme is using to help describe the well-being of the UK. The full list of these domains and the current measures within each domain can be seen in the Annex 'Proposed domains and measures for Measuring National Well-being'. More information about the Programme can be found on the National Well-being page on the ONS website.

Governance is a far reaching subject and to cover it in its entirety would be difficult in a single article. Therefore this article includes some of the main components of the subject and gives references to further reading where appropriate.

A fundamental part of the work of government is to support a better life for its citizens and help build strong and resilient communities which in turn may improve the wellbeing of individuals. This was highlighted in the ONS National Debate on Measuring National Well-being. When people were asked what mattered most for the measurement of National Well-being, national governance was one aspect that people considered important.

This article illustrates involvement in democracy and trust in how the UK is run and includes information about the headline measures currently proposed for this domain of National Well-being:

- Percentage of registered voters who voted

- Percentage who trust in Parliament a lot or a fair amount
- Percentage who have trust in the national government

Key points

Democracy

- In 2012 over 6 in 10 (63 per cent) residents in Great Britain agreed that 'For all its faults, Britain's democratic system is one of the finest in the world' with a higher percentage of those over 60 (76 per cent) than those aged 18 to 24 (48 per cent) agreeing
- When asked to choose features of Britain's political system under a third (32 per cent) of residents aged 18 and over in Great Britain mentioned the 'role played by the Queen as one they liked the most and over half (53 per cent) mentioned 'the quality of our politicians' as one they liked the least

Civic engagement

- The proportion of adults aged 16 and over in England engaged in some form of civic participation (34 per cent), was lower in 2009–10 and 2010–11 than in previous years
- In 2011 those aged 18 and over in Great Britain with a GCSE or equivalent level qualification were more likely as those with a degree to agree with the statement 'politics and government seem so complicated that a person like me cannot really understand what is going on' at 65 per cent and 36 per cent respectively

Trust and accountability

- Less than a quarter (23 per cent) of people in the UK aged 15 and over tended to trust the UK Parliament in 2012 and just over a fifth (21 per cent) tended to trust the government: both of these were lower proportions than in some earlier years

Government spending

- In the UK in 2010, half (50 per cent) of GDP was spent by the Government on a variety of public services compared with the average of 46 per cent for 34 countries in the Organisation for Economic Development

e-government

- In 2007 about 78 per cent of basic government services in the UK were available online and this had risen to 98 per cent in 2010
- In 2011 approximately 4 in 10 users of the Internet aged 14 and over in Great Britain had used it to access information on central government services (40 per cent) and information on local services (38 per cent)

Democracy

'Government of the people, by the people, for the people' was the definition of democracy given by the United States president Abraham Lincoln in 1863. Democracy can be defined as a form of government where a constitution guarantees basic personal and political rights, fair and free elections, and independent courts of law.

Many people stated in the findings from the National Well-being debate that democracy was important. A quote from the debate described the UK as 'a largely incorrupt democracy, albeit imperfect'

Figure 1: Proportion of people who agree or disagree that Britain's democratic system is one of the finest in the world(1): by age, 2012 (2)

Great Britain

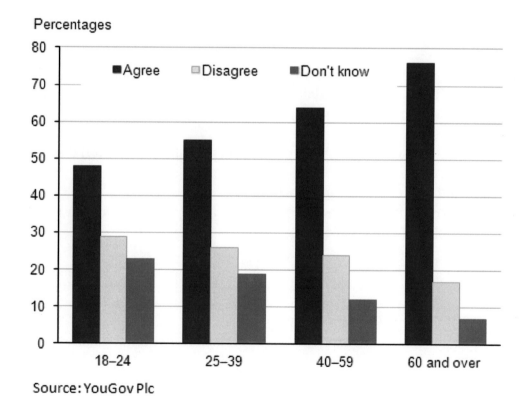

Source: YouGov Plc

Notes:
1. Respondents aged 18 and over were asked whether they agree or disagree with the statement 'For all its faults, Britain's democratic system is one of the finest in the world'. Agree is a total of those who agreed strongly or tended to agree. Disagree is a total of those who tended to disagree and disagreed strongly.
2. Fieldwork was carried out on 12 to 21 January. Total sample size was 5,160. The figures have been weighted and are representative of all adults in Great Britain.

In January 2012, adults aged 18 and over in Great Britain were asked in a survey conducted by YouGov whether they agreed with the statement 'For all its faults, Britain's democratic system is one of the finest in the world' (YouGov,2012).

- Over 6 in 10 (63 per cent) agreed strongly or tended to agree with the statement, while over 2 in 10 (23 per cent) tended to disagree or disagree strongly

There was considerable variation by age group (Figure 1):

- Under half (48 per cent) of those aged 18 to 24 reported that they agreed strongly or tended to agree with the statement, compared to just over three-quarters (76 per cent) of those aged over 60
- The proportion of those who stated that they didn't know also varied with 23 per cent of those aged 18 to 24 compared to just 7 per cent of those aged 60 and over

On the same survey, respondents were asked to choose up to three features of Britain's political system that they liked the most:

- Over a third (36 per cent) reported that they liked 'the coverage of politics on radio and television'
- Just under a third (32 per cent) liked the 'role played by the Queen'
- Under a quarter (23 per cent) liked 'the coverage of politics in the newspapers'

When asked to choose up to three features of Britain's political system that they liked the least:

- Over half (53 per cent) reported 'the quality of our politicians'
- Nearly 4 in 10 (39 per cent) chose 'the way peers are selected to be members of the House of Lords' and 'the quality of our political parties'

Figure 2: Satisfaction with the workings of democracy, (1) 2010

United Kingdom

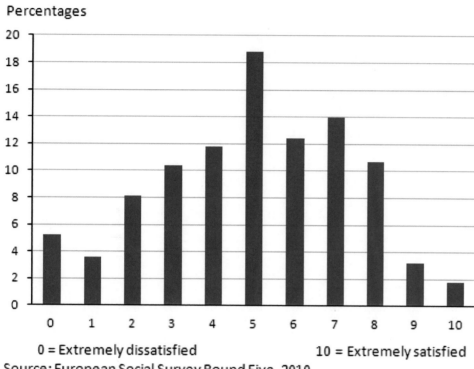

Percentages

0 = Extremely dissatisfied   10 = Extremely satisfied

Source: European Social Survey Round Five, 2010

Notes:
1. Respondents aged 15 and over were asked 'On the whole, how satisfied are you with the way democracy works in Britain (or the UK if in Northern Ireland), where 0 means extremely dissatisfied and 10 means extremely satisfied.

The European Social Survey (ESS) asked people aged 15 and over in the UK in 2010 to rate the way they felt democracy works in the UK on a scale of 0 to 10 where 0 was extremely dissatisfied and 10 was extremely satisfied (Figure 2) (ESS, 2010).

In 2010:

*   Over half (53 per cent) had levels of 'satisfaction with democracy' of 3 to 6 out of 10
*   30 per cent reported their satisfaction as 7 or more out of 10
*   However, a sizeable minority of the population were estimated to have very low ratings of 0 to 2 out of 10 (17 per cent)

One of the hallmarks of democracy in the UK is the election system. People can vote in person, by post or by proxy in regular elections of borough, county and parish councils, the London Assembly, mayoral elections, parliaments in Wales, Scotland and Northern Ireland, and the European and Westminster parliaments. The strength of enthusiasm for and engagement with the democratic process in the UK is vital to sustaining a healthy representative democracy.

According to the 2010 British Social Attitudes survey (BSA), 61 per cent of adults aged 18 and over in Great Britain agreed strongly or agreed with the statement 'Voting is the only way people like me can have any say about how the government runs things', while a quarter (25 per cent) of adults disagreed or disagreed strongly with this statement (BSA, 2010).

Figure 3: Voting turnout in UK General Elections (1)

United Kingdom

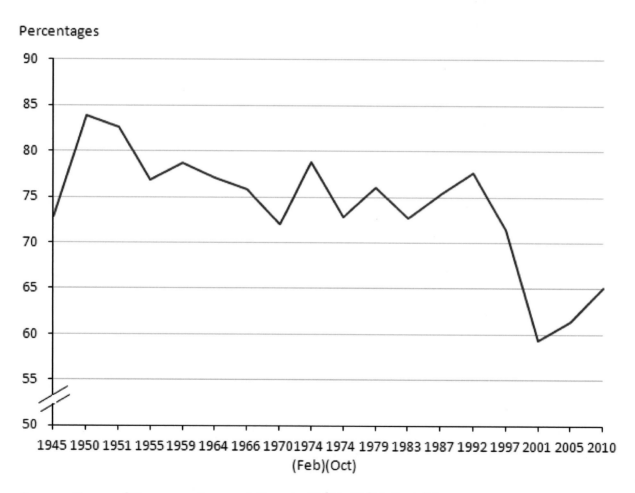

Source: House of Commons Research Papers 01/54, 05/33 & 10/37

Notes:
1.   Valid votes as a proportion of the electorate.

In 1950 voting turnout peaked with over 8 in 10 (83.9 per cent) of the electorate voting in General Elections[1] (Figure 3). By 1983, turnout was down to 72.7 per cent - and despite an improvement in participation in both 1987 and 1992, the General Elections in 2001 and 2005 had relatively low turnouts (59.4 per cent and 61.4 per cent respectively). In 2010 the turnout rose to 65.1 per cent.

Those that do use their votes are more likely to be from the older age groups with younger people less likely to vote. Data from the British Election Study shows that in 1964, 11 per cent of young people aged 18 to 24 and 19 per cent of those aged 25 to 34 were non-voters. Overall electoral turnout in 1964 was 77 per cent. During the 1970s and 1980s an average of around 25 per cent of those aged 18 to 24 and 19 per cent of those aged 25 to 34 were non-voters. Turnout in these two decades varied from 72 per cent to 79 per cent. Electoral turnout in 2005 was 61 per cent, and the proportion of people aged 18 to 24 and 25 to 34 who did not vote had risen to 55 per cent and 47 per cent respectively (2005 is the latest data on age available).

Notes

1. Voter turnout is measured by the number of people registered to vote. Non-voters are those registered but not voting.

Civic engagement

Civic engagement has three components:

*   Civic activism – which refers to involvement either in direct decision-making about local services or issues, or in the actual provision of these services by taking on a role such as a local councillor, school governor or magistrate
*   Civic consultation – which refers to active engagement in consultation about local services or issues through activities such as attending a consultation group or completing a questionnaire about these services
*   Civic participation – which covers wider forms of engagement in democratic processes, such as contacting an elected representative, taking part in a public demonstration or protest, or signing a petition

Figure 4: Participation in civic participation, civic consultation and civic activism (1)
England

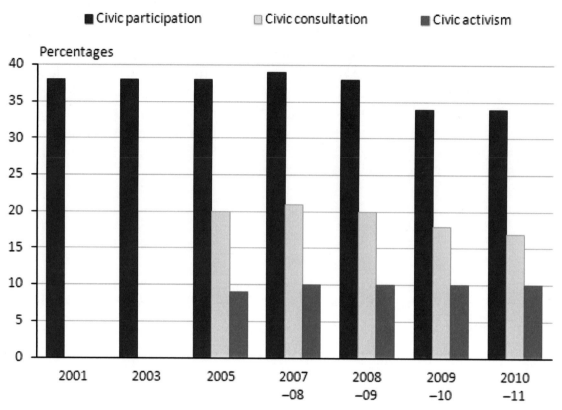

Source: Citizenship Survey, Department for Communities and Local Government

Notes:
1. In the 12 months prior to interview.

According to the Citizenship Survey run by the Department for Communities and Local Government (Figure 4) (DCLG, 2010-11):

- In 2010–11, around a third (34 per cent) of adults aged 16 and over in England engaged in some sort of civic participation at least once in the 12 months prior to interview; unchanged on 2009-10 but lower than in any year before (between 38 per cent and 39 per cent)
- Under a fifth (17 per cent) were involved in some sort of civic consultation in 2010–11 at least once in the 12 months prior to interview, lower than in all previous years (18 per cent to 21 per cent)
- The percentage of people reporting that they had engaged in civic activism during the previous year was 10 per cent in 2010–11, the same proportion as all previous years

Table 1

Public perception of civic participation[1], 2011[2]

Great Britain   Percentages

	Men	Women	All
Being active in politics is a good way to get benefits for groups that people care about like pensioners or the disabled	50	42	46
It takes too much time and effort to be active in politics and public affairs	39	35	37
Being active in politics is a good way to get benefits for me and my family	26	15	21

1 Adults aged 18 and over who strongly agreed or agreed with the statement.

2 Fieldwork was carried out on 4 and 5 December 2011. Total sample size was 1,699. The figures have been weighted and are representative of all adults in Great Britain.

YouGov Plc

YouGov asked adults aged 18 and over in Great Britain in 2011 to agree or disagree with statements about participation in politics (Table 1) (YouGov, 2011):

- Half of men (50 per cent) and 42 per cent of women strongly agreed or agreed with the statement that being involved in politics was a good way to benefit groups that people care about like pensioners and disabled
- Just over a quarter of men (26 per cent) and 15 per cent of women strongly agreed or agreed that involvement in politics was a good way to benefit them and their family
- However, over a third of both men (39 per cent) and women (35 per cent) felt that being involved in politics and public affairs took too much time and effort

Education may be a factor in developing an interest in politics and in turn participation in civic matters. The British Social Attitudes survey (BSA) asked adults aged 18 and over in Great Britain in 2011, whether they agreed or disagreed with the statement 'Sometimes politics and government seem so complicated that a person like me cannot really understand what is going on' (BSA, 2011):

- People with an O-level/GCSE or equivalent level qualification were more likely to strongly agree or agree with this statement (65 per cent) compared to those who had the higher qualification of a degree (36 per cent)

People were also asked how much interest in politics they have:

- 46 per cent of those with a degree reported a great deal or quite a lot of interest
- This compares with 24 per cent of people with an O-level/GCSE A-C or equivalent qualification

Trust and accountability

Trust in, and accountability of, national government and other institutions such as local councils and the justice system were key concerns reported during the National Well-being debate.

In the simplest sense, government accountability means that the Government is answerable for its performance or results. Much of the public's trust rests upon the Government being openly accountable for its decisions, actions and mistakes. A loss of public trust in the Government may result when the Government operates in secret or refuses to disclose information to the public.

Figure 5: Trust in parliament and government (1)

United Kingdom

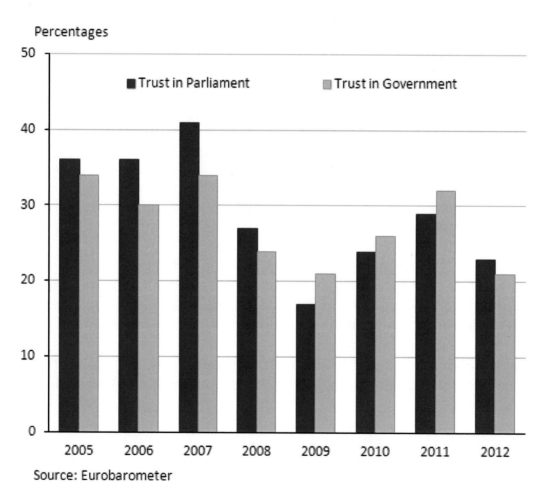

Source: Eurobarometer

Notes:

1. Respondents aged 15 and over were asked if they 'tend to trust' or 'tend to not trust' the UK parliament and government. Percentages are for those who answered 'tend to trust'. Fieldwork was carried out in May and June in 2005; March and May in 2006; April and May in 2007; March and April in 2008; June and July in 2009 and May in 2010 to 2012.

According to the Standard Eurobarometer survey, less than a quarter (23 per cent) of people aged 15 and over in the UK 'tended to trust' the UK parliament in 2012, while just over a fifth (21 per cent) 'tended to trust the government (Figure 5). Since 2005, trust in the UK Parliament peaked in 2007 at 41 per cent but then declined sharply to 17 per cent in 2009. Similarly, in 2007 the proportion of people that 'tended to trust' the Government, stood at over a third (34 per cent) but fell to just over a fifth (21 per cent) in 2009. These proportional declines may have been due to the UK parliamentary expenses scandal and the start of the financial crisis (Eurobarometer, 2012).

Trust in the political system and satisfaction with living in the UK or Great Britain or one of the constituent countries is related.

Figure 6: Trust in the political system (1) compared with satisfaction with living in the UK or Great Britain or constituent countries (2), 2011–12 (3)

Great Britain

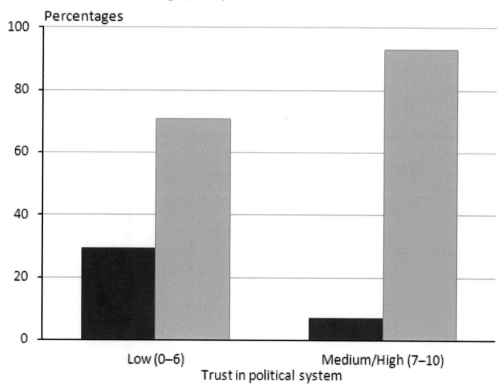

Source: Opinions and Lifestyle Survey, Office for National Statistics

Notes:
1. Adults aged 16 and over were asked 'How much do you personally trust the political system?' where nought is 'not at all satisfied' and 10 is 'completely satisfied' .
2. Adults aged 16 and over were asked 'How satisfied are you living in this country? where nought is 'not at all satisfied' and 10 is 'completely satisfied' . ''This country' refers to the UK, Great Britain or one of the constituent countries. All respondents were asked when answering questions about 'this country', what country or countries

were you thinking of?' This data only includes respondents who answered UK, Great Britain or one of the constituent countries.

3.   Data are for September 2011 and January and May 2012.

Of adults aged 16 and over in Great Britain who reported a medium/high trust (7 to 10 out of 10) in the political system, 7 per cent reported a low satisfaction (0 to 6 out of 10) with living in the UK or Great Britain or one of the constituent countries (Figure 6). However, of those reporting a low trust in the political system, nearly 3 in 10 (29 per cent) reported a low satisfaction for living in the UK or Great Britain or one of the constituent countries. However, it must be noted that 71 per cent reported a medium/high satisfaction with living in the UK or Great Britain or one of the constituent countries, despite a low trust in the political system.

Figure 7: Satisfaction with living in UK or Great Britain or constituent countries (1) compared with life satisfaction (2), 2011–12 (3)

Great Britain

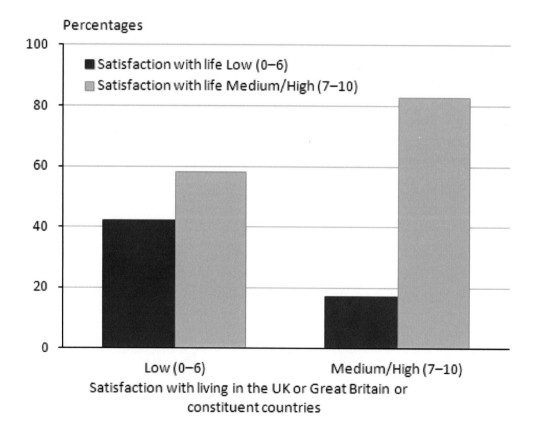

Source: Opinions and Lifestyle Survey, Office for National Statistics

Notes:

1.   Adults aged 16 and over were asked 'How satisfied are you living in this country? where nought is 'not at all satisfied' and 10 is 'completely satisfied' . ''This country' refers to the UK, Great Britain or one of the constituent

countries. All respondents were asked when answering questions about 'this country', what country or countries were you thinking of?' This data only includes respondents who answered UK, Great Britain or one of the constituent countries.

2. Adults aged 16 and over were asked 'How satisfied are you with your life nowadays?' where nought is 'not at all satisfied' and 10 is 'completely satisfied' .

3. Data are for September 2011 and January and May 2012.

Of adults aged 16 and over in Great Britain who reported a medium/high (7 to 10 out of 10) satisfaction for living in the UK or Great Britain or one of the constituent countries, 17 per cent reported a low satisfaction with life (Figure 7). However, of those reporting a low satisfaction for living in the UK or Great Britain or one of the constituent countries, 42 per cent reported a low life satisfaction. However, it must be noted that 58 per cent reported a medium/high satisfaction with life despite a low satisfaction for living in the UK or Great Britain or one of the constituent countries.

Associated with people's trust in parliament is their trust in politicians. Adults aged 18 and over in Great Britain were asked on the British Social Attitudes survey 'How much do you trust politicians of any party in Britain to tell the truth when they are in a tight corner?' (BSA, 2010).

*   In 2000 just over 1 in 10 (11 per cent) reported that 'politicians told the truth almost always or most of the time when in a tight corner' compared with 46 per cent who reported that they told the truth almost never
*   In 2010, 7 per cent reported that politicians told the truth just about always or most of the time. However, those that reported 'almost never' increased by 10 percentage points to 56 per cent

Trust in the Criminal Justice System (CJS) was another issue raised in the National Well-being debate. The CJS is an important part of society, and it is expected to be fair, impartial, efficient and effective.

Table 2: Public confidence in the Criminal Justice System, (1) 2007/08

England and Wales and Northern Ireland (Percentages)

	England and Wales	Northern Ireland
Respects the rights of people accused of committing a crime and treats them fairly	80	82
Treats people who come forward as witnesses well	69	68
Effective in bringing people who commit crimes to justice	44	43
Deals with cases promptly and efficiently	42	37
Effective at reducing crime	38	38
Meets the needs of victims of crime	36	37
Effective at dealing with young people accused of crime	25	29

Source: Crime Survey for England and Wales, Office for National Statistics (formally the British Crime Survey, Home Office), Northern Ireland Crime Survey, Department of Justice

Table notes:
1. Data in the table is for adults aged 16 and over who answered 'very' or 'fairly confident' or 'very' or 'fairly effective'. The unweighted base for the headline measure for England and Wales (effective in bringing people who commit crimes to justice) was 36,425, other unweighted bases for the other measures were similar.

According to a report compiled by the Ministry of Justice with data from the Crime Survey for England and Wales[2] (formerly known as the British Crime Survey), less than half (44 per cent)

of adults aged 16 and over in England and Wales in 2007/08 (the latest data available for these measures[3]) reported that they were very or fairly confident that the CJS was effective in bringing people who commit crimes to justice (Table 2). A larger proportion of adults (80 per cent) felt very or fairly confident that the CJS respected the rights of people accused of committing a crime and treated them fairly. Just under 7 in 10 (69 per cent) felt very or fairly confident that the CJS treated people who came forward as witnesses well. Similarly in Northern Ireland less than half (43 per cent) of adults reported that they were very or fairly confident that the CJS was effective in bringing people who commit crimes to justice, with over four-fifths (82 per cent) very or fairly confident that the CJS respected the rights of people accused of committing a crime and treated them fairly (CSEW, 2007/08).

Although most people live in relative safety, the challenges to peace and security are ever increasing. Many of these challenges, including the risk of terrorism and cybercrime, are becoming increasingly sophisticated. They may have an impact on people's sense of security and in turn their general well-being.

Figure 8: Selected challenges to the security of UK citizens (1), 2011

United Kingdom

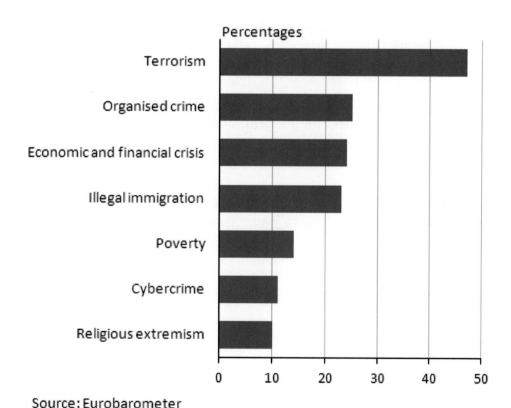

Source: Eurobarometer

Notes:

1. Respondents aged 15 and over were asked in June 2011, 'What do you think are the most important challenges to the security of UK citizens at the moment?'

People aged 15 and over in the UK were asked on a Eurobarometer Survey in 2011 to identify the most important challenges to the security of UK citizens (Figure 8) (Eurobarometer, 2011):

- Nearly half (47 per cent) identified terrorism and a quarter organised crime (25 per cent)
- The recent economic and financial crisis and illegal immigration were reported by just under a quarter (24 per cent and 23 per cent respectively)
- 14 per cent reported poverty as an important challenge
- Around 1 in 10 people reported that Cybercrime and religious extremism was a challenge to security at 11 per cent and 10 per cent respectively

 People were asked on the same survey if the UK was doing enough to 'fight' some of these challenges:

- Nearly two-thirds (64 per cent) agreed that the UK was doing enough to fight terrorism
- Half (50 per cent) agreed that the UK was doing enough to fight organised crime
- Just over 4 in 10 (41 per cent) agreed that the UK was doing enough to fight cybercrime

Notes

1. The Criminal Justice System (CJS) is responsible for detecting crime and bringing offenders to justice; carrying out the orders of court, such as collecting fines; and supervising community and custodial punishment. Criminal justice agencies include the police, the Crown Prosecution Service, the courts, the prison service, the probation service, and the youth justice service.

2. The British Crime Survey (BCS) is now known as the Crime Survey for England and Wales (effective from 1 April 2012) to better reflect its geographical coverage. While the survey did previously cover the whole of Great Britain it ceased to include Scotland in its sample in the late 1980s. There is a separate survey – the Scottish Crime and Justice Survey – covering Scotland.

3. 2007/08 was the last time these measures were used. A new set of questions were developed and entered into the survey in 2007/08 and these have been used from then onwards. These new measures are:

    - Confident that the CJS is effective
    - Confident that the CJS is fair

    For more information see Table D50 Crime Statistics - period ending September 2012

Government spending

Government spends money to provide goods and services and redistribute income, which in turn may have some effect on the well-being of some of its citizens. The economy as a whole and its relation to measuring national well-being was covered as a Measuring National Well-being domain article in its own right in October 2012[1]. However, for the purposes of this article it is worth having a look at the UK's government expenditure compared to the other member states of the Organisation for Economic Co-operation and Development (OECD).

General government spending[2] as a share of GDP provides an indication of the size of the government across countries. However, the large variation in these ratios highlights different approaches to delivering public goods and services and providing social protection not necessarily differences in resources spent.

Figure 9: General government expenditures as a percentage of GDP, 2010 (1)

OECD 34

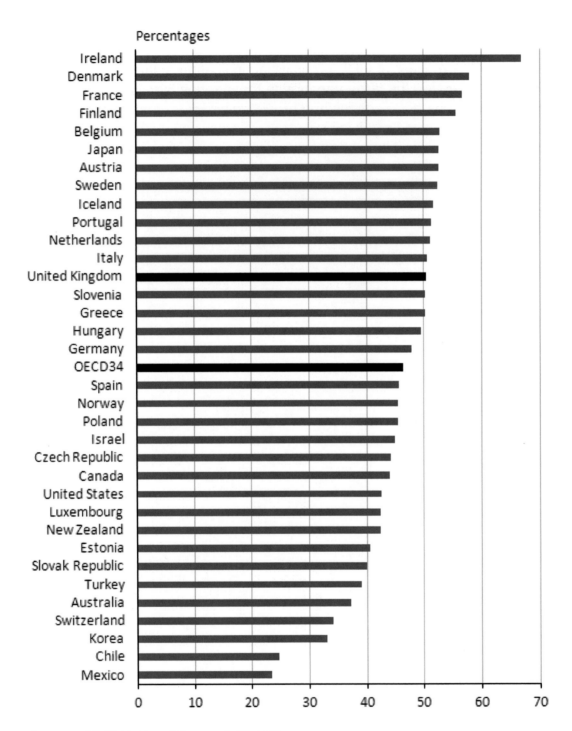

Percentages

Source: OECD National Accounts Statistics

Notes:

1. Data for Australia, Chile, Korea and New Zealand are for 2009.

On average, government expenditures across the 34 countries of the OECD represented 46 per cent of GDP in 2010 according to OECD National Accounts Statistics (Figure 9). This compares with 50 per cent of GDP in the UK. In general, countries from the European Union (EU) tend to have a higher ratio than other OECD member countries. Ireland (67 per cent), Denmark (58 per cent), and France (57 per cent) spend the most as a share of GDP. Mexico and Chile spend the least, 23 per cent and 25 per cent of GDP respectively (OECD, 2010).

Government finances a variety of public goods and services, for example, providing benefits, building public infrastructure or subsidising alternative energy sources. However it must be noted that other factors, such as an ageing population or a high level of national debt requiring substantial amounts of interest payments, also influence the size and structure of general government expenditures.

Figure 10: General government expenditure (1), 2010

United Kingdom and OECD31 (2)

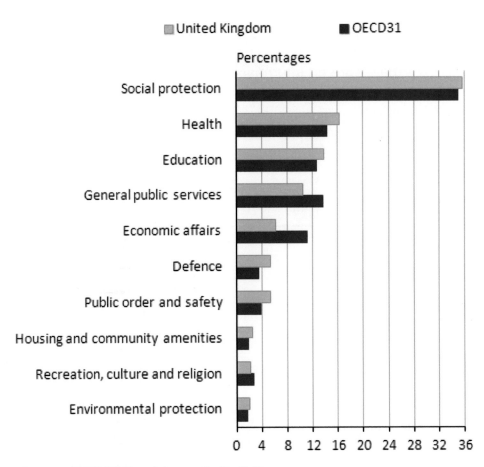

Source: OECD National Accounts Statistics

Notes:
1.   By Classification of the Functions of Government (COFOG).
2.   Data for Australia, Chile and Mexico are not available.

Figure 10 shows a comparison of the proportion of spending on different functions between the UK and 31 of the 34 member states of the OECD. Social protection was the largest category of expenses in both the UK and the OECD31, representing over one third of total expenditures in 2010. Aside from social protection, OECD member countries spent the most on health (14 per cent), general public services, which include interest payments on debt (14 per cent) and education (13 per cent). In general, OECD member countries spend the least on environmental protection and housing and community amenities. Aside from social protection, the UK spent the most on health (16 per cent), Education (14 per cent) and general public services (11 per cent) (OECD, 2010).

How the UK acts and is perceived abroad was mentioned in the National well-being debate as the following quote demonstrates;

'Knowing that the UK is meeting its international obligations and providing leadership on poverty reduction, climate change, combating AIDS, fighting major causes of mortality etc.'

An important obligation is the UK's expenditure on International Development Assistance. In 2010, UK Official Development Assistance (UK ODA) accounted for 0.57 per cent of Gross National Income (GNI), equivalent to £8,452 million.

Table 3
Public perception on UK Overseas Development Assistance
Great Britain

	18–24	25–39	40–59	Aged 60 and over	All aged 18 and over
The UK's development assistance to poorer countries helps us to protect our national interests and long-term security, and the government is right to protect it from public spending cuts	39	34	28	22	29
Much development assistance is wasted and does little or nothing to promote British interests; it should be radically reduced	30	46	59	67	54
Don't Know	31	20	13	11	16

1 Adults aged 18 and over were asked which of the statements in the table above come closest to your view.
2 Fieldwork was carried out on 24 and 25 June 2010. Total sample size was 2,481. The figures have been weighted and are representative of all adults in Great Britain.
Source: YouGov Plc/Chatham House survey

Adults aged 18 and over in Great Britain were asked in a survey conducted by YouGov in June 2010 which of two statements on UK ODA they felt came closest to the way they felt. Just under 3 in 10 (29 per cent) felt that the statement 'The UK's development assistance to poorer countries helps us to protect our national interests and long-term security, and the government is right to protect it from public spending cuts' was closest to their view (Table 3). However agreement with this statement decreased with age, with just under 4 in 10 (39 per cent) of those aged 18 to 24 and around 2 in 10 (22 per cent) of those aged over 60 (YouGov, 2010).

Over half of all adults (54 per cent) reported that the statement 'Much development assistance is wasted and does little or nothing to promote British interests; it should be radically reduced' came closest to the way they felt. Agreement with this statement increases with age with 3 in 10 (30 per cent) of those aged 18 to 24 reporting that the statement came closest to their view compared to nearly 7 in 10 (67 per cent) of those aged 60 and over.

Notes

The economy

1. Government expenditures data are derived from the OECD National Accounts Statistics, which are based on the System of National Accounts (SNA), a set of internationally agreed concepts, definitions, classifications and rules for national accounting. In SNA terminology, general
2. government consists of central, state and local governments and social security funds.

e-government

e-government is the use of information technology by government to interact with citizens, businesses and other governments. The Internet has transformed the way in which many UK citizens interact with banks, shops, travel companies, airlines, the media and a whole host of social groups. It has also changed the way that people interact with government and the way government interacts with its citizens.

Interacting with public authorities' online makes obtaining information and downloading and submitting forms easier for some people than by, for example, queuing at a post office or government office. In 2010 nearly half (48 per cent) of adults aged 16 to 74 in the UK used the Internet for interaction with public authorities in the 12 months prior to interview, compared with 41 per cent in the EU-27 according to Eurostat statistics. The highest proportions of people interacting online with public authorities were in Denmark (78 per cent) and Sweden and Finland (both 68 per cent), while the lowest percentage was in Romania (8 per cent) (Eurostat, 2010).

Figure 11: Availability of e-government online (1)

UK and EU-27

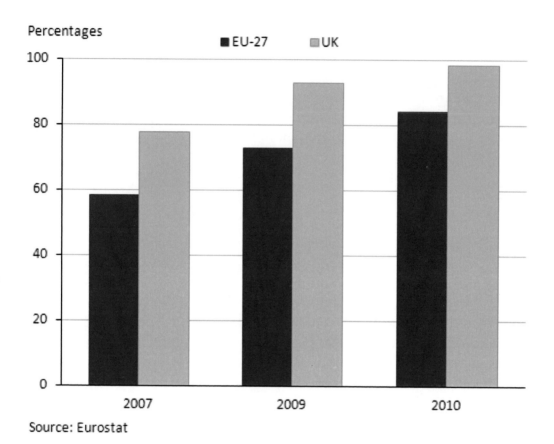

Source: Eurostat

Notes:

1. The indicator shows the percentage of the 20 basic services which are fully available online i.e. for which it is possible to carry out full electronic case handling. For example if in a country 13 of the 20 services were measured as being 100 per cent available online and one service was not relevant (e.g. does not exist), the indicator is 13/19 which is 68.4 per cent. Measurement is based on a sample of URLs of public web sites agreed with Member States as relevant for each service.

Figure 11 shows a comparison of the availability of e-government services over time. Between 2007 and 2010, the proportion of 20 basic e-government services[1] which were fully available online in the UK rose from 78 per cent to 98 per cent. Over the same period the percentage of e-government services in the EU-27 overall, rose from 58 per cent to 84 per cent. In 2010, the UK ranked second after six countries that had 100 per cent availability online (Austria, Ireland, Italy, Malta, Portugal and Sweden).

According to the ONS Opinions and Lifestyle Survey, people had different reasons for using the Internet to interact with public authorities:

- Almost a third (32 per cent) of Internet users aged 16 and over in Great Britain in 2011 obtained information from public authority websites
- Over a quarter downloaded official forms or submitted completed forms (26 per cent and 27 per cent respectively)

However it must be noted that over half (56 per cent) of Internet users did none of these things.

Looking at the online use of government services in more detail, Figure 12 contains data for 2005 and 2011 from the Oxford Internet Survey run by Oxford University.

Figure 12: Use of online government services (1)

Great Britain

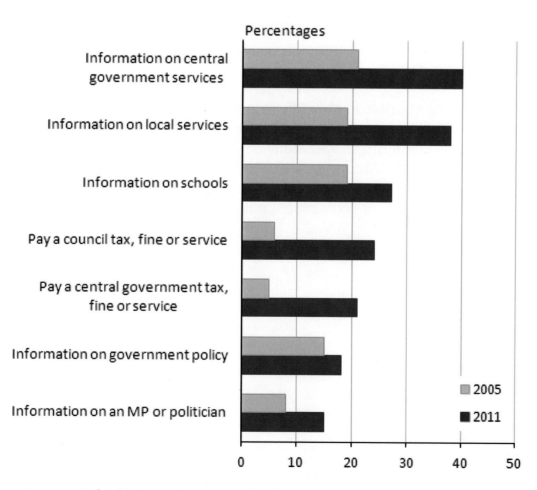

Source: Oxford Internet Survey, Oxford University

Notes:

1. Current users of the Internet at time of interview, aged 14 and over.

Online use of government services by current users of the Internet aged 14 and over in Great Britain increased between 2005 and 2011 (OXIS, 2011):

- Looking for information on central government services and looking for information on local services, both increased by 19 percentage points to 40 per cent and 38 per cent respectively
- Paying council tax, a fine or paying for a service increased by 18 percentage points to 24 per cent
- Paying a central government tax, fine or service increased by 16 percentage points to 21 per cent

As previously mentioned, less than half of all adults in the UK interact with government online. There could be many reasons for this including not having an internet connection. According to the ONS Opinions and Lifestyle Survey (ONS, 2012):

- 20 per cent of households in Great Britain did not have Internet access at home in 2012
- Over half (54 per cent) of all households with no Internet access reported that they did not need the Internet
- Over a fifth (22 per cent) reported a lack of skills

The Accenture Digital Citizen Pulse Survey reported that a quarter of respondents in the UK indicated that they were not aware of ways to interact digitally with government or they did not want the government to access personal data.

The Internet is enabling people to participate in civic affairs in a new environment. According to the 2011 Oxford Internet Survey, the most common online civil participation activity carried out by internet users aged 14 and over in Great Britain was signing a petition online at 14 per cent, twice the proportion of that in 2007 (7 per cent). Around 1 in 10 users performed other civic activities online such as sending a message supporting a political cause (9 per cent), commenting on politics in a social media environment (9 per cent) or contacting a politician (8 per cent) (OXIS, 2011).

Notes

1. The 20 basic e-government services are:

    - Income taxes
    - Job search
    - Social security benefits
    - Personal documents (passport and driver's license)
    - Car registration (new, used, imported cars)
    - Application for building permission
    - Declaration to the police (e.g. in case of theft)
    - Public libraries (availability of catalogues, search tools)

- Certificates (birth and marriage): request and delivery
- Enrollment in higher education/university
- Announcement of moving (change of address)
- Health related services (interactive advice on the availability of services in different hospitals; appointments for hospitals)
- Social contributions for employees
- Corporate tax: declaration, notification
- VAT: declaration, notification
- Registration of a new company
- Submission of data to statistical offices
- Customs declarations
- Environment-related permits (including reporting)
- Public procurement

About the ONS Measuring National Well-being Programme

NWB logo 2

This article is published as part of the ONS Measuring National Well-being Programme.

The programme aims to produce accepted and trusted measures of the well-being of the nation - how the UK as a whole is doing. It is about looking at 'GDP and beyond' and includes:

- greater analysis of the national economic accounts, especially to understand household income, expenditure and wealth
- further accounts linked to the national accounts, including the UK Environmental Accounts and valuing household production and 'human capital'
- quality of life measures, looking at different areas of national well-being such as health, relationships, job satisfaction, economic security, education environmental conditions
- working with others to include the measurement of the well-being of children and young people as part of national well-being
- measures of 'subjective well-being' - individuals' assessment of their own well-being
- headline indicators to summarise national well-being and the progress we are making as a society

The programme is underpinned by a communication and engagement workstream, providing links with Cabinet Office and policy departments, international developments, the public and other stakeholders. The programme is working closely with Defra on the measurement of 'sustainable development' to provide a complete picture of national well-being, progress and sustainable development.

Find out more on the Measuring National Well-being website pages.

Background notes

2. Details of the policy governing the release of new data are available by visiting www.statisticsauthority.gov.uk/assessment/code-of-practice/index.html or from the Media Relations Office email: media.relations@ons.gsi.gov.uk

Copyright

This document is also available on our website at www.ons.gov.uk.

References

1. BSA, 2010 & 2011 - British Social Attitudes

2. CSEW, 2007/08 - Crime Statistics and Smith (2010) Public confidence in the Criminal Justice System: Findings from the British Crime Survey 2002/03 to 2007/08, Ministry of Justice

3. DCLG, 2010–11 - DCLG - Citizenship Survey

4. ESS, 2010 - European Social Survey

5. Eurobarometer, 2011 & 2012 - Eurobarometer

6. Eurostat, 2010 - Eurostat

7. OECD, 2010 - OECD: Statistics

8. ONS, 2012 - Internet Access: Households and individuals

9. OXIS, 2011 - Oxford Internet Surveys

10. YouGov, 2010, 2011 & 2012 - Yougov archives

Proposed domains and measures for Measuring National Well-being

More information about these proposed domains and measures can be found in 'Measuring National Well-being, Summary of Proposed Domains and Measures' which can be found http://www.ons.gov.uk/ons/guide-method/user-guidance/well-being/publications/index.html.

RFT - Domains and measures (24.5 Kb Excel sheet)

Proposed domains and measures for Measuring National Well-being
United Kingdom

Proposed domain and measure	Source
Individual Well-being	
Percentage with medium and high rating of satisfaction with their lives overall	ONS/SWB APS UK
Percentage with medium and high rating of how worthwhile the things they do are	ONS/SWB APS UK
Percentage who rated their happiness yesterday as medium or high	ONS/SWB APS UK
Percentage who rated how anxious they were yesterday as low or very low	ONS/SWB APS UK
Our Relationships	
Average rating of satisfaction with family life out of 10	Eurofound UK
Percentage who were somewhat, mostly or completely satisfied with their social life	BHPS UK
Percentage who said they had one or more people they could really count on in a crisis	BHPS UK
Health	
Healthy life expectancy at birth	ONS UK
Percentage who reported a long term illness and a disability	ONS/APS UK
Percentage who were somewhat, mostly or completely satisfied with their health	BHPS UK
Percentage with some evidence indicating probable psychological disturbance or mental ill health	BHPS UK
What we do	
Unemployment rate	ONS/LFS
Percentage who were somewhat, mostly or completely satisfied with their job	BHPS UK
Percentage who were somewhat, mostly or completely satisfied with their amount of leisure time	BHPS UK
Percentage who were somewhat, mostly or completely satisfied with their leisure time	BHPS UK
Percentage who volunteered in the last 12 months	BHPS UK
Where we live	
Crimes against the person (per 1,000 adults)	ONS/CSEW England and Wales
Percentage who felt very or fairly safe and walking alone after dark	ONS/CSEW England and Wales
Percentage who accessed green spaces at least once a week in England	Natural England; England
Percentage who agreed or agreed strongly that they felt they belonged to their neighbourhood	BHPS UK
Personal finance	
Percentage of individuals living in households with less than 60 per cent of median income after housing costs	FRS, DWP UK
Mean wealth per household, including pension wealth	ONS/WAS GB BHPS UK
Percentage who were somewhat, mostly or completely satisfied with their income of their household	BHPS UK
Percentage who report finding it quite or very difficult to get by financially	BHPS UK
Education and skills	
Human capital – the value of individuals' skills, knowledge and competences in the labour market	ONS UK
Percentage with 5 or more grades A*–C incl English and Maths	DfE; WG;SG; NIDoE
Percentage ok UK residents aged 16 to 64 with no qualifications	ONS/LFS UK
The economy	
Real household income per head	ONS UK
Net National Income of the UK (£ million)	ONS UK
UK Net National debt as a percentage of Gross Domestic Product	ONS UK
Consumer Price Inflation index (2005=100)	ONS UK

Measuring National Well-being - The Natural Environment

Author Name(s): Jawed Khan and Kahwei Hoo; Office for National Statistics

Abstract

The article is published as part of the Office for National Statistics (ONS) Measuring National Well-being programme. The programme aims to produce accepted and trusted measures of the well-being of the nation – how the UK as a whole is doing. This article explores in more detail the aspects of the Natural Environment that are considered important for measuring National Well-being. It includes information on the environmental assets available to us, how they are used and the pressure that places on the natural environment.

Introduction

Well-being is determined by physical and non-physical factors. The ability of a society to produce and consume goods and services determines its standard of living, but in the long-run even more critical is its ability to build and maintain the natural environment that meets basic needs like food, water, clean air and ensure the same for future generations. When ONS conducted a national debate on well-being in 2011, 73 per cent of respondents mentioned the environment, including local green space and nature, as an important factor in well-being, only behind health, family and friends, and job security.

The negative impacts of human activity and economic growth on the natural environment and ecosystem services are an important concern. Therefore, environmental problems such as pollution, loss of green spaces, and waste from the process of producing and using natural resources are an important consideration when looking at National Well-being. The use of land and the protection of the countryside and wildlife are also important issues that have to be addressed in order to ensure that an environmentally sound world is passed on to future generations.

In the recent ONS Report on the Consultation of Proposed Domains and Measures (788 Kb Pdf), the domain 'Natural Environment' is described as an important contextual domain for measuring National Well-being. The four headline measures proposed to measure the natural environment domain are:

- The extent of protected areas,
- Per cent of energy consumption by renewable means,
- Air pollutants,

- Greenhouse gas emissions.

This article provides an overview of the UK stocks of environmental assets including protected areas; how they provide goods and services by looking at the use of physical assets – it focuses almost exclusively on material well-being - including renewable energy; and the pressures of this use on the natural environment in terms on air pollutants and greenhouse gas emissions.

Key Points

Natural Resources

- In 2010, the area covered by the UK woodlands increased by two-and-a-half times the area covered in 1924,
- The total extent of protected areas in the UK has more than doubled during the last decade, from 3.5 million hectares in 2000 to just over 7.5 million hectares in 2011,
- The upper range of the UK's total oil reserves halved from 5 billion tonnes in 1990 to 2.5 billion tonnes in 2010,
- Cod, a popular food in the UK, has been reduced from around 168,000 tonnes in 1964 to around 53,000 in 2010,
- The population of the wild birds in the UK has remained relatively stable between 1970 and 2010.

Uses of Resources

- Imports accounted for 80 per cent of the total timber supply in the UK,
- In 2010, only half of the fish stocks were harvested sustainably and at full reproductive capacity,
- In 2010, 3.2 per cent of the total energy consumption was from renewable sources, although the amount has increased over 5 times since 1990,
- The UK is third from the bottom out of all EU 27 countries in terms of renewable energy consumption as a percentage of gross final energy consumption.

Pressure on the Natural Environment

- Between 1990 and 2010 the emissions from PM_{10} fell by 54 per cent from 0.31 million tonnes to 0.14 million tonnes,
- In the UK, during the last two decades, greenhouse gas emissions per head have fallen by 3.9 tonnes of CO_2 equivalent,
- Based on the emissions estimated up to and including 2010, UK is on course to meet its Kyoto Protocol target for greenhouse gas emissions.

Natural Resources

The Natural Environment is the stock of our physical natural assets or resources available from the natural environment (such as soil, forests, water and bio-diversity) which provide flow of services that benefit people (such as pollinating crops, climate regulation or the benefits of walking in green spaces).

Land

Figure 1: Land Use 2008

United Kingdom

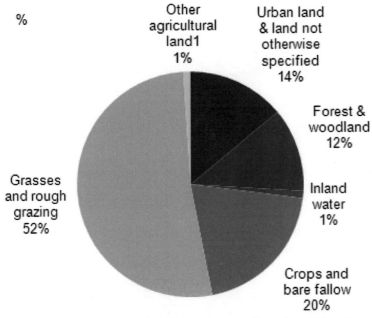

%

Other agricultural land1
1%

Urban land & land not otherwise specified
14%

Forest & woodland
12%

Inland water
1%

Grasses and rough grazing
52%

Crops and bare fallow
20%

Source:Department for Environment, Food and Rural Affairs, Ordanance Survey, Forestry Commission, Forest Service

Nature provides us with a number of environmental assets such as land, woodlands, mineral and energy resources, water, and fish resources. The land area of the UK includes surfaces enclosed by all inland borders including all inland waters. Figure 1 shows that in 2008, agricultural land (grasses and rough grazing, crops and bare fallow, other agricultural land) covered around 73 per cent of the total of UK land area. The remainder of the UK land area was forest and woodlands, urban land and inland water which accounted for around 12 per cent, 14 per cent and 1 per cent respectively.

Woodlands

Figure 2 shows that in 2012, woodlands covered 3.1 million hectares, 12.8 per cent, of the UK land area. This is more than two-and-a-half times the area covered in 1924 when these statistics were first collected by the Forestry Commission. Much of the increase between the 1950s and 1980s was at least partly related to increased investment in woodlands as a result of tax advantages. The apparent increase in 2012, compared with 1995-99, can largely be attributed to improved technology that has enabled more accurate identification of woodlands.

Figure 2: Woodland Area; 1924 to 2012

United Kingdom

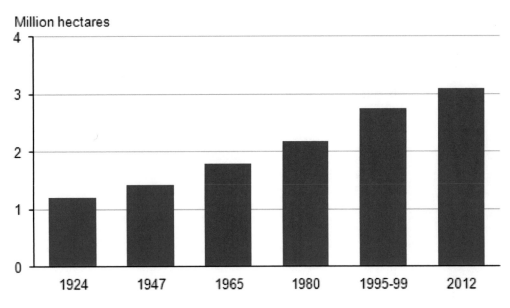

Source: Forestry Commission

The UK woodlands provide various economic and environmental benefits to individuals in terms of eco-system services. The UK National Ecosystem Assessment (June 2011) estimated the following economic value of various ecosystem services from forestry:

- Provisioning services – timber at £96 million per annum,
- Regulatory services – carbon storage is estimated at £680 million in 2009, compared with £124 million in 1945,
- Cultural Services – over £20 billion of direct expenditures associated with annual 2.86 billion outdoor recreational visits in England.

Protected Area

Figure 3: Land and Sea Protected Areas; 1980 to 2011

United Kingdom

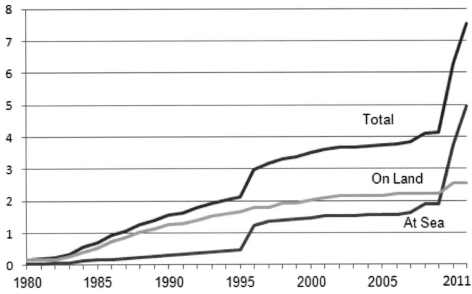

Million Hectares

Source: Joint Nature Conservation Committee

Protected areas are locations that are conserved because of landscape, ecological and/or cultural reasons. In the UK, there are some protected areas which have international designations, such as World Heritage Sites, and some areas, including our National Parks, which have national designations. Protected areas also include Marine Protected Areas, which are zones of the seas and coasts where wildlife is protected from damage and disturbance.

The total extent of protected areas in the UK has more than doubled during the last decade, from 3.5 million hectares in 2000 to just over 7.5 million hectares in 2011 (see figure 3). The main reason for this increase is due to an increase in marine area following the designation of inshore and offshore marine sites under the Habitats Directive – the area of marine protected areas increased by more than 3 million hectares between 2009 and 2011. The extent of protected areas on land has increased by more than half a million hectares since 2000. In 2011, total protected area on water and land was around 5 million hectares and 2.5 million hectares respectively.

Protected areas are highly valued by people for their recreational and cultural services. It is out of the scope of this article to look at how people access these areas and use green spaces but the Measuring National Well-being – Where we live article include measures and information looking at how people interact with the access and local environment.

Mineral and energy resources

Mineral and energy resources are defined as deposits of oil resources, natural gas resources, coal and peat resources, non-metallic minerals and metallic minerals. Mineral and energy resources are a type of environmental asset that can be extracted and used for economic activity but cannot be renewed.

Oil and Gas reserves

Figure 4: Estimated remaining recoverable oil reserves: 1990 to 2010(1)

United Kingdom

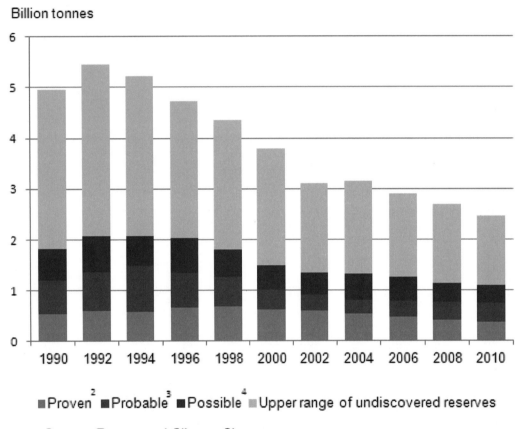

Billion tonnes

Proven[2] Probable[3] Possible[4] Upper range of undiscovered reserves

Source: Energy and Climate Change

Notes:
1. The categories 'proven', 'probable' and 'possible' are based on confidence levels.
2. Proven reserves are known reserves which have a better than 90 per cent chance of being produced.
3. Probable reserves are known reserves which are not yet proven but which are estimated to have a greater the 50 per cent chance of being technically and commercially producible.
4. Possible reserves are those reserves which at present cannot be regarded as 'probable' but are estimated to have a significant but less than 50 per cent chance of being technically and commercially producible.

Figure 4 shows that in the UK, the upper range of the UK's total oil reserves was estimated to be 2.5 billion tonnes at the end of 2010, 121 million tonnes lower than in 2009. This was due to a fall in the upper range of undiscovered reserves of 103 million tonnes to 1.4 billion tonnes, together with a fall in total discovered reserves – proven, probable and possible - of 18 million tonnes to 1.1 billion tonnes. In 2010, proven, probable and possible reserves stood at 374 million tonnes, 377 million tonnes, and 342 million tonnes respectively. It is best practice to concentrate on proven and probable reserves as the possible reserves are quite volatile. In 2011, proven and probable reserves stood at 788 million tonnes; however, there are no estimates available on the possible and upper range of undiscovered reserves.

Estimates of remaining UK oil reserves are uncertain, but reserves do show an overall decline between 1990 and 2010. This suggests that remaining reserves are being depleted faster than new discoveries are being made. In 2010, the level of oil extraction amounted to 63 million tonnes – the lowest since records began in 1989 - approximately 5 million tonnes lower than in 2009.

Estimates of the remaining UK gas reserves paint a similar picture. Figure 5 shows an overall decline between 1995 and 2010 in gas reserves, suggesting that remaining reserves are also being depleted faster than new discoveries are being made. In 2010, level of gas extraction amounted to 55 billion cubic tonnes – the lowest since 1992, approximately 2 billion cubic metres lower than in 2009.

Figure 5: Estimated remaining recoverable gas reserves; 1990 to 2010

United Kingdom

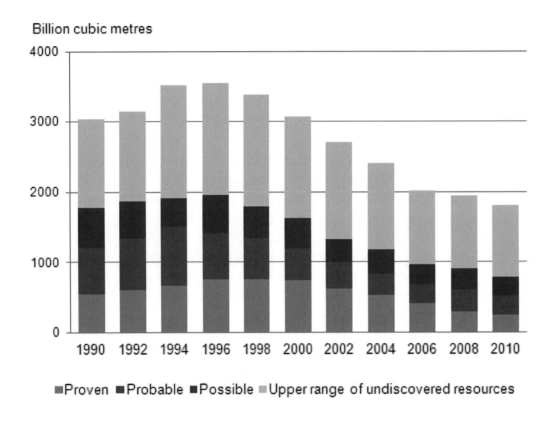

Source: Department of Energy and Climate Change

Coal

The Coal Authority estimates economically recoverable and minable coal resource in current operations and those in the planning or pre-planning process at 320 million tonnes in underground mines and 120 million tonnes in surface mines. In addition there are some 250 million tonnes at closed underground mines still in licence. The tonnage in identified prospects is 2,030 million tonnes suitable for underground mining and 780 million tonnes suitable for surface mining.

In addition to these conventional mining resources, the Coal Authority has licensed some 3,500 million tonnes of coal in offshore conditional licences for potential underground coal gasification operations.

Fish Stocks

Fish are a vital element of the ocean's ecosystem. The level of spawning stock biomass – the total weight of all sexually mature fish in a population – is used to determine whether the population of each stock is at a sustainable level. To prevent over exploitation of fish stocks, there has to be a balance between fishing activities and the natural ability of fish stocks to regenerate.

Figure 6: North Sea Fish Stocks; 1964 to 2010

United Kingdom

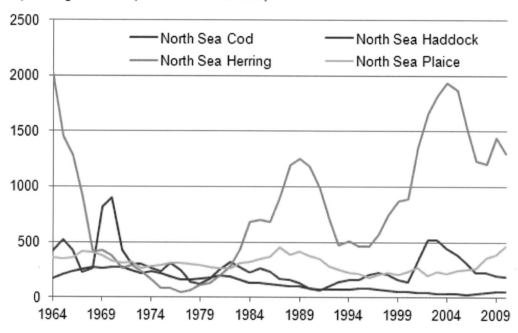

Source: Department for Environment, Food and Rural Affairs, Centre for Environment, Fisheries and Aquaculture Science

Figure 6 shows that the population of the North Sea fish stocks has fluctuated substantially between 1964 and 2010 and the trend has varied from species to species. Cod, a popular food in the UK, is caught throughout the North Sea and because of over fishing has been reduced to very low levels. In 1964 the stocks of cod in the North Sea were estimated at around 168,000 tonnes but by 2006 stocks had fallen to an all time low of 29,000 tonnes, a decrease of 83 per cent. Numbers had recovered slightly by 2010 with stocks standing at around 53,000 tonnes.

North Sea Herring paints a similar picture as they were also seriously over fished in 1970s and between 1964 and 1977 herring stocks declined by around 98 per cent, from just over 2 million tonnes to 48,000 tonnes. This led to a ban on fishing of herrings between 1978 and 1982 and although there was some recovery in the late 1980s, numbers declined again during the 1990s. This decline was due to a combination of excessive fishing and low numbers of young fish entering the stock. Due to management actions stocks started to recover from the mid 1990s and rose to around 1.9 million in 2004. The recent decline from 2005 could be attributed to environmental factors.

Biodiversity

Conserving biodiversity is essential to ensure that ecosystems are resilient and continue to deliver the services that secure the variety of life on earth. This includes ensuring the sustainability of forestry, fisheries, wildlife and agriculture.

Figure 7: Wild bird populations; 1970 to 2010(1)

United Kingdom

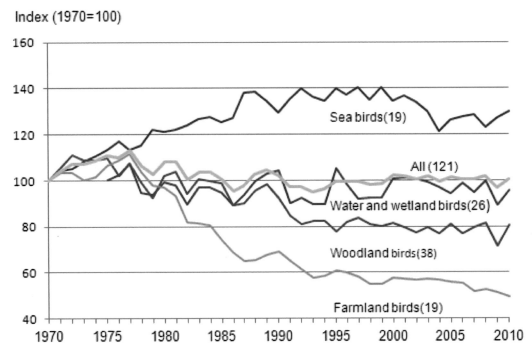

Source: Departement for Environment, Food and Rural Affairs, British Trust for Ornithology (BTO), Royal Society for the Protection of Birds (RSPB)

Notes:
1.   Figures in brackets show the number of species

Wildlife provides cultural services and wild bird populations are an indicator of the general state of wildlife and biodiversity. They occupy a wide range of different habitats and as they tend to be near to or at the top of the food chain, they can reflect changes in insects, plants and other aspects of the environment. Figure 7 shows that overall the population index of wild birds in the UK, which measures the population of 121 species, has remained relatively stable between 1970 and 2010. However, the trends of different species vary.

The farmland bird population has seen a significant decline between 1970 and 2010 and reached its lowest level in 2010. This is driven by a combination of land management changes and intensification of farming that took place over a long period of time. More recent declines are thought to be related to a combination of additional factors including disease, weather and climate change. Recent cold winters and wet springs are known to have had a negative impact.

The woodlands bird population also experienced a decline over the same time period but it recovered slightly in 2010. However, the seabird populations have increased over this time period and were around 30 per cent higher than in 1970.

Use of Resources

Natural resources such as timber are used to produce goods and services consumed by individuals. We are dependent on natural resources for food and as the population and economy grows, more goods and services are produced. As a result more material is being extracted from earth's natural resources and all extraction of non-renewable resources is known as depletion. This article now looks how we consume our natural resources, focussing on a number of consumption indicators.

Consumption

Wood Consumption

Figure 8: Apparent Consumption of Wood(1), 1999 to 2011

United Kingdom

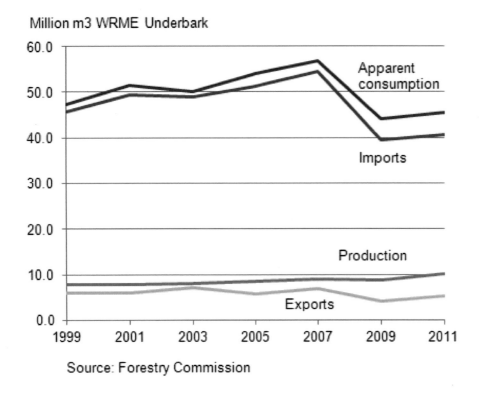

Source: Forestry Commission

Notes:

1.   Excludes recovered paper

The UK apparent consumption – production and imports minus exports - of wood has followed the trend in imports over the years reflecting the fact that a lot of wood and wood products in the UK are imported. Figure 8 shows that apparent wood consumption has generally decreased since 2007 due to a reduction in imports. This was due to fall in demand mainly in the construction sector due to the contraction of UK economy. However, imports still accounted for 80 per cent of the total timber supply (production + import) in the UK.

Between 1999 and 2011, apparent consumption decreased by 1.8 million cubic metres Wood Raw Material Equivalent (WRME) underbark[1], driven by the reduction in imports but slightly offset by a small upward trend in production over the time period (see figure 8).

Fish harvesting

Figure 9: Percentage of fish stocks harvested sustainably and at full reproductive capacity: 1990 to 2010(1)

United Kingdom

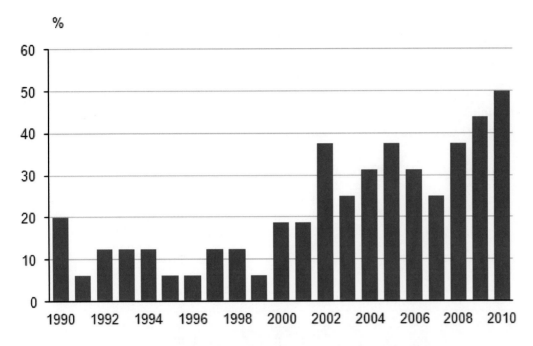

Source: Department for Environment, Food and Rural Affairs,
International Coucil for the Exploration of the Sea, Centre for the
Environment, Fisheries and Aquaculture Science

Notes:

1. Based on 16 stocks for which accurate time series are available derived from stock assessment reports by International Council for the Exploration of the Sea

Figure 9 reflects a positive picture in the use of fish stocks in recent years. Between 2007 and 2010, the percentage of fish stocks harvested sustainably and at full reproductive capacity has grown significantly from 25 per cent to 50 per cent.

However, the fish stocks represented in figure 9 do not represent the whole biodiversity in the sea. In 2010, only half of the fish stocks were harvested sustainably and at full reproductive capacity. There are a significant number of fish stocks that are known to be at risk of not being harvested sustainably. They are not considered in this analysis because UK does not have sufficient consistent data to include in the above indicator. As such, the usefulness of the above indicator as a measure of the overall sustainability of fishing activity is limited.

Energy consumption

Increasing the contribution of renewable resources to future energy consumption is one way to protect the environment. Renewable energy is energy that is naturally replenished. It is sourced from natural resources such as sunlight, wind and water (hydro). In 1997, the UK signed up to the Kyoto Protocol which includes a legally binding target to reduce the emissions of greenhouse gases. Renewable energy is seen as part of the solution to achieve the target. The use of renewable energy technology is environmental friendly since it produces relatively less pollution and secures renewable resources.

Renewable energy has both direct and indirect economic benefits. In the long term, it insulates the economy from fossil fuel price spikes and supply shortages. However, it is the conventional fuels that continue to dominate the generation of energy in the UK.

Figure 10: Energy Consumption by Source: 1990-2010

United Kingdom

Million tonnes of oil equivalent (Mtoe)

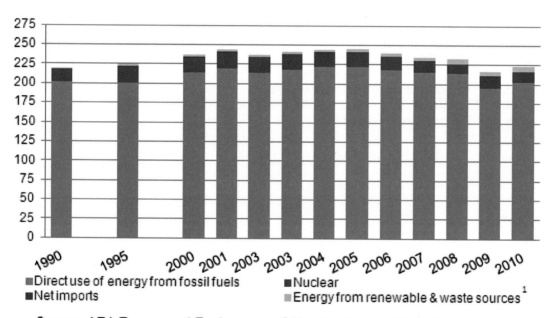

Source: AEA Energy and Environment, Office for National Statistics

Notes:

1. Renewable sources include solar photovoltaic, geothermal and energy from wind, wave and tide, hydroelectricity, wood, straw, liquid biofuels and sewage gas. Landfill gas, poultry litter and municipal solid waste combustion have also been included within this definition.

Figure 10 shows the source of total energy consumption. Since 1990, fossil fuels have remained the main source of energy despite an increase in the use of renewable energy from 1.3 Mtoe to 7.1 Mtoe in 2010.

Figure 11: Percentage of energy consumption from renewable and waste sources

United Kingdom

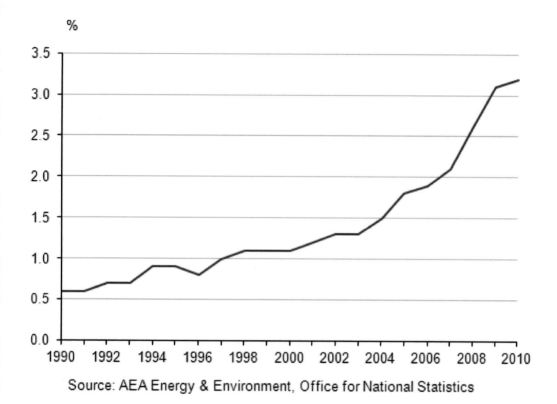

Source: AEA Energy & Environment, Office for National Statistics

Figure 11 shows that in 2010, 3.2 per cent of the total energy consumption was from renewable sources, although the amount has increased over 5 times since 1990.

Of the renewable & waste energy used in 2010:

- 45 per cent was from waste sources such as landfill gas, sewage gas, municipal solid waste & poultry litter,
- 20 per cent from wood & straw,
- 18 per cent from liquid bio-fuels, bioethanol & biodiesel,
- and 17 per cent from renewable generation from hydroelectric power, solar photovoltaic, geothermal aquifers & energy from wind, wave & tide.

The UK has a target to supply 15 per cent of its energy consumption from renewable sources by 2020 under the EU Renewable Energy Directive. The latest data[2] (2011) for the UK shows that we attained 3.8 per cent against the Renewable Energy Directive measure.

Figure 12: Progress against EU Renewable Energy Directive, 2010 (1)(2)

EU Comparison

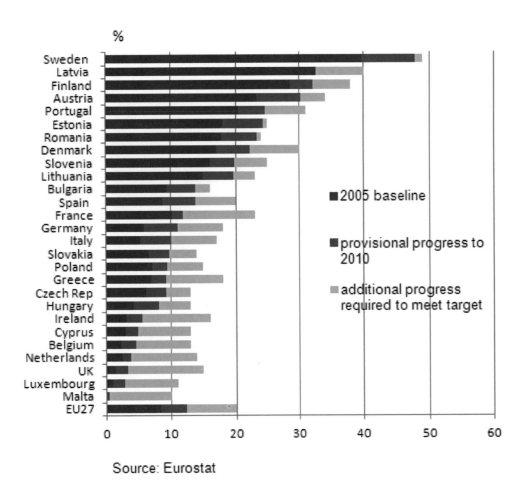

Source: Eurostat

Notes:

1. Data for Belgium, France and Hungary relate to 2009
2. Renewable energy consumption as a percentage of capped gross final energy consumption

Figure 12 shows the renewable energy targets for the UK and other EU countries that they need to achieve under the EU Renewable Energy Directive. Each country has its own target depending on the basis of the 2005 share of each country plus both a flat-rate increase of 5.5 per cent per Member State as well as a GDP-weighted additional increase. It shows that the UK is third from the bottom out of all EU 27 countries in terms of renewable energy consumption as a percentage of gross final energy consumption.

Notes

1. Wood Raw Material Equivalent is the amount of wood required to produce a product – this enables to add volumes of different wood products. Cubic metres underbark relates to volume in cubis metres without bark.

2. Source: Department for Energy and Climate Change

Pressures on the Natural Environment

The use of natural resources in economic production and household consumption has adverse effects on the natural environment in terms of greenhouse gases and air pollutants that can have a knock on effects on human well-being.

Air Pollutants

Air pollutants are an indicator of air quality. The main pollutants of concern in the UK are particulate matter (PM), oxides of nitrogen, sulphur dioxide, carbon dioxide, ground level ozone and ammonia. Road transport, large fuel-burning plants such as power stations, and agriculture are key sources for one or more of these pollutants.

Air pollution has both direct and indirect costs to the economy. Health provision in terms of prescription charges and care services is the direct cost, whereas lower productivity resulting from air pollution is the indirect cost to the economy. Moreover, reduction in life expectancy resulting from air pollution is a loss in human capital. It is estimated that air pollution reduces life expectancy in the UK by an average of six months with an estimated equivalent health cost of up to £19 billion each year. It also has a detrimental effect on the UK's ecosystem and vegetation.

PM and Ozone are two pollutants thought to have the greatest impacts on public health through long-term exposure. PM that is less than 10 microns in diameter or about one-seventh of the thickness of a human hair are known as PM_{10} and are more likely to have a toxic effect as they can be breathed more deeply into the lungs.

Figure 13: Total PM10 Emissions: 1990 to 2010

United Kingdom

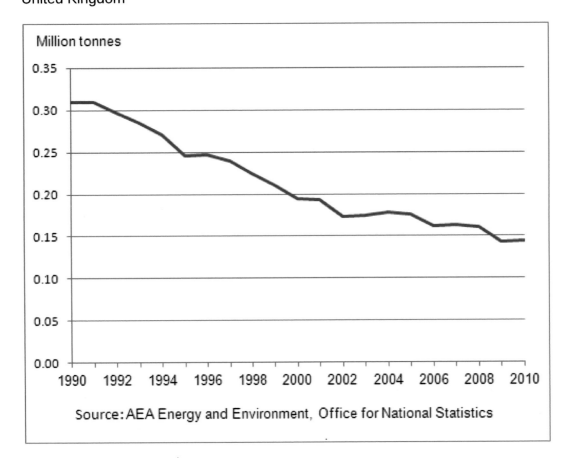

Source: AEA Energy and Environment, Office for National Statistics

Figure 13 shows that emissions of PM_{10} in the UK have been generally falling since the 1990s, and the rate of decline has accelerated since 1990. Between 1990 and 2010 the emissions from PM_{10} fell by 54 per cent from 0.31 million tonnes to 0.14 million tonnes. The steady decline was attributable to a move away from coal to gas in both electricity generation and domestic and commercial combustion, and also the introduction of emission standards for road vehicles.

Greenhouse Gases

The presence of water vapour, carbon dioxide, methane, nitrous oxide and ozone in the atmosphere keep the Earth's surface about $33^{o}C$ warmer than it would be without them. Without this natural 'greenhouse effect' the average temperature of the Earth's surface would be around $-18^{o}C$ and arguably without complex higher life forms.

There is overwhelming scientific evidence, however, that greenhouse gas emissions from human activities are the main cause of observed climate change over the past century and especially the last few decades. Environmental and societal impacts of climate change are already seen and are projected to worsen during this century as emissions continue.

The UK has both international and domestic targets for reducing greenhouse gas emissions. The Kyoto Protocol requires that UK greenhouse gas emissions are reduced by 12.5 per cent below base year levels over the period 2008-12. This equates to annual emissions of 682.4 million tonnes CO_2 equivalent ($MtCO_2e$) on average over the period. Based on emissions estimated up to and including 2010, the UK is on course to meet its Kyoto Protocol target. The UK Climate Change Act requires that UK greenhouse gas emissions are reduced by at least 80 per cent below base year levels by 2050 (equivalent to 154.2 $MtCO_2e$ on the basis of the latest estimates).

Figure 14: Greenhouse Gas Emissions (Kyoto basket): 1990 to 2011(1)(2)

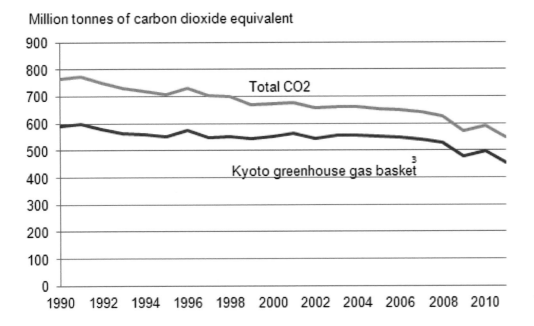

Million tonnes of carbon dioxide equivalent

Source:Deprtment of Energy and Climate Change

Notes:
1. Kyoto basket total includes emissions from the UK, Crown Dependancies and UK overseas Territories, as well as emissions from flights between the UK, Crown Dependancies, and Overseas Territories
2. Figures shown for 2011 are provisional.
3. Kyoto greenhouse gas basket consists of emissions of carbon dioxide, methane, nitrous oxide, hydrofluorocarbons, perfluorocarbons and sulphur hexafluoride

Figure 14 shows that UK greenhouse gas emissions have been declining gradually since 1990. In 2009, there was a fall in emissions resulting from a significant fall in energy consumption across all sectors, most probably related to the contraction of the UK economy during the year, together with an increase in the use of nuclear power rather than coal and natural gas for electricity generation. This was then followed by an increase in emissions in 2010 resulting from a rise in residential gas use during the year, which saw very low temperatures, combined with fuel switching away from nuclear power back to coal and gas for electricity generation. Provisional estimates show that UK greenhouse gas emissions declined in 2011, compared with 2010.

Emissions of CO_2 represented 84 per cent of the total UK greenhouse gas emissions in 2010, and have followed the same trend as overall greenhouse gas emissions. Between 1990 and 2010, overall emissions of UK greenhouse gases fell from 766.4 million tonnes of CO_2 equivalent to 590.4 million tonnes of CO_2 equivalent, or by 23 per cent, driven mainly by reductions in the energy supply and industrial process sectors.

Figure 15: Greenhouse Gas Emissions Per Head: 1990 and 2010

EU Comparison

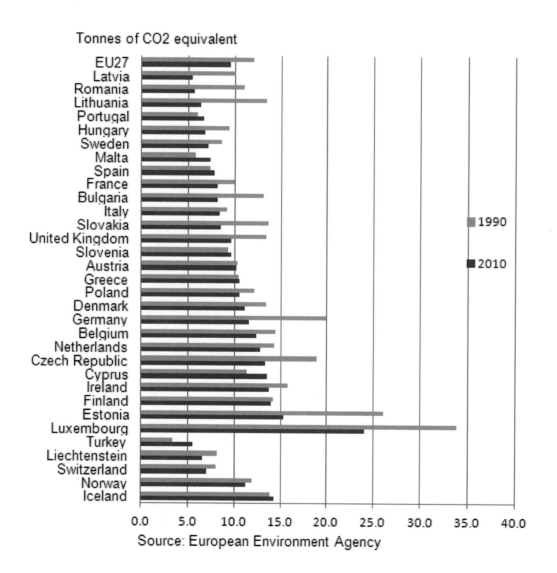

Source: European Environment Agency

Greenhouse gas Emissions per head show significant differences across European countries (figure 15). In 2010, UK's greenhouse gas emissions per head were 9.5 tonnes of CO_2 equivalent, almost similar to EU average of 9.4 tonnes of CO_2 equivalent. In the UK, during the last two decades, greenhouse gas emissions per head have fallen by 3.9 tonnes of CO_2 equivalent. Low levels of emissions in countries such as Latvia and Sweden are because around half of their electricity is produced from renewable sources; whereas, higher level of emissions in countries such as Luxembourg is due to high level of road fuel exports.

Figure 16: Greenhouse Gas Emissions Intensity(1)

United kingdom

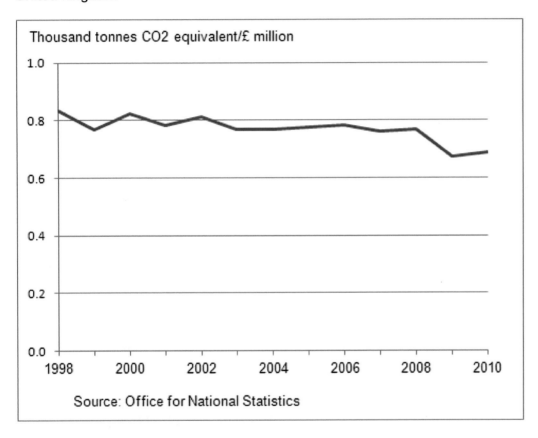

Source: Office for National Statistics

Notes:
1. Output is based on calculations using the constant price measure of Gross Value Added, the contribution of individual industry groups to Gross Domestic Product.

The level of greenhouse gas emissions created per unit of economic output, also known as emissions intensity, can be used to examine whether or not economic growth is causing emissions. Figure 16 shows a reduction of 15.7 per cent between 1997 and 2010, which could be due to a decline in UK's manufacturing sector and thus moving away to the service sector. Another reason of this decline could be related to the relocation of production abroad. Department for Environment, Food and Rural Affairs Statistics shows that in 2009, greenhouse gas emissions associated with imported goods were estimated at 477 million tonnes CO_2 equivalent, compared with 285 million tonnes CO_2 equivalent in 1990.

A significant reduction in 2008 could be due to the recession that reduced economic activity and an increase in 2010 could be attributed to an increase in economic growth combined with cold weather at the beginning and end of 2010 that increased the UK energy consumption.

About the ONS Measuring National Well-being Programme

NWB logo 2

This article is published as part of the ONS Measuring National Well-being Programme.

The programme aims to produce accepted and trusted measures of the well-being of the nation - how the UK as a whole is doing. It is about looking at 'GDP and beyond' and includes:

- greater analysis of the national economic accounts, especially to understand household income, expenditure and wealth
- further accounts linked to the national accounts, including the UK Environmental Accounts and valuing household production and 'human capital'
- quality of life measures, looking at different areas of national well-being such as health, relationships, job satisfaction, economic security, education environmental conditions
- working with others to include the measurement of the well-being of children and young people as part of national well-being
- measures of 'subjective well-being' - individuals' assessment of their own well-being
- headline indicators to summarise national well-being and the progress we are making as a society

The programme is underpinned by a communication and engagement workstream, providing links with Cabinet Office and policy departments, international developments, the public and other stakeholders. The programme is working closely with Defra on the measurement of 'sustainable development' to provide a complete picture of national well-being, progress and sustainable development.

Find out more on the Measuring National Well-being website pages.

Background notes

1. Details of the policy governing the release of new data are available by visiting www.statisticsauthority.gov.uk/assessment/code-of-practice/index.html or from the Media Relations Office email: media.relations@ons.gsi.gov.uk

Copyright

References

1. uknea.unep-wcmc.org/Resources/tabid/82/Default.aspxBateman,I. et al. (2011), Chapter 22: Economic Values from Ecosystems. In: The UK National Ecosystem Assessment Technical Report. UK National Ecosystem Assessment, UNEP-WCMC, Cambridge

2. DECC, UK emissions statistics

3. DECC, UK Performance against emissions reduction targets: 2011 provisional figures

4. DEFRA (2007), The Air Quality Strategy for England, Scotland, Wales and Northern Ireland (Volume 1)

5. DEFRA (2010), Measuring Progress Sustainable Development indicators 2010: Land use

6. DEFRA (2011), Wild bird populations in the UK 1970-2010 National Statistics Release

7. DEFRA (2012), Statistical Release: UK's Carbon Footprint 1990 – 2009

8. DEFRA, North Sea fish stocks and stocks of North East Atlantic mackerel

9. DEFRA, Sources and impacts of air pollution

10. DEFRA, Sustainability of fish stocks around the UK

11. DEFRA, Wild Bird Populations in UK, 1970-2010

12. European Environment Agency (2011), Greenhouse gas emissions in Europe: a retrospective trend analysis for the period 1990–2008

13. European Environment Agency, EEA Greenhouse Gas – Data Viewer: Emissions per capita

14. European Renewable Energy Council (2008), Renewable Energy Roadmap 20% by 2020

15. Eurostat, Share of renewable energy in gross final energy consumption

16. Forestry Commission, Forestry Statistics 2012

17. JNCC, C1. Protected sites

18. ONS (2010), Social Trend, England: Palgrave Macmillan

19. ONS, Measuring National Well-being: Summary of Proposed Domains and Measures, July 2012

20. ONS, UK Environmental Accounts 2012

Measuring National Well-being: Life in the UK, 2012

Author Name(s): Abigail Self, Jennifer Thomas and Chris Randall, Office for National Statistics

Abstract

Measuring National Well-being: Life in the UK 2012 provides a unique overview of well-being in the UK today. The report is the first snapshot of life in the UK to be delivered by the Measuring National Well-being programme and will be updated and published annually. Well-being is discussed in terms of the economy, people and the environment. Information such as the unemployment rate or number of crimes against the person are presented alongside data on people's thoughts and feelings, for example, satisfaction with our jobs or leisure time and fear of crime. Together, a richer picture on 'how society is doing' is provided.

Executive summary

Two years ago, the ONS launched the Measuring National Well-being (MNW) programme. The aim is to 'develop and publish an accepted and trusted set of National Statistics which help people understand and monitor well-being'. Traditional measures of progress such as Gross Domestic Product (GDP) have long been recognised as an incomplete picture of the state of the nation. Other economic, social and environmental measures are needed alongside GDP to provide a complete picture of how society is doing.

The Economy

During the first part of the millennium, incomes and GDP were rising and debt levels were rising slowly. The recession in 2008 led to a sharp fall in GDP and impacted on income and debt levels at both the national and household level. Real income has fallen as inflation has grown faster than incomes, and the public sector debt ratio has increased. GDP has started to recover, but at a slower rate than before the recession.

- Real household actual income per head (RHAI) in the UK grew from £16,865 to £18,159 between 2002 and 2008, before falling to near 2005 levels in 2011 (£17,862).
- UK Public Sector Net Debt grew between 32.5% and 42.8% of GDP between 2003 and 2008 before rising to 65.7% in 2011.
- GDP per head increased during the first part of the millennium, fell by 6.1% between 2007 and 2009, before rising again between 2009 and 2011.

People

The recession has led to a higher proportion who are unemployed, with a particular impact on the young, and in 2009/10 more than 1 in 8 (12.3%) of us were finding it quite or very difficult to manage financially. Life satisfaction presents a more resilient picture, having remained broadly stable throughout the last decade and the most recent figures for those who report being somewhat, mostly or completely satisfied with their social life and job standing at 67% and 77.8% respectively and satisfaction with our family life averaging 8.2 out of 10 (where 1 is very dissatisfied and 10 is very satisfied). In terms of our health which is one of the most important influences on our well-being, our 'healthy' life expectancy has increased as has our overall satisfaction with our health.

- There has been a shift from employment to unemployment since the beginning of the recession, with the young being the worst affected. In Jun-Aug 2012 the UK unemployment rate for those aged 16-24 was 20.5% compared with 7.9% for those aged 16 and over.
- In the 2009/10 in the UK, 12.3 per cent were finding it quite or very difficult to manage financially.
- In 2011, just over three-quarters (75.9 per cent) of people aged 16 and over in the UK rated their overall life satisfaction at the medium or high level.
- Healthy life expectancy at birth in 2008-2010 was age 63.5 for males and 65.7 for females, in the UK, increases of 2.8 and 3.3 years respectively since 2000-02.
- In the UK in 2009/10, 68.3 per cent were somewhat, mostly or completely satisfied with their health.

The Environment

Long term progress is being made with protecting our local and global environment. More than half of us visited our natural environment at least once a week in the 12 months prior to interview in 2011/12 and nationally, the proportion of protected areas, including land and sea has increased. Globally, emissions and energy consumption have fallen and use of renewable energy has increased during the last decade.

- In England in 2011/12, over half of us visited our natural environment at least once per week in the 12 months prior to interview.
- The total extent of land and sea protected in the UK through national and international protected areas increased from 3.7 million hectares in 2005 to over 7.5 million hectares in 2011.
- Emissions of carbon monoxide, the most prevalent air pollutant, has more than halved since 2000.
- Use of renewable and waste sources more than doubled between 2000 and 2010 from 2.7 million tonnes of oil equivalent (Mtoe) to 7.1 Mtoe.

Background

The Measuring National Well-being programme began in November 2010 with a six month National Debate, asking, 'what matters', to understand what measures of well-being should include. Following 175 events, with 2,750 people and 34,000 responses received online or via other channels, ONS developed a framework for measuring national well-being. The framework consists of 10 areas or 'domains', including areas such as Health, Education and What we do; and 40 headline measures of well-being, for example, the unemployment rate, satisfaction with our health, or levels of crime. These measures and others have been used to describe life in the UK 2012, under the headings, the Economy, People and the Environment, and can be seen in the interactive wheel of measures[1].

Future plans

'Better policies for better lives' were words used by the OECD to describe the importance of going beyond GDP when measuring progress and national well-being. The snapshot of life in the UK presented is only based on a small selection of headline indicators. There is more to do to fully understand national well-being and what actions are needed to improve it. In particular, there is an important story in what lies beneath - where are the deviations from the norms and why, are there particular sub groups, for example, age groups, ethnic groups, those that are vulnerable for some reason or some other cluster which can be identified which differs considerably from others? Are there any particular geographical areas where things could be improved? Are we looking at the right measures?

The next phase of the Measuring National Well-being programme is to identify and explore in more detail those areas which deviate from 'norms' and to:

- Review and further refine domains and measures of well-being and the criteria used to select them;
- Develop means of appropriately assessing whether domains and/or measures are getting better or worse;
- Research drivers of well-being

Notes

1.   http://www.ons.gov.uk/ons/interactive/well-being-wheel-of-measures/index.html

Introduction and background

In November 2010, the ONS set up the Measuring National Well-being (MNW) programme. The aim is to 'develop and publish an accepted and trusted set of National Statistics which help people understand and monitor well-being'.

This report begins with a background to well-being, the MNW programme and next steps. This is followed by an examination of life in the UK 2012, which looks at well-being under three broad headings including: Economic, Social and Environmental well-being.

What is National Well-being?

The well-being of the nation is influenced by a broad range of factors including economic performance, quality of life, the state of the environment, sustainability, equality, as well as individual well-being.

Measuring 'how a country is doing' has until now largely rested on traditional economic measures such as Gross Domestic Product (GDP). But economists and statisticians have always acknowledged that GDP does not capture everything that determines society's well-being and was not designed to do so. For example, fuel consumed in traffic jams adds to GDP but is unlikely to increase well-being; the environment and skills of the nation's workers are important determinants of a nation's future economic well-being but are not adequately represented by existing economic statistics.

Through supplementing economic measures, such as GDP, with measures which reflect social and environmental well-being, national well-being looks at the state of the nation through a broader lens.

Why is National Well-being important?

'Better policies for better lives' were the words used by the OECD at the recent world forum on statistics, knowledge and policy, New Delhi, November 2012, to describe the importance of going beyond GDP when measuring progress and national well-being.

In particular, having a more complete picture of national well-being will lead to:

- better understanding of policy impacts on well-being;
- better allocation of scarce resources via more informed policy evaluation and development;
- comparisons between how different sub-groups of the population are doing, across a range of topics;
- more informed decisions on where to live, which career to choose, based on well-being information for that area/organisation;
- assessments of the performance of government;
- comparisons between the UK with other countries.

How is information on well-being being used?

Measures of national well-being as defined by the MNW programme are still very much under development. It is therefore unrealistic to expect to be able to provide evidence of any major decisions that have been heavily influenced by well-being at this stage. However, the examples that follow demonstrate that the foundations are very much in place in UK policy:

- Well-being data being made available at council and neighbourhood levels for more informed decision making: subjective well-being data have been analysed and promoted at the local level and modelled against the geo-demographic (ACORN) profile of residents in each neighbourhood. The analysis has highlighted variation in well-being between neighbourhoods, and enables comparisons with local data and knowledge by local authorities, councillors and communities. (Department for Communities and Local Government)
- Well-being of job seekers: questions on subjective well-being have been used to track well-being of job seekers allowance applicants. Those with poor mental health and low subjective well-being were found to take longer to find work. Recommendation that connections could be made between Job Centres and Mental Health trusts to address the issues. (Department for Work and Pensions)

- Impact of community learning: recently published research shows adult learning has substantial impact on life satisfaction, well-being and health, including mental health. Techniques from Green Book Annex on social cost-benefit analysis were used to value the improvement to life satisfaction resulting from an adult learning course. This better understanding will lead to more informed decisions when allocating budget for Community Learning. (Business Innovation and Skills)
- Well-being and the National Citizen Service: a pilot for the National Citizen Service evaluated the subjective well-being of young people before and after their participation in the service. The results show increases in subjective well-being among participants, before and after involvement, compared with a control group of peers over the same period. (Cabinet Office)

Separate initiatives to investigate well-being are being undertaken by the devolved governments. These include: the National Performance Framework, which forms part of the 'Scotland performs'[1] initiative and the recently published 'Analysis of subjective well-being in Wales: Evidence from the Annual Population Survey'[2]. These initiatives reflect the specific needs of the countries they represent.

Internationally, there is considerable interest in how a shared view of well-being and progress can be produced. The EU's 'GDP and Beyond' initiative, the Commission on the Measurement of Economic Performance and Social Progress (Stiglitz-Sen-Fitoussi commission) and OECD's project on 'Measuring progress of Societies' and Better Life initiative look to measure the progress of society according to the 'triple bottom line' of the economy, society and the environment.

What has the Measuring National Well-being programme delivered so far?

The MNW programme began with a six month national debate asking people, 'what matters', in order to understand what should be included in measures of national well-being. ONS ran 175 events around the UK, involving around 7,250 people and received more than 34,000 responses, some from organisations representing thousands more.

Figure 1:

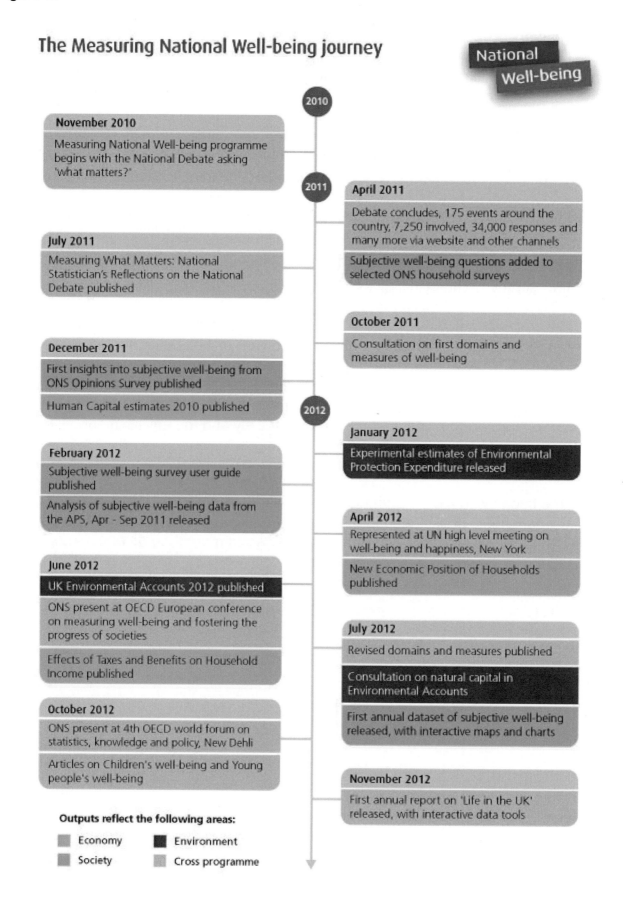

Analysis of the debate findings, existing research and international initiatives led to the development of a framework for measuring national well-being. The framework consists of a set of 10 areas or 'domains' and 40 headline measures of well-being. Headline measures reflect our quality of life, the state of the natural environment as well as the performance of the economy and people's assessment of their own well-being. The measures are grouped into a set of domains covering areas such as individual well-being, health, personal relationships and what we do. The domains and measures were consulted upon and will continue to be developed and refined throughout the programme. A summary of domains and measures and latest status is available in Annex A. An interactive 'wheel of measures'[3] has also been developed and shows the latest data for each measure.

Alongside the domains and measures, a range of supporting outputs have been published. Measures of economic well-being which better reflect the household and individual position, as opposed to the national picture have been published in outputs such as the 'Economic position of households'; Environmental Accounts have been published which measure the impact the economy has on the Environment; questions on individual well-being have been added to ONS household surveys; interactive maps and graphs[4] have been developed and a series of articles which provide more information on each of the domains have been published. A summary of the progress to date is provided in Figure 1. Links to the domain articles are provided in Annex B.

Future developments

Critical to the success of the MNW programme has been and will continue to be user engagement. ONS regularly consult with a broad audience including analysts, policy makers, academics, the public, the media and others, and will continue to do so. A National Statistician's Advisory Forum and a Technical Advisory Group have also been established.

The next phase of the MNW programme is to identify and explore in more detail those areas which deviate from 'norms' and to investigate what if any relationships exist between the factors affecting well-being.

In the short term, the MNW programme will:

- review and further refine domains and measures of well-being and the criteria used to select them;
- develop means of appropriately assessing whether domains and/or measures are getting better or worse;
- report on subjective well-being regression analysis;
- explore the social and economic position of different groups using 2011 Census data, to identify those at risk of social exclusion;
- further develop visual tools for better access to well-being data.

Longer term, the programme will:

- investigate international comparisons of economic well-being;
- analyse the distribution of real income, wealth, foreign direct investment and material well-being;
- develop experimental estimates of the value of childcare in household production;
- analyse social impacts on national well-being, including health, education, crime and personal relationships;
- further test the subjective well-being measures;
- further analyse the drivers of subjective well-being among different sub-groups of the population and over time;
- further explore social capital and latest statistical developments.

Notes

1. www.scotland.gov.uk/About/Performance/scotPerforms

2. www.wales.gov.uk/about/aboutresearch/social/latestresearch/ wellbeing/;jsessionid=E12847E54DBC1AD0B6F69108EE50C79E?lang=en

3. www.ons.gov.uk/ons/interactive/well-being-wheel-of-measures/index.html

4. www.ons.gov.uk/ons/interactive/well-being-interactive-graph/index.html

Life in the UK, 2012 - Key information

About this section

This section summarises well-being in the UK in 2012.

- Where possible, data are presented for the UK. Where this is not the case, the best available geography is used.
- Data are the latest available at the end of September 2012, with the exception of economy measures which reflect more up to date data published in the Measuring National Well-being: Economy article
- As a guide, trends in the data have been considered over a 10 year time period. Longer time periods are included where appropriate, for example, for changes in life expectancy. Shorter time periods reflect data availability.
- Objective data, for example the number of reported crimes, or the unemployment rate, are provided alongside data about how people think and feel, for example, fear of crime, or satisfaction with one's job. Data presented in this way lead to a richer understanding of life in the UK.

Key facts about the UK

- In 2012, the population of England and Wales, according to the 2011 Census figures was 56.1 million, with 53.0 million in England and 3.1 million in Wales.
- The UK population has grown from 59.1 million in mid-2001 to 62.3 million at mid-2010, the latest available estimate.
- The UK population is ageing. At the time of the 2011 Census, one in six of the population (16.4 %) were aged 65 and over in England and Wales. In 2011, there were 430,000 residents aged 90 and over compared with 340,000 in 2001. The median age of the population in England and Wales was 39.
- The UK economy is the seventh largest economy in the world. After adjusting for inflation Gross Domestic Product (GDP) was £1.4 trillion in 2011. The economy had grown by 0.9 per cent since 2010 but was still 2.3 per cent below its pre-recession peak in 2007.

The Economy - Introduction

The Economy section of this report will cover the measures proposed in the economy and personal finance domains. It will begin with an overview of the national economy, which affects our well-being by impacting on us financially. It will then discuss what this means for us personally, how it affects our income and wealth and how we feel about this.

The Economy - National Economy

"A sense that everybody has access to a good standard of living" (ONS, 2011, response to "what things matter to you?" from the National Debate)

The economy covers the set of activities related to the production and distribution of goods and services. Its performance will impact on all of us financially and will therefore affect our national well-being.

This section will discuss the four headline measures of economic well-being, namely Real[1] Net National Income (RNNI) per head; Real Household Actual Income (RHAI) per head; inflation rate (as measured by the Consumer Prices Index) and Public Sector Net Debt (PSND) as a percentage of Gross Domestic Product (GDP). It will also include GDP as a reference point for the other economic measures outlined above.

A wider and more comprehensive analysis of GDP and the four proposed measures of economic well-being is available in Measuring National Well-being: The Economy[2]. Unemployment is covered in the People section.

Economic measures and life satisfaction

It is widely reported that as GDP grows, the strength of the positive relationship between income and reported levels of happiness levels off. (Easterlin, 1974; Allin, 2007; Thomas and Evans, 2010). While critics of this paradox argue that this is due to the nature of GDP (Stevenson and Wolfers,

2008), time series data from multiple countries illustrate that despite large increases in GDP per capita, levels of life satisfaction have moved differently.

Figure 2: GDP per head, Real (1) Net National Income per head, Real Household Actual Income (2) per head and Life Satisfaction (3) over time

United Kingdom

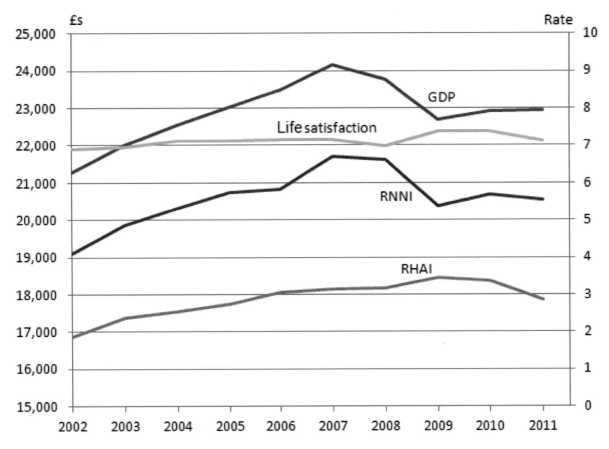

Source: Office for National Statistics, UKEA and Blue Book; World Database of Happiness

Notes:
1. 'Real' is calculated to exclude the effects of price inflation.
2. Real household actual income = Real household actual gross disposable income.
3. Life satisfaction data are as a proportion of Great Britain respondents who stated that they were fairly or very satisfied when answering the question: 'On the whole how satisfied are you with the life you lead?' – with the responses 1) not at all satisfied; 2) not very satisfied; 3) fairly satisfied; 4) very satisfied. This was then increased to a 10 point scale by linear stretch. For an explanation of linear stretch refer to Veenhoven, R. Trends in Nations, World Database of Happiness, Erasmus University Rotterdam, Introductory text hppt:// worlddatabaseofhappiness.eur.nl (2002-2011). The data used is for the Autumn quarter where available.

Figure 2 shows that over the last 9 years GDP per head, RNNI per head and RHAI per head have moved differently to life satisfaction in the UK, though over the past 4 years, RHAI has followed a similar pattern to life satisfaction. GDP per head increased during the first part of the millennium but, as a result of the global recession, it decreased sharply by 6.1% between 2007 and 2009. Since then, GDP has started to rise again albeit at a slower rate than it was growing previously.

National Income

"material living standards are more closely associated with NNI and consumption than with GDP" (Stiglitz, Sen and Fitoussi, 2009)

A more appropriate economic measure of well-being is RNNI per head (Stiglitz, Sen and Fitoussi, 2009). That is the total national income divided by the population.

Figure 2 shows that RNNI per head consistently grew between 2002 and 2007, following a similar pattern to GDP. Between 2008 and 2009, average incomes dropped by 5.8%. RNNI per head began increasing again in 2010, before falling again in 2011 whereas, GDP per head increased during this period.

Life Satisfaction

Life satisfaction remained broadly stable throughout the last decade. According to the World Database of Happiness, between 2007 and 2008, life satisfaction in the UK dropped by 0.17 points (from 7.15 - 6.98 out of 10) but appeared to recover more quickly than GDP or RNNI. Between 2008 and 2009 there was an increase of 0.4 points taking average life satisfaction to 7.38 out of 10. From 2009 onwards, life satisfaction fell once more, to 7.12 out of 10.

The fall in life satisfaction between 2007 and 2008 coincides with the beginning of the recession. This could perhaps be explained by an initial reaction to the news of the recession, whereby people were concerned about their finances and what the recession may mean for them. However, the recession was followed by a period when a person's income was not immediately affected, perhaps explaining the increase in life satisfaction between 2008 and 2009.

Household income

More recently, household incomes have begun to decrease and this is shown in the pattern of RHAI in Figure 2. RHAI per head measures the disposable income a household has left after deductions such as taxes and pensions. It is adjusted to include the extra benefit to households of goods and services that are free or subsidised, for example healthcare in the UK. This also allows better international comparisons of material well-being. RHAI moves more consistently with life satisfaction than RNNI per head and GDP per head.

'It gives me huge reassurance to know that I don't have to worry that I may not be able to pay for hospital treatment or educating my children and great reassurance to know that the majority of fellow citizens feel the same way' (ONS, 2011, response to the National Debate)

RHAI went through a sustained period of growth from 2002 until the recession in 2008 (from £16,865 to £18,159). At the beginning of the recession, growth in RHAI continued to grow, as employment did not fall as much as expected, given the size of the recession; mortgage payments fell due to low interest rates and taxes and benefits provided a stabilising effect[3]. Average household incomes peaked in 2009 but due to higher prices (inflation) and the ongoing recession, real household average incomes fell back in 2011 close to levels seen in 2005.

The fall in RHAI coincided with a second fall in life satisfaction that occurred in between 2009 and 2011 (from 7.38 to 7.12 out of 10) and is more indicative of how the individual's income was affected by the recession, than GDP or RNNI.

Rate of Inflation

The Consumer Prices Index (CPI) measures the changes in the average prices of goods and services in the UK. Changes in the CPI over a 12 month period are referred to as the rate of inflation[4]. The inflation rate decreases the real value of income and wealth.

Figure 3: Inflation rate measured by CPI (1)

United Kingdom

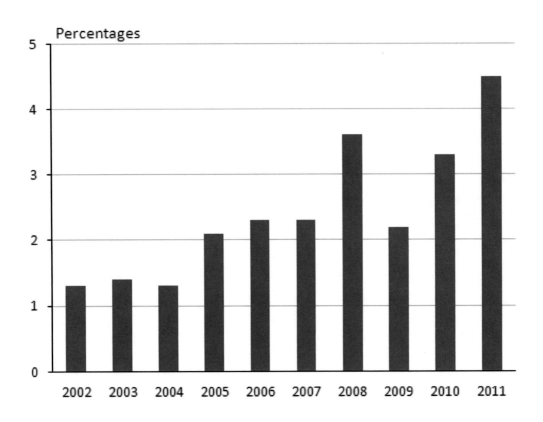

Source: Office for National Statistics

Notes:

1.   Consumer Prices Index.

The UK inflation rate grew steadily from around 1.3% in 2002 to around 3.6% in 2008 (Figure 3). Monthly figures show that by September 2008 the rate of inflation peaked at 5.2% but fell back to 1.1% in September 2009. Due to factors such as high oil and energy prices, the rate of inflation rose steadily from this point to peak at 4.5% in 2011. The effect of this has been to erode real incomes. This means that prices have been rising faster than people's incomes and over time, people have found their income will not stretch as far.

Public Sector Net Debt

Public Sector Net Debt (PSND) as a percentage of GDP[4] measures total financial liabilities (for example any type of debt the government owes), less any financial assets (such as bank deposits). Debt is an important measure of sustainability[5] as it indicates the extent to which the burden of paying for goods and services has been transferred from the present to the future.

Figure 4: Public sector net debt as a percentage of GDP (1)

United Kingdom

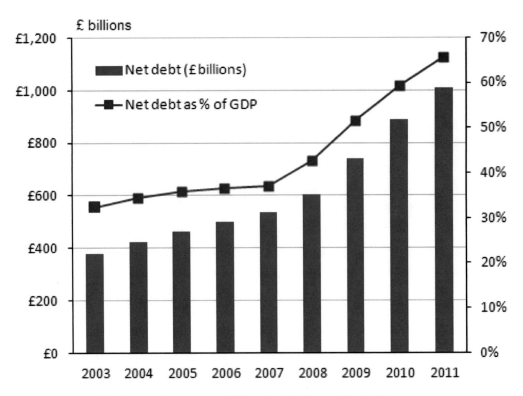

Source: Public Sector Finances, Office for National Statistics

Notes:
1.   Temporary effects of Financial interventions are excluded.

Figure 4 shows that UK PSND grew between 2003 and 2008 (rising from 32.5% to 42.8%) before accelerating in the past few years. It has increased from 42.8% of GDP in 2008 to 65.7% in 2011, when it exceeded one trillion pounds for the first time. If PSND is not reduced, the effect may be to limit spending possibilities for future generations due to the burden of debt interest payments.

Notes

1. All the economic indicators used in this section are "real", which means they have been calculated to exclude the effects of price inflation. This enables a more meaningful comparison of different time periods.

2. The economy

3. As employment falls, people pay less in the way of taxes (income tax) and claim more in the way of benefits (unemployment benefits). Therefore the income that people used to get from wages (minus the amount they paid in income taxes) is replaced by income from benefits – lessening the extent of any fall in income from unemployment.

4. It is constructed by measuring the change in the prices of a representative basket of goods and services. The changes in prices of different items are weighted by the relative proportion of household expenditure each good and service attracts. Overall, an average change is taken and then converted into a percentage form.

5. It does not include the temporary effects of financial interventions (e.g. bank bail outs) since, in the long run, it is intended that they will be reversed and will have negligible effects on PSND.

6. Sustainability in this context means whether the extent to which this level of well-being can last over time.

The Economy - Personal finance

"I would hate for someone to be worrying about whether they will have something to eat or a roof over their head. Also doing other things including recreation activities improves your mental well-being which in turn affects your general well-being but you can only do those things if you are in a good financial position." (ONS, Well-being)

Personal finance relates to the individual and household, both now and in the future. During the National Debate respondents were asked 'what things in life matter to you?' The importance of having adequate income or wealth to cover basic needs was highlighted by 45% of respondents. A wider and more comprehensive analysis of personal finance is available in Measuring National Well-being: Personal Finance[1].

Poverty

A household is currently described as in poverty if its income is less than 60% of the median[2] net household income, before and after housing costs[3]. Households with above average poverty rates include large families, workless households, lone parents and those without educational qualifications. In 2010/11 median income after housing costs in the UK was £359 per week, a rise from £277 per week in 1994/95 but a fall from £373 per week in 2009/10.

Figure 5: Income distribution for the total population (After Housing Costs) (1,2) 2010/11
United Kingdom

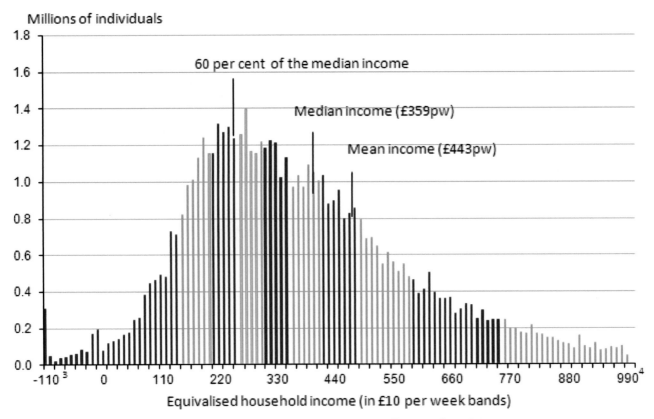

Source: Households Below Average Income, Department for Work and Pensions

Notes:
1. Equivalised household disposable income before deduction of housing costs (in £10 bands), using OECD equivalisation scale. The £10 bands are grouped into decile groups in alternating colours. For an explanation of linear stretch refer to Veenhoven, R. Trends in Nations, World Database of Happiness, Erasmus University Rotterdam, Introductory text available at www.worlddatabaseofhappiness.eur.nl
2. Negative incomes BHC (Before Housing Costs) are reset to zero, but negative AHC (After Housing Costs) incomes calculated from the adjusted BHC incomes are possible. Where incomes have been adjusted to zero BHC, income AHC is derived from the adjusted BHC income.
3. There were also an additional 0.3 million individuals with income below -£100 per week.
4. There were also an additional 3.0 million individuals with income above £1,000 per week.

Figure 5 illustrates that the income distribution for 2010/11 disposable incomes, which is the income left after housing costs are taken out, is not even. There is a much greater concentration of people at lower levels of weekly income, with nearly two-thirds of individuals living in households with a disposable weekly income lower than the mean of £443 per week[4] (DWP, 2012).

Figure 6: The percentage of individuals living in households with less than 60 per cent median income

United Kingdom

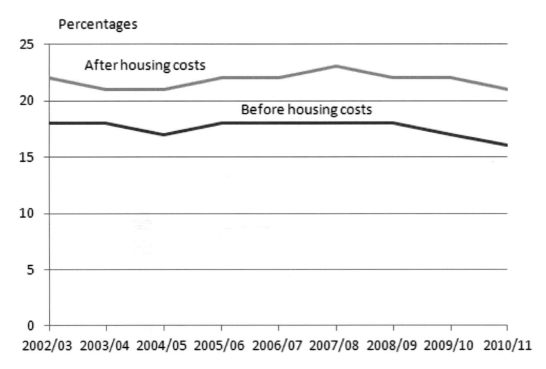

Source: Households Below Average Income, Department for Work and Pensions

In 2010/11, just over 1 in 5 (21%) people in the UK, lived in poverty after housing costs. Before housing costs this figure was 16%. Figure 6 shows that between 2002/03 and 2010/11 there was a small decrease in the proportion of individuals living in households where the income falls below 60% of contemporary median income, either before or after housing costs (from 18% to 16% and 22% to 21% respectively). The reduction in the percentage below the poverty rate between 2009/10 and 2010/11 is in part attributable to a fall in median income rather than any substantial improvement of the financial situation of the people at the bottom of the distribution. Usually reductions in poverty are driven by incomes at the bottom of the distribution growing faster than incomes in the middle (DWP, 2012).

Satisfaction with household income

While over 1 in 5 (21%) live in poverty after housing costs, figures from the Understanding Society Survey show that only 5.8% adults aged 16 and over in the UK were completely dissatisfied with their income. Those in the North East were most likely to report being completely dissatisfied with their income (6.9%) (Understanding Society, 2011).

Overall 57.2% were somewhat, mostly or completely satisfied with their income in 2009/10. People in Scotland were most satisfied, with 60% reporting being somewhat, mostly or completely satisfied with their income.

Table 1: Satisfaction with income of household (1)

United Kingdom (Percentages (2))

	2002/03	2003/04	2004/05	2005/06	2006/07	2007/08	2008/09
Responses							
Completely satisfied	11.1	11.2	10.1	9.7	9.7	9.6	8.5
Mostly satisfied	19.9	21.8	22.0	18.3	20.7	22.4	20.4
Somewhat satisfied	27.4	29.0	27.5	26.6	28.0	28.2	29.5
Neither satisfied nor dissatisfied	19.9	19.2	20.1	20.9	20.2	20.1	20.8
Somewhat dissatisfied	11.7	10.7	11.8	12.7	12.0	11.3	11.9
Mostly dissatisfied	5.9	5.0	5.1	6.9	5.6	5.2	5.3
Completely dissatisfied	4.1	3.1	3.4	5.0	3.7	3.2	3.6

	2002/03	2003/04	2004/05	2005/06	2006/07	2007/08	2008/09
omewhat, ostly ompletely atisfied	58.4	61.9	59.6	54.6	58.4	60.2	58.5

Source: British Household Panel Survey

Table notes:

1. Responses to " How dissatisfied or satisfied are you with.........The income of your household ?"
2. The percentages are of those who responded. Estimated percentages are based on the full sample adjusted to UK figures using cross-sectional weights.
3. Responses to earlier waves of the BHPS differ. However, they have always been on a seven point scale varying from completely (or very) satisfied to completely (or very) dissatisfied.

Figures from the earlier British Household Panel Survey show that between 2002/03 and 2008/09, those somewhat, mostly or completely satisfied with their household income fluctuated between 54.6 and 61.9% (Table 1). In 2008/09, in the middle of the recession, satisfaction dropped to 58.5% from 60.2% in the previous year. There has however been a steady decrease in those who are completely satisfied with their household income throughout the whole period, with a low of 8.5% in 2008/9.

Wealth

It is important to consider income jointly with wealth. Those who have recently had an increase in income may still be paying off debts, while those who have recently had a fall in income may be able to live off wealth.

Wealth can include home ownership, investment schemes, the ownership of shares and the accumulation of wealth, for instance through pensions. It is an important component in the financial position of households as it can be used to fund future consumption and can provide a 'safety net' against loss of income. Estimated median household wealth for Great Britain, including pension wealth, was £236, 973 in 2008/10, this was an increase of around 13% from 2006/08 (£210,313) (ONS WAS).

Figure 7: Total household wealth (1), 2008/10

Great Britain

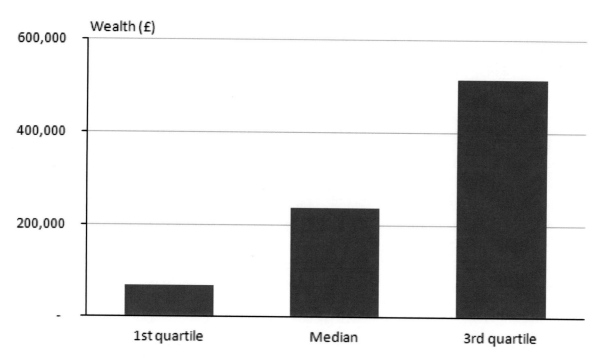

Source: Wealth and Assets Survey, Office for National Statistics

Notes:
1. Excludes assets held in Trusts (except Child Trust Funds) and any business assets held by households.

The median value of household wealth masks considerable variation in wealth for households (Figure 7). For example, in 2008/10, households a quarter of the way from the top of the distribution (third quartile) of all wealth had around eight times more wealth than those households a quarter of the way up the distribution from the bottom (first quartile) (ONS WAS).

Managing financially

Figures from the Understanding Society Survey show that in 2009/10, 12.3% of adults aged 16 and over in the UK found it quite or very difficult to manage financially. Adults in London were finding it hardest with 15.4% reporting such difficulty. People in the East of England, the South East and Northern Ireland were least likely to report that they found it quite or very difficult to manage financially, with around 11% reporting that they were finding it difficult (Understanding Society, 2011)..

Table 2: Managing financially (1)

United Kingdom (Percentages (2))

	2002/03	2003/04	2004/05	2005/06	2006/07	2007/08	2008/09
Responses							
Living comfortably	32.9	34.2	33.4	31.4	32.4	32.4	28.4
Doing alright	39.8	39.7	39.5	40.0	39.7	39.8	38.2
Just about getting by	21.7	21.3	21.5	22.7	21.8	21.8	25.8
Finding it quite difficult	4.1	3.5	4.1	4.1	4.2	4.3	5.4
Finding it very difficult	1.5	1.4	1.5	1.8	2.0	1.7	2.1
Finding it quite/ very difficult	5.6	4.9	5.6	5.9	6.2	6.0	7.5

Source: British Panel Household Survey

Table notes:

1. Responses to " How well would you say you yourself are managing financially these days? Would you say you are.... ?"

2. The percentages are of those who responded. Estimated percentages are based on the full sample adjusted to UK figures using cross-sectional weights.

3. Responses to earlier waves of the BHPS differ. However, they have always been on a seven point scale varying from completely (or very) satisfied to completely (or very) dissatisfied.

Data from the earlier BHPS[5] (Table 2), covering the period between 2002/03 and 2008/09, show that 7.5% of adults aged 16 and over in the UK found it quite or very difficult to manage financially in 2008/09, higher than in any year since 2002/03. During this period there was also a significant decrease in those who feel they are living comfortably (from 32.9% to 28.4%).

Personal finance measures indicate that the current economic downturn has influenced people's ability to cope financially and their feelings about their current financial situation. This is also reflected in expenditure trends that show that households are increasing spending on essential items such as food, housing and utilities while reducing spending on non essentials such as travel, recreation and eating out. In addition, in 2010, the number of households in fuel poverty in the UK had increased to around 4.8 million (approx 19% of all households), a fall of 0.7 million from the previous year. However, there had been an increase of about 1 million households in fuel poverty between 2008 and 2009, continuing an upward trend since 2004. Saving ratios have also increased in the UK suggesting that households are paying debts, borrowing less and saving more.

Notes

1. Measuring National Well-being - Personal Finance

2. The numerical value separating the higher half of a sample, a population, or a probability distribution, from the lower half. The median of a finite list of numbers can be found by arranging all the observations from lowest value to highest value and picking the middle one. If there is an even number of observations, then there is no single middle value; the median is then usually defined to be the mean of the two middle values.

3. This value of a specific income or 'poverty' depends on the number of individuals in the household, as larger households need more money (although not proportionately more) than smaller ones in order to achieve the same standard of living.

4. The mean is equal to the sum of the values divided by the number of values. The mean is the arithmetic average of a set of values, or distribution.

5. The British Household Panel Survey was replaced with the Understanding Society Survey in 2009. While the questions are similiar the methodology has changed to such an extent that it is not possible to compare the two.

People - Introduction

The People section of this report will cover the measures proposed in the following domains:

- Education and skills,
- Environment
- Governance,
- Health,
- Individual well-being,
- Our relationships,
- What we do,
- Where we live.

People - Labour market

"There is a strong evidence base showing that work is generally good for physical and mental health and well-being. Worklessness is associated with poorer physical and mental health and well-being" (Gordon Waddell, A Kim Burton, 2006).

Having a job is an essential element of well-being. It provides earnings which in turn contribute to a person's financial security. During the National Debate, job satisfaction and economic security were one of the main things that mattered most in people's lives and that should be included in measures of well-being. A large part of many adult's lives, at least between the ages of 16 and 64, is spent either working or looking for employment.

Figure 8: Rates of economic activity and inactivity (1)

United Kingdom

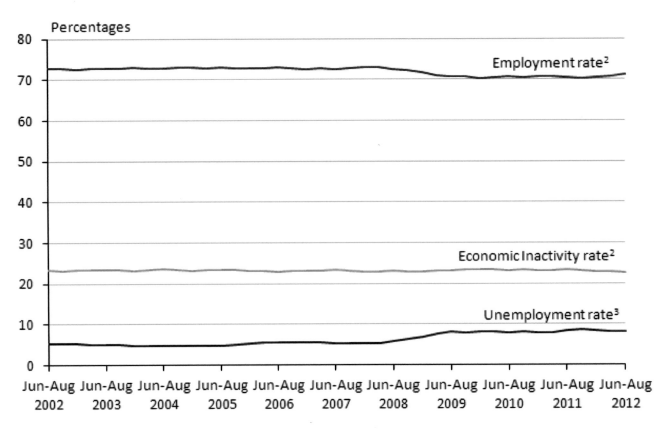

Source: Labour Force Survey, Office for National Statistics

Notes:
1. Data are seasonally adjusted.
2. Men and women aged 16 to 64.
3. Total unemployed as a percentage of economically active for all those aged 16 and over.

Over the last 10 years, the proportion of people of working age who are economically active has been generally stable. The employment rate for those aged from 16 to 64 for June to August 2012 was 71.3%, the highest figure since February to April 2009 and up 0.9% on a year earlier (Figure 8). The number of people in employment aged 16 and over was 29.6 million. The number of people in employment has not been higher since comparable records began in 1971, but the employment rate of 71.3%, for those aged from 16 to 64, is lower than the pre-recession peak of 73.0% recorded for March to May 2008. The unemployment rate for June to August 2012 was 7.9% of the economically active population, down 0.3% on a year earlier. There were 2.5 million unemployed people in June to August 2012, down 50,000 from a year earlier. The economic inactivity rate for those aged from 16 to 64 for June to August 2012 was 22.5%, down 0.8% on a year earlier. The number of economically inactive people aged from 16 to 64 was 9.0 million in June to August 2012 (ONS LFS).

Youth unemployment has risen in each of the last three recessions and the immediate years following their end. Around 1 in 5 (20.5%) people aged 16 to 24 in the UK were unemployed in June to August 2012, equivalent to 957,000 young people. This compares with peaks of 924,000 in 1993 and 1.2 million in 1984. In June to August 2012 nearly four times as many (3.71 million) young people were in employment than were unemployed (ONS, LFS).

Figure 9: Satisfaction with job (1), 2009/10

United Kingdom

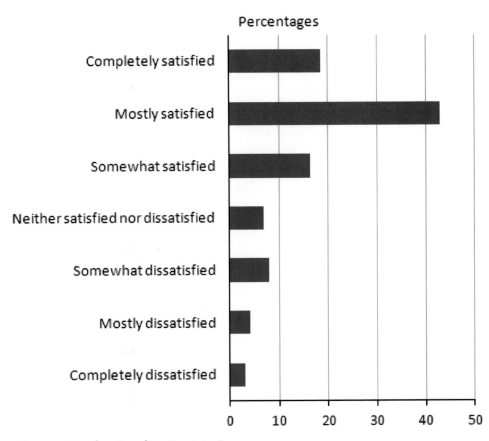

Source: Understanding Society Survey

Notes:
1. Responses to " How dissatisfied or satisfied are you with.........your job (if in employment)". The percentages are of those who responded.

For those that are working, job satisfaction may not only help make the working environment enjoyable and add to a person's well-being but may also improve productivity. Over three-quarters (77.8%) of people aged 16 and over in the UK with a job were somewhat, mostly or completely satisfied with their job according to the 2009–10 Understanding Society Survey (Figure 9). However it must be noted that over 1 in 5 (22.2%) were neither satisfied nor dissatisfied or were somewhat, mostly or completely dissatisfied with their job (Understanding Society).

Voluntary work can give people an increased sense of well-being, for example, by meeting new people and forging friendships while in a 'working' environment. The British Household Panel Survey asked adults aged 16 and over in the UK in 2008/09 how frequently they did unpaid voluntary work. Just under 1 in 5 (19.0%) did unpaid voluntary work several times a year or more. Of these 5.4% did voluntary work at least once a week, 7.6% at least once a month and 6.0% several times a year. However it must be noted that the majority of respondents (76.9%) reported that they almost never or never did any voluntary work.

People - Education

Educational qualifications

"Learning encourages social interaction and increases self-esteem and feelings of competency. Behaviour directed by personal goals to achieve something new has been shown to increase reported life satisfaction" New Economics Foundation (2009).

Employment and education are linked. Educational qualifications can give a person a good basis to gain employment in the sector of their choice. As well as showing discipline academically, it proves a sound knowledge of a person's chosen studies. Education and training was considered in the National Debate to be one of the most important things to include in measures of well-being.

Figure 10: Proportion of people with no qualifications (1): by selected years

United Kingdom

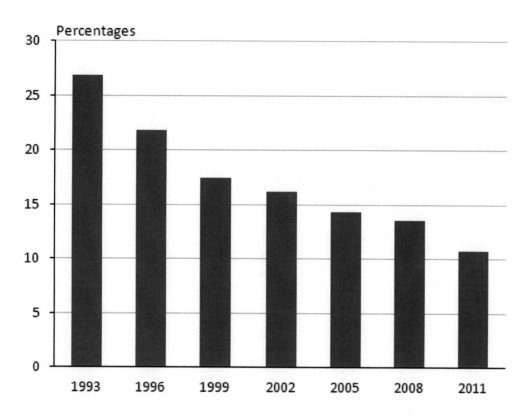

Source: Labour Force Survey, Office for National Statistics

Notes:

1.   Those aged 16 to 64.

Of the 40 million adults aged 16 to 64 in the UK in 2011, 35.4 million (89%) had some kind of formal educational qualification, but 4.3 million (11%) had no formal qualifications (Figure 10). In the last 18 years, the number of adults without any formal educational qualifications has more than halved from the 9.0 million (27%) in 1993. Large decreases occurred between 1993 and 1996 (1.3 million) and 1996 and 1999 (1.4 million) and between 2008 and 2011 (1.1 million). This is not, however, because the proportion of young adults without a qualification has been falling (it has remained broadly unchanged) but because older adults, where the proportion without a qualification is high, have been reaching pensionable age.

In 2010, a quarter (25%) of the UK population aged 22 to 64 had a degree as their highest qualification, while around a fifth had A levels (21%) or GCSE grades A* to C (20%).

Figure 11: Percentage hourly pay gap to employees with GCSE or equivalent level of education (1)
United Kingdom

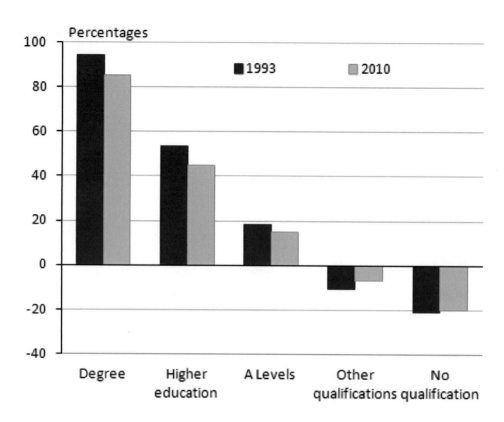

Source: Labour Force Survey, Office for National Statistics

Notes:
1. Respondents aged 22 to 64 in October to December.

People with the highest educational qualifications tend to earn more, however the pay gap comparing employees educated to around the GCSE or equivalent level with those educated to a higher level, was lower in 2010 than in 1993 (the earliest year for which data are comparable). According to the Labour Force Survey (October to December 2010), employees in the UK with a minimum of a degree, earned on average, around 85% more than employees educated to around GCSE level compared with 95% in 1993 (Figure 11). Those educated to around A Level or an equivalent qualification earned around 15% more per hour compared with 18% in 1993. The pay gap to employees with no formal educational qualification has been reasonably stable over time and these employees earned around 20% less than employees educated up to GCSE level in 2010[1] (ONS Pay Gap).

A measure of pupils' academic performance which focuses more on core skills is the proportion of pupils achieving at least five or more GCSEs at grade A* to C including English and mathematics. Just over half (52.9%) of pupils in the UK in their last year of compulsory education achieved this in 2009/10, compared to 47.7% in 2007/08 and 49.8% in 2008/09. This measure was achieved by a higher proportion of girls (57.1%) than boys (48.9%).

Human capital stock

"The well-being of modern society is dependent not only on traditional capital and labour but also on the knowledge and ideas possessed and generated by individual workers. Education is the primary source of this human capital." (Crocker 2002)

The stock of human capital is measured in the UK as the value of the qualifications of those in the labour market[2]. It can be used as a measure of an economy's future well-being, as the work on economic growth suggests that countries with higher levels of human capital, other things being equal, have greater potential output and income in the future.

Data from ONS shows the estimated value of human capital in the UK has increased from £14,460 billion in 2001 and peaked at £17,250 billion in 2009 before falling to £17,120 billion in 2010 (ONS Human Capital).

Figure 12: Human capital stock (1)

United Kingdom

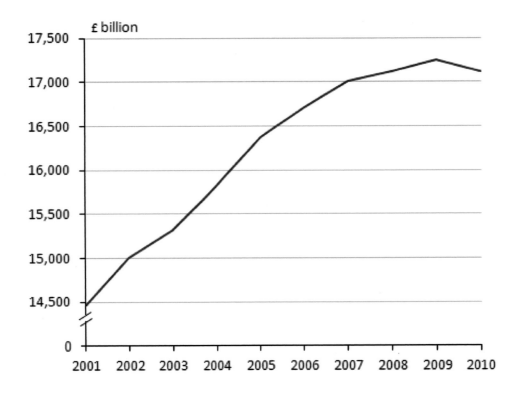

Source: Human Capital Estimates, Office for National Statistics

Notes:
1.   Figures in 2010 prices, labour productivity growth rate = 2% and discount rate = 3.5%.

Figure 12 illustrates the effect of the economic downturn on the UK's human capital stock as the total number of people employed decreased. The value of the UK's human capital stock increased steadily between 2001 and 2007, averaging annual growth of 2.8% (£425 billion). By 2009 the annual rate of growth had slowed to 0.8% (£130 billion) and its value fell by 0.75% (£130 billion) in 2010 (ONS Human Capital).

Notes

1. This analysis focuses on employees aged 22 to 64 because most people have completed their full-time education by this age.

2. The Organisation for Economic Cooperation and Development (OECD), defines human capital as the knowledge, skills, competencies and attributes embodied in individuals that facilitate the creation of personal, social and economic well-being. This is a broad definition, encompassing a range of attributes such as the knowledge, skills, competencies and health conditions of individuals.

People - Individual well-being

"Just generally how I feel - all things considered, how satisfied am I with my life as a whole these days?" (response to "What things matter to you?" from the National Debate).

An important component of national well-being is the subjective well-being of individuals, which is measured by finding out how people think and feel about their own lives. Since April 2011, ONS has included four monitoring questions of subjective well-being on their household surveys.

Table 3: Individual well-being measures (1)

United Kingdom (Percentages)

Indicator	Definition	Value (%)
Life satisfaction[2]	Percentage with medium/high rating of satisfaction with life overall	75.9
Worthwhile[3]	Percentage with medium/high rating of how worthwhile the things they do are	80.0
Happy yesterday[4]	Percentage with medium/high rating who rated their happiness yesterday	71.1
Anxious yesterday[5]	Percentage with medium/low rating who rated how anxious they were yesterday	60.1

Source: Annual Population Survey, Office for National Statistics

Table notes:
1. Respondents aged 16 and above. All questions were answered on an 11 point scale of 0 to 10 where 0 is 'not at all' and 10 is 'completely'.
2. Based on the question "Overall, how satisfied are you with your life nowadays?"
3. Based on the question "Overall, to what extent do you feel the things you do in your life are worthwhile?".
4. Based on the question "Overall, how happy did you feel yesterday?"
5. Based on the question "Overall, how anxious did you feel yesterday?"

Table 3 shows that in terms of overall reflections on the quality of our lives, the picture is positive. Just over three-quarters (75.9%) of people aged 16 and over in the UK rated their overall life satisfaction as medium or high[1] in 2011/12 and four-fifths (80.0%) felt that the things they do in their life are worthwhile.

When asked to reflect on their feelings during the preceding day, over 7 out of 10 (71.1%) people in the UK rated their happiness as medium/ high. In terms of anxiety people felt the day before, 4 out of 10 (40%) reported high anxiety.

These figures provide a helpful overall picture of individual well-being in the UK, but important differences exist in the levels of well-being reported by different groups in the population. For example, levels of well-being differ by age, health, relationship and employment status and where we live.

Figure 13: Subjective well–being by age group, 2011–12 (1,2,3)

United Kingdom

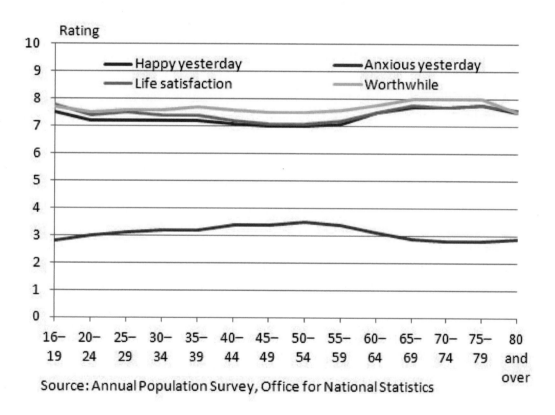

Source: Annual Population Survey, Office for National Statistics

Notes:
1. Data from April 2011 to March 2012.
2. All data weighted.
3. Non-respondents not included.

Figure 13 shows that well-being is highest for the young and old but is lower for the middle aged. Younger people aged 16 to 19 and older people aged 65 to 79 rated their life satisfaction highest between 7.7 and 7.8 out of 10 and felt that the things that they do were worthwhile (between 7.7 and 8.0 out of 10). Those in middle age (aged 40 to 59) were least satisfied with their lives, reporting a score of 7.1 to 7.2 out of 10 and also reporting the highest anxiety levels; 3.4 to 3.5 out of 10. Anxiety levels among the younger and older age groups were lower at 2.8 out of 10.

Many of the specific measures that are related to an individual's well-being are also related to each other such as age, employment status, marital status and health. ONS is currently analysing[2] the relationship between each measure and subjective well-being. Preliminary results suggest that for the measures available, self reported health, relationship status, employment status and ethnicity are most strongly related to subjective well-being. A methodological report providing more detailed results will be available in Spring 2013.

Notes

1. Experimental thresholds are still under evaluation. For 'Life satisfaction', 'Worthwhile' and 'Happy yesterday', medium/high is 7 to 10 on a 11 point scale, where 0 is not at all and 10 is completely. For 'Anxious yesterday', medium/low is 0 to 3 on the same scale.

2. Regression analysis - a statistical procedure that determines a relationship between one set of variables or measurements and another.

People - Health

During the National Debate, health was the most common response when individuals were asked what things in life mattered and what should be reflected in the measures of national well-being. The four headline measures of health currently include healthy life expectancy, self-reported health and a measure of mental illness. For a wider evaluation of health please refer to the Measuring National Well-being domain article on health[1].

Life expectancy

Over time there have been considerable improvements in life expectancy in the UK. Between 1930 and 2010, life expectancy at birth in the UK increased by around 20 years (or a third) for both sexes. In 1930 life expectancy was 58.7 years for males and 63.0 years for females, increasing to 78.1 years for males and 82.1 years for females in 2010 (ONS ST & ONS Health).

Increasing life expectancy has important implications for areas of government policy such as retirement age and healthcare provision. It is important to establish whether these extra years of life are being accompanied by increased periods in good health.

Figure 14: Life expectancy and healthy life expectancy (1) for males and females at birth

United Kingdom

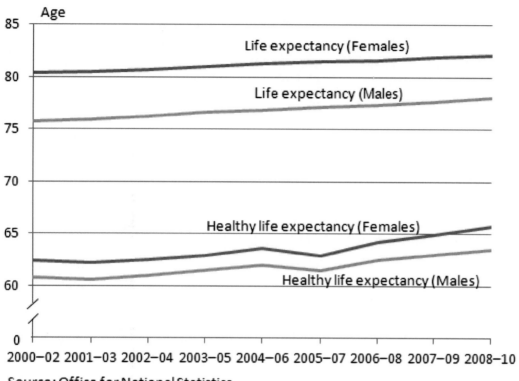

Source: Office for National Statistics

Notes:
1.   Healthy life expectancy based on five-point general health question; 2005–07 to 2008–10. Estimates for 2000–02 to 2004–06 are simulations based on original survey data.

Healthy life expectancies provide the number of years, or proportion of lifetime spent in very good or good health (Healthy life expectancy (HLE)). ONS estimates of HLE for males and females at birth between 2000–02 and 2008–10 in the UK have shown greater increases than life expectancy over the same period. HLE has increased by 2.8 years for males and by 3.3 years for females (Figure 14). Over this time, life expectancy rose by around 2.3 years for males and 1.7 years for females.

Another measure of healthy life expectancy is Disability-free life expectancy (DFLE) or the number of years spent free from a limiting persistent illness or disability. ONS estimates for DFLE for males and females at birth in the UK between 2000–02 and 2008–10, have risen by 3.6 years for males and by 2.3 years for females.

Increases in a lifetime spent in very good or good health or free from a limiting persistent illness may ultimately reduce the healthcare burden associated with an ageing population and has important implications for fitness for work beyond retirement age.

The World Bank published data about life expectancy at birth for all residents as well as for males and females for a large number of countries. Of the 193 countries for which they provide figures for 2010, the UK was ranked 20th with a life expectancy at birth of 80.4 years. Of these countries; San Marino, Japan, Hong Kong SAR, and Switzerland had the highest life expectancies (between 82.2 years and 83.2 years) in 2010. Lesotho and Sierra Leone had the lowest with life expectancies at birth of 47 years.

Satisfaction with health

Figures from the Understanding Society Survey report that in 2009/10, 68.3% of adults aged 16 and over in the UK were somewhat, mostly or completely satisfied with their health. Those in Northern Ireland were most satisfied with their health than those in the rest of the UK with 69.7% of respondents claiming to be somewhat, mostly or completely satisfied. They were also the most likely to report being completely dissatisfied with their health (5.6% compared with a national average of 4.2%).

Figures from the earlier BHPS show that the proportion of adults aged 16 and over in the UK that were satisfied with their general health increased between 2002/03 and 2008/09. In 2002/03, 66.7% reported being somewhat, mostly or completely satisfied with their health, compared with 70.2% in 2008/09 [2]

Figure 15: Self-reported health (1) and satisfaction with life overall (2), 2011/12

United Kingdom

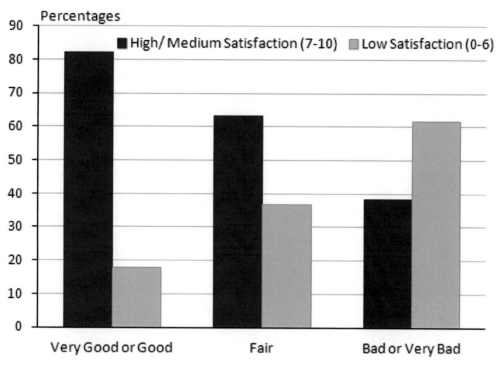

Source: Annual Population Survey, Office for National Statistics

Notes:
1. Individuals are asked to say whether their general health is very good, good, fair, bad or very bad.
2. Individuals were asked to rate how satisfied they were with their lives overall on a scale of 0 to 10 where 0 was 'not at all satisfied' and 10 was 'completely satisfied'.

People's own assessment of their health is associated with their assessment of overall life satisfaction; those who feel that they have good health are much more likely to report higher levels of subjective well-being and, conversely, those who report poor health are much more likely to report lower subjective well-being. Figure 15 shows that almost two thirds (61.7%) of those reporting bad health also reported low levels of well-being, compared to almost one in five (18.0%) of those reporting good health.

Disability

Physical health has a strong association with individual well-being. The number of adults aged between 16 and retirement age[3], who report a current disability has remained at approximately 1 in 5 since 2001 (fluctuating between 18.6 and 19.9%). Half of individuals reporting being long term disabled reported low overall life satisfaction. This compares to around 1 in 5 (19%) of those with no disability.

Mental health

'Mental health and well-being are fundamental to quality of life, enabling people to experience life as meaningful and to be creative and active citizens. Mental health is an essential component of social cohesion, productivity and peace and stability in the living environment, contributing to social capital and economic development in societies' (WHO, 2005).

Positive mental health can be described as people thinking and feeling good about themselves and feeling able to cope with their problems. This positivity is important to an individual's well-being. Mental health differs from mental illness. Mental illness covers a range of mental health problems which can cause marked emotional distress and interfere with daily function, including different types of depression and anxiety. These types of problems can also have a detrimental effect on an individual's well-being.

Table 4: Percentage (1) with some evidence indicating probable psychological disturbance or mental ill health indicated by a GHQ12 score of 4 or more (2)

United Kingdom (Percentages)

	2002/03	2003/04	2004/05	2005/06	2006/07	2007/08	2008/09
Score of 4 or more	20.0	19.3	19.3	20.6	20.0	19.5	20.5
Score of 11 or 12	2.8	2.8	3.0	3.1	3.0	3.1	3.5

Source: British Household Panel Survey

Table notes:
1. Percentages exclude missing and proxy values.
2. The GHQ-12 questionnaire concentrates on the broader components of psychological morbidity and consists of twelve items measuring general levels of happiness; depression and anxiety; sleep disturbance; and ability to cope over the last few weeks. The twelve items are rated on a four-point response scale, where a score of 0 is given to responses such as that the symptom is present 'not at all' or 'no more than usual' and a score of 1 is given to

responses symptom is present 'not at all' or 'no more than usual' and a score of 1 is given to responses such as 'rather more than usual' or 'much more than usual'. Consistent with analysis of other surveys, a GHQ12 score of 4 or more is referred to as a 'high GHQ12 score', indicating probable psychological disturbance or mental ill health.

Table 4 shows that between 2002/03 and 2008/09 around 1 in 5 (ranging from 19.3% and 20.5%) adults aged 16 and over in the UK indicated some element of psychological distress (scoring 4 or more). For the same period, between 2.8% and 3.5% reported a score of 11 or 12, indicating a much higher level of distress.

The Adult Psychiatric Morbidity Survey (APMS)[4] estimates the number of adults suffering from common mental disorders (CMDs) such as anxiety and depression. Results showed that in England in 2007 around 1 in 6 adults (17.6%) met the diagnostic criteria for at least one CMD in the week prior to interview. Between the surveys conducted in 1993 and 2000 there had been an increase in the prevalence of both mixed anxiety and depressive disorders and a slight increase in generalised anxiety disorders (from 7.5% to 9.4% and 4.4% to 4.7% respectively) , but there were only small changes between 2000 and 2007 (ONS, 2012, Health).

For a wider discussion of mental health including a discussion on positive mental health measures please refer to ONS Health.

Notes

1. Health

2. The British Household Panel Survey was replaced with the Understanding Society Survey in 2009. While the questions are similiar the methodology has changed to such an extent that it is not possible to compare the two.

3. Men aged 16-64, women aged 16-59.

4. The Adult Psychiatric Morbidity Survey (APMS) series provides data on the prevalence of both treated and untreated psychiatric disorder in the English adult population (aged 16 and over).

People - Our relationships

Leisure time

Leisure time may provide many health benefits, both physically and mentally. Obtaining and maintaining the correct balance between working life and home life can be beneficial to an individual's overall well-being.

Figure 16: Satisfaction with amount of leisure time (1), 2009/10

United Kingdom

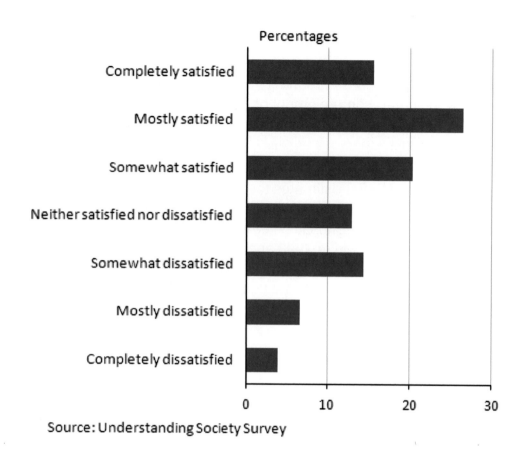

Source: Understanding Society Survey

Notes:

1. Adults aged 16 and over were asked 'How dissatisfied or satisfied are you with.........The amount of leisure time you have'. The percentages are of those who responded.

The Understanding Society Survey asked respondents 'How dissatisfied or satisfied are you with the amount of leisure time you have'. In the UK, in 2009/10, 62.3% of adults aged 16 and over reported that they were somewhat, mostly or completely satisfied, 12.9% were neither satisfied nor dissatisfied and 24.8% were somewhat, mostly or completely dissatisfied (Figure 16) (Understanding Society).

Social life

"The quality of a person's social life could have an even greater impact than diet and exercise on their health and well-being" (research by the Universities of Exeter and Queensland, Australia).

A social life can be an important part of someone's leisure time. Having a good social life with good social networks may increase a person's sense of well-being. According to the British Household Panel Survey (BHPS), nearly 7 in 10 (67.0%) adults aged 16 and over in the UK were somewhat, mostly or completely satisfied with their social life in 2008–09. Social life satisfaction varied by age. Those aged 16 to 24 and 55 and over were more likely to report that they were somewhat, mostly or completely satisfied with their social life (75.7% and 71.7 respectively). This compares with 58.2% of those aged 35 to 44, 62.1% aged 45 to 54 and 63.2% of those aged 25 to 34. This is consistent with the pattern of general life satisfaction discussed previously. Lower satisfaction with social life for these age groups may be due to people having less time for socialising because of work or family commitments. The presence of children in the family clearly has an effect. Three-quarters (75.2%) of couples with no children and 71.8% of couples with non-dependent children were somewhat, mostly or completely satisfied with their social life. This is higher than the equivalent figures for couples with dependent children (62.2%) and lone parents with dependent children (50.8%).

Relationships with family and friends

"The frequency of contact with others and the quality of personal relationships are crucial determinants of people's well-being. People get pleasure from spending time with others – be it family, friends or colleagues – and activities are typically more satisfying when shared with others. Furthermore, social networks provide material and emotional support in times of need" (Kahneman and Krueger, 2006).

Relationship with families and friends was another key measure identified in the National Debate. Adults in the EU-27 were asked on the Eurofound European Quality of Life Survey on a scale of 1 to 10 how satisfied they were with their family life where 1 was very dissatisfied and 10 was very satisfied. The average (mean) rating for the UK was 8.2, higher than the average for the EU-27 at 7.9. Denmark and Malta had the highest average rating at 8.8 and 8.7 respectively while Bulgaria and Macedonia had the lowest average ratings of 6.5 and 6.9 respectively (Eurofound).

Figure 17: Spending most days or everyday with family and friends (1): by age, 2011
England

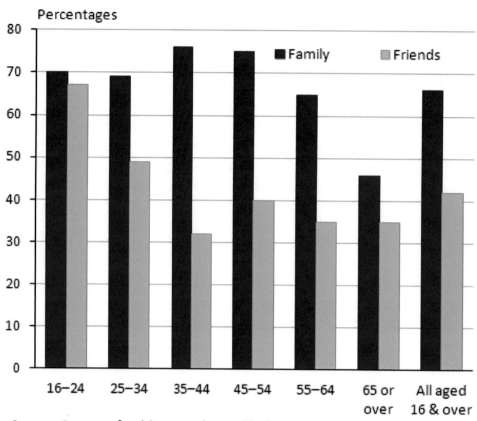

Source: Survey of public attitudes and behaviours towards the
environment, Department for Environment, Food and Rural Affairs

Notes:

1. Sample composed of 1,769 adults aged 16 and over.

The 2011 survey of public attitudes and behaviours towards the environment run by the Department for Environment, Food and Rural Affairs (Defra) asked people in England how often in the previous two weeks they had spent time together with family and friends. Two-thirds (66%) of respondents reported having spent time with family every day or most days during the two weeks prior to interview (Figure 17). This is an increase from 61% in 2007. Those aged 65 and over were much less likely to report spending time with family every day or most days (46%) than other age groups (Defra 2011).

Over 4 in 10 adults (42%) spent time with friends every day or most days. This was an increase from 37% in 2007. Proportionately, younger people were more likely to report spending time with friends than older people; 67% of 16 to 24 year-olds spent time with friends on most or every day in the two weeks prior to interview, compared with 35% of those aged 55 to 64 and 65 and over. The lowest proportion of people spending time with friends on most or every day was those in the 35 to 44 age group (32%). This may be due to having young children to look after and work commitments (Defra 2011).

Social connections

"Social connections, including marriage, of course, but not limited to that, are among the most robust correlates of subjective well-being. People who have close friends and confidants, friendly neighbours and supportive co-workers are less likely to experience sadness, loneliness, low self-esteem and problems with eating and sleeping..."– (Helliwell and Putnam, 2004).

Figure 18: Satisfaction with personal relationships compared with life satisfaction (1), 2011–12 (2)
Great Britain

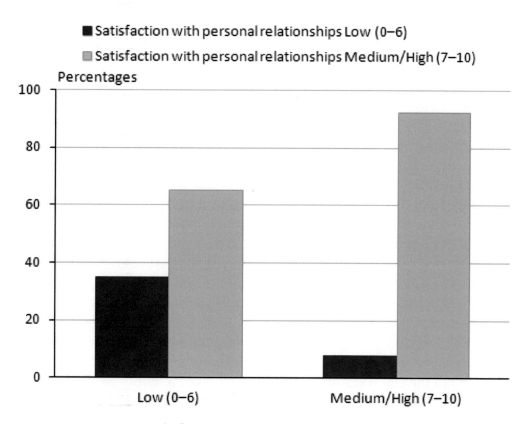

Source: Opinions and Lifestyle Survey, Office for National Statistics

Notes:
1. Adults aged 16 and over were asked 'Overall, how satisfied are you with your life nowadays?' and 'Overall, how satisfied are you with your personal relationships?' Where 0 is 'not at all satisfied' and 10 is 'completely satisfied' .
2. Data are for April, June & October 2011 and February 2012. There were different split trials (April & June – Mode effect, October – Order effect of the four headline questions and February – Show card effect). These trials may have had an impact on the resulting data.

Overall satisfaction with life and personal relationships are related. Of those who reported a medium/high satisfaction with life (7 to 10 out of 10), 92.3% also reported a medium/high satisfaction with their personal relationships (Figure 18). Conversely, 34.7% of those who reported a low satisfaction with life (0 to 6 out of 10) also had low satisfaction with their personal relationships. However it must be noted that 65.3% who reported a low satisfaction with life also had a medium/high satisfaction with their personal relationships, which indicates that there are other factors that impact on overall individual well-being.

Over 9 in 10 (96.8%) adults aged 16 and over in the UK reported on the British Household Panel Survey in 2007/08 that there was someone who they could really count on to help out in a crisis. Just under a quarter of adults (24.4%) had one person to rely on and nearly three-quarters (72.4%) had more than one person to rely on. However 3.2% of adults had no one at all to rely on.

Inadequate levels of social relationships may lead to people experiencing loneliness in life. However the feeling of loneliness is subjective and a person may experience this even when in the company of family and friends. In 2011–12[1], the ONS Opinions and Lifestyle Survey asked adults aged 16 and over in Great Britain on a scale of 0 to 10 how lonely they felt in daily life where 0 was not lonely at all and 10 was very lonely. Over a third (34.5%) of respondents who answered this question recorded not being lonely at all in their daily life (0 out of 10), while 3.1% recorded being completely lonely in their daily life (10 out of 10). However it must be noted that over 6 in 10 (62.4%) reported some degree of loneliness, scoring between 1 and 9.

Isolation can be a major factor in someone's feeling of loneliness and where people live can have an effect on people's sense of isolation. A feeling of belonging to a person's neighbourhood can influence people's sense of identity and may also contribute to an individual's sense of well-being. According to the 2009/10 Understanding Society Survey two-thirds (66.0%) of adults aged 16 and over in the UK strongly agreed or agreed that they felt they belonged in their neighbourhood. However, just over a quarter (25.7%) neither agreed or disagreed and 8.3% disagreed or strongly disagreed that they felt they belonged in their neighbourhood (Understanding Society).

Adults aged 18 and over in Great Britain were asked in a survey by YouGov in 2011 whether they or anyone else they knew felt isolated as a result of having difficulty accessing local shops and services. Around 1 in 20 (5%) of people reported feeling a sense of isolation, while just over 1 in 5 (22%) reported that they knew someone who felt a sense of isolation due to difficulty accessing local shops and services (YouGov).

Notes

1. Data for July & November 2011 and March 2012

People - Governance

"...... participation in political life (through voting or engaging in associations) is influenced by "solidarity incentives" that are "intangible costs and benefits of a social nature deriving, for example, from friendship, camaraderie, recreational activity, status, social pressure, or a sense of belonging" Knack (1992).

Trustworthy and honest public administration is fundamental for citizens' trust in democracy and the state. Having trust in parliament and a feeling that people have a voice or that they can help themselves has an effect on how we think and feel. Trust in, and accountability of, national government and the role of parliament were key concerns reported during the National Debate. In the simplest sense, government accountability means that the government is answerable for performance or results. Much of the public's trust rests upon the government being openly accountable for its decisions, actions and mistakes.

Figure 19: Trust in parliament and government (1)

United Kingdom

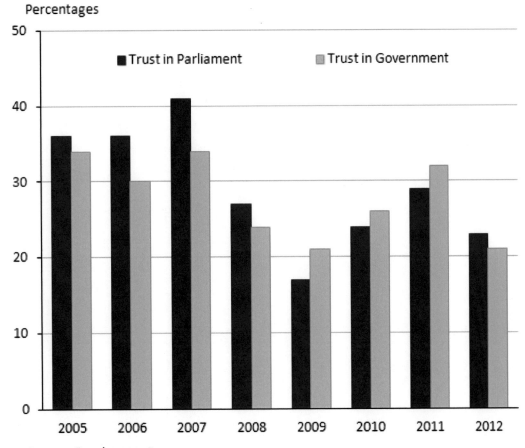

Source: Eurobarometer

Notes:

1. Adults aged 15 and over were asked if they 'tend to trust' or 'tend to not trust' the UK parliament and government. Percentages are for those who answered 'tend to trust'. Fieldwork was carried out in May and June in 2005; March and May in 2006; April and May in 2007; March and April in 2008; June and July in 2009 and May in 2010 to 2012.

According to the Standard Eurobarometer survey, less than a quarter (23%) of adults aged 15 and over in the UK 'tended to trust' the UK parliament in 2012, while just over a fifth (21%) 'tended to trust the government' (Figure 19). Since the question was first asked in 2005, trust in the UK Parliament peaked in 2007 at 41% but then declined sharply to 17% in 2009. This was mirrored by the proportion of people that 'tended to trust' the government, at over a third (34%) in 2007, falling to just over a fifth (21%) in 2009. These proportional declines coincide with the UK parliamentary expenses scandal and the start of the financial crisis (Eurobarometer).

According to the 2010 British Social Attitudes survey, 61% of adults aged 18 and over in Great Britain agreed strongly or agreed with the statement 'Voting is the only way people like me can have any say about how the government runs things', while a quarter (25%) of adults disagreed or disagreed strongly with this statement.

Figure 20: Voting turnout in UK General Elections (1)

United Kingdom

Percentages

Source: The International Institute for Democracy and Electoral Assistance

Notes:
1. Valid votes as a proportion of the electorate.

In 1950 voting turnout peaked with over 8 in 10 (83.6%) of the electorate voting[1] (Figure 20). By 1983, turnout was down to 72.8%. Despite an improvement in participation in both 1987 and 1992, the General Elections in 2001 and 2005 had relatively low turnouts (59.4% and 61.4% respectively). In 2010 the turnout rose to 65.8% (IDEA).

Notes

1. Voter turnout is measured by the number of people registered to vote. Non-voters are those registered but not voting.

People - Where we live

Living in local area

Adults aged 16 and over in Great Britain were asked on the ONS Opinions and Lifestyle Survey how satisfied they were overall with their local area (15 to 20 minutes walking distance from home), where 0 was not satisfied at all and 10 was completely satisfied. In October 2011 and February 2012, nearly 8 in 10 (79.3%) people reported a medium/high satisfaction (7 to 10 out of 10) with their local area, while 20.8% reported a low satisfaction (0 to 6 out of 10).

Crime

"The biggest impact of crime on people's well-being appears to be through the feeling of vulnerability that it causes" OECD

The 2008 Place Survey (the latest data available), run by the Department for Communities and Local Government (DCLG), asked adults aged 18 and over in England to select up to five priorities that would be important in making somewhere a good place to live. The most important factor reported was the level of crime (61%).

According to the Crime Survey for England and Wales (previously known as the British Crime Survey), between 2002/03 and 2011/12 household crime and personal crime had been generally falling. Household crime (per 1,000 households) has fallen by 29.2% while personal crime (per 1,000 adults aged 16 and over) has fallen by 26.2% (ONS CSEW).

However, people's perception of crime does not reflect the fall in actual crime. Since 1996, the Crime Survey for England and Wales asked adults aged 16 and over how much they think the level of crime has changed in their local area and in the country as a whole in the two years prior to interview (ONS CSEW).

Table 5: Perceptions of changing crime levels (1)

England and Wales (Percentages)

	National crime	Local crime
2001/02	64.6	51.0
2002/03	72.3	53.9
2003/04	65.2	48.5
2004/05	60.7	42.4
2005/06	62.7	42.0
2006/07	64.5	41.4
2007/08	65.3	38.9
2008/09	74.8	36.2
2009/10	66.4	30.6
2010/11	59.9	27.9

Source: Crime Survey for England and Wales, Office for National Statistics

Table notes:

1. Percentage of adults aged 16 and over reporting 'a little more' or 'a lot more' crime than two years ago.

The proportion of adults in England and Wales who thought that crime had increased nationally is higher than the proportion who thought that crime had increased in their local area. In 2010/11 just under 6 in 10 (59.9%) people reported that there was a little more or a lot more crime in England and Wales as a whole than two years ago, compared to under 3 in 10 (27.9%) who reported more crime in their local area (Table 5). The gap between perceptions of change in national and local crime levels widened between 2003/04 and 2008/09. It then narrowed slightly in 2009/10 and 2010/11, following a sharp increase in the proportion of adults who thought that crime had gone up nationally in 2008/09 and a decrease in the proportion who thought it had gone up locally (ONS, CSEW).

According to the 2010–11 Scottish Crime and Justice Survey, 23% of adults aged 16 and over in Scotland perceived that there had been an increase in the crime rate over the previous two years in their local area, while 9% perceived there had been a decrease in the crime rate in their local area. According to the 2010–11 Northern Ireland Crime Survey, over a third of respondents (35%) felt that crime levels in their local area had increased in the preceding two years; just under a quarter (24%) felt there was 'a little more crime', while 11% felt there was 'a lot more crime'

Feeling safe in a local area can be an important factor for a person's sense of satisfaction in the area around them. A good indicator of this is to find out whether a person feels safe walking alone after dark. According to the Crime Survey for England and Wales just over a third (34.1%) of adults aged 16 and over in 2010/11 reported that they felt very safe walking alone after dark, with 41% feeling fairly safe. However, around a quarter (24.3%) felt a bit or very unsafe (ONS, CSEW).

Housing and tenure

'We spend much of our lives in the home, our primary emotional connections are shaped in the domestic arena of the home; where we live and how we live are important determinants of our social position, physical health and individual well-being' (Rennie Short, 1999)

An individual's housing tenure and the level of their overall satisfaction with life are linked. Home ownership, either outright or through a mortgage, is the most common form of tenure in the UK. According to the 2010 General Lifestyle Survey just over two-thirds (68%) of households in Great Britain owned their own homes: with just under a third (32%) owning outright and 36% owning with a mortgage. Social renting describes those who rent from a local authority or housing association. In 2010, 10% of households rented from a council and 8% from a housing association. The remaining 13% of households rented from the private sector (ONS GLS).

Table 6: Life satisfaction (1): by selected housing tenure (2), 2011/12

United Kingdom (Percentages)

	Satisfaction with life	
	Low (0–6)	Medium/High (7–10)
Owned outright	19.0	81.0
Bought with mortgage or loan	20.1	79.9
Rented	32.2	67.8

Source: Subjective Well-being Annual Population Survey dataset, Office for National Statistics

Table notes:
1. Adults aged 16 and over were asked 'Overall, how satisfied are you with your life nowadays? where nought is 'not at all satisfied' and 10 is 'completely satisfied'.
2. Those who stated they were 'part renting/part mortgage', 'rent free' and 'squatting' are not included in the table due to small sample sizes.

According to the 2011/12 Subjective Well-being Annual Population Survey dataset (which are experimental data), a higher proportion of those who owned their property, either outright or with a mortgage, reported a medium/high level of life satisfaction (7 to 10 out of 10) than those with other tenures in the UK in 2011/12 (Table 6). Conversely, nearly a third (32%) of those who rented reported a low satisfaction with life (0 to 6 out of 10) compared with just under a fifth (19%) of those who owned their accommodation outright and a fifth (20%) of those who owned their accommodation with a mortgage.

The Environment - Introduction

"The environment is the basic foundation of individual wellbeing. Often referred to as natural capital, the environment functions and interacts with human systems, social systems, and the built environment. Environmental wellbeing is embedded within many of the dimensions of the wheel because of people's continual direct interaction with their physical surroundings" Washington State University.

In the National Debate, just under three-quarters (73%) of respondents mentioned the environment as an important factor in well-being. Responses about the environment were for both the local environment and the global environment. Responses about the local environment included having access to open, green space within walking distance of the recipient's home and the quality of the local area. Global environment factors included air quality and climate change. The natural environment has a role to play to ensure sustainable supply of natural goods like food, water, minerals, raw materials, and to maintain intangible factors such as critical ecosystem services that provide benefits for human welfare.

The Environment - The natural environment

The 2008 Place Survey (the latest data available), run by the Department for Communities and Local Government (DCLG), asked adults aged 18 and over in England to select up to five priorities that would be important in making somewhere a good place to live. Just under a quarter (23.3%) reported that access to nature was important in making somewhere a good place to live (DCLG Place Survey).

Figure 21: Frequency of visiting the natural environment (1), 2011/12

England

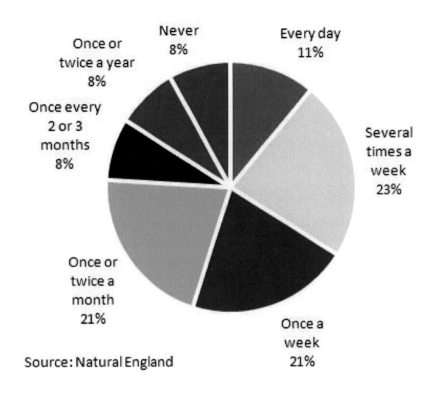

Source: Natural England

In 2011/12, over half (55%) of adults aged 16 and over in England reported that on average, they visited the outdoors away from home at least once a week in the 12 months prior to interview (Figure 21). Just over a third (34%) reported that they visited the outdoors, away from home, several times a week or more often, while 11% reported that they visited on a daily basis. Under 1 in 10 (8%) stated that they had not visited the natural environment in the previous 12 months; this was equivalent to around 3.5 million adults. Almost 2 in 5 (38%) of those who did not take a visit to the natural environment in the last 12 months were aged 65 and over. Just over two-thirds (68%) of people who visited at least once per week were between the ages of 25 and 64, with those aged between 25 and 44 the most likely to have frequently visited the outdoors in the last 12 months (36%) (Natural England).

Figure 22: Extent of United Kingdom nationally and internationally important protected areas (1,2)

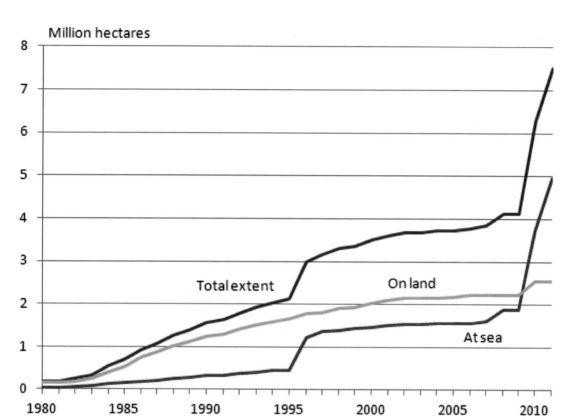

Source: Joint Nature Conservation Committee based on its own data and data from the Countryside Council for Wales, Natural England, Northern Ireland Environment Agency and Scottish Natural Heritage

Notes:
1. The demarcation between the protected areas on land and at sea is mean high water (mean high water spring in Scotland). The calculations to create the indicator split the terrestrial and marine components of coastal sites between the 'on land' and 'at sea' lines shown.
2. Based on calendar year of site designation.

The UK has a responsibility to ensure the conservation and enhancement of habitats and species in both a national and international context. Designation of protected areas[1] is a key mechanism for biodiversity conservation. The overall total extent of land and sea protected in the UK through national and international protected areas has increased from just under 0.2 million hectares in 1980 to just over 7.5 million hectares in December 2011 (Figure 22). Since 2000 the total extent of protected areas has more than doubled, from 3.5 million hectares. A large contribution to this has been from the marine environment following the designation of inshore and offshore marine sites under the Habitats Directive[2] – the area of marine protected areas increased by more than 3 million hectares between 2009 and 2011.The extent of protected areas on land has increased by more than half a million hectares since 2000 (JNCC).

Notes

1. A 'protected area' is defined by the International Union for Conservation of Nature as a clearly defined geographical space, recognized, dedicated and managed, through legal or other effective means, to achieve the long-term conservation of nature with associated ecosystem services and cultural values

2. For more information see http://ec.europa.eu/environment/nature/legislation/habitatsdirective/index_en.htm

The Environment - Air quality

Air pollution

"Pollution can affect well being both through an awareness of the adverse health and ecosystem effects of pollution as well as through the direct health effects" (Carmen Lawrence, 2011).

Air pollutants can have a detrimental impact on the quality of the air we breathe. Many everyday activities produce air pollutants which can harm the environment and in turn affect human health.

Figure 23: Emissions of selected air pollutants (1)

United Kingdom

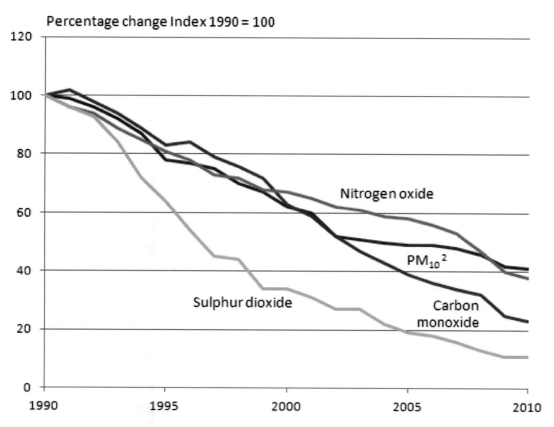

Source: Department for Environment, Food and Rural Affairs; AEA Energy and Environment

Notes:
1. Covered by the UK Air Quality Strategy.
2. Particulate matter that is less than 10 microns in diameter.

Emissions of the major air pollutants in the UK have generally been falling since the 1970s, and the rate of decline has accelerated since 1989. Carbon monoxide (CO) is the most prevalent air pollutant, the largest source being road transport. Emissions of carbon monoxide fell by 77% between 1990 and 2010 (Figure 23). The probable reason for this was that exhaust emissions standards were introduced for petrol cars in the early 1990s, which in most cases meant fitting a catalytic converter to reduce pollutants. Road transport is the main source of nitrogen oxides (NOx) which have similar effects to sulphur dioxide. Emissions fell by 62% between 1990 and 2010, again mainly as a result of catalytic converters being fitted on cars.

Sulphur dioxide (SO2) is an acid gas that can affect both human and animal health, and vegetation. UK SO2 emissions are dominated by combustion of fuels such as coal and heavy oils in power stations and refineries. Emissions fell by 89% between 1990 and 2010, largely as a result of the reduction in coal use by power stations.

Particulate matter is derived from both human-made and natural sources and are small enough to be inhaled into the deepest parts of the lung. In the UK the biggest human-made sources are fuel combustion and transport. Total emissions of particulate matter fell by 59% between 1990 and 2010, partly because of the reduction in emissions from power stations, the installation of equipment to reduce or eliminate airborne pollutants and increased efficiency and use of natural gas for electricity generation (Defra 2010).

Greenhouse gases

The Earth's climate is driven by energy from the Sun, which is absorbed by the planet's surface. Greenhouse gases in the atmosphere, mainly water vapour, carbon dioxide, methane and nitrous oxide, help to keep the Earth warmer by preventing some of this energy from escaping. Without this natural 'greenhouse' effect the Earth would be around 33°C colder than it is, with a global average temperature of about -18°C. Extra greenhouse gases are emitted by human activities and are dominated by carbon dioxide, methane, nitrous oxide and ozone. Of these, carbon dioxide has the largest long-term effect on the climate. The overwhelming scientific consensus is that man-made greenhouse gases are very likely responsible for most of the global warming seen over the 20th century.

Carbon dioxide (CO2) accounted for about 83% of the UK's man-made greenhouse gas emissions in 2010. In 2011, an estimated 40% of carbon dioxide emissions were from the energy supply sector, 26% from transport, and 15% from each of the business and residential sectors. Between 2010 and 2011, provisional estimates indicate that CO2 emissions decreased in the residential sector by 22% (19 million tonnes), 6% (12 million tonnes) from the energy supply sector, 8% (6 million tonnes) from the business sector, and 1% (2 million tonnes) in the transport sector.

Since 1990, there has been a decrease in UK carbon dioxide emissions of around 23%. This fall in emissions has been accompanied by a decrease in overall energy consumption over the period, of around 5%. On a temperature corrected basis[1], energy consumption has fallen by around 6% between 1990 and 2011. A number of factors explain this effect, such as changes in the efficiency in electricity generation and switching from coal to less carbon intensive fuels such as gas (DECC, 2010).

Notes

1. The temperature corrected series of total inland fuel consumption indicates what annual consumption might have been if the average temperature during the year had been the same as the average for a long term period

The Environment - Renewable energy

"With consistent climate and energy policy support, renewable energy sources can contribute substantially to human well-being by sustainably supplying energy and stabilizing the climate". (Professor Ottmar Edenhofer, Co-Chair of Intergovernmental Panel on Climate Change Working Group III in 2011).

Renewable energy is seen as environmentally friendly and may add to the well-being of future generations.

Use of energy from renewable and waste sources has more than doubled between 2000 and 2010, from 2.7 million tonnes of oil equivalent (Mtoe) to 7.1 Mtoe, an average of 10% each year. This was due to an increase in road transport biofuels and wood energy consumption, driven by increases in direct energy use in the electricity, water and waste, and consumer expenditure industry groups.

In 2010, use of renewable and waste energy increased by 0.5 Mtoe (6.8%) compared with 2009. As a result, 3.2% of total energy consumption was from renewable sources in 2010. Of the renewable and waste energy used in 2010, 45% was from waste sources such as landfill gas, sewage gas, municipal solid waste (MSW) and poultry litter, 20% from wood and straw, 18% from liquid bio-fuels, bioethanol and biodiesel, and 17% from renewable generation from hydroelectric power, solar photovoltaic, geothermal aquifers and energy from wind, wave and tide (ONS MNWB Environment).

About the ONS Measuring National Well-being Programme

NWB logo 2

This article is published as part of the ONS Measuring National Well-being Programme.

The programme aims to produce accepted and trusted measures of the well-being of the nation - how the UK as a whole is doing. It is about looking at 'GDP and beyond' and includes:

- greater analysis of the national economic accounts, especially to understand household income, expenditure and wealth
- further accounts linked to the national accounts, including the UK Environmental Accounts and valuing household production and 'human capital'
- quality of life measures, looking at different areas of national well-being such as health, relationships, job satisfaction, economic security, education environmental conditions

- working with others to include the measurement of the well-being of children and young people as part of national well-being
- measures of 'subjective well-being' - individuals' assessment of their own well-being
- headline indicators to summarise national well-being and the progress we are making as a society

The programme is underpinned by a communication and engagement workstream, providing links with Cabinet Office and policy departments, international developments, the public and other stakeholders. The programme is working closely with Defra on the measurement of 'sustainable development' to provide a complete picture of national well-being, progress and sustainable development.

Find out more on the Measuring National Well-being website pages.

Background notes

1. Details of the policy governing the release of new data are available by visiting www.statisticsauthority.gov.uk/assessment/code-of-practice/index.html or from the Media Relations Office email: media.relations@ons.gsi.gov.uk

Copyright

1. Allin P (2007) 'Measuring societal wellbeing',*Economic & Labour Market Review* vol 1, no 10, pp 46–52, Available at http://www.ons.gov.uk/ons/guide-method/user-guidance/well-being/publications/previous-publications/index.html

2. DECC - Department of Energy and Climate Change

3. Defra 2010 - DEFRA: Statistics

4. Defra, 2011 - Survey of public attitudes and behaviours towards the environment DEFRA: Statistics

5. DWP, 2012 - DWP: Households Below Average Income

6. Eurobarometer - Eurobarometer

7. Eurofound - www.eurofound.europa.eu/

8. IDEA - www.idea.int/

9. JNCC - www.jncc.defra.gov.uk/

10. Natural England - www.naturalengland.org.uk/

11. ONS CSEW - Crime in England and Wales

12. ONS GLS - General Lifestyle Survey index

13. ONS Health - Health Expectancies at birth and age 65 in the United Kingdom index

14. ONS Human Capital - Jones R and Fender V (2011): *Human Capital Estimates, 2010*, ONS.

15. ONS LFS - Labour Force Survey

16. ONS MNWB Environment - Natural Environment

17. ONS Pay Gap - Earnings by qualification in the UK index

18. ONS, ST - Social Trends index

19. ONS, WAS - Wealth and Assets

20. ONS, Well-being - Measuring National Well-being index

21. Stevenson, B., and Wolfers, J. (2008). Economic growth and subjective well-being: Reassessing the Easterlin paradox. Available at http://bpp.wharton.upenn.edu/betseys/papers.asp

22. Stiglitz, J., Sen, A., and Fitoussi, J-P. (2009) Report by the Commission on the Measurement of Economic Performance and Social Progress.

23. Understanding Society, 2011 - Understanding Society: Early findings from the first wave of the UK's household longitudinal study

24. Veenhoven, R. Trends in Nations, World Database of Happiness, Erasmus University Rotterdam, www.worlddatabaseofhappiness.eur.nl (2002-2011)

25. WHO, (2005) WHO, Mental health action plan for Europe: Facing the challenges, building solutions, WHO European Ministerial Conference on Mental Health, Helsinki, Finland, 12–15 January 2005.

26. YouGov - Yougov archives

Annex A: Measuring National Well-being Programme Domains and Measures

The Domains and Measures

Table 1 shows a list of the current domains and measures being used by the Measuring National Well-being Programme.

Table 1: List of Domains and Measures, November 2012

RFT- Annex A Table 1 (38 Kb Excel sheet)

The measures are largely the same as those published in July, however some minor amends have been made which are listed in table 2.

Table 2: Summary of amendments to measures since July 2012

RFT Annex A Table 2 (31.5 Kb Excel sheet)

How the measures were selected

The domains and measures were developed based on responses to the National Debate, which took place between November 2010 and April 2011, existing research and international initiatives. After identifying approximately 3,000 potential measures, a number of criteria, as set out in Measuring What Matters[1], the National Statistician's report on the findings from the National Debate were applied. These specified that measures must be:

- statistically robust - that is they meet the standard statistical requirements of accuracy, reliability and validity;
- available for the UK;
- policy relevant;
- internationally comparable;
- have a time series and are likely to be available in the future;
- shown and compared for countries in the UK, regions of England, and smaller geographic units where required;
- able to be analysed in ways which show distribution of outcomes for individuals or households, e.g. analysis for poorest and richest households, by age group or by marital or employment status

The measures were then grouped into sensible domains and a number of other considerations were employed. These included;

- effective coverage of the domains; without overlap or duplication;
- provision of a coherent and consistent picture within the domains;
- relevance for measuring well-being or an aspect that can be shown to be related to well-being;
- relevant stakeholder endorsement;
- whether they are rated highly against other potential measures for measuring well-being;
- sensitivity to effective policy interventions without being readily susceptible to manipulation; and
- likely to receive public acceptance, interest and understanding.

In October 2011, ONS published a set of proposed domains measures of national well-being for consultation[2], and received nearly 1,800 responses. Overall there was broad support for the domains and measures proposed. Suggestions received were mainly concerned with the placement of measures within domains and the adoption of additional measures to complement those already included. For a more detailed account please refer to the Report on the Consultation on Proposed Domains and Measures[3].

Future development

The domains and measures will continue to be developed throughout the programme. The next steps which will further consider the findings from the consultation and include a review of both the measures and the criteria used to select them will be published in Spring 2013.

Should you wish to feedback on the domains and measures or any element of the Measuring National Well-being programme please email: nationalwell-being@ons.gov.uk

.

Notes

1. Measuring National Well-being index

2. Measuring National Well-being - Discussion paper on domains and measures

3. Measuring National Well-being index

Annex B: Measuring National Well-being programme publications

Below is a list of outputs released by the Measuring National Well-being programme since November 2010. Publications are grouped under the area to which they relate and are listed with the most recent first. They are published here Measuring National Well-being

The Economy

The effects of taxes and benefits on household income 2010/11 (Jun 2012)

Comparisons of UK and EU at risk Poverty Rates 2005-2010 (Jun 2012)

Quarterly Household Release, Q4 2011 (Apr 2012)

Human Capital estimates 2010 (Dec 2011)

People

First Annual ONS Experimental Subjective Well-being Results (Jul 2012)

Subjective well-being survey user guide (12 month dataset) (Jul 2012)

Measuring National Well-being - Households and families (Apr 2012)

Analysis of experimental subjective well-being data from the Annual Population Survey, April - September 2011 (Feb 2012)

Subjective well-being survey user guide (Feb 2012)

Measuring National Well-being - Population (Jan 2012)

Initial investigation into Subjective Well-being data from the ONS Opinions Survey (Dec 2012)

Measuring subjective well-being (Jul 2011)

The Environment

UK Environmental Accounts 2012 (Jun 2012)

World Environment Day article 2012 (May 2012) UK Environmental Accounts

Developments in Environmental Protection Expenditure Accounts (Jan 2012)

Domain articles

Measuring National Well-being - The Natural Environment, 2012 (Nov 2012)

Measuring National Well-being - Governance, 2012 (Oct 2012)

Measuring National Well-being - The Economy (Oct 2012)

Measuring National Well-being - Personal finance (Sep 2012)

Measuring National Well-being - Health (Jul 2012)

Measuring National Well-being - Where we live (Jul 2012)

Measuring National Well-being - Education and skills (Jul 2012)

Measuring National Well-being - What we do (Mar 2012)

Measuring National Well-being - Our relationships (Feb 2012)

Measuring economic well-being (Jul 2011)

Domains and measures

Measuring National Well-being - summary of proposed domains and measures (Jul 2012)

Report on the Consultation on Proposed Domains and Measures (Jul 2012)

Consultation on proposed domains and measures of national well-being: responses received (Jun 2012)

Initial findings from the consultation on proposed domains and measures of national well-being (Feb 2012)

Measuring National Well-being - Discussion paper on domains and measures (Oct 2011)

Cross-programme

Measuring National Well-being - Children's well-being, 2012 (Oct 2012)

Measuring National Well-being - Measuring young people's well-being, 2012 (Oct 2012)

Is there more to life than GDP and happiness (Feb 2012)

Measuring what Matters: National Statistician's Reflections on the National Debate on Measuring National Well-being (Jul 2011)

Findings from the National well-being debate (Jul 2011)

Developing a framework for understanding and measuring national well-being (Jul 2011)

Measuring children's and young people's well-being (Jul 2011)

Measuring National Well-being - the Contribution of Longitudinal Studies (Jul 2011)

Interactive content

Measuring National Well-being - Interactive wheel of measures (Nov 2012)

Measuring National Well-being - Interactive graphs (Nov 2012)

Measuring National Well-being - Interactive tool (Jul 2012)

Measuring National Well-being - Interactive map (Jul 2012)

this page is intentionally blank

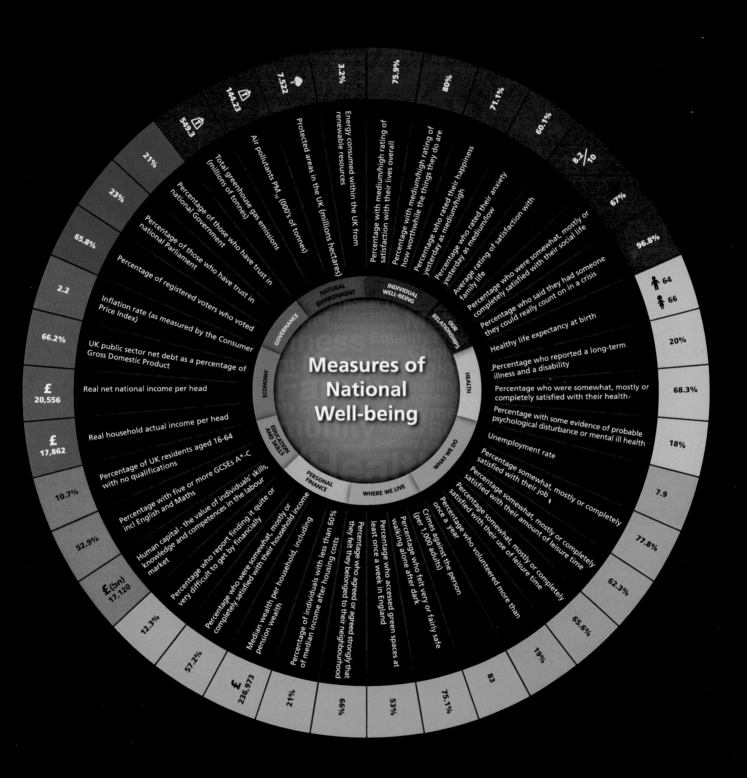

Energy consumed within the UK from renewable resources — 3.2%
Protected areas in the UK from (millions hectares) — 7.522
Air pollutants PM₁₀ (000's of tonnes) — 144.23
Total greenhouse gas emissions (millions of tonnes) — 5493
Percentage of those who have trust in national Government — 21%
Percentage of those who have trust in national Parliament — 23%
Percentage of registered voters who voted — 65.8%
Inflation rate (as measured by the Consumer Price Index) — 2.2
UK public sector net debt as a percentage of Gross Domestic Product — 66.2%
Real net national income per head — £ 20,556
Real household actual income per head — £ 17,862
Percentage of UK residents aged 16-64 with no qualifications — 10.7%
Percentage with five or more GCSEs A*-C incl English and Maths — 52.9%
Human capital - the value of individuals' skills, knowledge and competences in the labour market — £(bn) 17,120
Percentage who report finding it quite or very difficult to get by financially — 12.3%
Percentage who were somewhat, mostly or completely satisfied with their household income — 57.2%
Median wealth per household, including pension wealth — £ 236,973
Percentage of individuals with less than 60% of median income after housing costs — 21%
Percentage who agreed or agreed strongly that they felt they belonged to their neighbourhood — 66%
Percentage who accessed green spaces at least once a week in England — 53%
Percentage who felt very or fairly safe walking alone after dark — 75.1%
Crimes against the person (per 1,000 adults) — 83
Percentage who volunteered more than once a year — 19%
Percentage somewhat, mostly or completely satisfied with their use of leisure time — 65.6%
Percentage somewhat, mostly or completely satisfied with their amount of leisure time — 62.3%
Percentage somewhat, mostly or completely satisfied with their job — 77.8%
Unemployment rate — 7.9
Percentage with some evidence of probable psychological disturbance or mental ill health — 18%
Percentage who were somewhat, mostly or completely satisfied with their health — 68.3%
Percentage who reported a long-term illness and a disability — 20%
Healthy life expectancy at birth — 64 / 66
Percentage who said they had someone they could really count on in a crisis — 96.8%
Percentage who were somewhat, mostly or completely satisfied with their social life — 67%
Average rating of satisfaction with family life — 8.2/10
Percentage who rated their anxiety yesterday as medium/low — 60.1%
Percentage who rated their happiness yesterday as medium/high — 71.1%
Percentage with medium/high rating of how worthwhile the things they do are — 80%
Percentage with medium/high rating of satisfaction with their lives overall — 75.9%

NATURAL ENVIRONMENT
INDIVIDUAL WELL-BEING
GOVERNANCE
OUR RELATIONSHIPS
ECONOMY
HEALTH
EDUCATION AND SKILLS
WHAT WE DO
PERSONAL FINANCE
WHERE WE LIVE

Measures of National Well-being

Measuring what matters:
Understanding the nation's well-being

More data and interactive version
available at: www.ons.gov.uk/well-being

Data are the latest available
at September 2012

this page is intentionally blank

Measuring National Well-being - Population

Author Name(s): Louise Barnes

Abstract

This article examines the composition of growth in the population of the UK in recent years and the projected changes using the latest available data.

Introduction

As this article was being planned, the population of the world was estimated to have reached 7 billion on 31st October 2011. The Executive Director of the United Nationals Population Fund, Dr Babatunde Osotimehin, said:-

"A world of 7 billion is both a challenge and an opportunity. Globally, people are living longer healthier lives and choosing to have smaller families. But reducing inequalities and finding ways to ensure the well-being of people alive today – as well as the generations that follow – will require new ways of thinking and unprecedented global cooperation" (UN, 2011).

Within the UK the future population challenge is both one of growth and ageing. Recent projections based on 2010 population estimates suggest that, not only will the UK population continue to grow, reaching nearly 72 million by 2031, but also that the estimated number of residents aged 65 and over will be larger than the number aged under 16 years by 2023 (ONS, 2011).

This illustrates the importance of population statistics in understanding the well-being of the country. They provide contextual information on the size and demographic profile of the population, including use in the analysis of specific domains of well-being that will be reported in subsequent articles. Population statistics are also used to scale other statistics, so that comparisons can be made on a 'per head of population' basis. All of this information is crucial to allow for planning of the infrastructure, services, economy and environment of the UK.

This article is published as part of the ONS Measuring National Well-being Programme. The programme aims to produce accepted and trusted measures of the well-being of the nation - how the UK as a whole is doing.

Key points

Population profile

- The estimated population of the world passed the 7 billion mark on 31st October 2011 and is projected to exceed the 10 billion mark by 2100
- The estimated resident population of the UK was 62.3 million in mid-2010[1] , an increase of 470,000 (0.8 per cent) on the previous year and the highest annual growth rate since mid-1962
- The latest 2010-based national population projections show that the UK's population is projected to reach 67.6 million by 2021 and increase further to 71.8 million by 2031
- There are more females than males in the UK population; 31.6 million females compared with 30.6 million males in 2010
- The number of people aged 65 and over is projected to become larger than the number aged under 16 in about 2023

Population change

- Between mid-2001 and mid-2010, net natural change (the difference between births and deaths) went up from 62,000 between 2001 and 2002 to 243,000 between 2009 and 2010
- Between 2009 and 2010, net natural change added 3.9 people and net migration and other changes added 3.7 people for every 1,000 resident in the UK
- In 2010, in the UK, there were approximately 810,000 live births and approximately 560,000 deaths
- An estimated 339,000 people emigrated from the UK in the year to December 2010 while the estimate of long-term international immigration to the UK in the same period is 591,000
- During the year ending September 2010, England experienced a relatively small net loss to other countries in the UK of around 3,500 people, with an outflow of 96,100 and an inflow of 92,600 people
- In 2010/11 there were 702,520 National Insurance Number (NINo) registrations to adult overseas nationals entering the UK, an increase of 132,800 registrations (23 per cent) compared with 2009/10

Notes

1. Mid-2011 population estimates for England and Wales will be available autumn 2012 while the first set of release tables from the 2011 Census will be available in July 2012. For details of the proposed running order of the 2011 Census outputs see:Census 2011

Population Profile

The population of the world has increased from 2.5 billion in 1950 to 6.9 billion in 2010. It was estimated that the population of the world passed 7 billion on 31st October 2011. Projected growth shows an increase to 9.3 billion in 2050 and 10.1 billion by 2100. Compared to 2011, when less than 8 per cent of the population of the world were estimated to be aged 65 or over, by 2100 it is projected that over 22 per cent will be in this age group. By contrast, in the UK the percentage of the population aged 65 or over is estimated to be approximately 17 per cent in 2011 and is projected to reach nearly 28 per cent by 2100. Growth in population in the UK is shown in Table 1 and the age distribution of this growing population in Table 2 below.

Figure 1

Average percentage growth rate (1) UK, Europe and the World

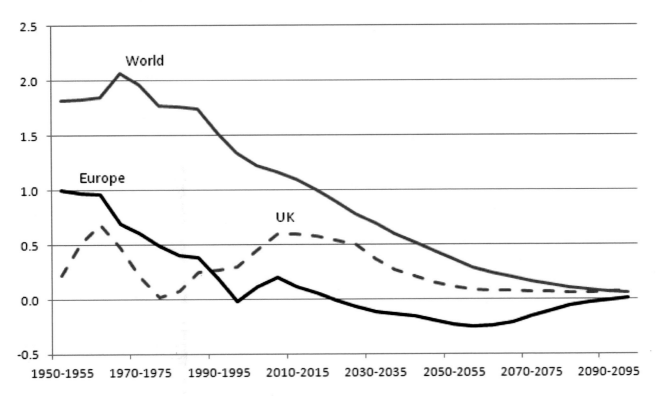

Source: Population Division of the Department of Economic and Social Affairs of the United Nations Secretariat, World Population Prospects

Notes:
1. Average exponential rate of growth of the population over a given five-year period, it is calculated as $\ln(Pt/Po)/t$ where Po is the population at the begining of the period, Pt is the population at period end an t is the length of the period. It is expressed as a percentage.

According to the United Nations 'World Population Prospectus' (UN, 2011) the United Kingdom's pattern of population growth rates is different to those of Europe or the world as a whole (Figure 1). Average growth rates in the world were above 1.5 per cent for the five-year periods from 1950–1955 to 1990–1995 and reached a peak of nearly 2.1 per cent on average in the period 1965–1970. Between 1995–2000 and 2005–2010 there has been a steady decline in the average growth rate of the world population to an average of 1.2 per cent. This decrease in the average growth rate is projected to continue so that it will be less than an average of 0.1 per cent in the last twenty years of the 21st century.

Neither Europe nor the UK has experienced the large average growth rates seen in the world as a whole. In Europe there was a steady decline in the average growth rate from 1.0 per cent in 1950–55 to an average decrease of 0.02 per cent in 1995–2000. After small increases in average growth rates over the next ten years, it is projected that there will be negative growth rates in Europe in each five year period between 2020–2025 and 2090–2095.

Table 1

Population (1) of the United Kingdom

Millions

	United Kingdom	England	Wales	Scotland	Northern Ireland
1901	38.2	30.5	2.0	4.5	1.2
1911	42.1	33.6	2.4	4.8	1.2
1921[2]	44.0	35.2	2.7	4.9	1.3
1931[2]	46.0	37.4	2.6	4.8	1.2
1951	50.2	41.2	2.6	5.1	1.4
1961	52.7	43.5	2.6	5.2	1.4
1981	56.4	46.8	2.8	5.2	1.5
1991	57.4	47.9	2.9	5.1	1.6
2001	59.1	49.5	2.9	5.1	1.7
2009	61.8	51.8	3.0	5.2	1.8
2010	62.3	52.2	3.0	5.2	1.8
2011	62.7	52.7	3.0	5.3	1.8
2016	65.3	54.9	3.1	5.4	1.9
2021	67.6	57.0	3.2	5.5	1.9
2026	69.8	59.0	3.3	5.6	2.0
2031	71.8	60.8	3.3	5.7	2.0

Table source: Office for National Statistics

Table notes:

1. Data for 1901 to 1961 are enumerated Census figures, 1981 to 2010 are mid-year estimates, and 2011 onward are national projections based on mid-2010 population estimates[3].

2. Figures for Northern Ireland are estimated. The population at the Census of 1926 was 1,257 thousand (608 thousand males and 649 thousand females).

3. Population estimates and projections – the estimated and projected populations are of the resident population of an area, that is all those usually resident there, whatever their nationality. Members of HM Forces stationed outside the UK are excluded; members of foreign forces stationed in the UK are included. Students are taken to be resident at their term-time addresses. Figures for the UK do not include the population of the Channel Islands or the Isle of Man.

Table 1 shows the estimated resident population of the UK was 62.3 million in mid-2010, an increase of 470,000 (0.8 per cent) on the previous year and the highest annual growth rate since mid-1962. The rate of population growth has become considerably faster since the mid-2000s. Between 1980 and 2000 the annual growth rate averaged 0.2 per cent, adding an estimated 127,800 people per year. Between 2001 and 2005 the average rate of population growth had increased to about 0.5 per cent (about 280,500 people per annum) and between 2006 and 2010 the average rate had further increased to 0.7 per cent per annum (about 419,400 extra residents per annum). Of the 62.3 million people resident in the UK in mid-2010, an estimated 52.2 million (84 per cent) were in England, 5.2 million (8 per cent) were in Scotland, 3.0 million (5 per cent) in Wales and 1.8 million (3 per cent) in Northern Ireland.

The latest 2010-based national population projections (ONS, 2011), show that the UK's population is projected to reach 67.6 million by 2021 and increase further to 71.8 million by 2031. The 2010-based national population projections for England suggest that the population will hit the 57.0 million mark by 2021 and increase further to 60.8 million by 2031. The 2010-based population projections for Wales suggest that the population will increase to 3.3 million by 2031, while the population for Scotland and Northern Ireland are projected to rise to 5.7 million and 2.0 million respectively.

Data from Eurostat shows by 2045 the UK's population is projected to become the highest in Europe at 75.0 million followed by Germany (72.9 million) and France (72.8 million[1]) (EU, 2011).

You may also be interested in:-

Population pyramids for sub national population estimates and projections
The structure of the population varies across the UK. Using the latest population estimates and projections data, this interactive graph allows you to compare national, regional and local populations in terms of size and structure. Animation is used to overlay the graphs for easier comparison as well as visualising changes over time. Sub-national Population Projections

Population estimates for UK, England and Wales, Scotland and Northern Ireland, mid-2010 population estimates

Mid 2010 population estimates are available at national level by age and sex and sub nationally (local authority/health area) by five year age group and sex. These include additional selected age groups and broad components of population change. The population estimates reflect the local authority administrative boundaries that were in place on 30 June of the reference year of the tables. Population Estimates for UK

Super Output Area mid-year population estimates for England and Wales, Mid-2010 Release

Population estimates for Lower and Middle Layer Super Output Areas in England and Wales by age and sex. These estimates are consistent with the local authority population estimates. The methodology used to produce the LSOA and MSOA estimates differs to the method used to produce the local authority mid-year estimates, and is subject to further development. Population and migration theme pages >Population change > Population estimates.

Ward Level mid-year population estimates for England and Wales (experimental), Mid-2010 Release

Shows mid-year estimates for wards. The ward estimates available to download or view are for (Census Area Statistics) CAS wards and 2010 wards. Ward estimates for other age groups are available on request. Population Estimates for UK

Population Estimates of the Very Elderly, 2010

Population of the very elderly (including centenarians) by gender, single year of age (90 to 104) and by age groups (90-99, 100+ and 105+) for the UK and England & Wales. Focus on Older People

National Population Projections, 2010-based extra variants

National population projections by age and sex for the UK and constituent countries. Includes information on the principal (main) and variant (alternative scenario) projections for each country together with details of the fertility, mortality and migration assumptions on which they are based Population and migration theme pages > Population change > Population estimates.

Population pyramids for variant population projections for the United Kingdom

An animated population pyramid graphic that allows you to compare different national population projections with each other. In addition to the principal (main) projection, the variant projections available for comparison are based on alternative assumptions of future fertility, mortality and migration. Animation makes it easier to see the impact of the differing assumptions on future population structures. This interactive census timeline brings to life how sensitive the size and structure of population is to major events and social change. You'll see how pandemics, medical breakthroughs, wars and social change have shaped, and continue to shape, the population of England and Wales (see Interactive content on ONS homepage).

The number of people in each age group within the population depends on how many people are born in a particular period and how long they live, as well as the numbers and ages of migrants moving to - and from - the country.

Table 2

Population:(1) by sex and age

United Kingdom

Thousands

	1971	1981	1991	2001	2010	2011	2016	2021	2026
Males									
Under 16	7,318	6,439	5,976	6,077	5,943	5,982	6,315	6,684	6,787
16–24	3,730	4,114	3,800	3,284	3,847	3,835	3,642	3,465	3,657
25–34	3,530	4,035	4,432	4,215	4,128	4,235	4,750	4,850	4,601
35–44	3,271	3,409	3,949	4,382	4,378	4,295	4,054	4,350	4,840
45–54	3,354	3,121	3,287	3,856	4,215	4,301	4,496	4,209	3,971
55–64	3,123	2,967	2,835	3,090	3,599	3,608	3,654	4,088	4,287
65–74	1,999	2,264	2,272	2,308	2,572	2,632	3,063	3,164	3,241
75–84	716	922	1,146	1,308	1,501	1,532	1,695	1,960	2,345
85 and over	126	141	212	312	460	482	602	757	938
All ages	27,167	27,412	27,909	28,832	30,643	30,902	32,271	33,526	34,667
Females									
Under 16	6,938	6,104	5,709	5,786	5,665	5,708	6,031	6,380	6,479
16–24	3,626	3,966	3,691	3,220	3,638	3,627	3,481	3,336	3,518
25–34	3,441	3,975	4,466	4,260	4,013	4,095	4,476	4,566	4,369
35–44	3,241	3,365	3,968	4,465	4,456	4,362	4,046	4,201	4,565
45–54	3,482	3,148	3,296	3,920	4,332	4,424	4,648	4,343	4,031
55–64	3,464	3,240	2,971	3,186	3,743	3,756	3,819	4,282	4,507
65–74	2,765	2,931	2,795	2,640	2,827	2,886	3,325	3,437	3,521
75–84	1,443	1,756	1,972	1,987	1,993	2,006	2,100	2,354	2,762
85 and over	359	462	661	817	951	970	1,074	1,211	1,401

All ages	28,761	28,946	29,530	30,281	31,619	31,833	33,000	34,110	35,153

Table source: Office for National Statistics

Table notes:
1.   Mid-year estimates for 1971 to 2010; 2010-based projections from 2011 to 2026.

There are more females than males in the overall UK population; 31.6 million females compared with 30.6 million males in 2010 (Table 2). In 2010, males outnumbered females up to age 34; while at older ages females outnumber males, reflecting the higher life expectancy of females. The difference in the numbers of males and females decreased from the early 2000s onward.

The average age of the UK population continues to increase gradually (ONS, 2011a). In 1985, there were around 690,000 people in the UK aged 85 and over, accounting for 1 per cent of the population. Since then the numbers have more than doubled reaching 1.4 million in 2010 (2 per cent of the UK population). By 2035 the number of people aged 85 and over is projected to be two and-a-half times larger than in 2010, reaching approximately 3.5 million and accounting for 5 per cent of the total population.

In terms of planning, one area of concern is the growth in the numbers in the 'oldest old' age groups as it is likely that they will make more use of health and social care services. Over the last 30 years the number of centenarians (people aged 100 years or more) in the UK has increased five fold from an estimated 2,500 in 1980 to 12,640 in 2010 (ONS, 2011b). The estimated number of centenarians in the UK increased by 84 per cent between 2000 and 2010, the largest percentage increase of 86 per cent, occurred in England and Wales, while the smallest increase was in Northern Ireland at 47 per cent. Current population projections suggest the number of centenarians in the UK will be approximately 100,000 by 2035, almost eight times the 2010 estimate (ONS, 2011a).

You may also be interested in:-

UK Population Pyramid
What does the structure of the UK's population look like? How many males and females are currently at school age, working age or at retirement age? How has that picture changed over time and how is it projected to change? Based on the latest ONS population estimates and projections data, this highly interactive, animated graphic allows you to explore these questions and more (see Interactive content on ONS homepage).

Animated map of ageing in the UK
An interactive mapping tool which allows you to analyse the age structure of the population at the local authority level more easily. You can see how the population has aged over time and is projected to continue to age by selecting from a list of indicators of population ageing, such as median age. Animating the map brings the data to life (see Interactive content on ONS homepage).

England and Wales Population Pyramid
This interactive, animated graphic shows how the age structure of England and Wales has changed in the past and how it is projected to change in the future, using the latest official population estimates and projections data (see Interactive content on ONS homepage).

Figure 2

Population(1) aged under 16 and 65 and over

United Kingdom

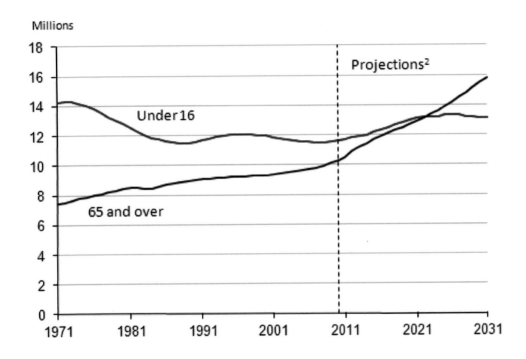

Source: Office for National Statistics, National Records of Scotland, Northern Ireland Statistics and Research Agency

Notes:
1. Mid-year estimates for 1971 to 2010.
2. 2010-based projections for 2011 to 2031.

Figure 2 shows the estimated and projected number of residents in the UK in two age groups, under 16 and 65 and over. There was a decrease in the number of those aged under 16 between 1971 and 1989 from 14.3 million to 11.5 million followed by relatively stable numbers over the next two decades. The number of residents under the age of 16 is projected to rise from 11.6 million in 2010 to 13.1 million in 2031. For the older age group there is a steady increase in numbers from 7.4 million in 1971 to 10.3 million in 2010, followed by a higher projected rate of growth which leads to a increase from 10.5 to 15.8 million between 2011 and 2031. The number of people aged 65 and over is projected to become larger than the number aged under 16 in about 2023.

Notes

1. It should be noted that Eurostat methods/assumptions for population projections may differ from those used for ONS population projections.

Population change

Table 3

Population change(1)

United Kingdom

Thousands

	Population at start of period	Annual averages		Net natural change	Net migration and other[2]	Overall change
		Live Births	Deaths			
1951–1961	50,287	..	..	..	..	..
1961–1971	52,807	..	..	..	..	..
1971–1981	55,928	..	..	..	..	..
1981–1991	56,357	..	..	102	6	108
1991–2001	57,439	731	631	100	68	167
2001–2010	59,113	737	582	155	195	350
2001–2002	59,113	663	601	62	143	205
2002–2003	59,319	682	605	77	156	233
2003–2004	59,552	707	603	104	186	290
2004–2005	59,842	717	591	127	267	394
2005–2006	60,235	734	575	159	190	349
2006–2007	60,584	758	571	187	214	401

2007–2008	60,986	791	570	220	192	413
2008–2009	61,398	787	570	217	177	394
2009–2010	61,792	797	554	243	227	470

Table source: Office for National Statistics

Table notes:

1. Mid-year estimates for 1951-1961 to 2009-2010.
2. 'Other changes' at UK level includes changes in the population due to changes in the number of armed forces (both foreign and home) and their dependents resident in the UK.

In the two decades between 1981 and 2001, net natural change (the difference between births and deaths) was the main driver behind population growth (Table 3). Between 2001 and 2010, the effect of net inward migration and other changes on overall population begins to be more noticeable with an average annual increase of 195,000 compared to an increase of 155,000 from net natural change.

Annual changes in the UK between mid-2001 and mid-2010 show an increasing trend in the number of live births and a decreasing trend in the number of deaths. This resulted in net natural change increasing from 62,000 between 2001 and 2002 to 243,000 between 2009 and 2010.

Over the same time period, the estimated contribution to population change of net migration has varied. In each year between 2001 and 2007, net migration was higher than net natural change with the largest increase of 267,000 between 2004 and 2005, coinciding with the A8 accession countries[1] joining the European Union. However, net natural change was again larger than net migration and other changes between 2007 and 2010. Between 2009 and 2010, net natural change added 3.9 people for every 1,000 residents in the UK and net migration and other change added 3.7 people.

In general, the size of net natural change (the difference between births and deaths) has been driven by changes in the numbers of births rather than in the numbers of deaths. While there are obvious increases in deaths related to the two world wars and to the Spanish influenza outbreak, just after the First World War, the numbers do not vary by as much as those for births.

Figure 3

Births(1,2) and deaths(1)

United Kingdom

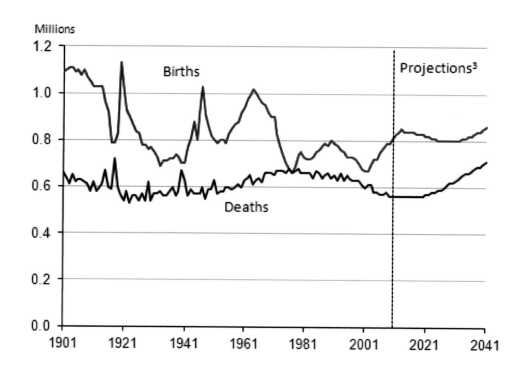

Source: Office for National Statistics

Notes:
1.   Data for 1901 to 1921 exclude Ireland which was constitutionally part of the UK during this period.
2.   Data from 1981 exclude the non-residents of Northern Ireland.
3.   2010-based projections for 2010 to 2041.

The two world wars had a major impact on births. There was a substantial fall in the number of births during the First World War, followed by a post-war 'baby-boom' with the number of births reaching 1.1 million in 1920, the highest number of births in any single year during the 20th century (Figure 3). Births then decreased and the number remained low during the 1930s' depression and World War Two. A second 'baby-boom' occurred after World War Two, followed by a further boom during the 1960s.

From about 1990, the number of births fell gradually to its lowest level of 668,800 in 2002, and then increased each year to 2010. In 2010 in the UK there were approximately 810,000 live births, an increase of 20,000 (2.9 per cent) compared with 2009. There were approximately 560,000 deaths in the UK in 2010 compared with 656,000 in 1901. The increase in population combined with the lower number of deaths has resulted in large declines in mortality rates (ONS, 2011c). In 2010, mortality rates in England and Wales were the lowest on record at 6,406 deaths per million for males and 4,581 per million for females. These improvements in mortality are mainly driven by medical advances.

You may also be interested in:-

Death registrations summary tables, England and Wales, 2010
Presents data on death registrations in England and Wales and contains data for death rates, cause of death data by sex and age and death registrations by area of residence. Deaths

Birth summary tables, England and Wales, 2010

The tables contain data for numbers of live births, fertility rates, percentage of births outside marriage, sex ratio, mean age of mother, area of usual residence of mother and country of birth of mother and father. Births

Figure 4

Long-term international migration into and out of the UK, 2010

United Kingdom

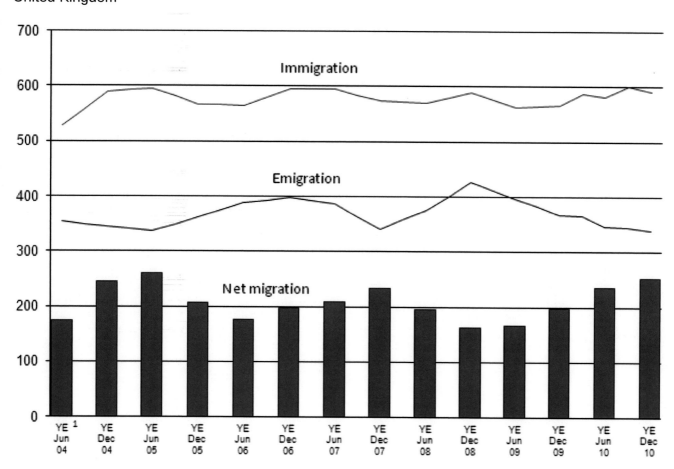

Source: Office for National Statistics

Notes:

1. YE = Year ending.

Population numbers also change because of emigration from and immigration to the UK. An estimated 339,000 people emigrated from the UK in the year to December 2010 (ONS, 2011d). This continues the decline since the year to December 2008 when total emigration from the UK was estimated at 427,000 (Figure 4). The final estimate of long-term international immigration[2] to the UK in the year to December 2010 was 591,000; this level has been broadly maintained since 2004 (ONS, 2011e).

Since Poland and seven other central and eastern European countries (collectively known as the A8) joined the EU in May 2004, around 66 per cent of all A8 citizens migrating to the UK have been Polish citizens. Between the year ending December 2003 and the year ending December 2010 the Polish-born population of the UK increased from 75,000 to 532,000. More recently immigration of Polish people had declined. Immigration was highest in 2007 at 96,000 Polish citizens, but has declined to 39,000 in 2009 (ONS, 2011f).

In addition to births, deaths and international migration, changes in population numbers in areas within the UK occur because residents move from one area to another (internal migration). Population gains and losses due to internal migration have important implications for housing planning as well as for the provision of welfare services. Estimates are based on information on re-registrations with NHS doctors and other sources.

Table 4

Movements between the UK countries, 2010(1)

Thousands

Destination	Country of origin				
	United Kingdom	England	Wales	Scotland	Northern Ireland
United Kingdom		96.1	48.5	41.3	11.2
England	92.6		46.5	37.6	8.5
Wales	50.4	48.5		1.5	0.4
Scotland	43.4	39.5	1.6		2.3
Northern Ireland	10.7	8.1	0.5	2.2	

Table notes:

1. Based on patients re-registering with NHS doctors in other parts of the United Kingdom.
2. *Source: National Health Service Central Register*

During the year ending September 2010, England experienced a relatively small net loss to other countries in the UK of around 3,500 people with an outflow of 96,100 and an inflow of 92,600 people (Table 4). Scotland and Wales experienced small net gains of around 2,100 people and 1,900 people respectively, while Northern Ireland experienced a net loss of approximately 400 people.

At a regional level within England, London experienced the most population movement overall during the year ending September 2010 (ONS, 2011g). Around 209,600 people moved from the capital to elsewhere in England while 164,000 people moved into the area, resulting in a net loss of 45,600 residents. The majority of those moving out of London moved to the adjacent regions of the South East and the East of England.

You may also be interested in:-

Long-Term International Migration, November 2011

For annual statistics on flows of international migrants to and from the UK and England and Wales, follow the *International Migration* link on the Population and migration theme pages

Internal Migration by local authorities in England and Wales mid-2010

For data on Internal migration, by Local Authority and Government Office Regions in England and Wales, follow the *Migration within the UK* link on the <u>Population and migration theme pages</u>

Table 5

National Insurance number registrations to adult overseas nationals entering the UK: by year and region

United Kingdom

Number

	2005/06	2006/07	2007/08	2008/09	2009/10	2010/11
All[1]	653,630	696,260	723,290	681,260	569,720	702,520
England	579,520	607,950	636,880	607,880	515,120	636,450
North East	10,930	13,330	12,230	11,480	9,310	11,390
North West	48,810	51,120	51,180	42,940	34,140	46,370
Yorkshire and the Humber	36,500	41,330	42,160	37,770	29,940	36,740
East Midlands	38,720	40,720	38,450	32,990	28,270	34,760
West Midlands	42,040	47,230	46,630	43,900	36,250	47,680
East of England	52,780	52,730	51,790	52,210	42,340	51,240
London	235,440	240,930	272,710	275,610	249,230	301,100
South East	80,240	79,330	82,830	77,870	61,970	76,290
South West	34,060	41,230	38,900	33,110	23,670	30,880
Wales	16,640	16,720	16,350	14,480	10,760	15,130
Scotland	41,400	51,890	52,410	46,260	36,330	41,540
Northern Ireland	16,060	19,680	17,640	12,630	7,530	9,390

Table source: Work and Pensions

Table notes:

1. Excludes overseas residents. Totals may not sum due to rounding method used.

National Insurance Number (NINo) registrations tell us about individuals entering the UK who have registered; they do not tell us whether those individuals are still in the UK. In 2010/11 there were 702,520 NINo registrations to adult overseas nationals entering the UK, an increase of 132,800 registrations (23 per cent) compared with 2009/10 (Table 5). There were 301,100 registrations within the London region (43 per cent of all registrations). The North East and Northern Ireland had the fewest registrations with 11,390 and 9,390 respectively.

In the year 2009/10, four out of every five NINo registrations were made by adult overseas nationals aged 18 to 34, while 55 per cent of NINo registrations to adult overseas nationals were made by men, this proportion increased slightly from 53 per cent in the previous year. In 2009/10, in Northern Ireland, 7,500 applications for National Insurance numbers were made by adult overseas nationals, of which 1,600 (22 per cent) were made by Polish Nationals.

Notes

1. Accession eight otherwise known as the A8. The eight A8 countries are; Czech Republic, Lithuania, Estonia, Poland, Hungary, Slovakia, Latvia and Slovenia, and joined the EU on 1 May 2004. Nationals of the A8 countries are allowed to enter the UK to look for and to take up employment or self-employment.

2. International migration estimates. An international migrant is defined as someone who changes his or her country of usual residence for a period of at least a year, so that the country of destination becomes the country of usual residence.

Background notes

1. Details of the policy governing the release of new data are available by visiting www.statisticsauthority.gov.uk/assessment/code-of-practice/index.html or from the Media Relations Office email: media.relations@ons.gsi.gov.uk

Copyright

www.nationalarchives.gov.uk/doc/open-government-licence/ or write to the Information Policy Team, The National Archives, Kew, London TW9 4DU, or email: psi@nationalarchives.gsi.gov.uk.

This document is also available on our website at www.ons.gov.uk.

References

1. DWP, 2011 - National Insurance number allocations to adult overseas nationals entering the UK. Full report available at: DWP: National Insurance Number Allocations to Adult Overseas Nationals entering the UK

2. *EU, 2011* - 1st January population: by sex and 5 year age groups (table proj_10c2150p), available at: Eurostat

3. *ONS, 2011* - National Population Projections, 2010-based projections available at: National Population Projections

4. *ONS, 2011a* - Older People's Day, 2011. Statistical bulletin available at: Focus on Older People

5. *ONS, 2001b* - Population estimates of the very elderly, 2010 available at: Population Estimates for UK

6. *ONS, 2011c* - Mortality rates in England and Wales, available at: Deaths

7. *ONS, 2011d* - Migration Statistics Quarterly Report November 2011, available at:Migration Statistics Quarterly Report

8. *ONS, 2011e* - Provisional IPS estimates of long-term international migration December 2010; Polish People in the UK both available at:Migration statistics reference tables

9. *ONS, 2011f* - A summary of the number of Polish People in the UK is available at: Migration Statistics Quarterly Report

10. *ONS, 2011g* - NHSCR Inter-regional migration movements, year ending September 2010 available at: Internal Migration (NHSCR) Interregional Movements

11. *UN, 2011* - The 2010 Revision of the World Population Prospectus is the twenty-second round of global demographic estimates and projections undertaken by the Population Division of the United Nations Division of the United Nations Department of Economic and Social Affairs of the United Nations Secretariat. The world population prospects are used widely throughout the United Nations and by many international organisations, research centres, academic researchers and the media. Available at: UN: World Population Prospects

About the ONS Measuring National Well-being programme

NWB logo 2

This article is published as part of the ONS Measuring National Well-being Programme.

The programme aims to produce accepted and trusted measures of the well-being of the nation - how the UK as a whole is doing. It is about looking at 'GDP and beyond' and includes:

- greater analysis of the national economic accounts, especially to understand household income, expenditure and wealth
- further accounts linked to the national accounts, including the UK Environmental Accounts and valuing household production and 'human capital'
- quality of life measures, looking at different areas of national well-being such as health, relationships, job satisfaction, economic security, education environmental conditions
- working with others to include the measurement of the well-being of children and young people as part of national well-being
- measures of 'subjective well-being' - individuals' assessment of their own well-being
- headline indicators to summarise national well-being and the progress we are making as a society

The programme is underpinned by a communication and engagement workstream, providing links with Cabinet Office and policy departments, international developments, the public and other stakeholders. The programme is working closely with Defra on the measurement of 'sustainable development' to provide a complete picture of national well-being, progress and sustainable development.